Praise for Kouzes and Posner's
The Leadership Challenge, 3rd Edition

"Leadership books are a dime a dozen, and most don't last a week let alone years. *The Leadership Challenge* has lasted because it is research based, it is practical, and it has heart! Believe me, Jim and Barry have hard evidence for what we usually think of as a soft topic. This book especially shines when ordinary folks can take these practices and work them into our lives on a moment-by-moment basis. Both authors are leaders in their own right, which doesn't hurt a bit. Why offer a new revision? Practically speaking, Jim and Barry have piles of new data to share, new real-life examples to tell, and updates given the wild and crazy new economy."

> —Tom Peters, management guru, founder and chairman, Tom Peters Company, and author of *In Search of Excellence*

"Based upon evidence collected from around the world and over decades, *The Leadership Challenge* provides practical guidance on how to lead and inspiration to make the effort."

> —Jeffrey Pfeffer, professor, Stanford Business School, and author of *The Human Equation: Building Profits by Putting People First*

"Kouzes and Posner are correct—leadership hasn't changed, but the context in which leaders operate has shifted dramatically. And that makes all the difference, as the two authors, who have conducted perhaps the most important research on leadership, describe in eloquent language and instructive case studies. If you read their first book, it's time to go back to the classroom and place your knowledge about leadership in a new context. If you didn't read the first edition, reading this book may be the most important thing you do this year to develop yourself as a leader!"

> —Janelle Barlow, president, TMI, US, and coauthor of *A Complaint Is A Gift*, *Emotional Value*, and *Smart Videoconferencing*

"Kouzes and Posner have written a book of reaffirmation. They have reaffirmed—with scholarship, stories, and their own ability to express ideas clearly—what it takes to lead. They return again and again to the essential qualities and values that enable one person to influence others, the capacity to reach and touch one another as caring, compassionate human beings."

> —David Lawrence, M.D., chair/CEO, Kaiser Foundation Health Plan, Inc.

"Kouzes and Posner give us breadth and depth with real-world examples of everyday leadership from everyday people who are meeting the extraordinary challenges of our time. A book of exceptional, real-world insight on what it takes to be a leader in our most complex and challenging times."

— Regis McKenna, chairman, The McKenna Group,
and author of *Total Access*

"*The Leadership Challenge* has been my primary leadership text since 1988. It is the blueprint for getting others to want to do what we are convinced needs to be done and is required reading for anyone who aspires to be a next-generation leader."

— Andy Stanley, founding pastor, North Point Community Church

"In *The Leadership Challenge*, chairs, deans, and provosts will find inspiration as well as practical suggestions that fit well with the difficult situations with which leaders in the academy struggle."

— Ann Lucas, professor of organization development, Fairleigh Dickinson University, and author of *Strengthening Departmental Leadership* and *Leading Academic Change*

"This is perhaps the most comprehensive field guide ever written for leaders. The principles are powerful, and have been a key part of my personal journey as a leader for years."

— Patrick Lencioni, president, The Table Group, and author of *The Five Temptations of a CEO*

"Jim and Barry have done the most practical, comprehensive, and inspiring research on leadership that I have ever read. Instead of another version of 'celebrity leadership,' *The Leadership Challenge* helps us gain practical wisdom from real leaders at all levels in many types of organizations. Every leader can relate to the knowledge in this book!"

— Marshall Goldsmith, cofounder of the Financial Times Knowledge Dialogue and the Alliance for Strategic Leadership, coeditor of *Coaching for Leadership*, and one of *Forbes* five top executive coaches

"Twenty years of research back this twenty-first century expression of core leadership practices. Inspiring stories and practical suggestions build your commitment to action, help you become the leader you want to be."

— Geoff Bellman, consultant and author of *Getting Things Done When You Are Not In Charge*

"By closely attending to the rich stories of thousands of successful leaders, the authors offer those who would be leaders—or would be better leaders—a treasure trove of insights about what makes a good leader. These qualities, as applicable to improving a public school as a private corporation, lie waiting within each of us."

> —Roland S. Barth, educator, author, former teacher, principal, and founding director of the Harvard University's Principals' Center

"The latest edition of *The Leadership Challenge* is pragmatic, humanistic, and inspirational. It is brimming over with collective wisdom and stories of leadership that are absolutely aligned with today's global needs. If ever a book gave meaning to the phrase 'leading with integrity,' this is it. I recommend this book to anyone who is serious about leading anything or anyone!"

> —Sue Cheshire, managing director, The Academy for Chief Executives (UK)

"Jim Kouzes and Barry Posner present an inspiring treatise on leadership and its importance on developing the maximum potential of the individual."

> —Joseph R. Bronson, executive vice president and chief financial officer, Applied Materials, Inc.

"Jim Kouzes and Barry Posner have taken a great book and made it even better in the new, third edition. Executives and students often ask me for a short list of the best books on leadership. For almost two decades, I have consistently recommended this remarkable collection of simple-but-powerful lessons. The new volume is thoroughly updated to recognize key changes in the leadership environment in recent years, but still retains its key strength—its clear and practical exposition of the best practices of successful leaders."

> —Lee Bolman, Marion Bloch/Missouri Chair in Leadership, Bloch School of Business and Public Administration, University of Missouri-Kansas City, and coauthor of *Leading With Soul* and *Reframing Organizations: Artistry, Choice, and Leadership*

"*The Leadership Challenge* is in a class by itself among leadership publications. The Five Practices of Exemplary Leadership—passionately yet practically described by the authors— really resonate with those in the helping professions and illustrate how professional leaders can provide much-needed vision and support for caregivers."

> —Judith Skelton-Green and Beverley Simpson, designers and facilitators, the Dorothy M. Wylie Nursing Leadership Institute, Toronto, Canada

"*The Leadership Challenge* answers the greatest challenge leaders face—knowing what to do to deliver value. Kouzes and Posner turn research into practical ideas that leaders at all levels can use. Full of practical tools and wonderful cases, it offers easy access to concepts that will build personal and organizational leadership depth. When the book first came out, it affected my thinking on leadership, and it continues to do so."

    —Dave Ulrich, professor, School of Business, University of Michigan, and author of *The Boundaryless Organization*

"People act like people everywhere. That's why leaders face the same challenges everywhere. *The Leadership Challenge* contains universal insights that spiritual leaders can use to become more effective in their own leadership journey."

    —Reggie McNeal, director of leadership development for the South Carolina Baptist Convention

"If you can have only one book on leadership, *The Leadership Challenge* has to be it. Kouzes and Posner reinforce their timeless principles with the stories of people who are actually leading in today's world. This third edition is beautifully written and eminently useful."

    —Terry Pearce, founder, Leadership Communication; senior vice president, Charles Schwab and Co.; author of *Leading Out Loud;* and coauthor of *Clicks and Mortar*

"No one who reads this book will ever shrink from an opportunity to lead. A truly inspiring work."

    —Leonard L. Berry, distinguished professor of marketing, Texas A&M University, and author of *Discovering the Soul of Service*

"Essential keys for the development of inspired and compassionate leadership during challenging times."

    —J. Peter Read, chairman, Grocery Outlet Inc.

"This is not a book about charismatic leaders who bedazzle their followers. It's about leaders who bring out the skills, capacities, and values of their partners and together realize shared dreams and goals."

    —Brian O'Connell, founding president, INDEPENDENT SECTOR, and professor of public service, University College of Public Service, Tufts University

"Employee fears and uncertainty during recessionary periods can disable organizations that are managed, but not led. Because *The Leadership Challenge* is so incisively relevant in the current environment, U.S. Venture Partners intends to provide a copy to every one of its portfolio CEOs."

—Irwin Federman, general partner, U.S. Venture Partners

"*The Leadership Challenge* hits the 'top ten' book category for leaders and managers at all levels. I continually use it with leaders and organizations in multiple countries."

—Bruce McNicol, president, Leadership Catalyst, Inc., and best-selling coauthor of *The Ascent of a Leader*

"If you read only one book on leadership, this is the one to read. If you read it more than a year ago, you need to read it again. It will stimulate new thoughts and (more important) inspire you to action. A true classic, extraordinarily well written, now in an invigorating new edition."

—David H. Maister, author of *Practice What You Preach* and coauthor of *First Among Equals*

"In this new edition of *The Leadership Challenge*, Kouzes and Posner have managed something very subtle and very important. They've reconciled what would appear to be the conflict between the more-crucial-than-ever role of enduring, immutable principles in a world that is changing at an ever-faster rate. It's a paradox, and they've handled it masterfully. Anyone who aspires to a position of leadership—that is, anyone who hopes to have followers—must read this book."

—John Guaspari, president, Guaspari Associates, and author of *Switched-On Quality: How to Tap Into the Energy Needed for Fuller and Deeper Buy-In*

"Want to increase your professional and personal ROI? Then read this book, use this book, and give this book to others. The ROI on your leadership will be significant, visible, and bankable."

—Sharon A. Winston, senior vice president, Lee Hecht Harrison

Third Edition

JAMES M. KOUZES

BARRY Z. POSNER

Third Edition

JOSSEY-BASS
A Wiley Imprint
www.josseybass.com

FIRST PAPERBACK EDITION PUBLISHED IN 2003.

Published by Jossey-Bass
A Wiley Imprint
989 Market Street, San Francisco, CA 94103-1741   www.josseybass.com

Page 459 constitutes a continuation of this copyright page.

Jossey-Bass books and products are available through most bookstores. To contact Jossey-Bass
directly call our Customer Care Department within the U.S. at 800-956-7739, outside the U.S.
at 317-572-3986 or fax 317-572-4002.

Jossey-Bass also publishes its books in a variety of electronic formats. Some content that appears
in print may not be available in electronic books.

Interior design by Yvo.

Library of Congress Cataloging-in-Publication Data

Kouzes, James M., 1945–
  The leadership challenge / by James M. Kouzes and Barry Z. Posner.—
3rd ed.
      p. cm.—(The Jossey-Bass business and management series)
Includes bibliographical references and index.
  ISBN 0-7879-5678-3 (alk. paper)
  ISBN 0-7879-6833-1 (pbk.)
  1. Leadership. 2. Executive ability. 3. Management. I. Posner,
Barry Z. II. Title. III. Jossey-Bass business & management series
  HD57.7 .K68 2002
    658.4'092—dc21   2002009871

Printed in the United States of America

THIRD EDITION
HB Printing   20 19 18 17 16 15 14 13 12 11
PB Printing   10 9 8 7 6 5 4 3

THIS BOOK

IS DEDICATED TO

DONNA BURNS KOUZES

WHOSE LOVING SPIRIT

LIVES ON IN THESE PAGES

CONTENTS

PART 3

INSPIRE A SHARED VISION

PART 4

CHALLENGE THE PROCESS

PART 7

LEADERSHIP FOR EVERYONE

PREFACE

Everyone's Business

Leadership for Today and Tomorrow

The Leadership Challenge is about how leaders mobilize others to want to get extraordinary things done in organizations. It's about the practices leaders use to transform values into actions, visions into realities, obstacles into innovations, separateness into solidarity, and risks into rewards. It's about leadership that creates the climate in which people turn challenging opportunities into remarkable successes.

Certainly there are no shortages of challenging opportunities today. In these extraordinary times, the challenges seem to be increasing—and through our responses, we have the potential to profoundly change the world in which we live and work.

When we published the first edition of this book in the late 1980s, the entrepreneurial spirit was blossoming. When the second edition was released in the mid-1990s, the flower of inventiveness was in full bloom. Then, as we turned the corner on the second year of the new millennium, it all seemed to wither and wilt. The freshness was gone, and people began wondering if what was true about leadership seven, fifteen, or twenty years ago still applied and whether leadership mattered at all. How is leadership different today? Will it be different tomorrow? Does leadership make a difference?

LEADERSHIP IN A NEW CONTEXT

As part of our research for this significantly revised and updated version of *The Leadership Challenge* we asked leaders the same question being asked of us: "What's new, and what's different?" The responses were identical. Whether in their early twenties, late seventies, or anywhere between, leaders told us that the fundamentals of leadership are the same today as they were in the 1980s, and they've probably have been the same for centuries. Yet the leaders were quick to add that while the *content* of leadership has not changed, the *context* has—and, in some cases, it has changed dramatically. What is this new context, and what are the implications for the practice of leadership? From heightening uncertainty across the world to an intense search for meaning, our connections as people and as leaders are part of this context.

Heightened uncertainty. All our lives were forever altered by the horror unleashed on September 11, 2001. Commercial jets as weapons of mass destruction. Our collective psyche resists: it remains nearly incomprehensible. Within minutes we came to feel much less safe and much less secure than when we had awakened that morning.

Even before these barbaric acts of terrorism, markets and consumers were jittery. After a thrilling eight-year joy ride, the New Economy's bubble had burst. Once high-flying icons of the Internet disappeared or disappointed. Stocks and sentiments descended, layoffs began in earnest, and people wondered if the good times would ever roll again. No wonder that more people than ever before are asking, "How do I lead during times of chaos and uncertainty?"

People first. Through the grief and anguish of all the tragedies, something truly amazing emerged. Sharp-elbowed bond traders on Wall Street, who once seemed more driven by greed than good, were seen openly weeping on television. CEOs of companies around the globe were advising us to "put families first." Acting as if they were one huge extended family, people across the United States and around the world began to come to each other's aid. They lit candles, held vigils, mourned, marched, sent money, gave blood, donated food and clothing, and went to religious services.

Tragedy is often a force that brings people together, and one of massive proportions shows us how connected we really are. The times seem to be showing us that we need to reconsider our priorities. Instead of placing work at the top of our agendas, perhaps we should put family and friends in the number one spot.

Will this shift to more compassion and collaboration last, or is it temporary? Will life return to the hypercompetitive, 24/7/365 world of September 10, 2001? Will profits replace people as number one on the corporate hit parade? Not according to what we've learned. The competencies of self-awareness, self-management, social awareness, and interpersonal skills are ascendant. Today there's much more demand for leaders who are exemplary coaches and individuals who show respect for people from many different cultural backgrounds. Team players are more valued than ever. We aren't naive enough to say that the brand-meism of the 1990s is gone forever, but we are certain of one thing. If you want to place a winning bet on who will be successful as a leader in these times, bet on the more collaborative person who values people first, profits second.

We're even more connected. A decade ago we noted that technology had connected us into an electronic global village. That seems like an absurdly provincial statement to us, now that the Internet and wireless technology have shrunk the globe to the size of a mobile phone. You wake up in Beijing knowing that you can check your personal digital assistant and link to your office, whether it's in Berlin or Boston. And, thanks to these links, you can send an electronic order today to a factory half-a-world away, and the factory can manufacture and ship the goods you want by tomorrow.

Being globally connected means much more than it did in the 1990s. Although the Internet has been exploited for its commercial capabilities—buying, bill paying, bartering, and brokering—its purpose, according to its inventors, is to help people work together. It's about enabling everyone to be more collaborative and cooperative. It's about sharing and supporting, not just buying and selling. It's a lesson being learned; the potential is there for leaders to reinvent how they use this powerful technology. So are the challenges. For instance, with access to information only a keystroke away, how do you lead in a globally connected world where hierarchy has become totally irrelevant? How do you use technology to give power away, not concentrate it in the hands of those with the central servers? How do you stay connected yet not invade people's privacy and personal space? How do you use instant messages, pagers, PDAs, mobile phones, and e-mail to stay in touch—without letting them rule your life? How do you lead a diffuse network of people scattered all over the planet, many of whom you may never meet? And how do you not allow technology to replace the most precious human moment—face-to-face contact?

Social capital. We have written earlier that knowledge had replaced land and financial capital as the new economic resource. Knowledge-added is the new value-added, we said, whether in goods or services. Well, guess what? Intellectual capital is no longer supreme. It's still true that those with educational degrees have higher incomes and more opportunity, and it's still true that an organization's fitness to compete is dependent upon the mental fitness of the workforce. Even so, there's a new champ in the ring. It's social capital—the collective value of people who know each other and what they'll do for each other. It's human networks that make things happen, not computer networks. And leaders who get extraordinary things done will be those who are right there in the middle of them.

The tragedy of September 11 reinforced this on a global scale. We are indeed all connected and our alliances are key. Social capital is amassed over years of investing in building relationships. Cash flow may the measure of our ability to finance our work, but social capital is the measure of our ability to put that cash to good use. How do you help leaders learn that it's as much the human heart as the human head that makes the world go round?

Global economy. Social connection and social capital extend far beyond national boundaries. The network we're talking about is global. So is the economy. Capital flows easily and instantly from one nation to another, creating a kind of volatility that is very new to the world. The health of the markets in Tokyo affects the health of the markets in the New York. A horrendous disaster in New York's financial district causes markets around the world to plummet, erasing billions of dollars in asset value.

From an economic perspective the world is boundaryless—and the implications for leadership extend beyond pure economics. The implications are cultural as well. With global economics comes a global workforce, a fact of life for which many executives are ill-prepared. English may be the language of business, understood whatever the accent; custom and culture, however, are far from uniform. Despite the electronic linkages—or perhaps because of them—the world may be connected but it is far from a community. For all the talk of the global economy, the world is a pretty parochial place. There are more countries in the world today than a decade ago. Fierce tribal rivalries threaten domestic and international peace, and special interest lobbying tears at our sense of community. There are more products and services than a decade ago, breaking the marketplace into ever smaller bits. Whether your organization is large or small, public sector or private, service or goods, you're likely to have constituents from many countries—and even in your own country, from many segments. Each expects to be treated with respect—just as you do. Global leadership means global understanding. How do you lead in a world that is so fragmented? How can a leader unite such a diverse and disparate constituency?

Speed. Speed is a direct consequence of the technologies that connect us. We've been cranking up the pace for centuries now. The transcontinental railroad was one of the most significant innovations of the nineteenth century in Europe and the United States. Automobiles and highways, then airplanes and radar, sped up our expectations. The Internet changed our concept of mail. "Snail mail" was replaced by the instant message, one that beeps and flickers, saying, "Read me now. Answer me now." We've come to expect an instant response when we order, when we eat, when we work.

Much of this has improved our lives, and it's lowered the costs of doing business. Yet it's also created a hurry-up culture and not everything—such as quality human relationships—can be hurried. How do you lead an organization that has to balance the importance of being responsive to family, employees, colleagues, customers, clients, and stockholders with the importance of "quality time" with those same individuals?

A changing workforce. Back in the 1990s, employers and employees alike were redefining the social contract. The largest employers had shed jobs at a record pace, and the contingent workforce was on the rise. More people were self-employed by choice. Students were told to expect to change careers many times in their lives, and becoming an entrepreneur was a status sought by millions. Toward the later part of the 1990s many young people were jumping to Internet start-ups and a chance at the IPO jackpot. Ethnic, gender, generational, and lifestyle diversity was on the rise, and it foreshadowed even more sweeping changes in the new millennium.

There's no going back to the days of a stable, homogeneous workforce. A diverse society brings a diverse workforce. And with a more diverse workforce comes a demand for a more customized approach to work. How do leaders embrace individual uniqueness and create wholeness out of diversity? How do leaders make an asset out of difference, and find a common purpose with which all can identify?

We also have to face another truth. Most of today's workers seriously question whether organizations are going to be loyal to their employees. They hear all this talk about how the organization wants loyal customers and committed employees, yet they don't experience life on the job as a reciprocal relationship. It seems to many that the notions of loyalty and job security have gone the way of the dodo bird. A certain distrust and wariness has crept into the workplace, and yet we know that trust is the foundation of any good relationship—and fundamental to getting extraordinary things done. How do you build a workplace where people can trust each other and trust the institution? How can you create a society in which people believe that they will be treated with dignity and respect regardless of the circumstances? After people have been torn apart by mergers, acquisitions, restructurings, and the attendant layoffs, when everyone assumes things won't last forever—how do leaders create commitment? How can leaders deliver on the promise of offering exciting and meaningful work and treating even the most temporary of workers with dignity and respect?

Even more intense search for meaning. In the last half-decade a countervailing force has arisen to combat what seemed to be an ever-expanding sense of cynicism. Younger workers aren't giving in to the idea that they don't make a difference. Aging baby boomers are back to exploring their souls. More and more of us are on a quest for greater meaning in our lives. Whether you call it spirituality, religion, faith, or soul, there's clearly a trend toward a greater openness to the spiritual side within the walls of business. Values and virtues are discussed more openly, and people worry about the legacy they are leaving. Though we still don't match the levels of faith we had in the 1940s and 1950s, recent crises have contributed to even stronger faith-based initiatives. Not so long ago, it would've been surprising to see a cover story in *Fortune* magazine on religion in business; when one appeared in 2001, it was an interesting but not astonishing development. Business schools have long offered courses and executive seminars on ethics in business; now some are sponsoring gatherings of students and executives to examine the role of faith in the workplace. Books on spirituality are regularly on the bestseller lists. Mainstream television shows address these issues. There's a growing yearning for a sense of higher purpose. How can leaders provide a climate for people to bring their souls to work, not just their heads and hands? How do leaders balance the spiritual side of life with the secular purpose of organizations? How do leaders show respect for all faiths, and not become proselytizers of one best way? How can leaders offer more hope in an increasingly cynical world?

With all these questions, there are countless opportunities to make a difference. Opportunities to restore hope and create a sense of meaning in our lives. Opportunities to rebuild a sense of community and increase understanding among diverse peoples. Opportunities to turn information into knowledge and improve the collective standard of living. Opportunities to apply knowledge to products and services, creating extraordinary value for the customer. Opportunities to weave the innocence and wisdom of different generations into our workplace and into our products and services. Opportunities to use the tools of technology to weave a web of human connection. Opportunities to find a better balance in our always-on, 24/7/365 lives. Opportunities to provide direction and support during uncertain times.

More than ever there is need for people to seize these opportunities to lead us to greatness. *The Leadership Challenge* is about those who do. It is about how traditional systems of rewards and punishments, control and scrutiny, give way to innovation, individual character, and the courage of convictions. It offers a set of leadership practices based on the real-world experiences of thousands of people who have answered the call for leadership.

What we have discovered, and rediscovered, is that leadership is not the private reserve of a few charismatic men and women. It is a process ordinary people use when they are bringing forth the best from themselves and others. What we've discovered is that people make extraordinary things happen by liberating the leader within everyone.

WHO SHOULD READ THIS BOOK?

The fundamental purpose of *The Leadership Challenge* is to assist people—managers and individual contributors alike—in furthering their abilities to lead others to get extraordinary things done. Whether you are in the private sector or public, an employee or a volunteer, on the front line or senior echelon, a student or a parent, we have written this book to help you develop your capacity to guide others to places they have never been before. We believe you are capable of developing yourself as a leader far more than tradition has ever assumed possible.

While *The Leadership Challenge* is written to strengthen your abilities and uplift your spirits, the principles and practices described in it are based solidly in research. The book has its origins in a research project we began in 1983. We wanted to know what people did when they were at their "personal best" in leading others. These were experiences in which, in their own perception, they set their individual leadership standards of excellence. We started with an assumption that we didn't have to interview and survey star performers in excellent companies to discover best practices. Instead, we assumed that by asking ordinary people to describe extraordinary experiences we would find patterns of success. And we did.

Thus, this book is not about being in a *position* (as if leadership was a place) but about having the courage and spirit to make a significant difference. It is about leadership and how ordinary people exercise it—and in the process become leaders. In it, we present stories of regular people, from all walks of life, who got bigger-than-life results.

The leaders we've worked with and learned from have asked us many questions about enhancing their leadership capabilities:

- What values should guide my actions as a leader?
- How do I best set an example for others?
- How do I articulate a vision of the future when things are so unpredictable?
- How do I improve my ability to inspire others toward a common purpose?
- How do I create an environment that promotes innovation and risk?

- How do I build a cohesive and spirited team?
- How do I share power and information and still maintain accountability?
- How do I put more joy and celebration into our efforts?
- What is the source of self-confidence required to lead others?
- How do I go about improving my leadership abilities?

In *The Leadership Challenge,* we offer guidance in answering these questions and more, for anyone with the desire to lead.

Leaders do exhibit certain distinct practices when they are doing their best. This process varies little from industry to industry, profession to profession, community to community, country to country. Good leadership is an understandable and a universal process. Though each leader is a unique individual, there are patterns to the practice of leadership that are shared. And that can be learned.

A FIELD GUIDE FOR LEADERS

Think of *The Leadership Challenge* as a field guide to take along on your leadership journey. We have designed it to describe what leaders do, explain the fundamental principles that support these leadership practices, provide actual case examples of real people who demonstrate each practice, and offer specific recommendations on what you can do to make these practices your own and to continue your development as a leader.

The first two chapters introduce you to our point of view about leadership. In Chapter One we describe the Five Practices of Exemplary Leadership revealed in our research.[1] Through examples from leaders we discuss the actions they took to get extraordinary things done. We conclude Chapter One with the Ten Commitments of Leadership—fundamentals for applying these leadership practices in your setting.

The leader's tale, however, is only half the story. To be a leader you have to have constituents. In Chapter Two we describe the results of our survey of the characteristics that people most admire in their leaders. In the twenty-plus years that we've been conducting our research, we've seen striking consistency in four qualities people believe are essential to exemplary leadership.

We tell you what those characteristics are, and we present to you the foundation on which all great leadership is built.

In Chapters Three through Twelve we explore the Five Practices, each in a pair of chapters. The discussions are built on the results of our research around the globe, and also draw on the research of other scholars. We illustrate each practice with case examples that we think best exemplify it. Each chapter concludes with a set of recommended actions, steps you can personalize to put the practice and commitment to use in your organization.

Those familiar with the first two editions of *The Leadership Challenge* will notice a reordering of some chapters. When we wrote those two editions we approached leadership descriptively. When we began our conversations for this edition, we asked ourselves, based on what we've learned, how would we present our research differently? We knew the Five Practices had not changed—nothing in our research told us that there was a magical sixth practice that would revolutionize the conduct of leadership, and nothing in our research suggested that any of the Five Practices were now irrelevant. We decided that we'd begin the leadership story from the inside and move outward, that we'd be more *prescriptive* in our telling of the leader's tale. In this edition, we describe leadership first as a personal journey of exploration and then as a rallying of others.

Having said that, short of starting with the first two chapters, there is no sacred order to this book. Go wherever your interests are. We wrote this material to support you in your leadership development. Just remember that each practice is essential. While you might skip around in the book, you can't skip any of the fundamentals of leadership.

When successful leaders talk about their personal best achievements, they talk about the importance of being clear about values and standing for principles. In Chapter Three we demonstrate that finding one's voice is the necessary first step to becoming an exemplary leader. In Chapter Four we discuss how leaders serve as role models for what constituents are expected to be and do, and how leaders set the example by their deeds and not just their words.

In Chapter Five we talk about how leaders look beyond the horizon of present time and imagine how things could ideally be several years ahead. Leaders have a sense of direction and a purpose beyond the present moment. Yet even the clearest vision is not enough to transform organizations. Unless the vision can be effectively communicated, people will not enlist in making the dream a reality. In Chapter Six, we show how effective leaders are positive and expressive in communicating and are able to forge a shared agenda.

When successful leaders talk about their personal best achievements, they talk about searching for opportunities to innovate and change things. In Chapter Seven, we identify the real motivator as the meaningfulness of the challenge, not the material rewards of success. The source of most innovation is external to the leader's organization, so the leader must always stay open to accepting ideas from any and every source. Innovation brings risk. As described in Chapter Eight, leaders accept the mistakes that result from experimentation and make every effort to learn from them. They also build commitment to change and renewal through a process of incremental improvement and small wins; they develop resiliency and hardiness in others to make them more capable of dealing with uncertain and troubling times.

The leaders we studied are involved and in touch with those they lead. They care deeply about others, and they often refer to their workplace as a community, and to those with whom they work as family. We explore these ideas in Chapter Nine as we examine how leaders foster collaboration and build effective teams. In Chapter Ten we show how leaders create a climate in which it is possible for others to do their best, and we describe what leaders do to enable others to be in charge of their own lives, how leaders turn constituents into leaders.

In Chapters Eleven and Twelve, we discuss how leaders sustain the commitment to achieve the extraordinary by recognizing individuals, building social support, and celebrating team successes. Leadership is hard work, and it's also great fun. Leadership, we've discovered, is about caring, about heart, and about love.

In Chapter Thirteen, we discuss how leadership is a learnable set of practices, accessible to anyone. We show you that leadership is everyone's business, and that the first place to look for leadership is within yourself. In so doing we hope to demystify it, and show how everyone has the capacity to lead. We talk about the contrasts and contradictions of leadership and how leaders learn to strike a balance. We also offer guidance on how you can continue your own growth and development. And we promise that if you read to the very end of this book, we'll tell you the secret to success in life.

Finally, for those who wish to know more about how we conducted our research, the Appendix describes a source of detailed information on our research methodology, statistical data, and highlights of validation studies by other scholars of our leadership paradigm—all available on the Web.

Within these thirteen chapters, Five Practices, and Ten Commitments is woven a core theme. Whatever the time, whatever the circumstances, *leadership is a relationship*. Whether it's one-to-one or one-to-many, business as usual or challenges in extraordinary times, leadership is a relationship between those who aspire to lead and those who choose to follow. North, south, east, and west, success in leadership, success in business, and success in life has been, is now, and will be a function of how well we work and play together. We're even more convinced of this today than we were twenty years ago.

THE FUTURE OF LEADERSHIP

The domain of leaders is the future. The leader's unique legacy is the creation of valued institutions that survive over time. The most significant contribution leaders make is not simply to today's bottom line; it is to the long-term development of people and institutions so they can adapt, change, prosper, and grow. We hope this book contributes to the revitalization of organizations, to the creation of new enterprises, to the renewal of healthy communities, and to greater respect and understanding in the world. We also fervently hope that it enriches your life and that of your community and your family.

Leadership is important not just in your own career and within your own organization. It's important in every sector, in every community, and in every country. We need more exemplary leaders, and we need them more than ever. There is so much extraordinary work to be done. We need leaders who can unite us and ignite us.

In the end, we realize that leadership development is ultimately self-development. Meeting the leadership challenge is a personal—and a daily—challenge for all of us.

Santa Clara, California   James M. Kouzes
June 2002   Barry Z. Posner

Third Edition

PART ONE

What Leaders Do and What Constituents Expect

1
THE FIVE PRACTICES OF EXEMPLARY LEADERSHIP

Leadership is ultimately about creating a way for people to

contribute to making something extraordinary happen.

Alan Keith, Lucas Digital

Vision, conviction, and courage made the difference—

for all of us.

Lindsay Levin, Whites Limited

Whites, a car dealership and repair group based in the southeast part of London, was no worse than its competitors, but probably no better, either. Though the firm seemed busy enough, deeper analysis revealed negligible profits, mediocre employee morale, outdated financial systems, and low customer retention rates. As with lots of similar businesses, much of the structure and systems at Whites had remained substantially unchanged for many years. Each of the three departments—sales, service, and parts—operated largely independently, frequently blaming the others for any problems. Performance measures centered on efficiency and the cost of overhead, with insufficient attention paid to the customer's experience. This is a situation all too familiar to businesses around the globe, large and small.

"What do our customers really think of us?" was the starting point for Managing Director Lindsay Levin. If the customers didn't feel about the business as she wanted them to, she wanted to know why: "I wanted to get Whites to the point where we could be totally confident that every customer would have an excellent experience dealing with us. I didn't want it to be okay; I wanted it to be amazing—every time." And so she started talking about this question with everyone.[1]

Lindsay had no illusions about the size of the task facing her, especially as a twenty-nine-year-old woman without so much as a streak of grease under her fingernails. She took over the reins of this family business (founded by her great-grandfather), only a few years out of college. Although she had worked in various parts of the business as a teenager, mostly over the summer and holidays, to this day she still knows little about automobile engines and the product side of the enterprise.[2] What she does know, she says now, "is that this business is really all about people. And that our ability to deliver amazing customer service is all about people, and making them feel motivated, empowered, and trusted. They need to feel that they know what is at stake and how they make a difference. If we are not really committed to our own people, how can we expect them to be committed to our customers? My vision for Whites is of a company where everyone is treated with respect, feels involved and valued, and sees continuous improvement as part of their job, where people are free to get on and move the business forward with the minimum of bureaucracy, taking responsibility for their actions without fear of blame."

One of the ways Lindsay got started was to hold focus groups of customers, videotaping the proceedings and playing them back to the employees. The results were electrifying. They revealed that comfortable assumptions about the job Whites was doing were not supported by the evidence. It was all the more powerful because employees recognized individual customers making complaints and could identify themselves as the subject of some of those complaints. Concerns ranged from poorly finished repairs and mistakes in billing to basic failures of communication such as not letting people know when their cars were ready to be picked up. Customers felt like a commodity. They didn't care which department they were talking to, they just wanted their car repaired.

As a first step, Lindsay asked people to talk about changes they would like to see happen and to form small voluntary teams to implement them. Initially these weren't earth-shattering shifts, they were tasks like redoing the kitchen and cleaning up the workshop—yet the response was enthusiastic and immediate. Some projects did take longer than expected, but they put people into the right frame of mind about working as a team. "Getting something concrete done got people over the 'I've heard it all before' reaction," recalls Lindsay: "It was an essential preliminary to changing attitudes and mindsets."

Once the teams had a few successes under their belts, they had the confidence to move on to bigger projects like building a new vehicle storage compound and, ultimately, to making fundamental changes in working practices. Most notably, they began operating as integrated and self-managing units in direct contact with customers rather than as traditional functional divisions. "As a result," says Lindsay, "a very new way of working in teams developed." It also transformed relationships—with customers who can now put a face to a name and talk to "their" technician, just as technicians get to know "their" customers personally. This has created such strong bonds that it is not unusual for employees to drop in on their days off to check progress on a particular vehicle.

Lindsay also made a commitment to training: "Vehicle repair is becoming a knowledge process, calling for brain as much as brawn." Sixteen hours a month—10 percent of time—was, and continues to be, devoted to training. She admits that it is expensive and that pulling people off the job is not always popular, but it's a long-term strategy that pays off in two directions. One is that skills transfer is a reality and the people who have been on training courses (covering both technical and people skills) go on to train others on the job. The other is the bottom-line effect, where revenue and growth have more than doubled, contributing to many awards both inside and outside the industry.

Lindsay also realized that you can never stop communicating, nor do enough communicating with people. In the early days, she would sometimes meet with all the technicians and parts people and be greeted with a wall of silence. "I'd have to be really proactive to get anything back from them." A big learning point for Lindsay and the leadership team was, as she says: "that it's easy for the manager to say, 'Well, I tried to get input from people but nobody wanted to contribute.' To succeed, you've got to keep persevering and going back." This level of commitment was required before people would really open up and be honest with Levin, other directors, managers, and even their peers:

I talk very much from the heart, from the soul. This was initially a very strange thing to do in the motor [car] business, because it's a very macho culture. You have to open up your heart and let people know what you really think and believe. This means talking about your values and the values in your organization. The key is being able to align these two—personal and organizational values—and being at home in your skin, and being honest with yourself. You may have a set of values or mission stuck up on the wall, but if it's not what you're about, then everyone in the business will know, and it's a complete waste of time, and you'd probably be better off not to do anything. Be honest with yourself about what really matters to you and motivates you. And you've got to make sure that what you're doing in your business is aligned with what you're really all about.

Lindsay knows the critical importance of doing what you say you'll do and leading from the front. She told us about a very recent incident where her actions in working with a new salesperson set an example for others and gave testimony to not only her values but also reinforced key organizational values in the process:

I went to our sales department and there was a new salesperson hired. There were a whole bunch of things he should have been shown as a new person, and hadn't been. Fairly simple things, like where to get the company telephone directory. So I sat down with him for half an hour, at his desk, and showed him where to get all the information, got on the Internet with him and showed him a whole bunch of mundane things. And I know that I'm chatting with this guy, and he's a great guy, and that my time with him will not only make an impression on him but also on others in the organization who notice how I just chose to spend half an hour coaching someone on how to do a better job.

Lindsay also makes sure that they do all kinds of things to recognize success at Whites. All managers take time out to say thank you personally to people at every opportunity. Each month twenty-five to fifty "Going the

Extra Mile" awards are given throughout the organization. Get three and trade them in for a gold pin with a winged W. Get three in a row and you've earned a dinner certificate. These awards are generated by anyone in the organization, recognizing the contribution, the "extra mile" taken by someone else in pursuit of serving the customer. "It uplifts everyone's hearts," says Lindsay, to see what people are doing on their own: like traveling up to Scotland to help a customer whose car has broken down, delivering a car after midnight to a customer who was returning home from an overseas flight, or rearranging one's own schedule so that a teammate can attend a child's celebration at school. The fact that this recognition is public makes all the difference, according to Lindsay, because you can't pay people to care. Lindsay herself writes lots of personal memos to congratulate people on achievement, signed with a smiley face. This has become a Lindsay trademark and people talk about how many "smileys" they have received.

"We really try very hard at Whites," says Lindsay, "to make certain that we are *zapping* and not *sapping* people. Zapping means giving people positive strokes—boosting their motivation by recognizing a job well done and giving them the confidence to push themselves further." She believes you need to zap people on a regular basis. "If everyone is doing a great job, what's the problem in letting them know that?" Lindsay also appreciates that in difficult and challenging circumstances, sometimes all people need is to be supported and propped up. "This can be as simple as asking people how they are feeling or taking them out for a cup of coffee. Putting a bit of time aside to acknowledge the efforts they are making, and also that change can be difficult, makes a big difference to how people feel."

"I knew I'd never be able myself to make all the changes that I thought were necessary to revolutionize the business and make it truly customer, and people, focused," says Lindsay, reflecting on her experience and the still-ongoing transformation at Whites. But these things were, and are, very important to her, and that comes across to people. She knows that if people trust her and she trusts them, then there are few limits to what they can accomplish. Further, Lindsay notes: "You can then expect people to take responsibility. We assume the best in people, that they want to do a good job, that they'll check up, get on with it, and honor the responsibility they've been given so that everybody's playing their part."

Lindsay demonstrates exemplary leadership skills, and she shows how to both build and guide a talented and committed team in accomplishing exceptionally challenging goals. She serves as a model for how other leaders can get extraordinary things done in a world of constant chaos and change.

LEADERSHIP FOR TODAY AND TOMORROW

Lindsay is a truly remarkable person, but her story is not. For over two decades we've been conducting research on personal-best leadership experiences, and we've discovered that there are countless examples of how leaders mobilize others to get extraordinary things done in virtually every arena of organized activity. We've found them in profit-based firms and nonprofits, manufacturing and services, government and business, health care, education and entertainment, work and community service. Leaders reside in every city and every country, in every position and every place. They're employees and volunteers, young and old, women and men. Leadership knows no racial or religious bounds, no ethnic or cultural borders. We find exemplary leadership everywhere we look.

Sometimes a leadership opportunity directly confronts you as it did with Lindsay Levin. Sometimes it knocks on your door and invites you to participate. When that happens, you have to be ready to seize the moment. Just take a look at what happened with Alan Keith, for example.

In 1991 the Turner Broadcasting System (TBS) wanted to launch the Cartoon Network. To make the Cartoon Network work, though, TBS needed instant programming to fill the hours of airtime. So it immediately went searching for acquisitions, and Hanna-Barbera Cartoons seemed like the ideal purchase. With its extensive library of classic cartoons developed over nearly forty years—including *The Flintstones, Scooby Doo,* and *The Jetsons*—Hanna-Barbera had just what the Cartoon Network needed, so TBS happily closed the deal. Along with the library, the acquisition of Hanna-Barbera included the company's animation studio. At that time the studio wasn't producing cool programming that appealed to the younger audience, but then–TBS chairman Ted Turner thought it could be turned around. He gave the Hanna-Barbera team two years to make that happen. If they couldn't, he'd close the studio down.

Alan Keith, chief accounting officer and controller for the Turner Distribution Company, was recruited to be part of the acquisition team. Alan assumed he'd be involved in it for a while, and then once the deal was completed he'd go back to his other responsibilities. But it turned out very differently. Instead, he was asked to take on the role of vice president of business operations of Hanna-Barbera, move to Los Angeles, and become part of the senior team there. The challenge: completely reinvent the Hanna-Barbera studios. "It became," Alan says, looking back, "one of the most compelling experiences I've ever had in my career. It was an environment where leadership was working at its best."

At the time of the acquisition a manufacturing philosophy ruled the studio. "It was about doing it cheaply, getting it out the door and getting it on the air as quickly as possible," Alan says. "Their whole drive, their whole motivation was not so much on creativity or quality but on volume." Like most factories, there was a highly centralized structure in which all decisions about creative issues were being made by one or two people, and all the work was divided into functional departments. Creativity had been dampened because of that system, and there was no free flow of ideas. Something had to be done quickly to revive a once great entertainment force.

The new team had to make a dramatic shift from a manufacturing mentality to a focus on *creativity*. It seems like an obvious thing when you're talking about animation, but, Alan says, "It was a huge struggle to get to the place where we could actually admit that all we really care about right now is bringing the right kind of creativity into this organization." And, as with so many simple yet profound shifts in perspective, "Once we were able to articulate it, so many things flowed from that statement."

"The vision," Alan explains, "was to ultimately be viewed as the world's leader in producing cartoon animation." But vision is one thing, action is another. "After scratching our heads for a little while . . . we decided to launch a shorts program. . . . This was really the unique and risky concept out of the whole idea. Animation's expensive to produce, and the only way it gets cost-effective is if you're producing long-run syndicated programs where you can amortize your cost over long periods of time. To produce a seven-minute short is an expensive proposition. To produce thirty-nine of them certainly adds to the risk."

Thus began a huge, real-time R&D effort. "We had an opportunity to produce thirty-nine unique, individual shorts, all different characters, all different stories. And then the Cartoon Network would air them repeatedly in different time slots, up against other programs, promote them in different ways, and collect lots of data on ratings and viewer feedback. That feedback ultimately gave us the indications of which handful were really the ones that seemed to appeal, and therefore were the ones we wanted to pursue."

To support this dramatic departure from the past, "We essentially turned the organization on its ear, and we questioned every paradigm that the business had about how it worked, how it was set up, how it was structured, and how it was operated," explains Alan. The old departmental structure gave way to highly decentralized production units and cross-functional teams. Each unit, focused on one of the shorts, would hire its own team and develop its own ideas. The support functions, depending on what they did, were assigned to work with different teams in the facility. What evolved was a much thinner yet stronger support system. The job of all those in leadership roles shifted from control to providing the backing for people to do what they were brought on to do. "It was fascinating to me," says Alan, "because it was such a radical process. And it involved a great deal of risk whether it would even work." It might have been a risk, but what resulted was a higher sense of accountability.

"Creative people by nature," Alan explains, "want some sense of ownership. They want some sense of empowerment and spirit. By focusing on the creator we were changing the whole leadership paradigm within our studio. . . . You can't make people trust change and trust the system. You have to actually create a system that is trustworthy, then people will begin to move much, much faster when you're trying to elicit change."

Part of creating a trustworthy system was getting to know the people he worked with, so Alan spent a lot of time with his employees. "We had times periodically throughout the year where managers were not allowed to have any appointments on their schedule other than those specifically set up by employees to come and talk to them about whatever was on their minds."

For Alan, this process of making deeper connections with people had a profound payoff. "To get the most out of people, you need to see them on more than a surface level. You really have to get to know what makes them tick. When you do that you're a little bit more human, and you create a system that's more trustworthy. Learning about their interests and passions made a huge difference in getting them connected to what we were trying to accomplish. It allowed me and it allowed others an opportunity to figure out how to motivate these people in order to do something that was absolutely extraordinary."

The entire climate of the studio changed. "We did everything from completely overhauling and doing a face-lift on the space so that it spoke to the creative spirit to encouraging anybody in the company—anybody that had an idea for a cartoon short—to come in and pitch their idea. It was an open system." Alan recalls how one woman in the purchasing department had an idea about how to liven up the look and feel of the place. She knew that the company wasn't going to spend gobs of money on new furniture because they didn't have it. "She said, 'The lobby needs to be redone because it's really tacky right now. I found a place that sells fabric. Let's just reupholster some of the existing furniture with some really wild, zany sixties-looking stuff because that's really the era of the furniture and it would liven it up.' It was those sorts of things that came out of a context of being fiscally responsible but yet coming up with great new ideas."

To teach people how to work in this new trusting system, lots of team building, lots of offsites, and other forms of training took place. Significant time, energy, and resources were spent on developing leadership within the organization, something to which Alan dedicated himself personally. One of the interventions Alan sponsored was a 360-degree feedback review process. This was done on a multi-year basis so that employees' perceptions could be tracked over time. It was a rigorous process involving quantitative data and written comments that each manager was required to review and then sit with employees and talk about. Alan set the example, later telling us: "I think that was probably one of the most significant ways that I showed I was walking the walk and talking the talk. I started with me when it came to getting the upward feedback."

Although turning around the Hanna-Barbera Studio was serious business, "We played a lot," Alan recalls. "The place was about creating animation for kids, so it should be a fun place to work. We had celebratory parties around the shows, and we'd bring in the costume characters." Individual recognition was also abundant. "It didn't matter if it was somebody in the legal department, human resources, or facilities. If a person did something that was incredibly useful or important to our mission, they were recognized. Sometimes it was in town hall meetings, and other times one-on-ones; whatever the method, people got recognized for their contributions."

There was also the company store. "We set up a store in our studio where employees could come and buy merchandise that we had created just for our production studio, unique merchandise that you couldn't buy elsewhere. We wanted people to feel it was really special to work there. We wanted employees to walk out the door at the end of the day wearing a really, really cool Hanna-Barbera T-shirt with one of our characters on it. We wanted people to stop them, talk about it, and say 'That's really cool. Where did you get that?'"

"A lot of this stuff sounds kind of silly," Alan remarks, "but from the time we acquired the company until I left, the whole face of the place changed. It was a very gray, dank-looking building when I first arrived. When I left, we had zany furniture in the lobby, the buildings were painted bright colors, and the conference tables had all of our characters' names engraved in them. It was like coming to work in a cartoon every day. That stuff happened organically as we started to really change the place."

The Hanna-Barbera turnaround was a huge success. It not only created programs and merchandise that have produced billions of dollars in revenue for the Cartoon Network, it also created a whole new, trustworthy system for producing cartoon animation. This new system had a lasting human impact as well. "To this day," says Alan, "a number of people who are no longer there maintain extremely close contact. There was a group of people working shoulder to shoulder for many years, figuring out how to make things work, and we developed a bond that is a very rare thing in the workplace."

Because of his success at Hanna-Barbera, Alan Keith was recruited by Lucas Digital Ltd. to become its chief administrative officer. "The purpose that I'm serving in this organization is one of change." And in that role he's applying the lessons he learned at Hanna-Barbera, trying to create another trustworthy system that will get even more extraordinary things done. What does he see as a key lesson? "Know what you value, be willing to take a risk, and lead from the heart—lead from what you believe in."

INTRODUCING THE FIVE PRACTICES

Faced with different cultures and difficult circumstances, Lindsay Levin and Alan Keith each seized the opportunity to lead. They chose a pioneering path and led their organizations to new summits of excellence. And although their cultures and circumstances are distinct, we learned some important lessons about leadership from Lindsay, Alan, and the thousands of others who told us their personal-best experiences. From them we learned what it takes to mobilize other people—by the force of their own free will and despite hard work and potential risk—to want to climb to the summit.

Through our studies of personal-best leadership experiences, we've discovered that ordinary people who guide others along pioneering journeys follow rather similar paths. Though each case we looked at was unique in expression, each path was also marked by some common patterns of action. Leadership is not at all about personality; it's about practice. We've forged these common practices into a model of leadership, and we offer it here as guidance for leaders to follow as they attempt to keep their own bearings and guide others toward peak achievements.

As we looked deeper into the dynamic process of leadership, through case analyses and survey questionnaires, we uncovered five practices common to personal-best leadership experiences. When getting extraordinary things done in organizations, leaders engage in these Five Practices of Exemplary Leadership:

- Model the Way.
- Inspire a Shared Vision.
- Challenge the Process.
- Enable Others to Act.
- Encourage the Heart.

These practices—which we discuss briefly in this chapter and then in depth in later chapters—aren't the private property of the people we studied or of a few select shining stars. They're available to anyone, in any organization or situation, who accepts the leadership challenge. And they're not the accident of a special moment in history. They've stood the test of time, and our most recent research confirms that they're just as relevant today as they were when we first began our investigation over two decades ago—if not more so.

Model the Way

Titles are granted, but it's your behavior that wins you respect. As Gayle Hamilton, a director with Pacific Gas & Electric Company, told us, "I would never ask anyone to do anything I was unwilling to do first." This sentiment was shared across all the cases that we collected. Exemplary leaders know that if they want to gain commitment and achieve the highest standards, they must be models of the behavior they expect of others. Leaders *model the way.*

To effectively model the behavior they expect of others, leaders must first be clear about their guiding principles. Lindsay Levin says, "You have to open up your heart and let people know what you really think and believe. This means talking about your values." Alan Keith adds that one of the most significant leadership lessons he would pass along is, "You must lead from what you believe." Leaders must find their own voice, and then they must clearly and distinctively give voice to their values. As the personal-best stories illustrate, leaders are supposed to stand up for their beliefs, so they'd better have some beliefs to stand up for.

Eloquent speeches about common values, however, aren't nearly enough. Leaders' deeds are far more important than their words when determining how serious they really are about what they say. Words and deeds must be consistent. Exemplary leaders go first. They go first by setting the example through daily actions that demonstrate they are deeply committed to their beliefs. Toni-Ann Lueddecke, for example, believes that there are no unimportant tasks in an organization's efforts at excellence. She demonstrates this to her associates in her eight Gymboree Play & Music centers in New Jersey by her actions. As just one example, she sometimes scrubs floors in addition to teaching classes.

The personal-best projects we heard about in our research were all distinguished by relentless effort, steadfastness, competence, and attention to detail. We were also struck by how the actions leaders took to set an example were often simple things. Sure, leaders had operational and strategic plans. But the examples they gave were not about elaborate designs. They were about the power of spending time with someone, of working side by side with colleagues, of telling stories that made values come alive, of being highly visible during times of uncertainty, and of asking questions to get people to think about values and priorities. Modeling the way is essentially about earning the right and the respect to lead through direct individual involvement and action. People first follow the person, then the plan.

Inspire a Shared Vision

When people described to us their personal-best leadership experiences, they told of times when they imagined an exciting, highly attractive future for their organization. They had visions and dreams of what *could* be. They had absolute and total personal belief in those dreams, and they were confident in their abilities to make extraordinary things happen. Every organization, every social movement, begins with a dream. The dream or vision is the force that invents the future. Lindsay Levin saw a new and even more responsive Whites Group; Alan Keith imagined people at Hanna-Barbera taking creativity seriously—and playfully—to rejuvenate and reenergize a decaying organizational culture.

Leaders *inspire a shared vision.* They gaze across the horizon of time, imagining the attractive opportunities that are in store when they and their constituents arrive at a distant destination. Leaders have a desire to make something happen, to change the way things are, to create something that no one else has ever created before. In some ways, leaders live their lives backward. They see pictures in their mind's eye of what the results will look like even before they've started their project, much as an architect draws a blueprint or an engineer builds a model. Their clear image of the future pulls them forward. Yet visions seen only by leaders are insufficient to create an organized movement or a significant change in a company. A person with no constituents is not a leader, and people will not follow until they accept a vision as their own. Leaders cannot command commitment, only inspire it.

To enlist people in a vision, leaders must know their constituents and speak their language. People must believe that leaders understand their needs and have their interests at heart. Leadership is a dialogue, not a monologue. To enlist support, leaders must have intimate knowledge of people's dreams, hopes, aspirations, visions, and values.

Leaders breathe life into the hopes and dreams of others and enable them to see the exciting possibilities that the future holds. Leaders forge a unity of purpose by showing constituents how the dream is for the common good. Leaders ignite the flame of passion in others by expressing enthusiasm for the compelling vision of their group. Leaders communicate their passion through vivid language and an expressive style.

And leaders are in all places. When he was named captain of the soccer team as a high school junior, Dave Praklet knew he would have to do something to inspire his teammates to always give 110 percent. As he explained to us: "I had to get personal with them and tell them how good it feels to win a league championship. Or how good it feels as you step on the field for a championship game—how the adrenaline sends a tingling feeling through your entire body. Recounting these memorable moments helped me inspire the team to want to work hard. They wanted to see what it feels like and play with your heart."

Whatever the venue, and without exception, the people in our study reported that they were incredibly enthusiastic about their personal-best projects. Their own enthusiasm was catching; it spread from leader to constituents. Their belief in and enthusiasm for the vision were the sparks that ignited the flame of inspiration.

Challenge the Process

Leaders venture out. None of the individuals in our study sat idly by waiting for fate to smile upon them. "Luck" or "being in the right place at the right time" may play a role in the specific opportunities leaders embrace, but those who lead others to greatness seek and accept challenge. Lindsay Levin, for instance, rose to the occasion when circumstances required her to take over the family business. In the process, she also found innovative ways to transform the business. Alan Keith succeeded in confronting a traditional culture with some radical new ideas.

Every single personal-best leadership case we collected involved some kind of challenge. The challenge might have been an innovative new product, a cutting-edge service, a groundbreaking piece of legislation, an invigorating campaign to get adolescents to join an environmental program, a revolutionary turnaround of a bureaucratic military program, or the start-up of a new plant or business. Whatever the challenge, all the cases involved a change from the status quo. Not one person claimed to have achieved a personal best by keeping things the same. All leaders *challenge the process*.

Leaders are pioneers—people who are willing to step out into the unknown. They search for opportunities to innovate, grow, and improve. But leaders aren't the only creators or originators of new products, services, or processes. In fact, it's more likely that they're not: innovation comes more from listening than from telling. Product and service innovations tend to come from customers, clients, vendors, people in the labs, and people on the front lines; process innovations, from the people doing the work. Sometimes a dramatic external event thrusts an organization into a radically new condition.

The leader's primary contribution is in the recognition of good ideas, the support of those ideas, and the willingness to challenge the system to get new products, processes, services, and systems adopted. It might be more accurate, then, to say that leaders are *early adopters* of innovation.

Leaders know well that innovation and change all involve experimentation, risk, and failure. They proceed anyway. One way of dealing with the potential risks and failures of experimentation is to approach change through incremental steps and small wins. Little victories, when piled on top of each other, build confidence that even the biggest challenges can be met. In so doing, they strengthen commitment to the long-term future. Yet not everyone is equally comfortable with risk and uncertainty. Leaders also pay attention to the capacity of their constituents to take control of challenging situations and become fully committed to change. You can't exhort people to take risks if they don't also feel safe.

It would be ridiculous to assert that those who fail over and over again eventually succeed as leaders. Success in any endeavor isn't a process of simply buying enough lottery tickets. The key that unlocks the door to opportunity is learning. In his own study of exemplary leadership practices, Warren Bennis writes that "leaders learn by leading, and they learn best by leading in the face of obstacles. As weather shapes mountains, problems shape leaders. Difficult bosses, lack of vision and virtue in the executive suite, circumstances beyond their control, and their own mistakes have been the leaders' basic curriculum."[3] In other words, leaders are learners. They learn from their failures as well as their successes.

Enable Others To Act

Grand dreams don't become significant realities through the actions of a single person. Leadership is a team effort. After reviewing thousands of personal-best cases, we developed a simple test to detect whether someone is on the road to becoming a leader. That test is the frequency of the use of the word *we*. In our interview with Alan Keith, for instance, he used the word "we" nearly three times more often than the word "I" in explaining his personal-best leadership experience.

Exemplary leaders *enable others to act.* They foster collaboration and build trust. This sense of teamwork goes far beyond a few direct reports or close confidants. They engage all those who must make the project work—and in some way, all who must live with the results. In today's "virtual" organization, cooperation can't be restricted to a small group of loyalists; it must include peers, managers, customers and clients, suppliers, citizens—all those who have a stake in the vision.

Leaders make it possible for others to do good work. They know that those who are expected to produce the results must feel a sense of personal power and ownership. Leaders understand that the command-and-control techniques of the Industrial Revolution no longer apply. Instead, leaders work to make people feel strong, capable, and committed. Leaders enable others to act not by hoarding the power they have but by giving it away. Exemplary leaders strengthen everyone's capacity to deliver on the promises they make. As a budget analyst for Catholic Healthcare West, Cindy Giordano would ask "What do you think?" and use the ensuing discussion to build up the capabilities of others (as well as educate and update her own information and perspective). She discovered that when people are trusted and have more discretion, more authority, and more information, they're much more likely to use their energies to produce extraordinary results.

In the cases we analyzed, leaders proudly discussed teamwork, trust, and empowerment as essential elements of their efforts. A leader's ability to enable others to act is essential. Constituents neither perform at their best nor stick around for very long if their leader makes them feel weak, dependent, or alienated. But when a leader makes people feel strong and capable—as if they can do more than they ever thought possible—they'll give it their all and exceed their own expectations. When leadership is a relationship founded on trust and confidence, people take risks, make changes, keep organizations and movements alive. Through that relationship, leaders turn their constituents into leaders themselves.

Encourage the Heart

The climb to the top is arduous and long. People become exhausted, frustrated, and disenchanted. They're often tempted to give up. Leaders *encourage the heart* of their constituents to carry on. Genuine acts of caring uplift the spirits and draw people forward. Encouragement can come from dramatic gestures or simple actions. When Cary Turner was head of Pier 1 Imports' Stores division, he once showed up in a wedding gown to promote the bridal registry. On another occasion, he promised store employees he'd parasail over Puget Sound and the Seattle waterfront if they met their sales targets. They kept their commitment; he kept his. As mayor of New York City, Rudy Giuliani wore different hats (literally) to acknowledge various groups of rescue workers as he toured ground zero after the World Trade Center towers were destroyed on September 11, 2001. But it doesn't take events or media coverage to let people know you appreciate their contributions. Terri Sarhatt, customer services manager at Applied Biosystems, looked after her employees so well that at least one reported that the time she spent with them was more valuable than the tangible rewards she was able to give out.

It's part of the leader's job to show appreciation for people's contributions and to create a culture of celebration. In the cases we collected, we saw thousands of examples of individual recognition and group celebration. We've heard and seen everything from handwritten thank-yous to marching bands and "This Is Your Life" ceremonies.

Recognition and celebration aren't about fun and games, though there is a lot of fun and there are a lot of games when people encourage the hearts of their constituents. Neither are they about pretentious ceremonies designed to create some phony sense of camaraderie. When people see a charlatan making noisy affectations, they turn away in disgust. Encouragement is curiously serious business. It's how leaders visibly and behaviorally link rewards with performance. When striving to raise quality, recover from disaster, start up a new service, or make dramatic change of any kind, leaders make sure people see the benefit of behavior that's aligned with cherished values. And leaders also know that celebrations and rituals, when done with authenticity and from the heart, build a strong sense of collective identity and community spirit that can carry a group through extraordinarily tough times.

LEADERSHIP IS A RELATIONSHIP

Leadership is an identifiable set of skills and practices that are available to all of us, not just a few charismatic men and women. The "great person"—woman or man—theory of leadership is just plain wrong. Or, we should say, the theory that there are only a *few* great men and women who can lead us to greatness is just plain wrong. We consider the women and men in our research to be great, and so do those with whom they worked. They are the everyday heroes of our world. It's because we have so many—not so few—leaders that we are able to get extraordinary things done on a regular basis, even in extraordinary times.

Our findings also challenge the myth that leadership is something that you find only at the highest levels of organizations and society. We found it everywhere. To us this is inspiring and should give everyone hope. Hope, because it means that no one needs to wait around to be saved by someone riding into town on a white horse. Hope, because there's a generation of leaders searching for the opportunities to make a difference. Hope, because right down the block or right down the hall there are people who will seize the opportunity to lead you to greatness. They're your neighbors, friends, and colleagues. And you are one of them, too.

There's still another crucial truth about leadership—more apparent to us this time around than it was before. It's something that we've known for a long time, but we've come to prize its value even more today. In talking to leaders and reading their cases, there was a very clear message that wove itself throughout every situation and every action: *leadership is a relationship.* Leadership is a relationship between those who aspire to lead and those who choose to follow.

Evidence abounds for this point of view. For instance, in examining the critical variables for success in the top three jobs in large organizations, Jodi

Taylor and her colleagues at the Center for Creative Leadership found the number one success factor to be "relationships with subordinates."[4] We were intrigued to find that even in this nanosecond world of e-everything, opinion is consistent with the facts. In an *on-line* survey, respondents were asked to indicate, among other things, which would be more essential to business success in five years—social skills or skills in using the Internet. Seventy-two percent selected social skills; 28 percent, Internet skills.[5] Internet literati completing a poll on-line realize that it's not the web of technology that matters the most, it's the web of people.

Similar results were found in a study by Public Allies, an AmeriCorps organization dedicated to creating young leaders who can strengthen their communities. Public Allies sought the opinions of eighteen- to thirty-year-olds on the subject of leadership. Among the items was a question about the qualities that were important in a good leader. Topping the respondents' list is "Being able to see a situation from someone else's point of view." In second place, "Getting along well with other people."[6]

Success in leadership, success in business, and success in life has been, is now, and will continue to be a function of how well people work and play together. We're even more convinced of this today than we were twenty years ago. Success in leading will be wholly dependent upon the capacity to build and sustain those human relationships that enable people to get extraordinary things done on a regular basis.

THE TEN COMMITMENTS OF LEADERSHIP

Embedded in The Five Practices of Exemplary Leadership are behaviors that can serve as the basis for learning to lead. We call these The Ten Commitments of Leadership. These ten commitments serve as the guide for our discussion of how leaders get extraordinary things done in organizations and as the structure for what's to follow. We'll fully explore each of these commitments in Chapters Three through Twelve. Before delving into the practices and commitments further, however, let's consider leadership from the vantage point of the constituent. If leadership is a relationship, as we have discovered, then what do people expect from that relationship? What do people look for and admire in a leader? What do people want from someone whose direction they'd be willing to follow?

THE FIVE PRACTICES AND TEN COMMITMENTS OF LEADERSHIP

PRACTICE	COMMITMENT

Model the Way

1. Find your voice by clarifying your personal values.
2. Set the example by aligning actions with shared values.

PART 3

Inspire a Shared Vision

3. Envision the future by imagining exciting and ennobling possibilities.
4. Enlist others in a common vision by appealing to shared aspirations.

PART 4

Challenge the Process

5. Search for opportunities by seeking innovative ways to change, grow, and improve.
6. Experiment and take risks by constantly generating small wins and learning from mistakes.

Enable Others to Act

7. Foster collaboration by promoting cooperative goals and building trust.
8. Strengthen others by sharing power and discretion.

Encourage the Heart

9. Recognize contributions by showing appreciation for individual excellence.
10. Celebrate the values and victories by creating a spirit of community.

Source: The Leadership Challenge by James M. Kouzes and Barry Z. Posner. Copyright © 2002.

2 CREDIBILITY IS THE FOUNDATION OF LEADERSHIP

Without credibility, you can't lead.

Brian Carroll, Challenge Bank, Australia

You can't follow someone who isn't credible, who doesn't truly believe in what they're doing—and how they're doing it.

Gayle Hamilton, Pacific Gas and Electric

Model the way, inspire a shared vision, challenge the process, enable others to act, and encourage the heart: these are the leadership practices that emerge from personal-best cases. But they paint only a partial picture. The portrayal can be complete and vivid only when we add in what constituents expect from their leaders. What leaders say they do is one thing; what constituents say they want and how well leaders meet these expectations is another. Leadership is a reciprocal process between those who aspire to lead and those who choose to follow. Any discussion of leadership must attend to the dynamics of this relationship. Strategies, tactics, skills, and practices are empty without an understanding of the fundamental human aspirations that connect leaders and constituents.

To balance our understanding of leadership, we investigated the expectations that constituents have of leaders. We asked constituents to tell us what they look for and admire in a leader. Their responses affirm and enrich the picture that emerged from our studies of personal bests. Clearly, those who aspire to lead must embrace their constituents' expectations.

WHAT PEOPLE LOOK FOR AND ADMIRE IN THEIR LEADERS

We began our research on what constituents expect of leaders more than two decades ago by surveying thousands of business and government executives. We asked the following open-ended question: "What values (personal traits or characteristics) do you look for and admire in your leader?"[1] In response to that question, respondents identified more than 225 different values, traits, and characteristics. Subsequent content analysis by several independent judges, followed by further analyses, reduced these items to a list of twenty characteristics, each with a few synonyms for clarification.

We've administered this questionnaire to over seventy-five thousand people around the globe, and we update the findings continuously. We distribute the checklist and ask respondents to select the seven qualities that they "most look for and admire in a leader, someone whose direction they would willingly follow." We tell them that the key word in this question is *willingly*. What do they expect from a leader they would follow not because they *have to,* but because they *want to?* We often ask respondents to imagine they are electing a leadership council of seven members and that there are twenty candidates in the running; these candidates are ideal qualities, not specific individuals.

The results of these surveys have been striking in their regularity over the years. It appears that a person must pass several essential tests before others are willing to grant the title *leader.* In Table 2.1, we present three sets of data gathered over the last two decades.

Although all characteristics receive some votes, and therefore each is important to some people, what is most striking and most evident is that, consistently over time and across continents, *only four* have continuously received over 50 percent of the votes. (For data on how these top four rank in different countries, see Table 2.2.) Some of the other qualities have flirted with consensus, but what people *most* look for and admire in a leader has been constant. As the data clearly show, for people to follow someone *willingly,* the majority of constituents must believe the leader is

- Honest
- Forward-looking
- Competent
- Inspiring

Table 2.1. Characteristics of Admired Leaders.

Characteristic	Percentage of Respondents Selecting That Characteristic		
	2002 edition	1995 edition	1987 edition
HONEST	88	88	83
FORWARD-LOOKING	71	75	62
COMPETENT	66	63	67
INSPIRING	65	68	58
Intelligent	47	40	43
Fair-minded	42	49	40
Broad-minded	40	40	37
Supportive	35	41	32
Straightforward	34	33	34
Dependable	33	32	33
Cooperative	28	28	25
Determined	24	17	17
Imaginative	23	28	34
Ambitious	21	13	21
Courageous	20	29	27
Caring	20	23	26
Mature	17	13	23
Loyal	14	11	11
Self-Controlled	8	5	13
Independent	6	5	10

Note: These percentages represent respondents from six continents: Africa, North America, South America, Asia, Europe, and Australia. The majority are from the United States. Since we asked people to select seven characteristics, the total adds up to 700 percent.
Source: The Leadership Challenge by James M. Kouzes and Barry Z. Posner. Copyright © 2002.

Table 2.2. Some Cross-Cultural Comparisons of the Characteristics of Admired Leaders.

Country	Percentage of Respondents Selecting Each Characteristic			
	Honest	Forward-looking	Competent	Inspiring
Australia	93	83	59	73
Canada	88	88	60	73
Japan	67	83	61	51
Korea	74	82	62	55
Malaysia	95	78	62	60
Mexico	85	82	62	71
New Zealand	86	86	68	71
Scandinavia	84	86	53	90
Singapore	65	78	78	94
United States	88	71	69	63

To understand the constituent's perspective even more fully, we expanded our work to include written case studies of the behaviors of admired leaders. People responded to questions about leaders with whom they had personal experience and for whom they had great admiration and respect. From these case studies (now numbering over a thousand) we collected specific examples of actions of respected leaders, information on the affective nature of admired leader–constituent relationships, and details about the types of projects or programs involved. These data came from sources in North America, Mexico, Western Europe, Asia, and Australia. Focus groups conducted subsequent to the collection of early cases further enabled us to determine the behaviors of admired leaders. Additionally, we conducted in-depth interviews with more than forty respected leaders and asked them to comment as constituents on the actions they believed exemplified quality leadership. Through a series of quantitative studies, we gained further insight into the leadership actions that influence people's assessments of credibility.[2]

These investigations of admired leader attributes reveal consistent and clear relationships with the stories we heard people tell us about their personal-best leadership experiences. The Five Practices of Exemplary Leadership and the characteristics of admired leaders are complementary perspectives on the same subject. When they're performing at their peak, leaders are doing more than just getting results. They're also responding to the expectations of their constituents, underscoring the point that leadership is a relationship and that the relationship is one of service to a purpose and service to people. As we weave the themes of being honest, forward-looking, competent, and inspiring into the text of the subsequent chapters on the practices, you'll see in more detail how exemplary leaders respond to the needs of their constituents. First, though, here's a closer look at each of the four attributes that have been selected by the majority of respondents over the last two decades.

Honest

In almost every survey we've conducted, honesty has been selected more often than any other leadership characteristic; overall, it emerges as the single most important ingredient in the leader-constituent relationship. The percentages vary, but the final ranking does not. Since the very first time we conducted our studies in the early 1980s, honesty has been at the top of the list.

It's clear that if people anywhere are to willingly follow someone—whether it be into battle or into the boardroom, the front office or the front lines—they first want to assure themselves that the person is worthy of their trust. They want to know that the person is truthful, ethical, and principled. When people talk to us about the qualities they admire in leaders, they often use "integrity" and "character" as synonymous with honesty. No matter what the setting, everyone wants to be fully confident in their leaders, and to be fully confident they have to believe that their leaders are people of strong character and solid integrity. That nearly 90 percent of constituents want their leaders to be honest above all else is a message that all leaders must take to heart.[3]

We—all of us—don't want to be lied to or deceived. We want to be told the truth. We want a leader who knows right from wrong. Yes, we want our team to win, but we don't want to be led—or *misled?*—by someone who cheats in the process of attaining victory. We want our leaders to be honest because their honesty is a reflection upon our own honesty. Of all the qualities that people look for and admire in a leader, honesty is by far the most personal. More than likely this is also why it consistently ranks number one. It's the quality that can most enhance or most damage our own personal reputations. If we follow someone who's universally viewed as being of impeccable character and strong integrity, then we're likely to be viewed the same. But if we willingly follow someone who's considered dishonest, our own images are tarnished. And there's perhaps another, more subtle, reason why honesty is at the top. When we follow someone we believe to be dishonest, we come to realize that we've compromised our own integrity. Over time, we not only lose respect for the leader, we lose respect for ourselves.

Just how do constituents measure a characteristic as subjective as honesty? In our discussions with respondents, we learned that the leader's *behavior* provided the evidence. Regardless of what leaders say about their own integrity, people wait to be shown; they observe the behavior. Consistency between word and deed is how people judge someone to be honest.

Honesty is strongly tied to values and ethics. We appreciate people who take a stand on important principles. We resolutely refuse to follow those who lack confidence in their own beliefs. Confusion over where the leader stands creates stress; not knowing the leader's beliefs contributes to conflict, indecision, and political rivalry. We simply don't trust people who can't or won't tell us their values, ethics, and standards.

Forward-Looking

More than 70 percent of our most recent respondents selected the ability to look ahead as one of their most sought-after leadership traits. People expect leaders to have a sense of direction and a concern for the future of the organization. This expectation directly corresponds to the ability to envision the future that leaders described in their personal-best cases. But whether we call that ability vision, a dream, a calling, a goal, or a personal agenda, the message is clear: leaders must know where they're going if they expect others to willingly join them on the journey.

Two other surveys that we conducted with top executives reinforce the importance of clarity of purpose and direction. In one study, nearly three hundred senior executives rated "developing a strategic planning and forecasting capability" as their most critical concern. When asked to select the most important characteristics in a CEO, these same senior managers ranked "a leadership style of honesty and integrity" first and "a long-term vision and direction for the company" second.[4]

By the ability to be *forward-looking,* people don't mean the magical power of a prescient visionary. The reality is far more down-to-earth: it's the ability to set or select a desirable destination toward which the company, agency, congregation, or community should head. Vision reveals the beckoning summit that provides others with the capacity to chart their course toward the future. As constituents, we ask that a leader have a well-defined orientation toward the future. We want to know what the organization will look like, feel like, be like when it arrives at its destination in six quarters or six years. We want to have it described to us in rich detail so that we'll know when we've arrived and so that we can select the proper route for getting there.

There is one significant finding about the quality of being forward-looking that's important to note. When we survey individuals at the most senior levels in organizations, the percentage of people who select forward-looking as a desired leader characteristic is around 95 percent. When we administer our checklist to people in frontline supervisory roles, the percentage of people selecting forward-looking is around 60 percent. This wide gap indicates an important difference in expectation that's clearly tied to the breadth, scope, and time horizon of the job. More senior people see the need for a longer-term view of the future than do those at the front lines of operations. This also suggests a major developmental need for individuals as they move into roles that are more strategic in nature.

Competent

To enlist in another's cause, we must believe that the person is competent to guide us where we're headed. We must see the leader as capable and effective. If we doubt the leader's abilities, we're unlikely to enlist in the crusade.

Leadership competence refers to the leader's track record and ability to get things done. It's the kind of competence that inspires confidence that the leader will be able to guide the entire organization, large or small, in the direction in which it needs to go. It doesn't refer specifically to the leader's abilities in the core technology of the operation. In fact, the type of competence demanded seems to vary more with the leader's position and the condition of the organization. While we demand a base level of under-standing of the fundamentals of the industry, market, or professional ser-vice environment, we also know that leaders can't be expected to be the most technically competent in their fields. Organizations are too complex and multifunctional for that ever to be the case. This is particularly true as people reach the more senior levels. For example, those who hold officer positions are definitely expected to demonstrate abilities in strategic plan-ning and policy making. If a company desperately needs to clarify its core competence and market position, a CEO with savvy in competitive mar-keting may be perceived as a fine leader. But in the line function, where peo-ple expect guidance in technical areas, these same strategic marketing abilities will be insufficient. A leader on the line or at the point of customer or client contact will typically have to be more technically competent than someone less engaged in providing services or making products. Yet it's not necessary that even the frontline leader have superior technical competence compared to the constituents. Much more significant is that the leader takes the time to learn the business and to know the current operation.

Relevant experience is a dimension of competence and one that is differ-ent from technical expertise. Experience is about active participation in situ-ational, functional, and industry events and activities and the accumulation of knowledge derived from participation. Experience correlates with success, and the broader your experience, the more likely you are to be successful across organizations and industries. An effective leader in a high-technology company, for example, may not need to be a master programmer, but must understand the business implications of electronic data interchange, net-working, and the World Wide Web. A health care administrator with experi-ence only in the insurance industry is more than likely doomed; the job needs extensive experience in the delivery of human services. There may be notable exceptions, but it is highly unlikely that a leader can succeed without both rel-evant experience and, most important, exceptionally good people skills.

A leader must have the ability to bring out the best in others—to enable others to act. In fact, new research is revealing that the ability to enable others to act has become the critical differentiator between success and failure in the executive ranks. We think it applies equally at all organizational levels, as well as to leaders in all settings. The most important competency a leader brings to the role is the ability to work well with others. As we pointed out in Chapter One, leadership is a relationship, and relationship skills are what shape success. The practices we discuss in this book—modeling, inspiring, challenging, enabling, and encouraging—are skills leaders must master if they're going to be considered competent.

Inspiring

We also expect our leaders to be enthusiastic, energetic, and positive about the future. We expect them to be inspiring—a bit of the cheerleader, as a matter of fact. It's not enough for a leader to have a dream about the future. A leader must be able to communicate the vision in ways that encourage us to sign on for the duration. We all long to find some greater sense of purpose and worth in our day-to-day working lives. Although the enthusiasm, energy, and positive attitude of a good leader may not change the content of work, they certainly can make the context more meaningful. Whatever the circumstances, when leaders breathe life into our dreams and aspirations, we're much more willing to enlist in the movement.

Inspiring leadership speaks to our need to have meaning and purpose in our lives. Further, being upbeat, positive, and optimistic about the future offers people hope. This is crucial at any time, but in times of great uncertainty, leading with positive emotions is absolutely essential to moving people upward and forward.[5] When people are worried, discouraged, frightened, and uncertain about the future, the *last* thing needed is a leader who feeds those negative emotions. Instead, we need leaders who communicate in words, demeanor, and actions that they believe we *will* overcome. Emotions are contagious, and positive emotions resonate throughout an organization and into relationships with other constituents. To get *extraordinary* things done in *extraordinary* times, leaders must inspire optimal performance—and that can only be fueled with positive emotions.

Some react with discomfort to the idea that being inspiring is an essential leadership quality. Some have even told us, "I don't trust people who are inspiring." No doubt this is a response to the crusaders who have led people to death or destruction. Others told us they were skeptical of their own ability to inspire others. Such lack of faith in others and in yourself is a terrible mistake. In the final analysis, leaders must uplift their constituents' spirits and give them hope if they're to voluntarily engage in challenging pursuits. Enthusiasm and excitement are essential, and they signal the leader's personal commitment to pursuing a dream. If a leader displays no passion for a cause, why should anyone else?

PUTTING IT ALL TOGETHER: CREDIBILITY IS THE FOUNDATION

Honest, forward-looking, competent, and inspiring: these are the characteristics that have remained constant during two decades of growth and recession, the surge in new technology enterprises, the birth of the World Wide Web, the further globalization of the economy, the ever-changing political environment, and the expansion and bursting of the Internet bubble. The relative importance of the most desired qualities has varied over time, but there has been no change in the fact that these are the four qualities people want most in their leaders. Whether we believe our leaders are true to these values is another matter, but what we would like from them has remained constant.

This list of four consistent findings is useful in and of itself—and there's a more profound implication revealed by our research. These key characteristics make up what communications experts refer to as "source credibility." In assessing the believability of sources of communication—whether newscasters, salespeople, physicians, or priests; whether business managers, military officers, politicians, or civic leaders—researchers typically evaluate people on three criteria: their perceived trustworthiness, their expertise, and their dynamism. Those who are rated more highly on these dimensions are considered to be more credible sources of information.

Notice how strikingly similar these three characteristics are to the admired leader qualities of honest, competent, and inspiring—three of the top four items selected in our survey. What we found in our investigation of admired leadership qualities is that more than anything, *people want leaders who are credible. Credibility is the foundation of leadership.*

Above all else, we must be able to believe in our leaders. We must believe that their word can be trusted, that they'll do what they say, that they're personally excited and enthusiastic about the direction in which we're headed, and that they have the knowledge and skill to lead.

Because this finding has been so pervasive and so consistent, we've come to refer to it as The First Law of Leadership:

If you don't believe in the messenger, you won't believe the message.

Credibility Makes a Difference

At this point, cynics might well say, "So what? I know people who are in positions of power and who are enormously wealthy, yet people don't find them credible. Does credibility really matter? Does it make a difference?"

It's a legitimate question, and we feel compelled to address it. But rather than ask about "top management" or "elected officials," we asked questions about people closer to home. We asked people to rate their immediate manager. As part of our quantitative research, using a behavioral measure of credibility, we asked organization members to think about the extent to which their immediate manager exhibited credibility-enhancing behaviors. We found that when people perceive their immediate manager to have high credibility, they're significantly more likely to

- Be proud to tell others they're part of the organization.
- Feel a strong sense of team spirit.
- See their own personal values as consistent with those of the organization.
- Feel attached and committed to the organization.
- Have a sense of ownership of the organization.

When people perceive their manager to have low credibility, on the other hand, they're significantly more likely to

- Produce only if they're watched carefully.
- Be motivated primarily by money.
- Say good things about the organization publicly but criticize it privately.

- Consider looking for another job if the organization experiences problems.
- Feel unsupported and unappreciated.

This evidence of the significant impact of leadership credibility on employee attitudes and behavior certainly provides clear dictates for organizational leaders. Credibility makes a difference, and leaders must take it personally. Loyalty, commitment, energy, and productivity depend upon it.

Credibility goes far beyond employee attitudes. It influences customer and investor loyalty as well as employee loyalty. In an extensive study of the economic value of business loyalty, Frederick Reichheld and his Bain & Company colleagues found that businesses concentrating on customer, employee, and investor loyalty generate superior results compared to those engendering disloyalty. They found further that disloyalty can dampen performance by a stunning 25–50 percent.[6] Loyalty is clearly responsible for extraordinary value creation. So what accounts for business loyalty? When they investigated this question, the researchers found that "The center of gravity for business loyalty—whether it be the loyalty of customers, employees, investors, suppliers, or dealers—is the personal integrity of the senior leadership team and its ability to put its principles into practice."[7] And what's true for bricks-and-mortar companies is just as true for the clicks companies. "In fact, when Web shoppers were asked to name the attributes of e-tailers that were most important in earning their business, the number one answer was 'a Web site I know and trust.' All other attributes, including lowest cost and broadest selection, lagged far behind. Price does not rule the Web; trust does."[8]

The Requirement and the Predicament of Being Forward-Looking

As much as we demand that leaders be credible before we will willingly follow them, credibility alone doesn't satisfy us; we demand something more from our leaders. We expect leaders to have a sense of direction, a vision for the future: we expect them to be forward-looking. Although we expect credible newscasters, for example, to be independent when reporting what's happening today, we expect leaders to have a point of view on today's events and to be firm about the destination of our national, organizational, or civic journey. We may want newscasters to be cool, reasoned, and objective, but we want leaders to articulate the exciting possibilities. Leaders don't just report the news; they make the news.

The dilemma is that leaders who are forward-looking are also biased—biased about the future. They aspire to change the way things are and guide us to a better tomorrow. But this very admirable and desirable leadership quality means that leaders often become the target of those who propose an alternative future. Thus when a leader takes a position on issues—when that leader has a clear point of view and a partisan sense of where the country, community, or company ought to be headed—that individual will be seen as less believable than someone who takes no stand. Consequently—ironic as it might seem—by the very nature of the role they play, leaders will always have their credibility questioned by those who oppose them.[9]

What does this mean for aspiring leaders? First, society places leaders in an awkward situation. We demand that they be credible, but we also contribute to undermining their credibility by expecting them to focus on a clear direction for the future. Leaders must learn how to balance their personal desire to achieve important ends with the constituents' need to believe that the leader has others' best interests at heart.

Second, because of this dilemma, leaders must be ever diligent in guarding their credibility. Their ability to take strong stands—to challenge the status quo, to point us in new directions—depends upon their being perceived as highly credible. Credibility matters as much to leaders as it does to other sources of information, if not more. If leaders ask others to follow them to some uncertain future—a future that may not be realized in their lifetime—and if the journey is going to require sacrifice, isn't it reasonable that constituents should believe in them? To believe in the exciting future possibilities leaders present, constituents must first believe in their leaders' trustworthiness, expertise, and dynamism.

This is not to suggest for one second that leadership is a popularity contest. It's totally unrealistic for any leader to expect 100 percent of potential constituents to willingly enlist.[10] Leaders have to learn to thrive on the tensions between their own calling and the voice of the people.

Opinions about those in leadership positions also tend to rise and fall with events. Americans generally have less confidence in many institutions now than they did in the 1970s when Gallup first began testing them. When times are good, people exhibit more confidence in their leaders; when times are bad, they show less. The more severe the events and the more compressed the time frame, the more cynical people are likely to become. And cynics have significantly less trust in their management than those who are upbeat. Nearly half of cynics doubt the truth of what management tells them, and only a third believe management has integrity. Three-quarters believe that top executives do pretty much what they want to no matter what people think.[11] And while most individuals believe that big government is low on the trust scale, many would be surprised to learn that only about 30 percent of the people on average have had confidence in big business over the last thirty years. With only a couple of exceptions, confidence in all institutions has tended downward since the 1970s.[12]

So it's understandable that in a period of drastic restructuring, with attendant layoffs and shrinking family incomes, the credibility of business, labor, church, and government leaders declines. A natural suspicion of power and the confluence of events—such as the financial and political scandals of the 1980s and 1990s, or the bursting of the Internet bubble, the drastic drop in stock portfolio values in mid-2001, and the Enron scandal in 2002—certainly explain a great deal about why leaders have lost credibility. Bad timing, bad times, and bad behavior can often tarnish trust.

Credibility problems aren't simply a function of the economic cycles, however. Even in the toughest of times, some leaders are held in extremely high regard, while others just fall out of respect. Some leaders stay true to their principles whatever the situation, and some are simply too weak, too amoral, too corrupt, or too mercenary to stand firm against the sirens of temptation or the gales of uncertainty. They have no strong bonds of belief that hold them firmly in place when they're lured by wealth, fame, or power, or are tossed about by turmoil, chaos, and disruptive change.

It would be absolutely reckless for leaders to attribute the majority of credibility gains or losses to the situation. Leaders must never take credibility for granted, regardless of the times or their positions. In any circumstance, credibility is one of the hardest attributes to earn and to sustain. It's personal—and the most fragile of human qualities. It's earned minute by minute, hour by hour, month by month, year by year. But it can be lost in very short order if not attended to. By and large people are willing to forgive a few minor transgressions, a slip of the tongue, a misspoken word, a careless act. But there comes a time when enough is enough. And when leaders have used up all of their credibility, it's nearly impossible to earn it back.

What Is Credibility Behaviorally?

Credibility is the foundation of leadership. Our data confirm this assertion time and time again. But what is credibility behaviorally? How do you know it when you see it?

We've asked this question of tens of thousands of people over nearly twenty years, and the response we get is always the same. Here are some of the common phrases people have used to describe how they know credibility when they see it:

- "Leaders practice what they preach."
- "They walk the talk."
- "Their actions are consistent with their words."
- "They put their money where their mouth is."
- "They follow through on their promises."
- *"They do what they say they will do."*

That last is the most frequent response. When it comes to deciding whether a leader is believable, people first listen to the words, then they watch the actions. They listen to the talk, and then they watch the walk. They listen to the promises of resources to support change initiatives, and then they wait to see if the money and materials follow. They hear the promises to deliver, and then they look for evidence that the commitments are met. A judgment of "credible" is handed down when words and deeds are consonant. If people don't see consistency, they conclude that the leader is, at best, not really serious, or, at worst, an outright hypocrite. If leaders espouse one set of values but personally practice another, we find them to be duplicitous. If leaders practice what they preach, we're more willing to entrust them with our career, our security, and sometimes even our life.

This realization leads to a straightforward prescription for leaders on how to establish credibility. It is:

DWYSYWD: Do What You Say You Will Do

This commonsense definition of credibility corresponds directly to one of the Five Practices of Exemplary Leadership identified in the personal best cases. DWYSYWD has two essential elements: *say* and *do*. To be credible in action, leaders must be clear about their beliefs; they must know what they stand for. That's the "say" part. Then they must put what they say into practice: they must act on their beliefs and "do." The practice of Modeling the Way links directly to these two dimensions of people's behavioral definition of credibility. This practice includes the clarification of a set of values and being an example of those values to others. This consistent living out of values is a behavioral way of demonstrating honesty and trustworthiness. We trust leaders when their deeds and words match.

To gain and sustain the moral authority to lead, it's essential to Model the Way. Because of this important connection between words and actions, we've chosen to start our discussion of the Five Practices with a thorough examination of the principles and behaviors that bring Model the Way to life. First, in Chapter Three, we introduce you to why it's essential to Find Your Voice—that unique expression of yourself that gives you the inner strength as a leader to *say* what you will *do*. Then, in Chapter Four, we'll take a look at how leaders Set the Example, the second half of the formula for establishing credibility. You'll see how leaders must focus on their own personal values and how they must build and affirm shared values. Throughout the chapters and the action steps, you'll also learn methods to align actions with values—the step in the process that communicates with deeds, not just words.

There are many more striking relationships between what leaders say they do when at their personal best and the attributes people look for and admire in their leaders. The leadership practice of Inspire a Shared Vision involves being forward-looking and inspiring. When leaders Challenge the Process, they enhance the perception that they're dynamic. Trust is also a major element of how leaders Enable Others to Act. In their descriptions of their personal bests, leaders said that they trusted others, which fostered others' trust in them. Likewise, leaders who recognize and celebrate significant accomplishments—who Encourage the Heart—increase their constituents' understanding of the commitment to the vision and values. When leaders demonstrate capacity in all of the Five Practices, they show others they have the competence to get extraordinary things done.

PART TWO

Model the Way

3 FIND YOUR VOICE

We lead from the essence of who we are as a person.

Lillas Brown, University of Saskatchewan

You have to believe in something yourself first, before you can get others to believe.

Ashraf Seddeek, Oracle Corporation

Max De Pree, former chairman and CEO of Herman Miller, the Michigan furniture maker, tells a moving story that well illustrates the connection between voice and actions:

> Esther, my wife, and I have a granddaughter named Zoe, the Greek word for "life." She was born prematurely and weighed one pound, seven ounces, so small that my wedding ring could slide up her arm to her shoulder. The neonatalogist who first examined her told us that she had a 5 to 10 percent chance of living three days. When Esther and I scrubbed up for our first visit and saw Zoe in her isolette in the neonatal intensive care unit, she had two IVs in her navel, one in her foot, a monitor on each side of her chest, and a respirator tube and a feeding tube in her mouth.

To complicate matters, Zoe's biological father had jumped ship the month before Zoe was born. Realizing this, a wise and caring nurse named Ruth gave me my instructions. "For the next several months, at least, you're the surrogate father. I want you to come to the hospital every day to visit Zoe, and when you come, I would like you to rub her body and her legs and her arms with the tip of your finger. While you're caressing her, you should tell her over and over how much you love her, because she has to be able to connect your voice to your touch."

Ruth was doing exactly the right thing on Zoe's behalf (and, of course, on my behalf as well), and without realizing it she was giving me one of the best possible descriptions of the work of a leader. At the core of becoming a leader is the need always to connect one's voice to one's touch.[1]

What power there is in connecting what we say to what we do, and what we do to what we say. In telling the story, Max articulates another important leadership lesson he learned from this traumatic experience: "There is of course a prior task—*finding* one's voice in the first place."[2]

Finding your voice is absolutely critical to becoming an authentic leader. If you can't find your voice, you'll end up with a vocabulary that belongs to someone else, mouthing words that were written by some speechwriter, or mimicking the language of some other leader who's nothing like you at all. As Max so eloquently reveals in this poignant story, if the words you speak are not *your* words but someone else's, you will not, in the long term, be able to be congruent—and therefore credible.

Voice in this context is both a noun and a verb. It encompasses words and speech. There's the message we want to deliver, and then there's the expression of that message. It's about *having* a voice and about *giving* voice.

To Find Your Voice you must engage in two *essentials:*

- Clarify your values
- Express your self

To become a credible leader, first you have to comprehend fully the values, beliefs, and assumptions that drive you. You have to freely and honestly choose the principles you will use to guide your actions. Before you can clearly communicate your message, you must be clear about the message you want to deliver. And before you can do what you say, you must be sure that you *mean* what you say.

Second, you have to genuinely express your self. The words themselves aren't enough, no matter how noble. You must authentically communicate your beliefs in ways that uniquely represent who you are. You must interpret the lyrics and shape them into your own singular presentation so that others recognize that you're the one who's speaking and not someone else.

CLARIFY YOUR VALUES

In our research studies and seminars, we've asked thousands of people to list the historical leaders they most admired—well-known leaders from the distant or recent past whom they could imagine following willingly. While no single leader receives a majority of the nominations, the two most frequently mentioned are Abraham Lincoln and Martin Luther King Jr. Other historical leaders who've made the list include Susan B. Anthony, Benazir Bhutto, César Chávez, Winston Churchill, Mahatma Gandhi, Mikhail Gorbachev, Nelson Mandela, Golda Meir, His Holiness the Dalai Lama, J. Robert Oppenheimer, His Holiness Pope John Paul II, Eleanor Roosevelt, Franklin D. Roosevelt, Mother Teresa, Margaret Thatcher, and Archbishop Desmond Tutu.

What do leaders like these have in common? In reviewing the list of the most admired leaders, one quality stands out above all else. The most striking similarity we've found—and surely it's evident to you—is that the list is populated by people with strong beliefs about matters of principle. They all have, or had, unwavering commitment to a clear set of values. They all are, or were, passionate about their causes. The lesson from this simple exercise is unmistakable. We admire most those who believe strongly in something, and who are willing to stand up for their beliefs. If anyone is ever to become a leader we'd willingly follow, one certain prerequisite is that they must be someone of principle.

David Pottruck, president and co-CEO of The Charles Schwab Corporation, summarizes it this way: "Virtually everyone I've ever met wanted to work with people of impeccable character. Just as my own character determines my personal ability to generate trust, so it is for the company as a whole. I wonder how many people think of building an entire company that has strength of character as its foundation. Such a company will be a compelling place to work."[3]

Remember the Kouzes-Posner First Law of Leadership?

If you don't believe in the messenger, you won't believe the message.

The observation that people most admire those leaders with clear and strong beliefs leads to the following corollary to our First Law:

You can't believe in the messenger if you don't know what the messenger believes.

People expect their leaders to speak out on matters of values and conscience. But how can you speak out if you don't know what to speak about? How can you stand up for your beliefs if you don't know what you stand for? How can you walk the talk if you have no talk to walk? How can you do what you say if you don't know what you want to say? To speak effectively, it's essential to find your own true voice. To earn and sustain personal credibility, you must be able to clearly articulate your deeply held beliefs.

Leaders who aren't clear about what they believe are likely to change their position with every fad or opinion poll. Without core beliefs and with only shifting positions, would-be leaders are judged as inconsistent and derided for being "political" in their behavior. Perhaps this is why so many people have become cynical about leadership.[4] They know that before politicians speak they've consulted their pollsters for exactly how to phrase their message. They know that senior executives have speechwriters to craft just the right language.

We all know deep down that people can only speak the truth when speaking in their own true voice. The techniques and tools that fill the pages of management and leadership books—including this one—are not substitutes for who and what you are.

Values Are Guides

In 1993 Lillas Brown was recruited to be the director of Business and Leadership Programs, a start-up operation in the University of Saskatchewan's Extension Division. She'd had a successful career as a corporate human resource development manager at Federated Cooperatives Ltd., a large retailer and wholesaler, but decided to make the switch to have an expanded role in working with people in a different setting. "I wanted to make a difference," says Lillas, "in the lives of leaders and their constituents in the workplace."

Lillas was new to the university system, and, she says now, "Like any new leader, I had to earn credibility. In any organization, credibility building is a process that takes time, hard work, devotion, and patience." But coming in as an outsider can be especially trying. There's more skepticism about your intentions and your abilities. This was even more true in Lillas's case, because one of the projects she initially took on was a leadership development program for department chairs. You can just hear the rumblings: "How can someone from retailing possibly help develop the skills of those in academia?"

"In the early years," Lillas says, "some naysayers dismissed my work, saying, 'This is a business model,' or 'You can't herd cats,' or 'Watch the fluff,' and so on. Painful as some of this was at the time, it not only contributed to my challenge, but it caused me to persevere. . . . It reinforced my intent to contribute to a more encouraging and nurturing culture than what I was experiencing."

Throughout this process Lillas turned to a simple method to aid her in staying the course. Every day she used personal journal writing for reflection and contemplation. "I use my journal to dialogue with the small still voice within," Lillas says. "Every evening I ask, 'What have I done today that demonstrates this value that is near and dear to me? What have I done inadvertently to demonstrate this is not a value for me? What do I need to do more of to more fully express my values?'" By daily clarifying and re-affirming her values, Lillas was able to strengthen her resolve to contribute. Increasingly, Lillas was able to win over even the most hardened skeptics and "accomplish what really mattered to the University and me while being more able to enjoy my life."

As Lillas's story illustrates, values are guides. They supply us with a moral compass by which to navigate the course of our daily lives. Clarity of values is essential to knowing which way, for each of us, is north, south, east, and west. The clearer we are, the easier it is to stay on the path we've chosen. This kind of guidance is especially needed in difficult and uncertain times. When there are daily challenges that can throw you off course, it's crucial that you have some signposts that tell you where you are.

The late Milton Rokeach, one of the leading researchers and scholars in the field of human values, referred to a value as an enduring belief. He noted that values are organized into two sets: means and ends.[5] In the context of our work on modeling, we use the term *values* to refer to our here-and-now beliefs about *how* things should be accomplished—what Rokeach calls *means values*. We will use *vision* in Chapters Five and Six when we refer to the long-term *ends values* the leader and constituents aspire to attain. It takes both. When sailing through the turbulent seas of change and uncertainty the crew needs a vision of what lies beyond the horizon, and they also must understand the standards by which performance will be judged. If either of these are absent, the vessel is likely to be lost at sea.

Values influence every aspect of our lives: our moral judgments, our responses to others, our commitments to personal and organizational goals. Values set the parameters for the hundreds of decisions we make every day. Options that run counter to our value system are seldom acted upon; and if they are it's done with a sense of compliance rather than commitment. Values constitute our personal "bottom line."

Values also serve as guides to action. They inform our decisions as to what to do and what not to do; when to say yes, or no, and really understand *why* we mean it.[6] If you believe, for instance, that diversity enriches innovation and service, then you should know what to do if people with differing views keep getting cut off when they offer up a fresh ideas. If you value collaboration over individualistic achievement, then you'll know what to do when your best salesperson skips team meetings and refuses to share information with colleagues. If you value independence and initiative over conformity and obedience, you'll be more likely to challenge something your manager says if you think it's wrong.

Values are empowering. We are much more in control of our own lives when we're clear about our personal values. When values are clear we don't have to rely upon direction from someone in authority. By knowing what means and ends are most important, we can act independently. We can also recognize a conflict between our own values and the values of the organization or society, and we can exercise choice about how to respond.

Values also motivate. They keep us focused on why we're doing what we're doing and the ends toward which we're striving. Values are the banners that fly as we persist, as we struggle, as we toil. We refer to them when we need to replenish our energy. Through them we can answer the question, Was it worth it?[7]

Personal Values Clarity Makes a Difference

Yes, values are guides, but how much difference does being clear about values make? Does it *really* matter? In research we conducted with our colleague Warren Schmidt, we set out to understand the relationship between personal values clarity and organizational values clarity.[8] The results of our research, summarized in the matrix in Figure 3.1, were reaffirming and surprising. They clearly indicate that values make a *significant* difference in behavior at work.

Figure 3.1. The Impact of Values Clarity on Commitment.

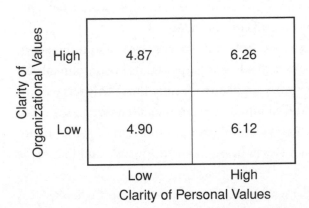

		Low	High
Clarity of Organizational Values	High	4.87	6.26
	Low	4.90	6.12

Clarity of Personal Values

Along the vertical axis is the extent to which people report being clear about their organization's values. Along the horizontal axis is the extent to which these same people report being clear about their own personal values. We then correlated these responses with the extent to which people said they were committed to the organization as measured on a scale of 1 (low) to 7 (high). We've organized the data into four cells, each representing a level of clarity from low to high on personal and organizational values. The numbers in each of the four cells represent the level of commitment people have to their organizations as it relates to the degree of their clarity about both personal and organizational values.

Take a look at where the highest level of commitment is. The people who have the greatest clarity about both personal and organizational values have the highest degree of commitment to the organization. Consistent with our previous research, we confirmed that individuals who are unclear about their own and the organization's values have only modest commitment and are apt to be particularly alienated from their work.

No surprises yet, but take another look. The lowest level of commitment is in the upper left corner—high clarity about organizational values but low clarity about personal values. Doesn't that make you a bit curious? It did us.

The second-highest level of commitment is in the bottom right corner—high clarity about personal values but low clarity about organizational values. What's significant and important here is that the people who know what they believe in but never have heard the corporate credo are *more likely* to stick around than those people who've heard the organizational litany but have never listened to their own inner voice. In other words, personal values are the route to loyalty and commitment.

How can this be? How can people who are very clear about their own values be committed to a place that has never posted its organizational values? Think about it. Have you ever had the feeling that "This place is not for me?" Have you ever walked into a place, immediately gotten the sense that "I don't belong here," and just walked right out? On the other hand, have you ever just known that you belong, can be yourself, and that "This is the right place for me."

It's the same way in the workplace. There comes a point when we just know whether it is or isn't a good fit with our values and beliefs, even if there was no lecture on the organization's values. We won't stick around a place for very long when we feel in our heart and in our soul that we don't belong.

Clarity about personal values is more important in our attitudes about work than is clarity about organizational values alone. Ultimately it's people who decide if the organization is a great place to work. Those individuals with the clearest personal values are better prepared to make choices based on principle—including deciding whether the principles of the organization fit with their own personal principles! The data also establish that sending the executive team off on a retreat to chisel out the organization's values, making corporate videos about those principles, conducting seminars on them, or handing out laminated wallet cards imprinted with the values all matter very little *unless* we also make sure that we ask individuals what they value and believe.

None of this is to say that shared values don't matter. On the contrary, based on a reading of our data and that of many others, shared values obviously matter a great deal.[9] People *want to* be part of something larger than themselves. What we're saying is this: people cannot fully commit to an organization or a movement that does not fit with their own beliefs. Leaders *must* pay as much attention to personal values as they do to organizational values if they want dedicated constituents.

Explore Your Inner Territory

Once, when discussing a list of most admired leaders, our conversation went something like this:

Jim: I think leadership begins with discontent.
Barry: That's too dismal a view for me. I think leadership begins with caring.
Jim: Okay, then, let's look up caring in the dictionary.

We grabbed one off the shelf, and opened it to "care." The first meaning: "suffering of mind: GRIEF."[10] There it was. Suffering and caring, discontent and concern, all come from one source. Deep within us all there is something we hold dear, and if it's ever violated we'll weep and wail. We'll fight to the death to secure it, grieve if we lose it, and shriek with joy when we achieve it.

In time, we realized that what we're both saying is *that leadership begins with something that grabs hold of you and won't let go.* This is where leaders must go to find their voice. To find your voice, you have to explore your inner territory. You have to take a journey into those places in your heart and soul where you bury your treasures, so that you can carefully examine them and eventually bring them out for display.

You *must* know what you care about. Why? Because you can only be authentic when leading others according to the principles that matter most to you. Otherwise you're just putting on an act. If you don't care, how can you expect others to do so? If you don't burn with desire to be true to something you hold passionately, how can you expect commitment from others? And until you get close enough to the flame to feel the heat, how can you know the source?

The answers to the question of values will come only when you're willing to take a journey through your inner territory—a journey that'll require opening doors that are shut, walking in dark spaces that are frightening, and touching the flame that burns. But at the end is truth.

John Robbins knows the joy and the pain of the inner journey. John is the founder of EarthSave International and chairman of Youth for Environmental Sanity (YES!). He's served on the boards of many nonprofit organizations dedicated to alleviating world hunger and to the health and welfare of all species, animal as well as human. He's the author of the best-selling books, *Diet for a New America* and *The Food Revolution.* Yet his role as a leader in these movements was not the path he was originally supposed to follow.

In his early years, John was groomed to become the chief executive of Baskin-Robbins, a company started by his father and his uncle. The pool in his backyard was in the shape of an ice cream cone, and his cats were named after ice cream flavors. Sometimes he ate ice cream for breakfast. As a young man, John scooped ice cream, loaded trucks, worked in franchising, marketing, merchandising, and every other aspect of what was at the time the world's largest ice cream company. But there was something stirring in him even in those early days that created a growing discomfort with the plan for his career.

John began to question the company's philosophies and found them to be out of synch with "something inside me that was very important to honor. And I didn't have a vocabulary for understanding it or expressing it. There was nothing in my parents' way of life or way of thinking that enabled me to understand what I was feeling, but the feelings were there, nevertheless, and they were just growing stronger as time went along."

It wasn't until John went off to college that he began to develop the words to express his own voice. He had the chance to hear and march with Dr. Martin Luther King Jr., and to protest the war in Vietnam. This was a very different direction from the one he'd known as a kid growing up in southern California. But compared to what he did after he graduated, these activities weren't the most radical. What he did next stunned his friends and family.

John was having a conversation with his dad, telling him about his deep concerns about the gap between rich and poor, about environmental deterioration, about living in a nuclear shadow. Then he said, "Do you understand, that for me, sensing these things as deeply as I do, inventing a thirty-second flavor just is not an adequate response."

John decided that the only route he could take that was true to himself was to cut the umbilical cord completely. He not only opted out of the company's succession, he refused any inheritance and any trust fund. He then set out to discover himself. He and his wife, Deo, spent the next ten years in a one-room log cabin on Salt Spring island off the coast of British Columbia. They lived on $1,000 a year, growing their own food and depending completely upon themselves and the earth. They meditated, did yoga, and gardened. And, as John put it, "I had to find my own ground in myself and a vocabulary for thinking about life and myself."

During this ten-year odyssey, John began to live by the values that culminated with the publication of *Diet for a New America*. He also started down a very public path of advocating for healthier choices about how we eat and for the welfare of all nature's creatures. He began to speak out about how animals are treated as they are prepared for our dinner tables, and how we can all make other choices when we shop and eat. He became active in his eloquence and his actions about the plight of the poor, and how our food habits contribute to world hunger. All this, from a one-time rich kid who grew up on ice cream.

Admittedly, John's case is not the norm. Few of us had the privileges that John had as a child, and even fewer of us have made or will make the choice to spend ten years in a one-room log cabin grounding ourselves. But his voice speaks so clearly and loudly that we can all learn from the powerful message in his life's story.

John urges all of us, "Make a statement with your life that's consistent with your heart, that gives voice to what you really feel is important. We don't have a lot of opportunities, most of us, to take stands—that are seen, anyway, that are visible. But my feeling is that you take it, whether it's seen or not, whether it's recognized or not, whether it's cheered or jeered. You do it because it's in you to do it, and because by doing it you're being true to who you are."

This is the common lesson we must all learn. To act with integrity, we must first know who we are.

Listen to the Masters

The internal exploration of our own inner territory to find our voice is often facilitated by listening carefully to the leaders we most respect. The leaders we personally admire are rich sources of information about our own values and beliefs. We chose them for a reason, so thinking more consciously about them can be extremely insightful.

In addition to asking people we've interviewed to tell us the historical leaders they admire, we've also asked them about individuals in their own lives who've been their leadership role models, and we've asked them to tell us what they've learned. Every interviewee has had an answer. The individual lessons vary, but the common learning is this: people try to model their behavior after those they admire and respect. When you listen carefully to the voices of your mentors and role models, you learn a lot about yourself.

When we asked Taylor Bodman, general partner at Brown Brothers Harriman in Boston about his historical and personal role models, he named six. He was able to tell us in great detail why he selected each person, what each did, how he felt about each, and what he learned from them. Here's just one abbreviated example:

> The fourth is a preacher at Harvard's Memorial Church. His name is Peter Gomes, and it's his storytelling that has made a difference to my own leadership practice. The thing about Gomes's stories—and of course he's often dealing with old texts—is how effectively he connects yesterday with today and tomorrow and where we're all going to end up. . . .
>
> I learned from Gomes that people burn out less from a lack of energy than from a lack of a sense of purpose. The insight changed the way I lead at work. I started to engage others in some large, obvious, and therefore long-absent questions, such as, "Why are we here?" and "What are we trying to do?" Observing Gomes also taught me that it is possible to honor the past and at the same time to make real the failings that lead us to want a better tomorrow.
>
> I have found for myself that stories can offer the perspective and meaning that generate energy in others. I try to do this at work. I try to determine the cause that is greater than ourselves and to convey it.

Taylor is typical of the people with whom we've spoken. The lessons are different, but the process is the same. We often learn how much we value something when we hear it from the mouth of a person we respect—and it resonates in our own heart.

We were talking to Phil Slater, author of *The Pursuit of Loneliness*, about teaching play writing, a past vocation. We commented that some writers think that finding your voice is about going off somewhere alone and listening only to one's inner voice: they think you have to develop your voice independent of others. To that he said, "Yes, I know. And they don't make very good writers."

The same can be said for leaders. If the only person you listen to is yourself, you're unlikely to discover your voice or your full potential. As Phil put it, "Finding your voice is about engaging with the world." When you engage with the world, and you try on other voices and other styles, you learn what fits you and what does not. Eventually your voice breaks through the noise and becomes recognizably you.

Clarity of values will enable you to feel more confident in your voice. Because clarity of values is so important to the process of finding your voice, we always ask participants in our workshops to record and make public their leadership principles. The details of this process are set forth at the end of this chapter in an action step titled "Write Your Credo." The exercise is no substitute for in-depth self-discovery, but it does provide a useful starting point for articulating your guiding principles.

EXPRESS YOUR SELF

Once you have a voice—the words you want to say—you must also give voice to those words. You must be able to express your voice so that everyone knows that you are the one who's speaking.

In this book we present a lot of scientific data to support our assertions about each of the practices. But leadership is also an art. And just as with any other art form—whether it's painting, playing music, dancing, acting, or writing—leadership is a means of personal expression. To become a credible leader you have to learn to express yourself in ways that are uniquely your own. As author Anne Lamott tells would-be writers in her classes:

> And the truth of your experience can *only* come through in your own voice. If it is wrapped in someone else's voice, we readers are suspicious, as if you are dressed up in someone else's clothes. You cannot write out of someone else's big dark place; you can only write out of your own. Sometimes wearing someone else's style is very comforting, warm and pretty and bright, and it may loosen you up, tune you into the joys of language and rhythm and concern. But what you say will be an abstraction because it will not have sprung from direct experience; when you try to capture the truth of your experience in some other person's voice or on that person's terms, you are removing yourself one step further from what you have seen and what you know.[11]

What's true for writers is just as true for leaders. You cannot lead through someone else's values, someone else's words. You cannot lead out of someone else's experience. You can only lead out of your own. Unless it's your style, your words, it's not you; it's an abstraction.

It's one thing to give voice to your words, it's another to give voice in tune, and with a personal style. If you're not the genuine article, can you really expect others to respect you? People don't follow your technique. They follow you—your message and your embodiment of that message.

In Your Own *Words*

One route to a true inner voice is in being more conscious about the words you choose and the words you use. Words matter. They're as much a form of expression for leaders as they are for poets, singers, and writers. Words send signals, and, if you listen intently, you may just hear the hidden assumptions about how someone views the world.

Take the following examples from an after-lunch speech we once heard a bank manager give to his employees. His intent was to motivate, but as we listened we heard more than that. We heard a fundamental belief system about how business functioned and what he believed to be important. Have a listen for yourself:

- "You've got to watch out for the headhunters."
- "Keep your capital and keep it dry."
- "We will act like SWAT teams."
- "We are going to beat their brains out."
- "Get the moccasin and the tom-tom going."
- "We won't tolerate the building of little fiefdoms."
- "There will be only a few survivors."

What is the main metaphor in these direct quotes from his speech? War. What this manager is saying is, "Business is a bloody war, and we're going to have to behave that way. It's kill or be killed." Contrast the bank manager's speech with the following words from Anita Roddick, founder of the Body Shop. These are phrases we've heard her use:[12]

- "We communicate with passion—and passion persuades."
- "I think all business practices would improve immeasurably if they were guided by feminine principles—like love, care, and intuition."
- "What we need is optimism, humanism, enthusiasm, intuition, curiosity, love humor, magic, fun, and that secret ingredient—euphoria."

- "I believe that service—whether it is serving the community or your family or the people you love or whatever—is fundamental to what life is about."

The organizational and business world that Anita paints contrasts dramatically with that of the bank manager. Hers is not about business as war, but about business as service and love. Anita and the bank manager are speaking in entirely different voices.

What's most important to understand is that Anita absolutely could not deliver the bank manager's words, and the bank manager could not deliver hers. We know this because we know them both. Their words are internally congruent for each of them. Each would be disingenuous and inauthentic if they spoke like the other.

To be a leader, you must confront this issue for yourself. You've got to awaken to the fact that you don't have to copy someone else, you don't have to read a script written by someone else, you don't have to wear someone else's style. Instead, you are free to choose what you want to express and the way you want to express it. In fact, we'd argue that you have a responsibility to your constituents to express yourself in a singular manner—in a way they would immediately recognize as yours.

The Three Stages of Self-Expression

Finding one's voice and finding one's unique way of expressing the self is something that every artist understands, and every artist knows that finding a voice is most definitely not a matter of technique. It's a matter of time and a matter of searching—soul-searching.

Several years ago we learned a valuable lesson about finding your voice from Jim LaSalandra, an artist friend of ours. Toward the end a walk through a gallery exhibiting a retrospective of Richard Diebenkorn's work, Jim made this observation: "There are really three periods in an artist's life. In the first, we paint exterior landscapes. In the second, we paint interior landscapes. In the third, we paint our selves. That's when you begin to have your own unique style." What applies to the art of painting applies just as well to the art of leadership.

Looking Out

When first learning to lead, we paint what we see outside ourselves—the exterior landscape. We read biographies and autobiographies about famous leaders. We observe master models and ask the advice of mentors. We read books and listen to audiotapes by experienced executives. We participate in training programs. We take on job assignments so that we can work alongside someone who can coach us. We want to learn everything we can from others, and we often try to copy their style.

We do all this to learn the fundamentals, and to acquire the tools and the techniques that others have learned from their experience. It's an absolutely essential period in a leader's development, and an aspiring leader can no more skip the fundamentals than can an aspiring painter. And we often return to this stage of finding our voice whenever we take on new and challenging roles—roles for which our previous experience has not prepared us.

Even though it's clear that authenticity comes only when you find your own authentic voice, sometimes when you're first developing your talents it can be quite useful to copy someone else's work. Author William Zinsser describes it this way:

> Never hesitate to imitate another writer. Imitation is a part of the creative process for anyone learning an art or a craft. Bach and Picasso didn't spring full-blown as Bach and Picasso; they needed models. Find the best writers in the fields that interest you and read their work aloud. Get their voice and their taste into your ear—their attitude toward language. Don't worry that by imitating them you'll lose your own voice and your own identity. Soon enough you will shed those skins and become who you are supposed to become.[13]

The same can be said for a leader's voice. It's useful to read, observe, and imitate the practices of leaders you admire. It's about learning the fundamentals. You'll discover over time what fits you, and what does not. As when trying on new clothes, you'll learn that on you some things look ridiculous and others bring out the best in you.

Even when you've been leading for a long time, it's important to stay open to learning from others on the outside. You never know when something might resonate. Taylor Bodman's story about pastor Gomes is just one example of continuously learning about ourselves by observing others.

Looking In

Somewhere along the way, you'll notice that your speech sounds mechanically rote, that your meetings are a boring routine, and that your interactions feel terribly sad and empty. You'll awaken to the frightening thought that the words aren't yours, that the vocabulary is someone else's, that the technique is right out of the text but not straight from the heart. While you've invested so much time and energy in learning to do all the right things, you suddenly see that they're no longer serving you well. The methods seem hollow. You may even feel like a phony.

In these moments you begin to stare into the darkness of your inner territory, and to wonder what lies inside. You say to yourself, "I'm not someone else. I'm a unique human being. But, *who* exactly am I? What is *my* voice?" For aspiring leaders, this awakening initiates a period of intense exploration, a period of testing, a period of invention. A period of going beyond technique, beyond training, beyond imitating the masters, and beyond taking the advice of others. Then, after exhausting experimentation and often painful suffering, there emerges from all those abstract strokes on the canvas an expression of self that is truly your own.

David Maister is considered by many to be the consultant's consultant. His entire practice is devoted to working with professional service firms, and he's highly regarded as a leader in his field.[14] Previously on the faculty at the Harvard Business School, David decided to go out on his own. "At the end of my first full year as a management consultant, at the age of thirty-nine, I decided to take stock," he reports.[15] He'd done well—at least that's what the bank account said. But David began to worry about his value to his clients. So he began an in-depth audit of his solo practice.

This internal audit was a turning point in David's career. David recalled that the health of a business is judged not only by the income statement but also by the balance sheet. So he asked himself what assets he had as a professional consultant. First he had his knowledge and skill, and then he had his client relationships. David began to realize that these were interdependent. If he relied only upon what he already knew, then he would only acquire clients who needed what he knew at that time. That, he surmised, was a finite number. Worse yet, his existing clients had already been served by what he already knew, so they were not likely to hire him again unless he learned more. Then it hit him. He hadn't learned anything new in his first year on his own.

"In sum," David concluded, "I learned that unless I actively worked at it, my career prospects would inevitably decline, even when (or perhaps especially when) I was making lots of money. Having a good current year financially was clearly a necessary condition for my success, but it was far from being a sufficient condition. Keeping my career moving forward, even staying level, was going to take conscious effort."[16]

David's story gives testimony to the fact that if you want to be hired or if you want to be followed, then you have to look within in order to improve and move on. You have to continuously ask yourself, How valuable am I—to my colleagues, to my customers, to my stockholders, to my partners in business?

Moving On

If, as David did, you're fortunate enough to experience an integrative turning point in your development—a point where you're able to merge the lessons from your outer and inner journeys—you move on to becoming an authentic leader, in whatever field you've chosen for yourself. You're able to recognize your own voice from the multitude of other voices ringing in your ears, and you find ways to express yourself in a singular style. You become the author of your own experience.

Anita Roddick is truly the author of her own experience. There's nothing cookie-cutter about her. For Anita the process of finding and expressing her voice was less a specific moment and more of a series of turning points. When we asked her to tell us the process she went through to find and express her singular voice, she said:

> My whole life, I went in the opposite direction to everyone else. I did the same thing when I opened my first shop, even though my ambitions at

that point were pretty basic. I just wanted to earn an honorable livelihood. With success came the sense that business has a responsibility to act as an agent for positive change. At some point, when you take such a position, you become a magnet, a kind of clearinghouse, for other people who share your convictions. And it happens over a while, so I can't say there was one flash of revelation. . . . I would say I am—and always have been—contrary, so my "true voice" would have been there from the beginning.

Egon Zehnder, founder and chairman emeritus of Egon Zehnder International, is also someone whose life has been marked by a series of turning points. It was his clarity of values that enabled him to move on at each juncture. For instance, following graduate school, he went to work for Spencer Stuart's U.S. executive search firm, and he was asked to start up the firm's offices in Europe. There came a point, however, when he had to confront his employer's practices as being too American and not well suited, in Egon's opinion, to the European culture. Spencer Stuart (with whom Egon is still good friends) didn't see it the same way, and suggested that Egon start his own company. Egon did just that. He moved on not for matters of money, or power, or prestige, but for matters of principle. He had the courage of his convictions. And Egon told us that this is how he wants to be remembered. He said that he wanted people to remember that "What Egon told us, he lived himself. He was open and he stuck to his principles all the way, even when life was very difficult. He was true to himself."

Unfortunately for many in leadership, development stalls in the artist's first period. It's still mostly about painting exterior landscapes, copying other people's styles, trying to mimic the great leaders. It's often based on the erroneous assumption that authentic leadership can come from the outside in. It cannot. It comes from the inside out. You have to be the author of your own story, not the reader of someone else's.

A BRIEF WORD ABOUT COMPETENCE

Having a voice and giving voice to your deeply-help beliefs requires competence. Words alone do not make a leader credible. Having a clear and authentic message is a necessary first step, yet the ability to consistently deliver the message and act on it requires a high level of skill. Before you can do the right things, you have to know how to do them. You cannot do what you don't know how to do, no matter how moral or noble the purpose.

To commit to doing something without the capacity to perform it is either disingenuous or stupid. There's nothing courageous about boldly saying you'll successfully launch a new product or turn around a factory if you have neither the skills nor the resources to do it. Leaders must be aware of the degree to which they actually have the capabilities to do what they say. And if they lack the competence they must dedicate themselves to continuously learning and improving.

Acquiring competence is all about being genuine. People who boast of being able to perform a task or achieve a goal or who make exaggerated claims of possessing noble attributes or desirable material goods are called phonies and fakes. People who actually possess the attributes or accomplish the results are called genuine.

Your value as a leader is determined not only by your guiding beliefs but also by your ability to act on them. To strengthen credibility you must continuously assess your existing abilities and learn new ones. And that takes time and attention.

Throughout this book, we'll talk about building your competence to lead in each of the Five Practices of Exemplary Leadership. We'll close each chapter with suggestions on how you can commit to the leadership challenge by offering suggestions on how to learn to lead and how to put what you learn into action. Here then is the first of a series of commitments and action steps that you can use to move yourself and others along the path to getting extraordinary things done.

COMMITMENT NUMBER 1:
FIND YOUR VOICE BY CLARIFYING
YOUR PERSONAL VALUES

Each and every one of us earns credibility as a leader on a daily basis. To be a leader, you have to Model the Way for others by demonstrating intense commitment to your beliefs with each and every action. Doing so begins by finding your voice—by clarifying your values and by expressing yourself in unique ways.

By finding your voice you take the first step along the endless journey to becoming a credible leader. By constantly asking yourself what value you bring to your constituents you'll always stay at the leading edge. This task brings us to the action steps you can take to find your voice and best present it.

• *Look in the mirror.*

Clarification of personal values begins with becoming more self-aware. A variety of opportunities are available, from sensitivity training groups to assessment centers to individual counseling. Whichever you choose, find some way to become better acquainted with who you are and how others see you. Self-knowledge can come from an internal search process, but we believe it needs to be supported with the advice and counsel of others. Someone needs to provide the mirror. Others cannot know our values unless we tell them, but they can observe our actions, and from our actions they infer our values. It's the ABCs of human action: *assumptions* (values) cause us to select certain *behaviors,* and those behaviors have *consequences.* By asking others to reflect back to us our behaviors, we can then better examine the assumptions that might be guiding our actions.

The option of 360-degree feedback, which is growing in popularity, suggests many possibilities. Ask your peers, managers, direct reports, spouse, friends, customers, and other constituents to give you feedback. There are many available tools you can use. For example, we have developed *The Leadership Practices Inventory* (LPI) to measure the leadership behaviors discussed in this book. But it's not the only available tool. Ask your human resources manager for some suggestions. Take advantage of these opportunities. And do it early in your career.

Feedback should be viewed as a gift, and if others offer this gift you should thank them. One way to thank them is to share with them the feedback they gave to you. Lisa Fink at United Medical Center in Cheyenne, Wyoming, talks about a time when she sat down with her staff and shared her LPI scores at the end of one of her regular staff meetings.

I explained the value that I saw in the 360-degree evaluation of frequency of behaviors and that their input was very important to me. I asked them to provide me with concrete suggestions as to how I could improve in this (Encouraging the Heart) practice. I left the room so they could talk for thirty minutes without me (this was not uncomfortable for me at all, by the way) and when I returned they had arrived at four simple suggestions that they felt would make them feel more valued and that would enable me to be more encouraging. . . .

I have to say that I was surprised! Pleasantly. I told them I would like to do this with each of the practices, and they felt it was valuable. The atmosphere and attitude has changed immensely in this department—immediately after that meeting.

Asking for feedback and concrete improvement suggestions, as Lisa did, can initially be somewhat scary and intimidating. As Lisa learned, however, the results can be valuable and pleasantly surprising. Leaders need these and other opportunities to have reflected back to them how their actions are received and how they affect others. After all, credibility is in the eye of the beholder, and only when we can see how others see us can we improve in ways that are responsive.

The time isn't of much value, though, if you aren't objective about yourself. Self-knowledge requires candor. You must get (and accept) honest, straightforward feedback, or you have no objective measure of yourself.

• *Take time for contemplation.*

When we asked John Robbins for his advice on developing ourselves as leaders, he responded:

I think people in this society need a spiritual practice. In order to find your voice and find the song that's within your heart and sing it with your life, you need some daily thing that you do regularly, whether you feel like it or not, that's nurturing your soul, a time of prayer, a time of contemplation. Some people do yoga and meditate, other people go run out in the woods or dance or pray or keep a journal. There're so many ways. And it can be one thing for a few years and another thing for another few years; it can change form. The form isn't the point.

Individuals have to find what works for them, but some way where you're answerable, not to society and not to making a living and not to other people's needs, but just to what's alive in you. What are you really feeling? What are the choices that you're making and surrendering into your living spirit?

In many churches, there's a tradition of giving 10 percent tithing. I find some value in that, if, who you're giving to is something you truly support and it reflects what you want to see more of. But how about giving . . . 10 percent of your day, some of your time, not just your money, but your time to the spirit as you understand that.

You may wonder how you can possibly take time out of your schedule to reflect and meditate. Like everything else that's important, you simply make it a priority. John is as busy as the rest of us. He's an author, he travels to lecture and speak, he's on the board of several organizations, and he has a family life. He still takes time for personal reflection every day. There's absolutely no way we can get to know ourselves if we don't take some quiet time. How you take time for yourself should fit your lifestyle. For some it may be a 10K run; for others, a quiet walk in the woods. For some it may be watching the sun set; for others, prayer. Whatever you choose to be your form of being alone, find some way of reaching a contemplative state in which you can hear your own voice speaking to you about what truly matters.

• *Write a tribute to yourself.*

Another way to begin the process of clarifying your values is to start with your ideal image of yourself—how you would most like to be seen by others. Try this exercise: Imagine that tonight you'll be honored as Leader of the Year. Hundreds of people will gather to pay tribute to your contributions to your family, your colleagues, your organization, and your community. Several people will make speeches praising your performance and your character.

What words or phrases would you most like to hear others say about you? How would you like to be remembered tonight? What descriptions would make you feel the proudest? If you could write these tributes yourself, what would you want them to say?

These descriptive adjectives and phrases may well be lofty and ideal. That's exactly the point: the greater the clarity of, belief in, and passion for our personal standards of excellence, the greater the probability we'll act in concert with them.

If you have trouble writing your tribute, you might start by recording your answers to some questions about what you most care about:

- What do you stand for? Why?
- What do you believe in? Why?
- What are you discontent about? Why?
- What brings you suffering? Why?
- What makes you weep and wail? Why?
- What makes you jump for joy? Why?
- What are you passionate about? Why?
- What keeps you awake at night? Why?
- What's grabbed hold and won't let go? Why?
- What do you want for your life? Why?
- Just what is it that you really care about? Why?

To write your tribute, and to lead, you need to answer these questions for yourself.

• *Record the lessons from the leaders you admire.*

As noted earlier, we've asked those we've interviewed to tell us the historical leaders they admire and why, and about people in their own lives who've been their leadership role models. The common refrain is this: people try to model their behavior after those they admire and respect. So another way to find your voice is to listen carefully to the voices of your mentors and role models.

- Which historical leaders do you most admire? Why? What values did they espouse and practice? How do these values show up in your own actions?
- Make a list of the individuals in your own life who've served as your leadership role models. What values did they espouse and practice? How do these values show up in your own actions?

We challenge you to do what Taylor Bodman did and come up with at least six historical and personal role models and write down for each: why you selected them, what they did, how you feel about each, and the lessons you gained from them. You'll learn a lot about yourself in the process of writing about others.

- *Write your credo.*

Here's an exercise we use in our workshops to get people started on writing their leadership philosophy. We call it the Credo Memo.[17] Follow these instructions, and you will record the beginnings of your leadership philosophy.

Imagine that your organization has afforded you the chance to take a six-month sabbatical, all expenses paid. The only hitch is that you may not take any work along on this sabbatical. And you will not be permitted to communicate to anyone at your office or plant while you are away. Not by letter, phone, fax, e-mail, or other means. Just you, a few good books, some music, and your family or a friend.

But before you depart, those with whom you work need to know the principles that you believe should guide their actions in your absence. They need to know the values and beliefs that you think should steer their decision making and action taking. After all, you'll want to be able to fit back in on your return.

You are permitted no long reports, however. Just a one-page Credo Memo. Take out one piece of paper and write that memo.

It usually takes about five to ten minutes to write a Credo Memo. We do not pretend that this exercise is a substitute for more in-depth self-discovery, but it does provide a useful starting point for articulating your guiding principles. To deepen the clarification process, identify the values you listed in your memo (usually they appear as key words or phrases) and put them in order of priority. Or rank them from low to high. Or place them on a continuum. Forcing yourself to express preferences enables you to see the relative potency of each value.

For an idea of how others have expressed their beliefs about leadership, people and organizations, see the following Credo Memo, written by Todd Shannon, division manager for Unilever.

> To: Sales Team
> Subject: Our Journey to Success
> In my absence please work towards our common end. Share ideas, thoughts and beliefs. Prioritize what must be done and act. Prioritize what is important and enjoy. Remember, we are in this together; win together and fail together. Applaud your colleagues when they succeed and uplift them when they don't. Always act and react with honesty, dedication and conviction. Also, look beyond what you can see and see the beyond. Congratulations on what is sure to be a wondrous journey for us all.

- *Engage in a credo dialogue and assessment.*

In addition to an internal dialogue reflecting on your values, an external dialogue with others about fundamental questions of values is also essential. So, once you've written your Credo Memo, read it aloud to some trusted colleagues. Ask them to assume that they know nothing about your values other than what you are reading to them. Ask them to listen for clarity and understanding. Then ask them to give you feedback on these questions:

- How clear was this to you?
- How well did you understand what I value as a leader?
- If this is all you had to guide your decisions and actions, what would you do?

- Would you be able to act without asking me what my expectations are?
- What do I need to clarify?

With their feedback, write another draft that you can share with your entire team.

Revisit your Credo Memo at least once a year to make sure it still represents your guiding principles. Although values are enduring beliefs, new self-knowledge continues to grow—don't hesitate to share it with others as you learn more about what's important to you.

As you evaluate your Credo Memo and as you change over time, ask yourself about each of the values you have recorded on your leadership credo.[18]

- Did I freely choose this value? If it is an organizational value, do I freely choose to accept it?
- Have I considered other alternatives to this value and explored them fully?
- Have I considered the alternative consequences of this value?
- Do I truly cherish this value? Is it something I prize? Am I passionate about it?
- Am I willing to publicly affirm that I hold this value?
- Am I willing to act on this value?
- Am I willing to act on this value repeatedly, over time, in a consistent pattern?

If your answers to all these questions are yes, then you are valuing your choices. If you have said no to any of them, then you might want to spend some time reexamining the values you have chosen.

• *Collect stories that teach values.*

It's reported that Abraham Lincoln loved *Aesop's Fables*. His other favorites were the King James Bible, *Pilgrim's Progress,* and Shakespeare's plays.[19] The pattern here? All are rich in moral tales, and all are rich in figurative language. Similarly, Martin Luther King Jr. was a student of the U.S. Constitution, a seminarian, and a student of the world's great philosophers.[20] These and all great leaders were students as well as teachers. No matter which leader's biography you read, you'll find they all were influenced by the lives and stories of others.

Former Secretary of Education William J. Bennett felt so strongly about values that he put together an edited volume entitled *The Book of Virtues: A Treasury of Great Moral Stories.*[21] Its intention was to offer stories from historic and modern times that teachers and families could use as a source of ideals and principles. His sections included such virtues as self-discipline, compassion, friendship, courage, and honesty. Lincoln and King may have come from different eras, King and Bennett may have been from different political parties, but they all share in common the love of stories that teach moral lessons.

Ask yourself these questions:

- What books or stories made the biggest impression on you as a child? What values did these books teach?
- What books or stories are you reading right now? What values do they teach?

We're sure you keep clippings that discuss important issues that have relevance to your organization. We're also sure that you often share these articles with your colleagues when you want to make a particular point. In addition to these clippings, we highly recommend that you create your own collection of stories that best present the values you believe should guide your own actions and those of others.

Label some file folders with the values about which you care deeply, and periodically update these folders with lists or collections of the stories that you select. Read them to yourself from time to time, and share them with your colleagues so they come to better understand what you believe.

- *Audit your ability to succeed.*

Your value as a leader and as an individual contributor is determined not only by your guiding beliefs but also by your ability to act on them. To strengthen credibility you must continuously assess your existing abilities and learn new ones. And that takes time and attention.

But competence alone does not determine the capacity to act on your values. You must also have the confidence that you can, in a given leadership situation, apply your skills and act on your beliefs. So yet another important aspect of self-knowledge is critical to leadership performance. It is perhaps the deepest belief of all—an honest trust and confidence in your own ability to competently meet the specific leadership challenges that confront your organization.

Your credo provides you with a good starting place. Beyond that, you must also identify the specific job-related competencies you need to master to lead your constituents. How do your abilities compare to what the situation, role, and tasks require? How well can you execute what you say you value? Where are there gaps? What specific knowledge, skills, and abilities do you have that will enable you to succeed in this environment? What do you need to acquire? What experiences do you need to sharpen these competencies? Who is the very best in the world in your field, and how do you compare to that person? What can you do to become the best? Would your constituents respond to these questions in the same way?

Audits are only as effective as the questions you ask. So stretch yourself beyond the usual questions. For Max De Pree, annual reviews with his managers were no-holds-barred sessions that examined some revealing questions. He'd ask some very unusual and intriguing questions, such as: "What should grace enable us to be?" And he'd ask some highly challenging ones, such as: "Why does this organization need you?"[22] Try answering *that* question for yourself.

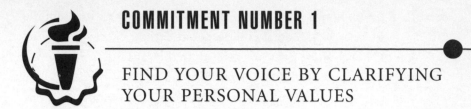

COMMITMENT NUMBER 1

FIND YOUR VOICE BY CLARIFYING YOUR PERSONAL VALUES

- *Look in the mirror.*

- *Take time for contemplation.*

- *Write a tribute to yourself.*

- *Record the lessons from the leaders you admire.*

- *Write your credo.*

- *Engage in a credo dialogue and assessment.*

- *Collect stories that teach values.*

- *Audit your ability to succeed.*

Source: The Leadership Challenge by James M. Kouzes and Barry Z. Posner. Copyright © 2002.

4 SET THE EXAMPLE

Leading means you have to be a good example, and live what you say. Only then can you persuade people honestly.

Tom Brack, SmartTeam AG

Being a good leader is not something that casually occurs. It takes great thought, care, insight, commitment, and energy. When it all comes together, it brings out the best of who you are.

Mary Godwin, Radius

Radius had accumulated approximately $70 million in debt that it could not pay, and creditors were threatening to put the company into bankruptcy. Mary Godwin was vice president of operations. Her role was to negotiate with product suppliers to continue building and shipping product under unusual business conditions, and negotiate debt-to-equity agreements with all of the suppliers to retire the debt. Also very important was keeping the operations team together, because they were responsible for the continued supply of product. Given the circumstances of the company it would have been very difficult to replace team members who left. Mary needed everyone (approximately twenty-five people) on the operations team to keep the activities going.

Early on the CEO asked Mary and other members of the senior management team whether they wanted to continue to try to keep the company afloat or choose to go the bankruptcy route. Several advisers to the company felt that it should go with bankruptcy. The senior management team did not feel that this would be the best thing for their employees, customers, or creditors and voted for working their way out of the debt.

Mary called a communications meeting with her team to talk about the situation. Before the meeting she was stymied over what she could tell everyone about what they were going to need to do, and to do this in a way that would not have everyone resign on the spot. She realized that the difficulty she was having in planning what to say stemmed from her doubts about whether they would really be able to pull off something like this—something that had never been done before. Mary was trying to figure out how she was going to keep *herself* from resigning. Acknowledging that it would have been a lot easier to leave, she explained:

> It came to me that if I wanted everyone else to be committed, then I had to be totally 100 percent, without doubt, committed personally. It was exhilarating. The rest became much easier. I told them that I was committed to seeing Radius through this challenging situation, that the company and I needed their help, and that I had great confidence in their ability to be successful with this project. Throughout the project I never asked anyone to do something that I wouldn't or couldn't do myself.

In the end, they met the deadline from their creditors to complete all the debt-to-equity settlements (over a hundred suppliers), kept the company from going into bankruptcy, and, most important to Mary: "the entire Operations team stayed on board through the whole process."

After her initial hesitation, Mary never let herself believe that they would not be successful. Her operations team had been through other challenging situations, and she believed that they were capable of getting the company on more solid ground. She also felt stimulated and challenged by implementing and organizing a $70 million debt-to-equity swap because it was something that hadn't really been done before.

What Mary realized was that before she could ask others to change she had to be willing to make those same changes and sacrifices herself. Only when she had come to a heartfelt conclusion to stay aboard and to do something that had never been done before could she ask her constituents to do the same. She also realized that it would be only through her actions that people would come to know the depth of her convictions:

> I had to follow through on commitments and show others by my actions how serious we were about our values and standards. My credibility depended upon this and so I had to set the example for others to follow. For example, if there was "bad news" to be delivered to the company, I would be the one to deliver it. If we needed to work on weekends, then I'd be there. I'd never let anyone on the team get "blamed" for something.

It's not enough for leaders to simply deliver a rousing speech or talk about lofty ideals or promising futures. Compelling words may be essential to lifting people's spirits, but leaders know that constituents are more deeply moved by deeds. Constituents expect leaders to show up, to pay attention, and to participate directly in the process of getting extraordinary things done. Leaders take every opportunity to show others by their own example that they're deeply committed to the values and aspirations they espouse. Leading by example is how leaders make visions and values tangible. It's how they provide the *evidence* that they're personally committed. And that evidence is what people look for and admire in leaders—people whose direction they willingly follow.

The *essentials* necessary to Set the Example are:

- Build and affirm shared values
- Align actions with values

In leading by example and practicing the essentials, leaders become the model for what the whole team (the group, the organization, the company) stands for, rather than just standing up for some personal or idiosyncratic set of values. In the process of setting an example, leaders endeavor to lead their constituents from "what I believe" to "what *we* believe." It isn't about doing everything all by yourself. Instead, as many people put it in describing their own personal best leadership experiences: "In the end, it wasn't about me, it was about what all of us did by working together." Leadership *is* a relationship.

BUILD AND AFFIRM SHARED VALUES

Shared values are the foundations for building productive and genuine working relationships. While credible leaders honor the diversity of their many constituencies, they also stress their common values. Leaders build on agreement. They don't try to get everyone to be in accord on everything—this goal is unrealistic, perhaps even impossible. Moreover, to achieve it would negate the very advantages of diversity. But to take a first step, and then a second, and then a third, people must have some common core of understanding. If disagreements over fundamental values continue, the result is intense conflict, false expectations, and diminished capacity. There could be no agreement on the specifications of quality, customer service, or any guiding principle.

The Power of Shared Values

Recognition of shared values provides people with a common language. Tremendous energy is generated when individual, group, and organizational values are in synch. Commitment, enthusiasm, and drive are intensified: people have reasons for caring about their work. When individuals are able to care about what they are doing, they are more effective and satisfied. They experience less stress and tension. Shared values are the internal compasses that enable people to act both independently and interdependently.

Organizations also benefit from shared values. As noted in Chapter Three, employees are more loyal when they believe that their values and those of the organization are aligned. They are more creative because they become immersed in what they are doing. The quality and accuracy of communication and the integrity of the decision-making process increase when people feel part of the same team.

Across a wide range of companies and industries, people whose personal values match those of their company feel significantly more strongly attached to their work and organization than do those who see little relationship in values. Not surprisingly, these two groups differ in the extent to which they find their management to be credible.[1] Studies across the globe yield similar results.[2]

When he was director of organization development for Alcoa Aluminum of Australia, Mike Leonard explained to us that the process of designing a new plant had begun with "developing a shared understanding of our basic philosophy about how we ought to be doing business. These values served to guide us, not only with actual physical construction and sociotechnical designs but also with the various recruitment, promotion, and compensation strategies." In Mike's case, values provided the common standard by which people could calibrate their decisions and actions. Like Mike, the other leaders we studied reported how essential it was that they and their teams were guided by a clear and agreed-upon set of values.

Important as it is that leaders forthrightly articulate the principles for which they stand, what leaders say and do must be consistent with the aspirations of their constituents. Leaders who advocate or stand for values that aren't representative of the collective will won't be able to mobilize people to act as one. Leaders set an example for all constituents based on a shared understanding of what's expected. Leaders must be able to gain consensus on a common cause and a common set of principles. They must be able to build and affirm a community of shared values.

A leader's promise is really an organization's promise—regardless of whether the organization is a team of two, an agency of two hundred, a school of two thousand, a company of twenty thousand, or a community of two hundred thousand. Unless there's agreement about what promises *we* can keep, leaders, constituents, and their organizations risk losing credibility.

In our own research, we've carefully examined the relationship between personal and organizational values. Our findings clearly reveal that when there's congruence between individual values and organizational values, there's significant payoff for leaders and their organizations.[3] Shared values do make a significant difference in work attitudes and performance:

- They foster strong feelings of personal effectiveness.
- They promote high levels of company loyalty.

- They facilitate consensus about key organizational goals and stakeholders.
- They encourage ethical behavior.
- They promote strong norms about working hard and caring.
- They reduce levels of job stress and tension.
- They foster pride in the company.
- They facilitate understanding about job expectations.
- They foster teamwork and esprit de corps.

When leaders seek consensus around shared values, constituents are more positive. People who report that their senior managers engage in dialogue around common values feel a significantly stronger sense of personal effectiveness than those individuals who feel that they're wasting energy trying to figure out what they're supposed to be doing.[4] As demonstrated in Chapter Three (see Figure 3.1), people tend to drift when they're unsure or confused about how they should be operating. The energy that goes into coping with, and possibly fighting about, incompatible values takes its toll on both personal effectiveness and organizational productivity.

Periodically taking the organization's pulse in regard to the clarity and consensus of its values is well worthwhile. It renews commitment. It engages the institution in discussion of values (such as diversity) that are more inclusive of a changing constituency. Once people are clear about the leader's values, about their own values, and about shared values, they know what's expected of them, can manage higher levels of stress, and can better handle the conflicting demands of work and their personal lives. Studies of public sector organizations also support the importance of shared values to organizational effectiveness. Within successful agencies and departments, considerable agreement, as well as intense feeling, is found among employees and managers about the importance of their values and about how those values could best be implemented.

What Shared Values Are Important?

Shared values make an enormous difference to organizational and personal vitality. Research confirms that firms with a strong corporate culture based on a foundation of shared values outperform other firms by a huge margin.[5]

- Their revenue grew more than four times faster.
- Their rate of job creation was seven times higher.
- Their stock price grew twelve times faster.
- Their profit performance was 750 percent higher.

Is there some particular value or set of values that's the springboard to organizational vitality? Consider these examples—three electronics companies, each of which has a strong set of values:[6] The first company prides itself on technical innovation and has a culture dominated by engineering values; it informally encourages and rewards activities such as experimentation and risk taking. The second company is much flashier; its important organizational values are associated with marketing, and the company gears itself toward providing outstanding customer service. The third company does things "by the numbers"; accounting standards dominate its key values, and energies are directed toward making the organization more efficient (by cutting costs, for example). Each of these companies is quite different and clearly communicates its own values. But all three companies compete in the same market, and all are successful, each with a different strategy. It's apparent, then, that successful companies may have very different values and that the specific set of values that serves one company may hurt another.

This view is supported by the research on companies that are "built to last." High-performing organizations, compared to like companies in their industry, had a very strong "core ideology" but didn't share the *same* core ideology.[7] The source of sustained competitive advantage for organizations *begins* with a values-based foundation—What are our basic principles? What do we believe in?—upon which management and leadership practices are built that reflect and embody these values.[8]

But questions such as What are our basic principles? and What do we believe in? are far from simple. Even with commonly identified values, there may be little agreement on the meaning of values statements. One study, for example, uncovered 185 different behavioral expectations around the value of *integrity* alone.[9] Leaders must engage their constituents in a dialogue about values. A common understanding of values comes about through that dialogue; it emerges from a *process,* not a pronouncement.

After all, if there's no agreement about values, then what exactly is the leader—and everyone else—going to model?

This is precisely what Marcello Bullara discovered when he took over the worldwide support operations manager position for the Pavilion PC division of Hewlett-Packard. He noted, as he traveled from one country to another, that it was not so important what the particular value was called or labeled but that everyone agreed on the importance and meaning of the values. One of his initial actions was to bring people together just for that purpose, so that they could arrive at common and shared understandings of what their key priorities and values were and what they meant in action:

> The key values that the team and I felt were most important to model were involvement, teamwork, communications, flexibility, and human relations. This set of values was discussed at great length and different people felt differently about what was the right set of five. In the end, I'm sure that it was far more important and constructive to have the discussion on what the key values should be, in order to further clarify the goal at hand, than it was to pick the magic set of five values. I am convinced that at least a dozen combinations of values would have allowed us to reach our goal, however, the process of deciding on one set of five was an extremely valuable unifying and clarifying experience.

For values to be truly shared, they must be more than advertising slogans. They must be deeply supported and broadly endorsed beliefs about what's important to the people who hold them. Constituents must be able to enumerate the values and must have common interpretations of how those values will be put into practice. They must know how the values influence their own jobs and how they directly contribute to organizational success.

Many senior executives have taken the shared values message to mean that they should set off on a weeklong retreat to formulate a corporate credo, then return home and announce it to constituents. We confess to having advocated this exercise ourselves at one time. Experience has taught us, however, that no matter how extensive top management's support of shared values is, leaders can't impose their values on organizational members. Consensus about values is more difficult to achieve than clarity, and without consensus it's hard to get consistent implementation of values throughout an organization. Leaders must be proactive in involving people in the process of creating shared values.

Imagine how much more ownership of the values there would be if leaders actively involved a wide range of people in their development. We now encourage leaders to invite everybody—or if that's not feasible, a representative group of constituents—to discuss the organization's values and see what critical themes emerge. Shared values are the result of listening, appreciating, building consensus, and practicing conflict resolution. For people to understand the values and come to agree with them, they must participate in the process: *unity is forged, not forced.*

A unified voice on values results from discovery and dialogue. Leaders must provide a chance for individuals to engage in a discussion of what the values mean and how their personal beliefs and behaviors are influenced by what the organization stands for. Leaders must also be prepared to discuss values and expectations in the recruitment, selection, and orientation of new members. Better to explore early the fit between person and organization than to have members find out late some sleepless night that they're in violent disagreement over matters of principle.

One word of caution: values should never be used as an excuse for the suppression of dissent. The dominant silent value at play in all organizational settings is the preference for freedom over enslavement.

ALIGN ACTIONS WITH VALUES

"I try to lead by example, by being what I want privates to be. And I expect as much out of them." So says Sergeant Jill Henderson, the first woman to win the Army's Drill Sergeant of the Year award. She can do push-ups with the best of them—thirty-five per minute—and she routinely works seventeen-hour days. Even in the rain and mud, she insists on wearing a crisply pressed uniform and spit-shined boots. Her values are clear, and she lives them. "I lead from the heart. The more I take care of people the more they take care of me." She tells her trainees in boot camp, "A soldier does all the work. If somebody looks down at you, remember inside that you are the one who carries out the mission. If you stay in the Army, you *will* become a leader. Just never forget where you came from." It's clear from her actions that Jill hasn't forgotten this for a second. It's not just words that she uses to convince and teach the privates she trains; it's her behavior—the match between what she demands of her people and what she demands of herself.

We can't stress enough the power of the leader's example. UCLA professor Donna McNeese-Smith, in her research on health care administrators, found that "the behavior most related to employee productivity was 'modeling the way.' If managers want productive employees they must set a good example, establish high standards, and then practice what they preach."[10] The same is true in industry: "Employees are proud when they can say their organization's leaders use actions to support their verbiage about quality. It's not just talk—they live their lives out in the same way."[11]

Leadership is a performing art. Leaders don't "act" in the same sense as Broadway performers, of course. However, they *enact* the meaning of the organization in every decision they make and in every step they take toward the future they envision. Leaders understand that they bring shared values to life in a variety of settings—in daily group meetings, one-on-one conferences, telephone calls, tours of facilities, and visits to clients, customers, suppliers, or community members.

There are five essential aspects to their behavior and actions that leaders need to be conscious about in their efforts to align shared values through the example of the actions they take.[12]

- Calendars
- Critical incidents
- Stories, analogies, and metaphors
- Language
- Measurements

Simple though these appear, each affords an opportunity to make visible and tangible to others a conscious commitment to a shared way of being. Modeling the way via these tools may appear rather basic and obvious. But it's all in the attention, the doing: it's their application that challenges aspiring leaders, and their lack of execution that fosters cynicism in constituents.

Calendars: Spend Time and Pay Attention

How you spend your time is the single clearest indicator, especially to other people, about what's important to you. If you say your top priority is your customers (or clients, patients, students, voters, or parishioners), then how much of your daily time do you spend with them? Is there a connection for you between how you allocate your schedule or calendar (time) and what you consider to be priorities and key values?

When Darryl Hartley-Leonard, then chairman of Hyatt Hotels Corporation, wanted to make sure that "customer service" was truly value number one and not just some executive pronouncement, he and other senior management officers spent time performing front-line employee jobs. Working alongside bell hops, desk clerks, switchboard operators, and the like, Darryl showed his respect and appreciation for their work. Beyond that, he underscored that customer service begins at the front line—and that he knew it!

You don't have to wait to be president or CEO to show people you're serious about your beliefs. Take this example from Greg Mills, of his personal best at Menlo-Atherton High School:

> Even though I was probably the most motivated to work out and play, I kept reminding myself that it was a team sport, and I couldn't do it all myself. I could set my own high standards, but I couldn't force my standards on other players. I wanted the team to decide how much they wanted to practice. As team captain, I decided to set an example for the team showing my dedication. . . . I led by example by being at every workout and working out hard. . . . I was usually the last one out of practice, and I always helped our coach pick up after practice. . . . If I told people to go to all the workouts, and I kept missing a few workouts a week, they wouldn't listen to me, as their confidence in me would diminish. . . . I also helped the younger players who didn't know much about the game . . . and tried to build up their confidence. . . . Most importantly, I kept telling myself water polo is a game that one should also have fun in. When I noticed the team getting too tense—or myself—I joked around with the players to relieve the tension.

Setting an example means arriving early, staying late, working out, and being there to show you care. It's about being the first to do something that everyone should value. Whether the value is family, teamwork, hard work, or fun, the truest measure of what leaders deeply believe is how they spend their time. Constituents look to this measure and use it to judge whether a leader measures up to espoused standards. Visibly spending time on what's important shows that you're putting your time and money where your mouth is. For example, by attending operating meetings in the field, leaders provide visible evidence of their concerns and the direction they want to pursue. That's why Logitech's worldwide vice president of human resources, Roberta Linsky, travels halfway around the world (from Fremont, California) to attend the Lunar New Year celebrations that take place in their manufacturing facility in Suzhou, China. Being there in person says more about how much Roberta values her constituents than any e-mail message, telegram, card, or video could ever do. What you do truly does speak more loudly about what you believe than what you say ever can.

Critical Incidents: Seize Opportunities to Teach

Consciously choosing to spend time on what's important to you is essential to sending the signal that you're serious about an issue. Yet even the most disciplined leaders can't stop the intrusion of the unexpected and the serendipitous. There are constant interruptions, brief interactions, and extraordinary variety—all of which are more extreme in an era of downsizing, global competition, and increased diversity. Critical incidents—chance occurrences, particularly at a time of stress and challenge—offer significant moments of learning for leaders and constituents. Critical incidents present opportunities for leaders to teach important lessons about appropriate norms of behavior.

Retired U.S. Army General H. Norman Schwarzkopf was a master at creating moments of learning during critical incidents. One event during Schwarzkopf's first day as a new division commander illustrates how a leader can turn a chance encounter into a classroom:

Although I'd delayed any sweeping changes, I *was* on the lookout for ways to establish myself as the leader from the moment I set foot on the base. The morning after we arrived I went out for a run. As I came up on the barracks area, a formation of troops raced by me, led by a guy who looked as if he belonged in the Olympics. . . . Stretching back into the distance were the soldiers who hadn't been able to keep pace. The leaders stopped in front of their barracks and were catching their breath as I jogged up. . . . I stopped and asked the company commander what they were doing. "Sir, we've just completed our five-mile run."

"That's terrific. But what about all those people back there?" I asked.

"Sir, those are guys who couldn't keep up."

"But you've run off and left them." The captain gave me a puzzled look. "Think of it this way," I said. "Suppose you're a new recruit. You come to your new unit, you're just out of basic training, and you're feeling great about being a soldier. But then you find out that your new unit does a lot more running than you're used to. And the very first day you're out with them, you run and you run until your legs give out and your lungs give out—but your unit keeps going and leaves you. What kind of unit cohesion does that build?"

The light dawned on the captain's face. After suggesting ways he might reorganize the morning run so that nobody was ever left behind, I jogged off, satisfied that I'd just taught a young officer . . . that cohesion at every level be developed. I knew the episode would get talked about around the base."[13]

Notice that Schwarzkopf was consciously *on the lookout* for ways to establish himself as a leader. His morning run was mainly for exercise, but he knew it could also become an opportunity if he stayed alert. Schwarzkopf recognized this chance encounter as an opportune moment for the captain and the soldiers to learn an important lesson about group cohesion. All that was required was the general's clarity of belief, perception that this was an opportunity, comfort in confronting someone about the behavior, and about five minutes of time.

Critical incidents are those events in leaders' lives that offer the chance to improvise while still staying true to the script. Although they can't be explicitly planned, it's useful to keep in mind that the way you handle these incidents—how you link actions and decisions to shared values—says volumes about what's important.

Stories, Analogies, and Metaphors: Use the Timeless Way to Teach Virtues

Critical incidents are often the most dramatic sources of moral lessons about what we should and should not value, about how we should and should not behave. They become stories that are passed down, whether around the base (as Schwarzkopf predicted), across the country, or from generation to generation.

While the leader's message is important, and how it is framed is critical, the process by which it is communicated is just as significant. Several people can present the same basic message and receive entirely different responses from their audience. How we educate and how our messages are communicated have much to do with whether what we say will be remembered, endorsed, and followed.

A leader's words "often assume their greatest impact as symbols rather than as literal meanings."[14] This is especially true when words are used to tell a story. Stories serve as a kind of mental map that helps people know, first, what is important (purpose and values) and, second, how things are done in a particular group or organization.

Two streams of research support and explain the greater impact of stories, and by extension metaphors and analogies, over rational discourse.[15] The first comes from the field of speech communications, where research shows that stories excite the imagination of the listener and create consecutive states of tension (puzzlement-recoil) and tension release (insight and resolution). Listeners are not passive receivers of information but are triggered into a state of active thinking as they puzzle over the meaning of the story and attempt to make sense of it, typically in reference to their own experiences and situations. Because this process is so engaging it fosters listeners' attention and holds their interest.[16]

Second, studies from social psychology explain why rhetorical devices like stories, analogies, and metaphors are a persuasive and effective means of communicating ideas. Statistical summaries, facts, and policy statements, because they are typically abstract and bland, lack impact and are treated as uninformative. In contrast, stories, analogies, and metaphors have a substantial impact on decision making.[17]

Jim Treyz, president of WellConnected, loves telling a story about something he experienced in his childhood. It goes something like this. There was a time in the history of The Walt Disney Company when the business was in need of an infusion of cash to fuel the growth that Walt Disney envisioned. The American Broadcasting Company was interested in the possibility of purchasing Disney, primarily to get the broadcasting rights for the now-famous Disney hour-long show, which would hold down a key ratings spot and bring Disney to all of America on ABC. The person responsible was Jim Treyz's dad, Ollie, who at the time was president of ABC. The negotiations were tough and acrimonious, but the turning point came when Ollie and Janet Treyz visited Disneyland to continue the negotiations. (Their boys, Jim and Don, about seven and ten years old at the time, stayed home.)

While Ollie Treyz and his staff were involved in discussions with Roy Disney, Walt—the company's president and its creative force—served as personal tour guide for Janet. It was a spectacular day, and one that she always remembered vividly. But it was what happened afterward that taught Jim a lesson he's never forgotten, and one that he's put into practice wherever he's worked. Soon after his parents returned home from Disneyland, a package arrived at the house. In the package were two original animation cels from Disney films. Each cel was personalized by Walt Disney, himself. One cel was of Jiminy Cricket, a character from *Pinocchio*. "Cricket" was Jim's boyhood nickname. The other was of *Donald's Train Ride*, for his brother, Don. Walt Disney had paid such close attention that day in Disneyland that he knew exactly which character to send to Jim and to his brother. As you can imagine the two boys were absolutely overjoyed and overwhelmed with their gifts, and their mom was thoroughly impressed with the personal attention given her sons by Walt Disney. Each inscription was exact, and personal.

And the ABC-Disney deal? Who do you suppose convinced Jim Treyz's dad that it was a good idea to buy Disney? You guessed it. Janet Treyz. And when Walt Disney wanted to buy the company back from ABC a few years later, who do you imagine was there to again to add her voice saying that this was the right thing to do? Right again. Janet Treyz. And many years later when the Walt Disney Company, with Michael Eisner at the helm, was negotiating to buy ABC, Ollie Treyz, long gone from ABC at the time, took great pleasure seeing the tables turn again. And all this was sealed decades before because one man paid a lot of attention to a guest and her two little boys back home.

When Jim Treyz grew up and became a businessman, he never forgot the moral of the story: personalized customer service makes all the difference in the world. Jim's own career is a testimonial to outstanding, personalized service to customers. Jim was general manager of International Business Services when Xerox won the Malcolm Baldrige Award in the Service category in 1997; he later became head of global sales and marketing at Citibank e-Business in Stamford, Connecticut, before he joined Well-Connected. Now he runs a company that specializes in customized one-to-one loyalty and personal relationship management services. He tells the "Disney story" to his prospects, his employees, his partners, and presumably anyone else who might listen, to impress upon them the power and importance of deeply personal attention. The Jiminy Cricket cel now hangs on the wall in his daughter Alex's room, and will carry the Disney story to other generations of family and friends.

When we're trying to communicate the values of an organization, what would have more of an impact on you? A policy statement that says "Thou shalt establish one-to-one relationships with customers," or the story told by Jim Treyz? If you said the story, you'd be exactly correct. In fact, research has shown that information is more quickly and accurately remembered when it is first presented in the form of an example or story.[18]

Language: Choose Words and Questions Deliberately

Harvard professor Shoshana Zuboff has observed that we're "prisoners" of our organizational vocabulary.[19] Zuboff's choice of words is conscious and none too strong. If you disagree, try talking about an organization for even a day without using the words *employee, manager, boss, supervisor, subordinate,* or *hierarchy.* You may find this exercise nearly impossible unless you've gotten comfortable with the language some organizations use today, like *associates, crew, team players,* or even *constituents.* We've all come to accept certain words we use as the reality of organizational life. Those words can trap us into a particular way of thinking about our roles and relationships. This is one of the reasons there are no managers at PSS/World Medical—there are sales leaders and operations leaders instead. Similarly, we worked with one multinational company that decided to rename its Division Management Team and call it the Division Leadership Team. This change sent a signal to everyone (and a constant message to the team members themselves) that their job was to lead, not manage, the organization.

Leaders understand and are attentive to language. They know the power of words. The words we choose to use are metaphors for concepts that define attitudes and behaviors, structures and systems. Our words evoke images of what we hope to create and how we expect people to behave. The wonder of the Magic Kingdom at Walt Disney World can be partially attributed to the deliberate use of language and metaphor. There are no employees at Disney World: everyone is a "Cast Member" hired not by a personnel department but by "Casting." There are no customers, only "Guests" (always capitalized). And in this family-oriented environment, everyone is on a first-name basis.

Questions, too, are quite powerful in focusing attention. When leaders ask questions, they send constituents on mental journeys—"quests"—in search of answers. The questions that a leader asks send messages about the focus of the organization, and they're indicators of what's of most concern to the leader. They're one more measure of how serious we are about our espoused beliefs. Questions provide feedback about which values should be attended to and how much energy should be devoted to them. What questions should leaders be asking if they want people to focus on integrity? On trust? On customer or client satisfaction? On quality? On innovation? On growth? On personal responsibility?

Questions frame the issue and set the agenda. In one of our workshops, we suggested that participants who wanted their constituents to stay focused on continuous improvement ask this simple question of every person attending their next group meeting: "What have you done in the last week to improve so that you're better this week than last?" We then recommended that they repeat this question for the next four weeks or more, predicting that it would take at least that many repetitions to sustain the focus.

About a month later, we heard from a participant in the workshop who had done what we recommended. He told us that the first time he asked the question, people looked at each other skeptically, apparently thinking, "Oh, this guy's just been to a seminar." The second time, some staff took him seriously and about 30 percent had a response. The third time, about 70 percent had something to report. And the fourth? Something very interesting happened: "They asked me what *I* had done in the last week to improve *myself* so *I* was better than I was last week." Questions can indeed be very effective tools for change!

Measurements: Recognize That What Gets Measured Gets Done

Brian Coleman, the tool and die manager, led a turnaround for the Ford Motor Company.[20] One of the tools that he and his team of union employees, based in Dagenham, England, developed was a simple device to measure car quality: "The workers would mark a tick on the outline of a car indicating the location of every defect that came down the line."

When they put the device to use, reports Brian, "I was shocked by the result. After only five hours there were more than fourteen hundred ticks on our drawing! I asked the team where we should begin, and they pointed to the area with the densest mass of ticks. Why? 'Because that's where we'll have the greatest impact,' they said. That's the opposite of what a management team would have chosen at the time."

For Brian and his team, that simple measuring device was a major factor in reducing the number of defects by over 70 percent and nearly doubling productivity in three months. In Brian's case, the value of quality, the specific goal of reducing defects, and the scoring mechanism all converged to produce results.

Research indicates clearly that measurement and feedback are essential to increase efforts to improve performance.[21] Score-keeping systems are essential to knowing how you're doing. Think about how Xilinx, a highly innovative company, uses the measurement of attrition and reporting of turnover by division units every ninety days to make certain that each manager is paying attention to retention and providing a workplace that makes people want to stay. Likewise, building a team-oriented, collective feeling at the Men's Wearhouse is facilitated by knowing that the company tracks the number of tickets written by each salesperson. If someone writes a lot more than others in the store, this suggests hogging the walk-in traffic, and that person gets counseled. If the behavior persists, the individual will probably be terminated.

Leaders can easily influence outcome by providing the tools for measuring progress. For example, if the organization's performance appraisal system fails to measure how well people perform against the standards of excellence set by corporate values, leaders can add clear performance measures that evaluate how well people are doing on quality, customer service, innovation, respect for others, contribution to profitability, fun, or whatever else is of critical value to the organization.

Rewards (discussed further in Chapter Eleven) are another tangible means of reinforcing values. Although increasing job satisfaction is a notable goal of rewards, the most important role of rewards in modeling is to reinforce the key values important to sustaining an adaptive culture. All support systems—incentive, recruitment, training, information, and the like—must be aligned with this purpose.

COMMITMENT NUMBER 2:
SET THE EXAMPLE BY ALIGNING
ACTIONS WITH SHARED VALUES

Leaders demonstrate their intense commitment to the values they espouse by setting an example: this is how they earn and sustain credibility over time. Setting an example is essentially *doing what you say you will do*. It begins with the clarification of personal values and an appreciation of how those values are played out in daily life. And it involves the building and affirming of values that leaders and constituents alike can embrace, an important step toward inspiring a vision, the topic of the next chapters.

The truest test of credible leadership is what leaders pay attention to and what they do. Leaders are measured by the consistency of deeds with words. In this sense, leadership is a performing art, one that you can improve with the action steps listed for this commitment. The essential repertoire of leaders includes how they spend their time, how they react to critical incidents, their stories, analogies, and metaphors, the language and questions they choose, and the measures they use. Application of these tools of leadership isn't haphazard. Although serendipity plays a role, leaders are constantly on the lookout for ways to establish themselves as leaders. They consciously manage the process of setting an example.

- *Create alignment around key values.*

Researchers have demonstrated that there are three central themes in the values of highly successful, strong-culture organizations:[22]

- High performance standards
- A caring attitude toward people
- A sense of uniqueness and pride

High-performance values stress the commitment to excellence, caring values communicate how people are to be treated, and uniqueness values tell people inside and outside how the organization is different from all others. These three common threads are central to weaving a values tapestry that leads to a shared commitment to greatness.

But how do you get there? A start is to ask constituents to write down what they believe the key values of the team (department, unit, or company) are. Try including some of your relevant customers, suppliers, vendors, and even shareholders in this discussion. Got lots of people? Send out a survey and find out what they think.[23] Share the findings among the group and find out how much agreement there is, or not. Clarify what is vital, and determine what is secondary. Present hypothetical situations involving potential value dilemmas and ask people to consider what actions they would take. Have them link their proposed actions back to key values. Take a recent organizational or team decision and analyze it in terms of agreement with shared values. National Football League referees go through a similar process every Monday morning, including fairly outrageous "*What would you do?*" scenarios. These sessions strengthen their confidence in their understanding of the rules and how they should be prescribed and their confidence that these values are being applied consistently across many different situations (often under intense scrutiny from thousands of screaming people, and the bright lights of television cameras).

Implicit in "What would you do" is another question, one that is at the root of values: Why? Why is an important question. Indeed, the Socratic question—"Why?"—is the *only* teacher behavior that is effective in raising the moral reasoning of schoolchildren.[24] A similar case can be made for leaders and their constituents. While we may feel that the importance of certain values should be self-evident, commitment is facilitated when people know that the values are not just their own individually but shared by others, endorsed and put into practice by their organization. Moreover, providing a rationale for the value helps people to remember that value and apply its logic to new and different situations and circumstances; this promotes a consistency in the interpretation and enactment of values.

Don't stop at creating alignment; acknowledge that even good ideas grow stale over time. Be sure to set a "sunset statute" for any formal (organizational) values statement. Whatever values you reach, make it known that you're going to review, change, or recommit to these values every two (or three or four) years. After all, it's likely that many people will have left the group since the original inception of your shared values statement and some of the new people may not feel included in this part of your organizational history. Certain values will endure and others will change (some slightly and some considerably), but the process of reviewing and prioritizing can only reinforce the team's unity of purpose and commitment to their (not yours) shared values.

- *Speak about shared values with enthusiasm and confidence—even drama.*

Talk about your common purpose and the importance of community. Let people know that they—and you—are in this together and develop a sense that "what we are doing is important," and that "all of our contributions make a difference." To do otherwise is to foster alienation. Constituents are attracted to leaders who are dynamic and energetic. They are filled with energy and enthusiasm themselves when their leader speaks with passion about shared beliefs. Your task is to keep people focused by constantly affirming publicly what *we all* stand for.

Researchers have documented the importance of speaking out on behalf of shared values and how it contributes to creating community. At an East

Coast university where there was a publicized incident of hate mail sent to an African American student, researchers randomly stopped students walking across campus and asked them what they thought of the incident. Before the subject could respond, however, a confederate of the researchers would come up and answer. One response was something like, "Well, he must have done something to deserve it." As you might expect, the subject's response was more often than not just like the confederate's. The confederate's alternate response was something like, "There's no place for that kind of behavior on our campus." The subject's response again replicated the confederate's.[25] This study illustrates clearly the importance of "affirming" and why it is that as leaders we must speak out strongly on behalf of our values and get others on the line to do the same.

And speaking strongly demands speaking with confidence. People look to leaders for guidance and need to feel that the leaders know what they are talking about. Speaking with confidence yourself builds the confidence of your constituents. Begin by doing your homework. Being prepared bolsters your natural self-assurance. When speakers are nervous and lacking in confidence they speak at a lower volume and make many speech errors—incomplete sentences, long pauses between words, and omitted portions of words or sentences. A more confident style will avoid these mistakes.

Research has also found differences between what are perceived as confident or powerful versus powerless styles of presentation. The powerless style includes speech hesitations as "ah," "you know," and "uh"; polite phrases like "please" and "thank you"; questioning voice tones at the end of declarative statements; and hedging phrases as "I think," "I guess," or "kinda." The powerful style lacks these qualities and instead portrays the speaker as more assuming, more goal directed, and more straightforward. In a study of these two styles, participants rated speakers using the powerful style as more potent and attractive, and more credible.[26]

Sometimes you need more than just a powerful style. Sometimes—particularly during times of change and transition—you need some drama to get a point across about a fundamental value and to make it memorable. We know of one executive team that went mountain climbing to teach team members about taking risks with one another. Jack Kahl, founder and former CEO of Manco, chose a less risky—but still dramatic—way to get employees working together: he promised them that if they achieved a stretch goal of $60 million, he would swim across the duck pond at corporate headquarters near Cleveland, Ohio. They reached the goal, and Jack followed through. He jumped in with the ducks and swam the width of the pond to the cheers of everyone. The event was such a hit that it has become a tradition, but now it's not just Jack who swims it; others are challenged to join in. Jack added some drama to the everyday life of the company and in doing so showed by example that he's good on his word. These actions weren't drama for drama's sake. Instead, they were designed to draw attention to critical values and priorities. Sometimes you have to go out of your way to get a point across. Jack Kahl even got wet.

- *Teach and reinforce through symbols and artifacts.*

Leaders pay heed to the informal channels by which organizational messages are conveyed. Foremost among these are the symbols and artifacts of workday life. Sometimes symbols represent time-honored traditions. For example, the mission church adorns the letterhead of Santa Clara University, signaling the Jesuit roots and credo of the institution.

Posters, pictures on walls, objects on desks, and buttons or pins on lapels can be much more than decorative items. Each can serve as a visible reminder of some key organizational value. Consider the situation at a high-technology company where the CEO handed out buttons at one critical point. Most of the company wore green "How Can I Help?" buttons; people on the critical path wore red "Priority" buttons. People with green buttons were to do anything to remove obstacles for those with red buttons. The CEO himself wore a green button. The buttons cost a total of $73.50; handing them out took fifteen minutes. But those hardware engineers with the red buttons got the message. As one engineer explained, "I think it was a way to make sure we understood how important what we were doing was."[27]

When organizations make major changes, they often proclaim new symbols and discard or destroy old symbols and artifacts in favor of the new. We need look no further than the toppling of the Berlin Wall and the statues of Lenin for dramatic evidence of this. On a smaller scale, when David Pottruck, president and co-CEO of The Charles Schwab Corporation, wanted to signal a change in the company's services, he called the senior management team together for a meeting whose theme was "Crossing the Chasm." In keeping with the idea of stepping out of the known to create a new way of doing business, one speaker—an engineer of the Golden Gate Bridge—made clear some of the challenges of building the bridge. At the conclusion of the meeting, the team boarded a bus to the San Francisco side of the Golden Gate Bridge. They saw with new eyes the challenges that spanning the roiling stretch of water involved. In walking the bridge, crossing what had once been a chasm, the team faced the idea of change together. The walk became a lasting memory for the entire team. And—in the form of a miniature of the Golden Gate Bridge, engraved to commemorate the occasion—the idea was brought back to those at Schwab as well.[28]

Leaders are attentive to the use of ceremonies, both official and spontaneous, in the reinforcement of shared values. Recognizing that initiation rites are ancient rituals essential to the maintenance of any strong culture, organizations often use ceremonies to mark the entry of people into the group.

The critical point is this: in the performing art of leadership, symbols and artifacts are a leader's props. They're necessary tools for making the message memorable and sustainable over time. Together with rituals, they're a means of keeping the vision and values present even when the leader is absent.

• *Lead by storytelling.*

When Stephen Denning was program director of Knowledge Management for the World Bank, one day he was sitting with a colleague over lunch and swapping work stories. Stephen's colleague, who had been working on a project in Zambia with the goal of improving health services to families, talked about a health worker who had logged on to the Web site for the Centers for Disease Control and found the answer to a question on how to treat malaria. Stephen didn't realize it at the time, but this very simple story was ultimately going to change his whole approach to persuading others about the vital role knowledge management could play within the World Bank.[29]

Stephen, who'd been having little success up to this point in convincing others in the World Bank that they had another role other than a financial one, decided to incorporate the Zambia anecdote into his presentations. In the weeks that followed, Stephen relates that the Zambia story was having unexpectedly positive results. He noticed that when he began his presentations with the Zambia story, "something was beginning to click" with his audiences. When he didn't use the Zambia story, Stephen explains, he found that the conversation ended up "in a tangle of debates about various aspects of the feasibility of the change idea."

Over the ensuing years Stephen learned how truly vital stories were to communicating essential messages within the World Bank, and within all organizations. Why storytelling? He says: "Nothing else worked. Charts left listeners bemused. Prose remained unread. Dialogue was just too laborious and slow. Time after time, when faced with the task of persuading a group of managers or front-line staff in a large organization to get enthusiastic about a major change, I found that storytelling was the only thing that worked."[30]

Stephen's experience with storytelling, in fact, is not remarkable, though the method is seriously underutilized. Why tell stories? We have already discussed how stories are teaching tools, powerful strategies for getting your point across, and more likely to be remembered by your constituents than policy pronouncements, lists, or statistics. David Armstrong, vice president at Armstrong International, offers some additional reasons in his book *Management by Storying Around* to show why storytelling is such an effective leadership practice: stories are simple, timeless, and can appeal to everybody regardless of age, gender, or race—and they are fun. And there are still more reasons: stories are a useful form of training, a good method for empowering people, great as a recognition device, a recruiting and hiring tool, a sales technique, and an excellent way to pass along corporate traditions.[31]

What makes for a good storyteller? To begin with, they tell personal stories. Tell a story that you know something about or give an example that you and your audience can personally relate to. What we communicate in stories (and examples) is remembered by others in proportion to its "vividness."[32] To be vivid, a story should be about a real person, have a strong sense of time and place, and be told in colorful and animated language.[33] It helps immensely if you can talk from a first-person perspective. Allow your emotions to surface as you speak; this brings excitement to your voice and increases your natural tendency to use gestures and to smile. If you are feeling truly excited about a particular activity or goal, show it. If you are deeply concerned about competitive threats, show it. Start your story by relating a heroic deed. Think of a clever title for the story that will capture people's attention and help them to remember (catalogue) it. Give your story a theme. Be willing to repeat this theme. Keep the story short. Use people's names. Verify all facts. Be sure to end your message or story with a conclusion that demonstrates concretely the intended message or lesson to be learned. (The old storytellers had good reasons for calling the ending "the moral of the story.")

Since the stories you tell should be about other people, about what they are doing to put shared values into practice and to demonstrate their commitment as "disciples," telling stories forces you to pay close attention to what your constituents are doing. Telling stories about others gives you the chance to reinforce that "everyone is a leader." Hearing or reading a story about similar people (people they can identify with) is also the most effective type of role model for stimulating an audience to learn how to take such actions themselves. By telling stories about other people, you can encourage their peers to also do the right thing. Moreover, people seldom tire of hearing stories about themselves and the people they know. These stories tend to get repeated and the lesson of the story gets spread far and wide. The moral? Be on the lookout for a good story!

• *Put storytelling on your meeting agendas.*

Capture as many examples of exemplary behavior in your organization as you can. Think of yourself as the chief historian for your team. The practice of observing and recording is important to building your skills in storytelling.

Start your storytelling by actually putting it on the meeting agenda. Make the only agenda item for one of your team meetings the telling of everyone's story about their most meaningful recognition. Make the only agenda item of another team meeting the telling of stories about other team members around the theme of "I heard something good about you." Be sure to tell any story in detail. It's the little things that often make the difference. If possible, figure out a way to reenact the incident. You might also use voice mail and e-mail as media for telling stories. Shorter stories are generally more useful than long ones in these formats, but they're still helpful ways to disseminate good news.

If you don't think you're a very good storyteller—and most of us have room for improvement—there must be someone in your organization who is. Spend some time talking with this person about how they came to be so good at it. Pick up whatever tips you can.[34]

What's the best movie you ever saw that tells a really compelling story? Watch it again. What lessons can you learn about storytelling, and how can you incorporate these lessons into your leadership practice? Buy a CD of one of your favorite children's stories. Then try reading the story yourself the way the professional did. Take a class in storytelling. Attend the next storytelling convention in your town. Sit in on a reading at a local bookstore featuring a fiction writer you like. Listen to how they read their stories. Take a page from their book and learn to express yourself in stories.

- *Ask questions.*

Every question you ask is another potential teaching opportunity. The key to good questions is to think about the "quest" in your *ques*tion: Where do you want to take this person with your question? What do you want this person to think about? Asking questions forces you to understand what you are trying to teach and achieve. Consider carefully the key (two or three) questions you want to ask about each and every action and decision that takes place.

Questions develop people. They help others escape the trap of their own paradigms by broadening their perspectives and taking responsibility for their own viewpoints. Asking good questions, rather than giving answers, also forces you to listen attentively to your constituents and what they are saying. This action demonstrates your respect for their ideas and opinions. If you are genuinely interested in what other people have to say then you need to ask their opinion, especially before giving your own. Asking what others think facilitates participation in whatever decision will ultimately be determined, and consequently increases support for the decision and reduces the risk that the decision might be undermined by either inadequate consideration or unexpected opposition.

Another by-product of asking other people for their ideas and listening to their suggestions is that such actions enhance self-worth. People feel more important when they know that they can come to you with their ideas and be given a fair hearing, and that you consult with them and value their counsel before making decisions which may affect them. Dennis Ham, university statistician for Curtin University (Western Australia) told us that the best way to locate and then solve problems was to ask questions. He typically begins providing service by asking his constituents questions like: What information do you require? What would you like to know more about that you don't know now? If you had information that you don't have now, what difference might it make?

• *Keep score.*

Hold yourself accountable by keeping score. Collect data from your constituents regarding your leadership practices and your commitments to shared values. In a broader way this is also another strategy for keeping in touch. Maintaining credibility requires you to seek 360-degree feedback: that is, feedback not only from your manager but from customers, vendors, peers, colleagues, associates (employees), and shareholders. And when you don't just collect the data but make that data public, you can ensure that all parties know that the feedback will be taken seriously.

When he was manager of human resource training at Westpac Bank (in Australia), Marcus Stafford regularly collected data from his constituents and found it invaluable. On one occasion, after assuming a new managerial position, the feedback showed him that while he was doing well on challenging and stretching people, they also said that they were not always able to complete each assignment with attention to detail. "This made me realize," said Marcus, "that I was inadvertently stressing activities or quantity over quality, and so we all got together and talked about the data and what it meant." Marcus explains: "You might not like the feedback. But it is the only way you can develop yourself as a leader. And this really validates that I care about and pay attention to what others think!" Marcus includes this feedback in the materials he submits to his manager as part of his own performance appraisal.

Tim Hendrix returned from one of our leadership workshops and shared his Leadership Practices Inventory data with his team at LSI Logic Corporation. As Tim, a senior equipment maintenance and operations manager, says, "It was terrific. We had one of the best conversations ever about leadership, where the team is heading, what each and every one of us needs to be doing better, and so on. We are definitely going to do this on a regular basis."

Want to up the ante? Tie your feedback directly to financial rewards. For example, to make certain that employees recognize the seriousness of their corporate values many companies are directly linking managers' bonuses with feedback from their constituents regarding their ability to manage against their values set.

· *Do a personal audit.*

To set the example, you need to really know what example you're setting. To see how you're modeling the way, take the time to watch your actions. Then, for even more of an impact, have your audit done by someone other than yourself. Make the results public. Explain what's right and working. Set in motion changes that will realign your actions and behaviors to be more consistent with shared values.

Audit your daily routines. Are you spending sufficient time on matters consistent with your shared values? Use your shared values as the basis for planning your weekly schedule. Let values be your guide, not old habits or the in-basket.

Audit your daily calendar. How much time are you spending modeling shared values? How do your appointments contribute to communicating and reinforcing shared values?

Audit the agendas for your meetings. What topics are discussed? What issue is first on the agenda? Is it product quality, customer retention, profitability, new business development, collaboration with vendors? What signal does that issue send about what people should consider to be important? The "primacy effect"—what comes first in a series of items—is a very powerful force in gaining attention. What goes last—the "recency effect"—is also crucial in getting people to retain what's important.[35] Do the ones related to your shared values have the right emphasis? Consciously facilitate the meeting agenda, being sure to schedule what's first and last based on what you consider to be the most important messages for people to understand and remember. Beyond auditing the agenda, make the sole topic of your next meeting be how each participant models the group's shared values. Be the first to describe what you have done.

Audit your questions. What questions do you typically ask in meetings, one-on-ones, telephone calls, and interviews? How do these questions help to clarify and gain commitment to shared values? Make a list of searching questions that correspond to each of the shared values. Every opportunity you have, ask others these questions, getting them to be more conscious about what they are doing to put values into practice. In your next interview, use your shared values as the basis for the interview questions. Whenever you start a new relationship with a supplier begin by giving them a copy of your credo and talking about the kind of organization you are, and how they should know this if they are going to be in business with you.

Audit how you deal with critical incidents: How did you respond to the most recent incident? To what extent did your actions teach lessons about the most important shared values?

Audit your internal memos, e-mail notes, and messages. How are you using them to foster commitment to shared values? Is your language (analogies and metaphors) compatible with your message?

Audit your in-basket. What percentage of your incoming mail relates to shared values? What might explain this?

Audit your rewards and recognitions. Who's being recognized? Do these people exemplify the values you want reinforced? When someone gets recognized have you made clear the value (or standard) on which the reward is based?

By these actions, you can find out about the example that you're really setting. Be sure it's what you intend.

COMMITMENT NUMBER 2

SET THE EXAMPLE BY ALIGNING ACTIONS WITH SHARED VALUES

- *Create alignment around key values.*

- *Speak about shared values with enthusiasm and confidence—even drama.*

- *Teach and reinforce through symbols and artifacts.*

- *Lead by storytelling.*

- *Put storytelling on your meeting agendas.*

- *Ask questions.*

- *Keep score.*

- *Do a personal audit.*

Source: The Leadership Challenge by James M. Kouzes and Barry Z. Posner. Copyright © 2002.

PART THREE

Inspire a Shared Vision

5 ENVISION THE FUTURE

What made the difference was the vision of how things

could be and clearly painting this picture for all to see

and comprehend.

Mark D'Arcangelo, Hitachi Semiconductor America

I am driven by concerns for the legacy I am leaving

my children.

Gail Mayville, Ben and Jerry's

While working as an administrative assistant at Ben and Jerry's, the ice cream company, Gail Mayville became aware of a problem. As a result of the company's rapid growth, the ice cream waste from its factory was overloading the local waste treatment plant. In fact, as Gail put it, "If we weren't able to find a solution to that problem, we would have been in danger of actually having to shut the facility down until we could figure out what to do with it." It wasn't in Gail's job description to do something about this problem. After all, she wasn't the president, manufacturing manager, or environmental manager. But that didn't matter to her. Something very important was at stake, and it wasn't just the factory or their jobs.

Having grown up on a farm in Vermont, Gail knew enough about pigs to figure they'd like to eat the rich ice cream mix. She boldly suggested to the company that it should buy some pigs, donate them to local farmers, put the waste into barrels, truck the barrels out to the farms, pour the creamy liquid into the troughs, and see if the pigs would eat it. Guess what? The pigs loved it!

The immediate problem was solved, the factory wasn't shut down, people's jobs were saved, and the company got some time to work on a more permanent solution. As a result of her initiative, Gail was appointed the company's first environmental manager. She worked on other projects, and she became an expert on recycling. Her knowledge and experience grew to the point where other companies sought her advice, and she eventually moved on to become an environmental consultant.

Gail's actions serve as yet another example of how leadership is a relationship and how leadership is everyone's business. The story serves as a reminder that it isn't necessary to have a title to take action on an important organizational problem. It's a reminder that visions come from relationships with others, be they children, coworkers, or community. Beyond this, it illustrates something about *why* people take action on a problem in the first place.

The risk of closing the factory may have been the presenting problem but a deeper, more compelling force propelled Gail into action. As she puts it, "For me, personally, I am driven by concerns for the legacy I am leaving my children, the environmental legacy." Her driving force was her intense interest in the kind of world she would bequeath to her children. She wanted to ensure that they would be able to enjoy a healthy and joyful life in the future.

Gail's story is not about one more ambitious person taking initiative in a crisis. Her story is about the connection between vision and action. When we feel passionately about the legacy we want to leave, about the kind of future world we want for ourselves and for others, then we are much more likely to voluntarily step forward. If we don't have the slightest clue about our hopes, dreams, and aspirations, then the chance that we'll take the lead is significantly less. In fact, we may not even see the opportunity that's right in front of us.

BEING FORWARD-LOOKING
DIFFERENTIATES LEADERS

As we reported in Chapter Two, people want leaders who are honest, forward-looking, competent, and inspiring. Three of the four qualities are the attributes that make a person credible:

For:	You Can Say:
• Honest	• Trustworthiness
• Competent	• Expertise
• Inspiring	• Dynamism

It's clear that *credibility is the foundation of leadership.* Yet there is one characteristic on the admired leader list that is *not* on the credible person list: *forward-looking.* The message thousands of people are sending is that unless they also believe an aspiring leader is forward-looking, they aren't likely to follow willingly. Just ask yourself, would you voluntarily enlist in a movement or join an organization in which the leaders have no idea where they're headed?

Gail Mayville and the thousands of other leaders in our studies share the characteristic of being forward-looking, of being concerned not just about today's problems but also about tomorrow's possibilities. They're able to *envision the future,* to gaze across the horizon of time and imagine the greater opportunities to come. They see something out ahead, vague as it might appear from a distance, and they imagine that extraordinary feats are possible and that the ordinary could be transformed into something noble.

The leaders we interviewed echo the perspective that bringing meaning to life in the present by focusing on making life better in the long run is an essential ingredient in getting extraordinary things done. All enterprises or projects, big or small, begin in the mind's eye; they begin with imagination and with the belief that what's merely an image can one day be made real.

THE IMPORTANCE OF HAVING A VISION

Despite the sometimes humorous references to "the vision thing," no serious contemporary treatment of leadership would suggest that a leader should be concerned only about short-term performance and not about the long-term creation of value. It's an accepted fact of a leader's life.[1]

No matter what term is used—whether *purpose, mission, legacy, dream, goal, calling,* or *personal agenda*—the intent is the same: leaders want to do something significant, to accomplish something that no one else has yet achieved. What that something is—the sense of meaning and purpose—has to come from within. No one can impose a self-motivating vision on you. That's why, just as we said about values, you must first clarify your own visions of the future before you can expect to enlist others in a shared vision. To create a climate of meaningfulness, first you must personally believe in something yourself. Before you can inspire others, you have to be inspired yourself.

Your passion for something is an indication of what you find worthy in and of itself. It's a clue to what you find *intrinsically* rewarding. Researchers in human motivation have long talked about two kinds of motivation—extrinsic and intrinsic.[2] We either do things because of external controls—the possibility of a tangible reward if we succeed or punishment if we don't—or we do things because of an internal desire. We do something because we feel forced, or we do something because we want to. We do something to please others, or because it pleases us. Which condition is more likely to produce extraordinary results?

On this, the research is very clear. External motivation is more likely to create conditions of compliance or defiance; self-motivation produces far superior results There's even an added bonus. People who are self-motivated will keep working toward a result even if there's no reward, but people who are externally controlled are likely to stop trying once the rewards or punishments are removed. As psychologist and motivational expert Edward Deci has so aptly put it, "Stop the pay, and stop the play."[3]

And you can't impose a self-motivating vision on others. It has to be something that has meaning to your constituents, not just to you. Leaders must foster conditions under which everyone will do things because they want to, not because they have to. One of the most important practices of leadership is giving life and work a sense of meaning and purpose by offering an exciting vision.[4]

BEING FORWARD-LOOKING
IN TIMES OF RAPID CHANGE

In this digital age where speed is so vitally important to business success, people often ask: "How can I have a vision of what's going to happen five or ten years from now, when I don't even know what's going to happen next week?"

Venture capitalist Geoff Yang has taken risks on many new technology companies that are expected to move at a rapid pace. What types of innovators is he willing to back? "Men and women with great vision," he says, adding, "They are able to recognize patterns when others see chaos in the marketplace. That's how they spot unexploited niche opportunities. And they are passionate about their ideas, which are revolutionary ways to change the way people live their lives or the way businesses operate. When they come to me they have conviction."[5] Vision is just as relevant to the nanosecond world of technology as it is to any other endeavor.

Look at it this way. Imagine you're driving along the Pacific Coast Highway heading south from San Francisco on a bright, sunny day. The hills are on your left; the ocean, on your right. On some curves, the cliffs plunge several hundred feet to the water. You can see for miles and miles.

You're cruising along at the speed limit, tunes blaring, top down, wind in your hair, and not a care in the world. Suddenly, without warning, you come around a bend in the road and there's a blanket of fog as thick as you've ever seen it. What do you do?

We've asked this question many, many times and we get the same answers:

- I slow way down.
- I turn my lights on.
- I grab the steering wheel with both hands.
- I tense up.
- I sit up straight or lean forward.
- I turn the radio off so I can hear better.

Then you go around the next curve in the road, the fog lifts, and it's clear again. What do you do? Relax, speed up, turn the lights off, turn the radio on, and enjoy the scenery.

This analogy illustrates the importance of clarity of vision, *especially* when you're going fast. How fast can you drive in the fog without risking your own or other people's lives? How comfortable are you riding in a car with someone else who drives fast in the fog? Are you able to go faster when it's foggy or when it's clear? It's obvious, isn't it? We're better able to go fast when our vision is clear. We're better able to anticipate the switchbacks and bumps in the road when we can see ahead. There are always going to be times when the sun hides behind the clouds or fog makes it difficult to maneuver, but when it comes to traveling at Internet speed it's definitely preferable to be able to see farther ahead.

Ken Kido, executive vice president, Washington Mutual Consumer Lending Division, adds to this point with another critical observation about the importance of vision and the volume of information to which we are now constantly exposed:

> A challenge in leadership today is maintaining a vision, because there are a lot of distractions. There's a lot of external noise out there that would cause people to not understand what you're all about, what your company's all about, what their unit's all about. . . . Because of voice mail, because of e-mail, because of all these different electronic means . . . people many times are in overload situations. You need leaders that can keep people focused on the two or three things that are most important to them, their unit, their business, their company.

Certainly the Internet has had a profound effect on commerce, education, entertainment, and family life. But a fundamental truth of leadership existed long before we wrote about it, has not changed since we first put words on paper, and will be around long after the Internet has become just another utility, as ubiquitous as the telephone. That universal truth? Constituents of all types demand that leaders be forward-looking and have a sense of direction. Leaders must develop this capacity to Envision the Future by mastering these *essentials:*

- Discover the theme
- Imagine the possibilities

We'll be discussing these two essentials in the rest of this chapter, but first a caveat. Even as we provide some structure for Envisioning the Future—the practice that most differentiates leaders from other credible people—we freely admit that it's more art than science. Our evidence underscores that the ability to articulate a clear vision of the future significantly contributes to getting extraordinary things done. Yet we'll be the first to confess that there are not five, seven, or ten steps to magically revealing your vision. What we can do, by taking a closer look at the leaders in our studies and the work of other researchers, is offer solid hints about how to engage in this process for yourself.

DISCOVER THE THEME

Unfortunately, just knowing that being able to envision the future is the difference between credible contributors and credible leaders doesn't make visions pop out of your head like bright lightbulbs. When we ask people to tell us where their visions come from, they often have great difficulty describing the process. And when they do provide an answer, typically it's more about a feeling, a sense, a gut reaction, a concern. When people first take on their roles as leaders—whether they're appointed or whether they volunteer—they often don't have a *clear* vision of the future for their teams and organizations.

At the beginning what leaders have is a *theme.* They have concerns, desires, questions, propositions, arguments, hopes, dreams, and aspirations—core concepts around which they organize their aspirations and actions. Leaders begin the process of Envisioning the Future by discovering their own themes. Everything else leaders say about their vision is an elaboration, interpretation, and variation on that theme. Fortunately, there are ways to improve your ability to articulate your own themes and ultimately your visions of the future.

Express Your Passion

Finding your vision, like finding your voice, is a process of self-exploration and self-creation. It's an intuitive, emotional process. There's often no logic to it. You just feel strongly about something and that sense, that intuition has yet to be fully explained.[6]

Exemplary leaders have a passion for their institutions, their causes, their technologies, their communities—something other than their own fame and fortune. We've said in our earlier writings that "caring is at the heart of leadership." In the context in which we wrote it at the time, we meant a caring for people. But we also know that true leaders care about something much bigger than themselves and much bigger than all of us. Leaders care about making a difference in the world.

If you don't care deeply for and about something and someone, then how can you expect others to feel any sense of conviction? How can you expect others to get jazzed, if you're not energized and excited? How can you expect others to suffer through the long hours, hard work, absences from home, and personal sacrifices if you're not similarly committed?

One of our favorite examples of sensing one's passion and making a difference comes from Tara Church, who, at age eight, founded Tree Musketeers. (As we write this, Tara is a student at Harvard Law School.) We love this story because it reinforces the point that you don't have to be the president of a country to think many years down the road. You just have to be concerned and passionate about the future.[7] Here's Tara's story in her own words.

I was eight years old when the world and my place in it turned inside-out. It was a lovely Friday afternoon in 1987 when my Brownie Girl Scout troop met to discuss an upcoming camping trip. This was not Brownie business as usual, however, because severe drought assailed California and we faced the difficult decision of whether to use paper plates or our traditional tin dishes on this outing. Since water was going to be difficult to come by at the campsite, paper plates seemed like the natural choice. My mother, our Girl Scout Leader, wanted us to make an informed decision as we laid out the pros and cons of disposable and reusable. She mentioned, almost off-handedly, that using excess paper wastes trees.

"Wastes trees?" someone asked. "What does that mean?"

"Don't trees just grow back?" another demanded.

My mother was not a scientist or (God forbid!) an environmentalist, but she told us what she knew about rainforest and old growth deforestation. Searching her memory for bits of information about the effects of forest destruction, she related a conversation she had had with someone on a plane about the hole in the ozone layer.

"If there aren't enough trees to fight pollution," she said, "it will all go up into the atmosphere and eat away the ozone layer. If the ozone layer isn't there to block the harsh rays of the sun, then the surface of the Earth will get very hot. Someone told me that scientists are already looking for ways for the human race to live underground after the atmosphere is gone."

It was as if a dark cloud had settled upon our little circle. Stifled by despair I looked around the room at twelve brows furrowed just like mine as each of us created a mental picture of dark underground caverns beneath the burning surface of the Earth. One of the girls cleared her throat and finally asked the question:

"Can you play soccer underground?"

We all agreed that it seemed unlikely. I sunk back into my gloom until a brilliant idea cut through like a sunbeam:

"We should plant a tree!"

Roughly two months later, thirteen of us sat around a freshly planted Sycamore, dubbed Marcie the Marvelous Tree, dreaming up a plan to save the environment. Planted in the middle of a barren strip of city land, skinny, rootbound Marcie was our hope for the future. Marcie had only a dozen or so leaves at the time, but I remember envisioning how majestic she would be, how much good she would do for the environment, how she would inspire people around the world to protect our Earth. . . .

My friends and I called ourselves TREE MUSKETEERS and launched a crusade to heal our local environment that carried us to the White House to accept an award from President Reagan in little over a year. In 1990 my eleven-year-old colleagues and I incorporated TREE MUSKETEERS as the world's first youth environmental organization. By 1997, when I attended the President's Summit for America's Future as a nonprofit delegate, we had developed a worldwide network of over two million young people. The President's Summit inspired us to dream of a massive, concerted effort to unify and quantify their work. The result was ONE IN A MILLION: a campaign to empower a million kids to dedicate a million volunteer hours to planting a million trees by end of 2000. The power of ONE IN A MILLION was the simple act of planting a tree. A Sycamore named Marcie changed my life and I have been blessed with the opportunity to share that magic with millions of kids.

In advising young leaders today, Tara offers the following advice based on her own experience: "Don't ever let anyone tell you that you can't make a difference. If we all work on our little parts of the planet, then neighborhood by neighborhood, state by state, nation by nation we *will* change the world. . . . I firmly believe that the TREE MUSKETEERS kids who are preparing to take over the helm of the organization are all but immune from the negative pressures which destroy many a young life . . . all because they are leaders whose place in society is defined by their passion and mission." These are powerfully inspiring words that should give us all hope for the future. In aiming for that future, we also need to look into the past.

Explore Your Past

Some rather surprising and intriguing research reported by Omar A. El Sawy of the University of Southern California extends our understanding of the relevance of our past experience to envisioning future.[8] El Sawy studied thirty-four chief executive officers, dividing them into two equal groups. Among the tests that he administered to the two subgroups was the Vista Test, which he devised to measure their time orientation. In one part of this test, the CEOs were asked to look ahead into their personal future—to "think of things that might (or will) happen to you in the future." In another part, they were asked to look into their personal past—to "think of the things that have happened to you in the past." In each case, they were asked to list ten events and to date each event.

One group listed the past events first; the other group listed the future events first. El Sawy then compared the length of the past and future time horizons for the two groups. As illustrated in Table 5.1, the CEOs who listed their past events first had significantly longer future time horizons—over four years longer—than the CEOs who listed future events first. The two groups had similar past time horizons, both with a maximum of about

Table 5.1. The Janus Effect.

	Looked Toward Future First	Reviewed Past First
Mean time in future	1.8 years	3.2 years
Maximum time in future	5.1 years	9.2 years
Minimum time in future	0.2 years	0.4 years

twenty years. El Sawy refers to the difference in future horizons as "the Janus Effect," after the two-faced Roman god of beginnings.

Of several plausible explanations for the Janus effect, El Sawy believes his research supports the "one-way-mirror hypothesis." This hypothesis states, "We make sense of our world retrospectively, and all understanding originates in reflection and looking backward. . . . We construct the future by some kind of extrapolation, in which the past is prologue, and the approach to the future is backward-looking."[9]

When we gaze first into our past, we elongate our future. We also enrich our future and give it detail as we recall the richness of our past experiences. So, to be able to envision the possibilities in the distant future, to enhance your ability to be forward-looking, look first into the past. When you do, you're likely to find that your central theme didn't just occur to you this morning. It's been there for a long time. For Gail Mayville and Tara Church, the concern for a healthy environment keeps repeating itself. For others it might be open computer architecture, self-managed investing, the wireless Web, e-commerce, virtual learning, fair housing, affordable health care, safe schools, religious freedom, equal rights, socially responsible business, or any number of possibilities. Search your past to find the recurring theme in your life.

In addition to identifying lifelong themes, there's another benefit to looking back before looking ahead: we can gain a greater appreciation for how long it can take to fulfill aspirations. We also realize that there are many, many avenues for us to pursue, and that there may actually be no end in sight. This life has many dreams with no endings, dreams that can occupy us for a lifetime in pursuing something greater.

None of this is to say that the past *is* our future. Adopting that extremely dangerous perspective would be not unlike trying to drive to the future while looking only in the rearview mirror. With that point of view, we'd drive ourselves and our organizations right off a cliff. What the Janus effect *does* tell us is that it's difficult, if not impossible, to imagine going to a place we've never experienced, either actually or vicariously. It's also virtually impossible to be passionate about it, because to be truly passionate about something you have to be willing to suffer for it. How would you know you'd be willing to suffer for it if you'd never taken part in it? Avail yourself of the richest set of experiences possible. The broader your experiences and the more vast your network of connections, the longer your time horizons are likely to be.

Pay Attention to Your Experiences

One of the accomplishments about which we're most proud is the fact that we wrote our second book, *Credibility: How Leaders Gain and Lose It, Why People Demand It,* on the Internet. In 1991–92, Barry was in Perth on sabbatical at the University of Western Australia; Jim was living in San Jose, California, and working with The Tom Peters Company in Palo Alto. We needed a fast and efficient way to send chapter drafts back and forth to each other. Express mail service was prohibitively expensive, and would have taken at least a week. The regular postal service, though affordable, was agonizingly slow and would've added several months to our schedule. Thank goodness the Internet was available to us. We just attached files to an e-mail message, and using a program called Kermit, we'd send the chapters halfway around the world.

We did this at a time—and it's not that long ago—when the Internet was not available to the general public. It was only available to research institutions, government agencies, and educational institutions, thanks to ARPAnet. We felt as if we were on the cutting edge, ahead of our time. We thought we were real pioneers.

Yet there was something we didn't do that could have changed the course of our lives, the lives of our families, and who knows what else. There was something we missed entirely. In a way, our eyes were closed, leaving us blind to the possibilities. If we'd been paying attention, if we'd really been *seeing* what was right in front of us, one of us would have jumped up and yelled, "WOW! Do you see what we're doing here? In seconds what we've composed on one desktop computer arrives on another computer half a world away. This is awesome! I bet there're millions of other people around the world who'd love to be able to do this. Why don't we write a business plan for a company that connects people virtually and allows them to communicate 24/7/365? And then let's find a venture capitalist willing to take a risk on this wacky idea." But neither one of us said that. Fortunately, others were paying attention and saw the potential of the technology.

Visions don't materialize magically in a sudden flash of light. They come, in part, from *paying attention* to what is right in front of us. That is why, as cultural anthropologist Jennifer James has observed, "the core skill for understanding the future is the willingness to see it—and see it in perspective."[10] The Internet (or its precursor) has actually been around since the late 1960s, when it was originally used for military research. It only became a viable commercial technology in the 1990s, some twenty-odd years after it was first conceived. It's a classic reason to look back before you look ahead; the technology and the talent may already exist in a laboratory or a garage somewhere.

There's another lesson from our own experience. To be able to have a vision of the future, you have to be able to see the big story: to see trends and patterns and not just one-off or one-time occurrences. We weren't the only ones using the Net back then. Thousands of others were using it; more and more were logging on every day. People were talking about it, but we weren't listening. Lots of little things were going on all around us, things that—had we paid attention—would have seemed like fingers pointing in the direction we were all headed. But we missed it.

One reliable explanation as to why we didn't see what was right in front of us is that we didn't really care. We didn't have the passion for the technology. We had the passion for something else. We had, and have, a passion for liberating the leader in everyone, and to us the Internet was simply a convenient and cool tool for doing just that. In contrast, Sky Dayton was paying attention to the Internet and in 1993 he came up with the idea for EarthLink, which is, as of this writing, the fourth-largest U.S. provider of Internet access. As Dayton commented to our colleague Richard Chang, "It was absolutely critical that everyone have a passion for the Internet and what we were doing."[11] Passion and attention go hand in hand. We don't see the possibilities when we don't feel the passion.

Immerse Yourself

As we acquire experience (in an organization, a profession, or an industry), we acquire information about what happens, how things happen, and who makes things happen. One of our Silicon Valley colleagues, a serial entrepreneur, is constantly looking for new businesses to start or to invest in. When we spoke with him about the process he goes through from concept to company, he talked about immersing himself in the technology and the industry. He gets a sense that something is going to make it big, so he learns as much as he can about it. He reads about it, talks to others about it, visits those engaged in it, and does whatever he can to understand the field of play. The longer our participation and the more varied our experiences, the broader and deeper our understanding is likely to be. For instance, there's a lot of talk these days about the need to be global. The implication for anyone who would lead in a global economy is that they need to spend some time traveling the world. After all, how can you imagine the possibilities of what your constituents might really need in Helsinki or Hong Kong if you've never been there? Sure, you can get connected on the Internet and send e-mail back and forth, but does that really give you the experience of what it's like to work and live there? Hardly. How can you be a leader in a global economy if you've never left home?

When we're presented with an unfamiliar problem in our work, we consciously (or unconsciously) draw upon our experiences to help us solve it. We select relevant information, make relevant comparisons, and integrate experience with the current situation. For the experienced leader, all of this may happen in a matter of seconds.[12] But it's the years of direct contact with a variety of problems and situations that equip the leader with unique insight. Listening, reading, smelling, feeling, and tasting the business—these tasks improve our vision. We begin to get an intuitive sense—a gut feel—for what is going to happen down the road. We can anticipate the future.

Many of the people we interviewed mentioned that the exercise of analyzing their personal-best leadership experiences was enlightening for them:

by highlighting key lessons from the past, they were able to generate insightful road maps for leadership highways still to be explored. Direct experience with the organization, the industry, or the profession is critical. It's the knowledge gained from direct experience and active searching that, once stored in the subconscious, becomes the basis for leaders' intuition, insight, and vision.

There's another significant aspect of immersing ourselves in something: we get inspired to do even more. Take the case of Don Bennett, who became the first amputee to climb Mount Rainier's 14,410-foot volcanic summit. That feat was the result of Don's passionate belief that the disabled were capable of doing more than others—and even they themselves—assumed. Don, a Seattle businessman at the time, set out to act on his belief, and had the inspiration to climb Mount Rainier.

But that's not the end of the story. It's really only the beginning, and it illustrates that action and vision are intimately connected. Here's how Don describes how he came up with the idea for the Amputee Soccer League and his sense of where visions come from:

> When I got off the mountain, I was in top shape. The best shape I'd ever been in my life. And so right away, because I'm doing one thing on the positive, my mind is thinking, "What can I do to stay in shape?" So where does it come from? I think there is a bolt of lightning in the middle of the night. All I had was the inspiration. I didn't know that much about soccer. I didn't know there were even two sizes of soccer balls. . . . So the next thing with the inspiration is "get out and start doing something." The doing part of it is picking up a phone, calling a few friends, and saying, "Why don't you meet me over on Mercer Island? I've got an idea here. I really feel it." So when they come over, I pull out a soccer ball. They already have their crutches, and we start kicking it. . . . Then things start happening.

Don's description of the process that he went through is typical of other descriptions we heard in our study: a moment of inspiration—a "bolt of lightning"—and then action (not planning, but action) to test out the idea. As Don said, "You've got to kick the ball around to get a feel for it. To see if you like it. . . . The inspirations come with kicking the ball."

Pigs, trees, mountain tops, or soccer leagues; where's the logic in these ideas? These were pure passion plays based on central themes in the lives of their creators. Gail Mayville was driven by her concern for the legacy she was leaving her children, and so she suggested pigs might help with the waste disposal problem. Tara Church was concerned about not wasting trees and needing clean air so kids could play soccer above ground, so she planted Marcie the Marvelous Tree. The vision of Tree Musketeers and what it could do for the world came later. Don Bennett was so enthusiastic after climbing Mt. Rainier that he got struck by a bolt of inspiration, picked up the phone, and invited some friends to get together and kick the ball around.

Envisioning the future is a process that begins with passion, feeling, concern, or an inspiration that something is worth doing. Your vision of the future may be fuzzy, but at least you're focused on a meaningful theme. You believe there's a better tomorrow, you act on your gut instincts and the vision gets a little clearer. You do something else that moves you, the vision gets a little clearer still. You pay attention to it, experience it, immerse yourself in it. You kick the ball around, plant a tree, buy some pigs, or write a letter. Get the process started and, over time, you see more detail in your dream. It's an iterative process, one that eventually results in something that you can actually articulate. After you've immersed yourself long enough, after you've gained enough experience, then you'll be able to answer your constituents' question, What's your vision of the future?

IMAGINE THE POSSIBILITIES

Leaders are possibility thinkers, not probability thinkers. *Probabilities* must be based upon evidence strong enough to establish presumption. *Possibilities* are not. All new ventures begin with possibility thinking, not probability thinking. After all, the probability is that most new businesses will fail and most social reforms will never get off the ground. If entrepreneurs or activists accepted this view, however, they'd never start a new business or organize a community. Instead, they begin with the assumption that anything is possible. Like entrepreneurs and other activists, leaders assume that anything is possible. It's this belief that sustains them through the difficult times.[13]

Turning this possibility thinking into an inspiring vision—and an inspiring vision that is shared—is the leader's challenge. In the context of leadership as a relationship, vision is about the *common good*, and not just about what the leader wants. *Vision*, as we use the term throughout the rest of this book, means *an ideal and unique image of the future for the common good*. It implies a choice of values and something that brings meaning and purpose to our lives.

Find Meaning in the Ideal

Visions are about hopes, dreams, and aspirations. They're about our strong desire to achieve something great. They're ambitious. They're expressions of optimism. Can you imagine a leader enlisting others in a cause by saying, "I'd like you to join me in doing the ordinary better"? Not likely. Visions necessarily stretch us to imagine exciting possibilities, breakthrough technologies, or revolutionary social change.

By focusing on the ideal we also gain a sense of meaning and purpose from what we undertake. It's one thing to go on an adventure just for the fun of it, it's another to do it because it feeds the soul. The visions of leaders are about making a difference in the world, about having an impact. Of course, the two aren't mutually exclusive; we should always have fun pursuing our dreams.

Dan Swisher, senior vice president of ALZA Pharma, managed to blend vision and fun even in trying times. When Dan attended a session of The Leadership Challenge Workshop, his new team had just recently pulled out of a slump caused by a failed merger.[14] The consultant running the workshop, Robert Thompson, focused the participants on creating a story about how the future looks and then working backward to create the strategy, tasks, and detail to accomplish it. Dan wrote, in part:

> Three years from now, I will be at a July 4 barbecue when someone will ask me, "Where do you work?" I will reply "ALZA" and be ready to explain where and what ALZA is when the person will say, "Oh, ALZA! That's a great company, I have a good friend who works there and raves about what a great company it is. I also own some stock that I bought three years ago . . . what a ride! Tell me what makes ALZA so special?"
>
> "That's easy," I say. "The people. The people. The people. ALZA is special because we attract bright, motivated employees who want to

make a difference. ALZA is special because we celebrate innovation. ALZA drug delivery technologies power the most successful brands in the industry. The vision of delivering the right drug to the right place at the right time is at the core of everything we develop. And ALZA is special because most importantly we benefit patients. Our products provide lasting benefits and treat significant human suffering."

Dan followed this up by sharing the story with his team and throughout the company. Just before that year's Fourth of July holiday, he even sent a voice mail out to everyone thanking them for their hard effort and encouraging them to look to the future, a time when, as he put it:

ALZA will be a household name, recognized as a pharmaceutical powerhouse with exciting products that truly advance patient care. Most importantly, ALZA will be recognized as a great place to work that attracts and retains the best talent in the industry. All that will be possible because of what all of us are achieving today.

In time, Dan's motto became a march. Everyone knew that their work for the next three years was all about the "barbecue." The theme was woven into the workday and used again at company functions; at the end of one evening, Dan was even given a barbecue hat and apron.

All the personal-best cases we collected were, like Dan's, about possibilities. They were about improving on the existing situation or creating an entirely new state of existence. The leaders were characterized by a dissatisfaction with the status quo and a belief that something better was attainable. They represent the choice of an ideal.

Ideals reveal our higher-order value preferences. They represent our ultimate economic, technological, political, social, and aesthetic priorities. The ideals of world peace, freedom, justice, a comfortable life, happiness, and self-respect are among the ultimate strivings of our existence—the ones that we seek to attain over the long term. They're statements of the idealized purpose that we hope all our practical actions will enable us to attain.

Take Pride in Being Unique

Visions communicate what makes us singular and unequaled; they set us apart from everyone else. Visions must differentiate us from others if we're to attract and retain employees, volunteers, customers, clients, donors, or investors.[15] There's no advantage in working for, buying from, or investing in an organization that does exactly the same thing as the one across the street or down the hall. Only when people understand how we're truly distinctive, how we stand out in the crowd, will they want to sign up with us.

Uniqueness fosters pride. It boosts the self-respect and self-esteem of everyone associated with the organization. The more proud we are of the place we shop, the products or services we buy, the school we (or our children) attend, the community in which we live, or the place we work, the more loyal we're likely to be. One of the best ways to discover the uniqueness in your organization's vision is to begin by asking why your customers or clients, internal or external, would want to buy your particular service or product, attend your program, or listen to your sermon.

One of our favorite answers to that question is this simple yet eloquent statement from Edward Goeppner, of the Podesta Baldocchi chain of flower shops: "We don't sell flowers, we sell beauty." Customers of a florist do exchange money for a dozen roses, but what they're really buying is something more than that: they want to beautify their homes, or express their love for others, or brighten the day. It doesn't take vision to sell a flower on a street corner, but it does take vision to sell beauty.

Uniqueness also enables smaller units within large organizations, or neighborhoods within large cities, to have their own vision while still being encompassed by the collective vision. Although every unit within a corporation, public agency, religious institution, school, or volunteer association must be aligned with the overall organizational vision, it can express its distinctive purpose within the larger whole. Every function and every department can differentiate itself by finding its most distinctive qualities. Each can be proud of its ideal and unique image of its future as it works toward the common future of the larger organization.

These days, with the latest and greatest available in a nanosecond at the touch of a key, it's become increasingly difficult to differentiate yourself from others. Log onto any Internet search engine, type in a key word, and up come hundreds, sometimes thousands of sites and offerings. And it's not just the speed and volume of information that creates problems. It's a sea of sameness out there. Towns around the world are looking the same. Whether you're in Greenwich, Connecticut, or Greenwich, England, you'll find Tower Records, The Gap, Starbucks, Citibank, and Wal-Mart. Everything begins to look and sound alike, and eventually it gets awfully boring. Businesses, new and old, must work harder and harder to differentiate themselves (and their products) from others around them. Business consolidation, the Internet, the information overload, the 24/7/365 always-on, everyone's-connected world means leaders must be even more attentive to ways in which they can be a beacon of light that cuts through the dense fog and steers people in the right direction.

Make Images of the Future

A beacon of light cutting through the fog. It's an image you can picture in your mind. In fact, leaders often talk about future issues in terms of foresight, focus, forecasts, future scenarios, points of view, and perspectives. Visual references, all. In our workshops and classes we often illustrate the power of images with this simple exercise. We ask people to think about the city of Paris, France, and to shout out the first thing that comes to mind. The replies that pop out—the Eiffel Tower, the Arc de Triomphe, the Seine, Notre Dame, good food, wine, romance—are all images of real places and real sensations. No one calls out the square kilometers, population, or gross domestic product of Paris. Why? Human memory is stored in images and sensory impressions, not in numbers. We recall images of reality, not abstractions from reality.

So what does this mean for leaders? It means that to envision the future, we must be able to draw upon that very natural mental process of creating images. When we invent the future, we need to get a mental picture of what things will be like long before we begin the journey. Images are our windows on the world of tomorrow. When talking about going places we've never been —whether to the top of an unclimbed mountain or to the pinnacle of an entirely new industry—we imagine what they'd look like. We picture the possibilities. Those who are more auditory by nature talk about a "calling."

All of us make efforts to see the future—not in some mystical sense but in a cognitive sense. We do it every time we plan a trip or put a little money in the bank for retirement. Although some people may have greater creative imagination than others, many of us have more than we may have assumed.

Visions are images in the mind, impressions and representations. They become real as leaders express those images in concrete terms to their constituents. Just as architects make drawings and engineers build models, leaders find ways of giving expression to their hopes for the future.

Look to the Future

Constituents want their leaders to be "forward-looking," to have "a long-term vision or direction." Yet the attention that senior management tends to devote to building a collective perspective on the future is woefully inadequate.[16] Leaders need to be proactive in thinking about the future, and this imperative increases with the leader's scope and level of responsibility. Naturally, all roles require attention to the present and the future; it's only the ratio that varies.

As we illustrate in Figure 5.1, when a leader's role is strategic (as it is for a CEO, president, or research scientist, for example), the time orientation

Figure 5.1. Mix of Present-Future Orientations of Leaders.

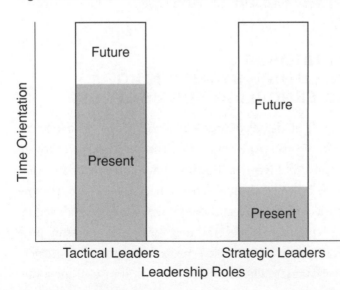

is longer term and more future-oriented than it is for a leader whose role is more tactical (for example, a production supervisor or operations manager). As a rule of thumb, we believe that most leaders should set for themselves the goal of developing their abilities to envision the future at least five to seven years ahead. At the more senior levels it should be at least ten, and executive leaders responsible for entire organizations in the national and international arenas have to look out twenty years and beyond.

Visions are reflections of our fundamental beliefs and assumptions about human nature, technology, economics, science, politics, art, and ethics. Two leaders in a single organization may have identical experiences and identical opportunities and yet have completely different visions of the organization's future. Why? They may operate under fundamentally different premises, different visions of the way the world works.

Visions are statements of destination, of the ends of our labor; they are therefore future-oriented and are made real over different spans of time. It may take three years from the time we decide to climb a mountain until we actually reach the summit. It may take a decade to build a company, a century to grow a forest, and generations to set a people free. For leaders of a community who envision neighborhoods so safe from crime that little children might once again walk alone to the corner store, aspirations may take a lifetime to achieve. The point is that leaders must think about the future and become able to project themselves ahead in time.

COMMITMENT NUMBER 3:
ENVISION THE FUTURE BY IMAGINING
EXCITING AND ENNOBLING POSSIBILITIES

The most important role of visions in organizational life is to give focus to human energy. To enable everyone concerned with an enterprise to see more clearly what's ahead of them, leaders must have and convey a focus.

In contrast, imagine how you would feel if you had to watch a slide show when the projector was out of focus and the images were blurred, vague, and indistinct. We've experimented with this in some of our leadership programs. The reaction is predictable. People express frustration, impatience, confusion, anger, even nausea. They avoid the situation by looking away.

When we ask them whose responsibility it is to focus the projector, the vote is unanimous: the leader—the person with the focus button. Some people get out of their chairs, walk over to the projector, and focus it themselves, but this doesn't change how they feel: they're still annoyed that the person with the button—the leader—wouldn't focus the projector. The leader's job is to keep the projector focused, to keep the "big picture," the overall purpose or vision of the organization, in view. This enables people to have a clear sense of what the future will look like when everyone has added their piece; with that in mind, they can contribute to the whole, efficiently and with confidence.

Whether you're leading a small department of ten, a large organization of ten thousand, or a community of a hundred thousand, shared vision sets the agenda and gives direction and purpose to the enterprise. As a leader, you must envision the future and then create the conditions for others to build a common vision together—one based on ideal and unique images of a common future. A vision spans years and keeps us focused on the future. And if it's to be attractive to more than an insignificant few, it must appeal to all who have a stake in it. In the next chapter we'll take a look at how a leader, by focusing the lens, inspires others to enlist in a common cause. First, in the action steps that follow, we offer some practical guidance in enhancing your own capacity to envision the future and to be open to the possibilities.

• *Read a biography of a visionary leader.*

Review a list of admired historical leaders (see our list in Chapter Three) or make your own. Select one person about whom you want to know more, go to the bookstore or library—virtual or physical—and get that person's autobiography or biography. Read it. Then read about the next person on your list. Or go to http://www.biography.com/ to locate excellent videotapes from A&E's Emmy Award–winning series *Biography*.

Pay particular attention to the stories your admired leaders share. Harvard professor Howard Gardner, in *Leading Minds,* comments, "Leaders achieve their effectiveness chiefly through the stories they relate. Here, I use the term *relate* rather than *tell* because presenting a story in words is but one way to communicate. In addition, in communicating stories, leaders *embody* those stories. That is . . . leaders . . . convey their stories by the kinds of lives they themselves lead and, through example, seek to inspire in their followers."[17] Visionary leaders aren't content to relate the existing stories; they create new ones. There's a practical lesson here for each of us. What can you learn from studying the biographies of your admired leaders about how to create new stories?

- *Think about your past.*

Remember that leaders with the longest time horizons are those who understand their past. Before you attempt to write your vision statement, look to your past for key messages about the direction you have chosen and the future to which you aspire. We especially like the "lifeline" exercise developed by Herb Shepard and Jack Hawley.[18] Here's an abbreviated version:

- Look backward in your past and record significant events in your life—turning points that have influenced the direction you have taken. Start as far back as you can remember and stop at the present time.
- Briefly record key events in your life that represent turning points or significant learning experiences. Many people find it useful to draw this as a *lifeline*—a graph that maps both the peaks and valleys, the highs and the lows. Others prefer to just list events. Whichever method works for you, give the technique a try.
- Next to each event, write a word or two identifying the experience.
- Now go back and review each peak event, making a few notes on why each was a high point for you.
- Analyze your notes. What dominant themes emerge? What patterns are revealed? What important personal strengths? What do these themes and patterns tell you about what you're likely to find personally compelling in the future?

Participants in our leadership workshops have found this exercise extremely revealing and useful as they prepare to clarify their visions of the future. We've also applied the process to the organization as well as the individual. By looking over the history of their organization, members begin to see the organizational strengths and weaknesses, the patterns and themes that have carried them to the present. They're then better informed about the foundation on which they're building the future.

• *Determine the "something" you want to do.*

Are you in your job *to do something*, or are you in your job *for something to do?* If your answer is "to do something," take out a sheet of paper and at the top write, "What I want to accomplish." Now make a list of all the things that you want to achieve on the job. For each item, ask yourself, "Why do I want this?" Keep on asking why until you run out of reasons. By doing this exercise, you're likely to discover those few higher-order values that are the idealized ends for which you strive.

Here are some additional questions that you can use as catalysts in clarifying your vision:

- How would I like to change the world for myself and our organization?
- How do I want to be remembered?
- If I could invent the future, what future would I invent for myself and my organization?
- What mission in life absolutely obsesses me?
- What's my dream about my work?
- What's my most distinctive skill or talent?
- What's my burning passion?
- What work do I find absorbing, involving, enthralling? What will happen in ten years if I remain absorbed, involved, and enthralled in that work?
- What does my ideal organization look like?
- What's my personal agenda? What do I want to prove?

Jack Haderle's personal best clearly reflected his desire to do something. In discussing his role as a U.S. Forest Service ranger responsible for the reforestation of Forest Hill (in the Tahoe National Forest) after a fire, he said that the work was about a "great cause. It's not about getting some product out. It's not about fixing something in a company that will only break again sometime in the future. It's about helping future generations, making life better for others in the long run." Jack knew what he wanted to accomplish. He also realized that the process could take many lifetimes. His truly was a future-oriented cause—something for his grandchildren and great-grandchildren.

• *Write an article about how you've made a difference.*

Your responses to the questions just posed should give you some clues to what you would like to accomplish in your life (and why). Now take it a step further. Imagine that it's ten years into the future and you've been selected to receive the "Fifty in Fifty Award"—a recognition as one of the fifty people who have made a difference in the last fifty years. Imagine that a national magazine has put together an article about the difference that you've made to your organization, family, constituents, or community. Write that article.

Don't censor yourself. Allow yourself this opportunity to record your hopes and dreams even if you find the process somewhat embarrassing. The more comfortable you are in discussing your innermost wishes, the easier it will become to communicate a vision to others. In writing your article, ask yourself the following questions:

- What's been your greatest contribution to your family?
- What's been your greatest contribution to those you've led?
- What's been your greatest contribution to your organization?
- What's been your greatest contribution to your community?
- What are you most proud of at this moment?

Then, once you've answered these and similar questions, project your answers into the future.

Writing such an article—and then reading it to your family, friends, or colleagues—is a very powerful way to clarify what's truly important to you. By looking back over your life and its potential, you come face to face with the legacy you want to leave and bring it into clearer focus.

To conclude this exercise, try to summarize in one sentence the legacy you want to leave in the same way that Gail Mayville expressed at the beginning of this chapter. Just fill in the blanks for yourself:

"For me, personally, I am driven by concerns for the legacy I am leaving _____, the _____ legacy."

- *Write your vision statement.*

Take all the information you've just gathered and write your *ideal and unique image of the future* for yourself and for your organization. We recommend that this statement be brief but not a one-liner. The one-liners come later. First, you need to practice expressing your hopes, dreams, and aspirations fully. As a general guideline, we tell people that Martin Luther King Jr.'s "I Have a Dream" speech was about seven minutes. Aim for something in the five- to seven-minute range. Any longer, and people are likely to lose interest. Much shorter, you won't be providing enough vivid detail for people to know where you really want to be ten or so years from now— what it truly feels like to be really be there.

Using your notes from your responses to the questions about the "something" you want *to do,* expand your vision by answering these questions:

- What is your ideal work community? What do you personally aspire to create?
- What is unique about your hopes, dreams, and aspirations? How is it distinctive compared to all the other visions of the future?
- When you project this into the future ten to fifteen years, what does it look like? What innovations and trends will influence that future? What vision will carry us forward into the future?
- What images come to mind when thinking of the future? What does it look like, sound like, taste like, feel like? What symbols or pictures best represent your vision of the future?
- How does this vision serve the common good? What's in it for others to align themselves with this vision?

Again, don't censor yourself. This is aspirational: it needs to be uplifting. Give voice to your dreams. Once you've written your vision, try drawing it, finding a picture that resembles it, or creating a symbol that represents it. Finally, create a short slogan of five to nine words that captures the essence of your vision. Something similar to Edward Goeppner's "We don't sell flowers, we sell beauty" is what we have in mind. A brief slogan is no substitute for a complete statement, but it does help others to remember the essential message and it can evoke images of a shared destiny.

After you've crafted your vision statement, revisit it periodically. Refine it and update it. The world changes, so be sure to adapt your stories to the changing times. Also keep in mind that while we're talking about *your* vision statement, we are definitely not suggesting that you impose your will on your constituents. Successful visions are *shared*. Much as we strongly encourage you to write and rehearse a consistent message to deliver to others, communicating a vision should be a *conversation*—not just a speech. What you articulate should provide others with the opportunity for dialogue.

- ### *Become a futurist.*

One of the leaders we interviewed said to us, "I'm my organization's futures department." We think all leaders should view themselves this way. Because being forward-looking is the differentiating leadership characteristic, you need to read about, think about, and talk about the long-term view, not only for your specific organization but for the environment in which you operate.

What percentage of your time is now devoted to creating a shared and outwardly focused long-term view of the future? Don't be surprised if your percentage is low. Researchers have found that the average time among senior executives is around 3 percent.[19] That's a pathetic number given the responsibility senior management has for the future success of their organizations. All leaders should strive to devote more time to creating a shared understanding of the future. That's your job!

Make it your business to spend some time studying the future. There are dozens of books and other sources of information available to expand your horizons; here are just a few:

- *The 500 Year Delta: What Happens After What Comes Next* by Watts Wacker and Jim Taylor, with Howard Means (New York: HarperBusiness, 1997).
- *The Art of the Long View: Planning for the Future in an Uncertain World* by Peter Schwartz (New York: Doubleday/Currency, 1991).
- *The Search Conference: A Comprehensive Guide to Theory and Practice* by Merrelyn Emery and Ronald E. Purser (San Francisco: Jossey-Bass, 1996).
- *Leading the Revolution* by Gary Hamel (Boston: Harvard Business School Press, 2000).

- *Thinking in the Future Tense: Leadership Skills for a New Age* by Jennifer James (New York: Simon & Schuster, 1996).
- *Where on Earth Are We Going?* by Maurice Strong (New York: Texere, 2001).

For more possibilities, see our Web site, http://www.leadershipchallenge.com/.

In addition, the following magazines address forward-looking issues: *American Demographics* discusses population patterns of the present and into the future, *Utne Reader* offers a digest of the alternative press, *Scientific American* covers developments in a variety of fields, and *Fast Company* serves up hip, hop, and hype on the leading edge of business. Thoughtful commentary on important cultural and social issues by thinkers around the world is included in *New Perspectives Quarterly,* while the *Economist* provides comprehensive coverage of world events along with periodic surveys on a variety of topics.

Finally, set up a futures research committee to study potential changes and developments in areas affecting your organization. Put together a team to continually track fifty or sixty publications that represent new thoughts on trends in your domain. Have team members abstract articles they think have relevance. A smaller team can then pull the abstracts into reports for use in planning and decision making. Or simply have all the people in your organization regularly clip articles from newspapers, magazines, and Web sites. Circulate the ideas generated and discuss the impact of trends on your products, services, technologies, and constituents. Use these discussions to help you and your organization develop the ability to think long term.

- *Test your assumptions.*

Assumptions are mental screens that expand or constrain what's possible. To determine their validity in regard to your vision, take the following steps:

- Make a list of the assumptions underlying your vision.
- Flesh out each assumption: ask yourself what you assume to be true or untrue about your constituents and your organization, about science and technology, about economics and politics, about the future itself.

- Ask a few close advisers to react to your assumptions. Do they agree or disagree with you? Why or why not?
- Ask people you think might have different assumptions to respond to yours.
- Test your assumptions by trying an experiment or two. Instead of struggling with words on paper, do something to act on your intuition. Do as Don Bennett did when he acted immediately on his inspiration to start the Amputee Soccer League. If you're inspired to do something, go try it. Then you'll see whether you really believe that you're on the right track. You'll also see whether others are as enthusiastic about the idea as you are.

Keep in mind that your assumptions may blind you to new solutions. Keep your eyes open and look around. Talk to people. Share your thoughts with others. Do some homework. Write your congressional representative or local newspaper. Go kick the ball around!

- *Rehearse with visualizations and affirmations.*

Once you've clarified your vision, one of the most effective things you can do to help you realize it is mental rehearsal—mentally practicing a skill, sequence of skills, or attitude using visual imagery or kinesthetic feelings. Mental rehearsal is used extensively in sports training to improve athletic performance. By visualizing yourself doing a move perfectly or reaching a desired goal, you increase your chances of making imagination become reality. Imagine what it will be like when you and your organization attain your vision. Rehearse this scenario over and over again.

Another practical technique is affirmation—a positive assertion that something is already so. It's a way of giving shape to that which you imagine for the future. An affirmation, sometimes called positive self-talk, can be made in writing, made silently, or spoken aloud. Whatever the mode, it's most effective in the present tense, as if the desired state already existed.

Write several affirmations about the ideal and unique image of your organization. Phrase your affirmation positively in terms of what you want. Make it short, and repeat it over and over to yourself. Here are a few leadership affirmations:

- I'm confident that I'm finding exciting opportunities as I accept these new challenges.
- I'm learning from my mistakes as I experiment with new ideas and methods.
- I'm creating enthusiasm as I communicate my vision of the future.

You might use these affirmations, and others, as part of a meditation for self-improvement. They are no substitute for personal conviction and a vision of substance, but they can help you focus your vision and create positive expectations about the future. And the more positive you feel about the future you envision, the better able you'll be to communicate positively with others.

COMMITMENT NUMBER 3

ENVISION THE FUTURE BY IMAGINING EXCITING AND ENNOBLING POSSIBILITIES

- *Read a biography of a visionary leader.*

- *Think about your past.*

- *Determine the "something" you want to do.*

- *Write an article about how you've made a difference.*

- *Write your vision statement.*

- *Become a futurist.*

- *Test your assumptions.*

- *Rehearse with visualizations and affirmations.*

Source: The Leadership Challenge by James M. Kouzes and Barry Z. Posner. Copyright © 2002.

6 ENLIST OTHERS

My enthusiasm, excitement, and commitment were contagious.

I spoke from the heart, with conviction and sincerity.

Sonya Lopes, Air Force Office of Special Investigations

Sharing the vision statement met with skepticism at first,

but as I kept coming back to parts of it over time, everyone

bought into the idea. People began to see it as a statement

about what we all wanted to build together.

Kevin Philbin, Solectron

Kevin Philbin was faced with implementing a new enterprise resource planning (ERP) system within Solectron, the world's largest contract electronics manufacturing services provider. ERP systems are designed to allow a company to use one system to track and manage many areas of business. They are notoriously complex to implement and often require significant customization. One early challenge Kevin ran into was that the plan he had inherited from the previous project manager was "very high-level and detailed." The team's response to it was generally, "We don't need to spend too much time reviewing it, because we've got real work to do." Because of the size of the plan and its dynamic nature, Kevin decided to put it on the network and on the team's Web site, reasoning that "anyone involved or interested in the project could see our plan. Also, I thought that by making our timelines broadly visible, we would get a higher level of commitment from everyone on the team." He soon realized that because the plan had been developed elsewhere and he was the one updating the plan, it was seen as *his* plan, not as *the team's* plan. As he put it, "Despite the fact that people had agreed to their assigned tasks, they didn't really feel a responsibility to check the project plan, to provide updates, or to use it as their map for progress."

Then Kevin made a change. As he says:

Instead of having just me present the plan to our management team, I proposed that we invite the whole team and have each person review their progress to date. While not everyone was crazy about having to present to management, it did begin instilling a sense of ownership in the plan, and it gave the team a chance to sit in the spotlight as we progressed.

We also started meeting every day at 10:00 A.M. to keep the project on track. After four months, I asked the team if we still needed the meeting; much to my surprise, their answer was yes. People felt that the meeting was a great way to get their issues addressed, to find out what's going on, to build a kind of team spirit, and continually reaffirm that we're all on the same track.

Kevin discovered how essential it is to find out what motivates each member of the team and why they want to be part of the project. Kevin notes that "the more you know about the people you work with, you find that you are more committed to each other's success, and how similar, after all, our hopes and aspirations for the project are." He developed what he calls a "mini-speech" to this effect: "I would repeat this vision of our group. I tried it out with different individuals on the team at first, to judge their reaction, and given positive feedback, I continued to hit upon this theme in our daily and weekly meetings. We got tremendous buy-in from this." Later, the team held a contest to select a name for their project. The winning name— GEARS, or Global Enterprise Applications & Resource System—subsequently became a unifying metaphor. As Kevin says, a company is like an engine: "We cannot move forward if any of the cogs are not working, and this system will be what allows us to work synchronously and effectively."

DEVELOP A SHARED SENSE OF DESTINY

In the personal-best cases that we collected, people frequently talked about the need to get buy-in on the vision, to enlist others in the dream. People talked about how they had to communicate the purpose and build support for the direction. Just as Kevin Philbin did, they found that it's not enough for a leader to have a vision. The members of the organization must understand, accept, and commit to the vision. When they do, the organization's ability to change and reach its potential soars.

Simply put, you have to teach others your vision. Teaching a vision—and confirming that the vision is shared—is a process of engaging constituents in conversations about their lives, about their hopes and dreams. Remember that leadership is a dialogue, not a monologue. Leadership isn't about imposing the leader's solo dream; it's about developing a *shared* sense of destiny. It's about enrolling others so that they can see how their own interests and aspirations are aligned with the vision and can thereby become mobilized to commit their individual energies to its realization. A vision is *inclusive* of constituents' aspirations; it's an ideal and unique image of the future for the *common* good.

When leaders effectively communicate a vision—whether it's to one person, a small group, or a large organization—that vision has very potent effects. We've found that when leaders clearly articulate their vision for the organization, constituents report significantly higher levels of a variety of positive reactions such as these:

- Job satisfaction
- Motivation
- Commitment
- Loyalty
- Esprit de corps
- Clarity about the organization's values
- Pride in the organization
- Organizational productivity

Clearly, teaching others about the vision produces powerful results.

Yet this leadership practice isn't always effectively employed. In fact, we've consistently found that inspiring a shared vision is the least frequently applied of the Five Practices of Exemplary Leadership. People also tell us that inspiring a shared vision is the leadership practice with which they feel the most uncomfortable. And when we ask people whether they consider themselves to be inspiring, only one in ten answers yes.

People generally don't see themselves as personally uplifting, and they certainly receive very little encouragement or training to be that way at work. What might have come naturally in youth has been dampened by the time they reach management ranks. But perhaps people underestimate themselves in this area: we've found that people's common perception of themselves as uninspiring is in sharp contrast to their performance when talking about their personal-best leadership cases or about their ideal futures. When relating hopes, dreams, and successes, people are almost always emotionally expressive. Expressiveness comes naturally when talking about deep desires for the future. People lean forward in their chairs, they move their arms about, their eyes light up, their voices sing with emotion, and they smile. They are enthusiastic, articulate, optimistic, and uplifting. In short, people *are* inspiring!

This contradiction is most intriguing. Why is it that people seem to see no connection between the animated, enthusiastic behavior they use in describing their dreams and their ability to lift others' spirits? We believe that most people have attributed something mystical to the process of inspiring a shared vision. They seem to see it as supernatural, as a grace or charm that comes from the gods. This assumption is far more inhibiting than any lack of natural talent for being inspirational. It's not necessary to be a famous, charismatic person to inspire a shared vision. What *is* necessary is believing and developing the skills to transmit that belief. This deeply felt belief, along with commitment and enthusiasm for it, is what mobilizes movements and energizes enterprises. It's this belief, genuinely displayed, that brings the vision to life for everyone.

In learning how to reach people, to move their souls and uplift their spirits—and our own—we look to a master of that art: the Reverend Dr. Martin Luther King Jr. On August 28, 1963, on the steps of the Lincoln Memorial in Washington, D.C., before a throng of 250,000, Martin Luther King Jr. proclaimed his dream to the world. As he spoke, and as thousands clapped and shouted, a nation was moved. That speech is among the most instructive of inspiring public presentations because of King's skill in moving his listeners. It also illustrates how the ability to exert an enlivening influence is rooted in fundamental values, cultural traditions, and personal conviction.

We play an audiotape of King's address in our leadership development programs. As participants listen, we ask them to imagine that they're communication researchers studying how leaders enlist constituents. We ask them to listen to the content as well as to the delivery and to notice the use of various rhetorical techniques. We ask them to place themselves on the steps of the Lincoln Memorial and attempt to get a feel for how the audience reacted as they listen to these words from King's "I Have a Dream" speech:

I say to you today, my friends, that in spite of the difficulties and frustrations of the moment I still have a dream. It is a dream deeply rooted in the American dream.

I have a dream that one day this nation will rise up and live out the true meaning of its creed: "We hold these truths to be self-evident; that all men are created equal."

I have a dream that one day on the red hills of Georgia the sons of former slaves and the sons of former slave owners will be able to sit down together at the table of brotherhood.

I have a dream that one day even the state of Mississippi, a desert state sweltering with the heat of injustice and oppression, will be transformed into an oasis of freedom and justice.

I have a dream that my four little children will one day live in a nation where they will not be judged by the color of their skin but by the content of their character.

I have a dream today.

I have a dream that one day the state of Alabama, whose governor's lips are presently dripping with the words of interposition and nullification, will be transformed into a situation where little black boys and black girls will be able to join hands with little white boys and white girls and walk together as sisters and brothers.

I have a dream today.

I have a dream that one day every valley shall be exalted, every hill and mountain shall be made low, the rough places will be made plains, and the crooked places will be made straight, and the glory of the Lord shall be revealed, and all flesh shall see it together.

This is our hope. This is the faith with which I return to the South. With this faith we will be able to transform the jangling discords of our nation into a beautiful symphony of brotherhood. With this faith we will be able to work together, to pray together, to struggle together, to go to jail together, to stand up for freedom together, knowing that we will be free one day.

This will be the day when all of God's children will be able to sing with new meaning, "My country 'tis of thee, sweet land of liberty, of thee I sing. Land where my fathers died, land of the pilgrim's pride, from every mountainside, let freedom ring."

And if America is to be a great nation this must become true. So let freedom ring from the prodigious hilltops of New Hampshire. Let freedom ring from the mighty mountains of New York. Let freedom ring from the heightening Alleghenies of Pennsylvania!

Let freedom ring from the snowcapped Rockies of Colorado!

Let freedom ring from the curvaceous peaks of California!

But not only that; let freedom ring from the Stone Mountain of Georgia!

Let freedom ring from every hill and molehill of Mississippi. From every mountainside, let freedom ring.

When we let freedom ring, when we let it ring from every village and every hamlet, from every state and every city, we will be able to speed up that day when all of God's children, black men and white men, Jews and Gentiles, Protestants and Catholics, will be able to join hands and sing in the words of that old Negro spiritual, "Free at last! Free at last! Thank God almighty, we are free at last!"[1]

What were the "techniques" you identified? Here are some of the observations that participants have made in commenting on King's speech:

"It was vivid. He used a lot of images and word pictures. You could *see* the examples."

"People could relate to the examples. They were familiar to them—for example, the spirituals, the songs, the traditions."

"His references were credible. It's hard to argue against the Constitution and the Bible."

"He talked about traditional values of family, church, country."

"He mentioned children—something we can all relate to."

"He appealed to common bonds."

"He knew his audience."

"He made geographical references to places the people in the audience could relate to."

"He included everybody: different parts of the country, all ages, both sexes, major religions."

"He used a lot of repetition: for example, 'I have a dream,' 'Let freedom ring.'"

"He said the same thing in different ways."

"He began with a statement of the difficulties and then stated his dream."

"He was positive and hopeful."

"He talked about hope for the future, but he also said people might have to suffer in order to get there. He didn't promise it would be easy."

"There was a cadence and a rhythm to his voice."

"He shifted from 'I' to 'we' halfway through."

"He spoke with emotion and passion. It was deeply felt."

"He was personally convinced of the dream."

After going through this process of hearing and then commenting on King's speech, participants in our leadership development programs recognize the ease with which they're able to identify what makes the speech so uplifting. They see that it's easy to decipher the code and that there's no mystery to its power. We then take the next step: going down the list of observations, we ask, "Can *you* do this in presentations to your own group?" We discuss with participants whether they feel they could get to know their audience, use examples that people can relate to and personal illustrations, and speak about traditional (company, industry, history, country) values. We ask them if they could find ways to appeal to common bonds, use images, word pictures, and repetition, and be positive and hopeful, and if they could make the shift from "I" to "we," speak with some emotion and energy, and have personal conviction about the dream. As we work our way through the list, participants say yes to nearly every question. When the "magic" of inspiration is revealed, most say that they could do more than they now do to awaken passion in others.

Fortunately, oratory skills as fine as King's are by no means necessary to enlist others. What matters isn't the eloquence of the speech but the appeal of the message to the audience. For that appeal to exist, leaders have to understand others' dreams, and they have to find common ground on which to build a shared dream. Whether they're trying to mobilize a crowd in the grandstand or one person in the office, leaders must practice these three *essentials* to Enlist Others:

- Listen deeply to others
- Discover and appeal to a common purpose
- Give life to a vision by communicating expressively, so that people can see themselves in it

LISTEN DEEPLY TO OTHERS

The first task in enlisting others is to identify our constituents and find out what their common aspirations are. No matter how grand the dream of an individual visionary, if others don't see in it the possibility of realizing their own hopes and desires, they won't follow. Leaders must show others how they, too, will be served by the long-term vision of the future, how their specific needs can be satisfied.

One talent leaders need to strengthen is the ability to sense the purpose in others. By knowing their constituents, by listening to them, and by taking their advice, leaders are able to give voice to constituents' feelings. They're able to stand before others and say with assurance, "Here's what I heard you say that you want for yourselves. Here's how your own needs and interests will be served by enlisting in a common cause." In a sense, leaders hold up a mirror and reflect back to their constituents what they say they most desire. When the constituents see that reflection, they recognize it and are immediately attracted to it.

Irwin Federman was the chief financial officer at Monolithic Memories when the board of directors decided to replace the CEO and urged Irwin to take on this position. The company was bleeding money badly, it wasn't clear how it was going to be able to survive in this very competitive industry, and they had neither the time nor the resources to search for a new CEO. Irwin's not an engineer, not even a very technical sort of person, he says, and he questioned the wisdom of putting someone like him at the top of this technology-dominated company (and industry). Still, within several months, with Irwin at the helm, the company turned itself around, going from negative to positive cash flows. The lesson, according to Irwin: "Good leaders listen, take advice, lose arguments, and follow." Irwin listened very carefully to what people were saying. Since he didn't have an engineering background, he had to take the advice of others (and, in the process, make them and not just him, responsible). He had to ask good (and tough) questions and be willing to lose arguments. In the end, says Irwin, "I couldn't ask them to follow me, if I wasn't willing to follow them in return."

Understanding leadership as a reciprocal relationship puts listening in its proper perspective. Leaders know that they can't do it alone. Leaders know that they don't have to have all the ideas or know all of the answers. One of the key characteristics of the leaders of companies who have been honored with America's highest award for quality is that they have impressive listening skills. As one senior executive explained, winning the Malcolm Baldrige Award required "10,000 leaders, and I needed to listen to every one of them."[2]

Leaders know very well that the seeds of any vision arise not from crystal-ball-gazing in upper levels of the organization's stratosphere but from images passed on from volunteers or frontline personnel about what the clients or customers really want or from manufacturing's mumblings about poor product quality. The best leaders, like Irwin Federman, are the best followers. They pay attention to weak signals and quickly respond to changes in the marketplace, whether overseas or just around the corner.[3]

Leaders find the common thread that weaves the fabric of human needs into a colorful tapestry. They develop a deep understanding of collective yearnings; they seek out the brewing consensus among those they would lead. They listen carefully for quiet whisperings and attend to subtle cues. They get a sense of what people want, what they value, what they dream about. Sensitivity to others is no trivial skill; rather, it is a truly precious human ability. But it isn't *complex:* it requires only receptiveness to other people and a willingness to listen. It means getting out of the office and spending time with people out in the field or on the factory floor or in the showroom or warehouse or back room. It means being delicately aware of the attitudes and feelings of others and the nuances of their communication.

To truly hear what constituents want—what they desperately hope to make you understand, appreciate, and include within the vision—requires periodically suspending regular activities and spending time listening to others. This means having coffee, breakfast, lunch, afternoon breaks—some unstructured time—with constituent groups (employees, associates, peers, advisers, shareholders, customers, and so on) and finding out what's going on with them and what they are hoping to achieve from their relationship with you (your product, your company, yourself). Some leaders put their desks right out on the office or factory floor to be close to the action and to the conversation. "I always refused to move into the executive office building," Bill Flanagan, Technology Group president for Amdahl, says, "because then I wouldn't be able to hear what was going on firsthand. I always ate in the same cafeteria, washed my hands in the same rest rooms, used the same entrances, often copied my own materials, just so that I would be available if anyone had something they wanted to share. This gave me lots of opportunities to share ideas with others, my constituents, to make certain we were all on the same page."

Doug Podzilni, president of Gourmet Source Food Brokers, makes a point of finding off-line time with people, often spontaneously, as in the example he describes here:

As a business manager traveling on the road with salespeople, I've found it's easy to fall into the trap of trying to fit more meetings into the day than the time allows. Recently, I surprised one salesperson by saying, "Let's stop and do something fun." We decided to go to a local ice cream parlor for a midafternoon snack. In that relaxed atmosphere, we talked about all sorts of things. As it turns out, this particular salesman had some serious personal issues on his mind. He took this opportunity to ask a few sensitive questions about his compensation, his future with the company, and the future of our division. He had been thinking about all of these questions for some time but had either not found the opportunity or had not felt comfortable in asking. I'm sure they were affecting his productivity and morale.

By taking the time to listen, Doug was able to find out information that this salesperson would never have revealed through formal communication channels. "Over chocolate sundaes," says Doug with a smile, "we addressed his concerns and strengthened the alignment between what he and the company were trying to achieve."

DISCOVER AND APPEAL TO A COMMON PURPOSE

Do you ask people why they stay? More likely, you worry about turnover and retention rates and why people leave the organization. But think about the vast majority of those who stay. Why do they? Why do you? The most important reason people give is that they like the work they are doing, that they find it challenging, meaningful, and purposeful.[4] Indeed, when we listen with sensitivity to the aspirations of others we discover that there are common values that link everyone together:[5]

- A chance to be tested, to make it on one's own
- A chance to take part in a social experiment
- A chance to do something well
- A chance to do something good
- A chance to change the way things are

Aren't these the essence of what most leadership challenges, as well as opportunities, are all about?

What people want has not changed very dramatically through the years. Even though job security is increasingly tenuous, regardless of industry or location, workers rank "interesting work" well above "high income." And quality of leadership ("working for a leader with vision and values") is more motivating than dollars. The most frequently mentioned measure of success in worklife? Would it surprise you to learn that "personal satisfaction for doing a good job" is cited between three and four times as often as "getting ahead" or "making a good living"?[6]

These findings suggest that there's more to work than is commonly assumed. There's rich opportunity for leaders to appeal to more than just the material rewards. Great leaders, like great companies and countries, create meaning and not just money. The values and interests of freedom, self-actualization, learning, community, excellence, uniqueness, service, and social responsibility truly attract people to a common cause.

There is a deep human yearning to make a difference. We want to know that we've done something on this earth, that there's a purpose to our existence. Work can provide that purpose, and increasingly work is where men and women seek it. Work has become a place where people pursue meaning and identity.[7] The best organizational leaders are able to bring out and make use of this human longing by communicating the meaning and significance of the organization's work so that people understand their own important role in creating it. When leaders clearly communicate a shared vision of an organization, they ennoble those who work on its behalf. They elevate the human spirit.

Leaders speak to people's hearts and listen to their heartbeats because, in the final analysis, common caring is the way in which shared visions get enacted. That's how David Clancy explained what Westpac's Commercial Banking organization in Australia was trying to accomplish by focusing on the question, "What does it mean to work here?" As head of that organization's Learning Resource Centre—which used to be called the Corporate Training Department—David had a vision: he and his colleagues had the job of making it possible for individuals to take responsibility for their own learning requirements and, in so doing, to discover what it is that they really care about—individually, as a team, and as an organization. John Evans, a partner in Cultural Imprint and an outside consultant with Westpac, studied a vast array of corporate "statements of vision" and found that they generally failed to compel people to action or personal responsibility. He contends that if people are to become committed to their organizations they need a cause to work for and a clear picture of what it means to work at their organization. Our research on what people expect from their leaders echoes this perspective: leaders uplift people's spirits.

Visions are not strategic plans. Contemporary management scholars all agree that *strategic planning* is not *strategic thinking*.[8] Strategic planning often spoils strategic thinking because it causes managers to believe that the manipulation of numbers creates imaginative insight into the future and vision. This confusion lies at the heart of the issue: the most successful strategies are visions; they are not plans. McGill University professor Harry Mintzberg explains that planning represents a "calculating" style, while leaders employ a "committing" style—one that "engage[s] people in a journey. They lead in such a way that everyone on the journey helps shape its course. As a result, enthusiasm inevitably builds along the way. Those with a calculating style fix on a destination and calculate what the group must do to get there, with no concern for the members' preferences. But calculated strategies have no value in and of themselves. . . . Strategies take on value only as committed people infuse them with energy."[9]

Leadership that focuses on a committing style is what leadership scholars have called *transformational leadership*. Transformational leadership occurs when, in their interactions, people "raise one another to higher levels of motivation and morality. Their purposes, which might have started out as separate but related, as in the case of transactional leadership, become fused. . . . But transforming leadership ultimately becomes moral in that it raises the level of human conduct and ethical aspiration of both the leader and the led, and thus it has a transforming effect on both."[10]

The most admired leaders speak unhesitatingly and proudly of mutual ethical aspirations. They know that people aspire to live up to the highest moral standards. So the first essential for enlisting others is to find and focus on the very best that the culture—group, unit, project, program, agency, community, organization, government, or nation—shares in common and what that means to its members. This communion of purpose, this commemoration of our dreams, helps to bind us together. It reminds us of what it means to be a part of this collective effort. It joins us together in the human family.

This sense of belonging is particularly key in tumultuous times, whatever the cause of the tumult. In the 1990s, the telecommunications industry took a quantum technological leap forward. As a consequence, competition became more fierce, downsizings more common, and customer needs changed dramatically. It was far from business as usual: people's talents had to drastically expand to meet the new demands. This was the situation facing AT&T branch manager Jack Schiefer and his leadership team as they set forth to grow their business throughout the Rocky Mountain states.

As Jack tells it, "We knew we had a problem as a team because we *weren't* a team. But none of us knew what to do to become one. We were too close to it." They began their quest to become a world-class sales organization with a leadership team offsite workshop based on *The Leadership Challenge.* A decade later, Jack still acknowledges and confirms that the team was acquiescent, but not totally committed. Then, as the discussion moved to the idea of a shared vision, "you could feel the energy change in the room from a very casual attitude to—all of a sudden—becoming electric." The difference came when the members of the group "became committed to a journey to find out what to do to become more effective as leaders and help our associates grow."

At first, "the horizon that we were looking at was maybe a month to three months." In looking up into space, they quickly saw that they needed a vision that would work, no matter what change was occurring, something that would stand the test of time. To get there, they shared with each other the heartfelt desires they each had for their Sales Center and for the kind of leaders they wanted to become. From that initial groundbreaking, the vision of a world-class sales organization, grounded in quality and reflecting a renewed commitment to their customers, their families, and each other, was born.

Theirs was much more than a one-time exercise to craft a slick-sounding statement; it was the creation of a new culture of success built on superior results and "value-based leadership." Has their vision work been helpful? In an industry where pricing has dropped through the floor, annual associate turnover has averaged 30 percent, and massive, gut-wrenching business-unit-wide reorganizations have occurred almost every year, Jack's team has continued to put up astonishing results. Jack feels so strongly about the sales center's vision and their continuing attention to it that he says, "you have nothing to lose and everything to gain by accepting the possibility that a shared vision and a commitment to it will allow your professional life and your personal life to be richer than they are today." With the zealousness of a converted skeptic (and a businessman interested in delivering results as cost-effectively as possible), he says, "inspiring a shared vision is the most efficient way to produce outstanding results."

GIVE LIFE TO A VISION

Clearly, shared vision is key—and to enlist others, leaders need to bring that vision to life. Leaders animate the vision and make manifest the purpose so that others can see it, hear it, taste it, touch it, feel it. In making the intangible vision tangible, leaders ignite constituents' flames of passion. By using powerful language, positive communication style, and nonverbal expressiveness, leaders breathe life (the literal definition of the word *inspire*) into a vision.

Use Powerful Language

Leaders make full use of the power of language to communicate a shared identity and give life to visions. Successful leaders use metaphors and other figures of speech; they give examples, tell stories, and relate anecdotes; they draw word pictures; and they offer quotations and recite slogans.

Review again the words of Martin Luther King Jr. Notice his use of visual and aural images: "the red hills of Georgia," "the prodigious hilltops of New Hampshire," "the heightening Alleghenies of Pennsylvania," "the jangling discords of our nation," and "a beautiful symphony of brotherhood." Read the specific examples: "where little black boys and black girls will be able to join hands with little white boys and white girls and walk together as sisters and brothers" and "a dream that my four little children will one day live in a nation where they will not be judged by the color of their skin but by the content of their character."[11] Notice the references to the Constitution and the quotations from anthems and spirituals. All these skillful uses of language give the listener a visceral feel for King's dream. They enable us to picture the future, to hear it, to sense it, to recognize it.

All of us can enrich language with stories, references, and figures of speech; in fact, doing so is a natural way of communicating. You need only think of how children tell each other stories, how they love to have stories told to them. Or consider the days before television, when people loved to imagine scenes described by a radio announcer. Even today's most popular video games take the players through stories or adventures.

Metaphors are plentiful in our daily conversations. We talk of computers as having memory, of time as money and knowledge as power. We talk about business as a game. Military metaphors are used in corporate strategy and sports vernacular in meetings. Metaphors and analogies are as common as numbers in organizations. Leaders make conscious use of metaphorical expressions to give vividness and tangibility to abstract ideas.

In this book, and in all our discussions of leadership, we use the journey metaphor to express our understanding of leadership. We talk about leaders as pioneers and trailblazers who take people on expeditions to places they've never been. We talk about vision as the beckoning summit. We talk about climbing to the top and about milestones and signposts. All of these metaphorical expressions are our way of communicating the active, pioneering nature of leadership.

As we described in Chapter Three, language is a powerful tool. Remember the contrast between the bank officer rallying his managers to take on the hostile competition and Anita Roddick joyfully liberating her people to make a difference at The Body Shop. Ken Wilcox, president and CEO for Silicon Valley Bank, which provides start-up funding to thousands of new ventures, explained how he learned about the power of language. An early vision statement for the bank was "50 in 5" and was meant to capture the drive to move the share price to $50 million within five years. "While it was a compelling rallying cry for our employees," he told us, "its problem was that it had very little relevance for our clients." For that reason, former president and CEO John Dean introduced a new vision statement, "Bringing our clients' vision to life by providing exceptional business solutions." As Ken puts it, "This brings us close to our customers, and makes our purpose and theirs one and the same." Leaders learn to master the richness of figurative speech so that they can paint the word pictures that best portray the meaning of their visions.

The shift in statements of vision and purpose for Silicon Valley Bank is one dramatic example of the difference in perspective between mercenaries and missionaries, a difference that was evident in the dot-com implosion at the start of this century. Those organizations and leaders who were driven only by money and revenue (and greed) were left behind in the marketplace by those companies compelled by a sense of purpose and a view, literally, of changing the landscape.

Practice Positive Communication

We want leaders with enthusiasm, with a bounce in their step, with a positive attitude. We want to believe that we'll be part of an invigorating journey. We follow people with a can-do attitude, not those who give sixty-seven reasons why something can't be done or who don't make us feel good about ourselves or what we're doing.

The leaders people most admire are electric, vigorous, active, full of life. We're reminded of our colleague Randi DuBois, one of the founders of Pro-Action, who gets people to stretch themselves by engaging in challenging physical tasks. Typically, her clients are nervous, even a bit scared at first. But people of all ages, all sizes, and all physical abilities have successfully completed the Pro-Action outdoor challenge courses. How does Randi succeed in leading these people? Her secret is very simple: she's always positive that people can do the course, and she never says never. She conveys very clearly that people have the power within themselves to accomplish whatever they desire. (Both authors know this from personal experience. We've been forty feet above the ground leaping off a small platform for an iron ring while Randi cheered us on.)

Less dramatic, and every bit as effective, is the positive attitude and communication style that Joan Carter exhibited when she took over as general manager and executive chef of the Faculty Club at Santa Clara University. Before Joan's arrival, both membership and sales had been seriously declining for several years, remaining customers were unhappy, the restaurant's balance sheet was "scary," and the staff was divided into factions.

Joan took all this in, and what she saw was a dusty diamond. "I saw a beautiful and historic building full of mission-era flavor and character that should be, could be, would be *the* place on campus." In her mind's eye, she saw the club bustling. She saw professors and university staff chatting on the lovely enclosed patio and enjoying high-quality, appealing yet inexpensive meals. She smiled as she envisioned the club assisting alumni in planning wonderful, personal, and professionally catered wedding receptions and anniversary celebrations. Joan could see a happy staff whose primary concern was customer satisfaction, a kitchen that produced a product far superior to "banquet food," and a catering staff that did whatever it took to make an event exceptional. She wasn't quite sure how the club had deteriorated to the extent it had, but that really didn't matter. She decided to ignore the quick fix and set out to teach everyone how unique and wonderful the club could be.

Over the next two years, as she talked with customers and worked with her staff, she instilled a vision of the club as a restaurant that celebrated good food and good company. As food and service quality began to improve, smiles became more prevalent among customers and staff and sales began to rise: 20 percent the first year and 30 percent again the next. When a top financial manager of the university asked how she had managed to turn the finances around so quickly and dramatically, Joan responded, "You can't turn around numbers. The balance sheet is just a reflection of what's happening here, every day, in the restaurant. I just helped the staff realize what we're really all about. It was always here," she said, "only perhaps a little dusty, a little ignored, and a little unloved. I just helped them see it."

Tap into Nonverbal Expressiveness

In explaining why particular leaders have a magnetic effect, people often describe them as charismatic. But *charisma* has become such an overused and misused term that it's almost useless as a descriptor of leaders. "In the popular media," notes leadership scholar Bernard Bass, "charisma has come to mean anything ranging from chutzpah to Pied Piperism, from celebrity to superman status. It has become an overworked cliché for strong, attractive, and inspiring personality."[12]

Social scientists have attempted to investigate this elusive quality in terms of observable behavior.[13] What they've found is that people who are perceived to be charismatic are simply more animated than others. They smile more, speak faster, pronounce words more clearly, and move their heads and bodies more often. They are also more likely to reach out and touch or make some physical contact with others during greetings. What we call *charisma,* then, can better be understood as nonverbal (and very human) expressiveness.

Similar reactions to nonverbal behavior are seen in the gestural language of children. The way children relate to each other nonverbally can be divided into five categories of interpersonal behavior: Attractive actions, threatening actions, aggressive actions, gestures of fear and retreat, and actions that produce isolation.[14] Children who become the leaders in their groups use attractive actions, not aggressive actions. At least in the world of the very young, real leaders—those who are naturally followed—aren't the young Rambos. The natural leaders are those who offer toys to others, lightly touch or caress, clap hands, smile, extend a hand, lean in to listen; they don't scratch, hit, or pull. Adults can learn much about leading from children: it's not aggression that attracts; it's warmth and friendship.

COMMITMENT NUMBER 4:
ENLIST OTHERS IN A COMMON VISION
BY APPEALING TO SHARED ASPIRATIONS

Leaders breathe life into visions. They communicate their hopes and dreams so that others clearly understand and accept them as their own. Leaders know what motivates their constituents. They show others how their values and interests will be served by a particular long-term vision of the future. Above all, they're convinced of the value of that vision themselves and share that genuine belief with others.

Leaders use a variety of modes of expression to make their abstract visions concrete. Through skillful use of metaphors, symbols, positive language, and personal energy, they generate enthusiasm and excitement for the common vision. In this commitment, we provide some action steps that you can take to increase your ability to enlist the support of others. Then, in the next chapters, we explore how you can successfully Challenge the Process en route to the extraordinary.

• *Get to know your constituents.*

Identify your constituents. Make a list of all the individuals or groups of individuals you want to enlist in your vision of the future. Your organizational managers and any direct reports are obviously on the list. In all probability, you'll also want your peers, customers, and suppliers to buy into your dream. Perhaps you'll want the support of the citizens of your local community. There are bound to be elements of your vision that will be of interest to the state and the nation in which you do business. You may even have a global vision. And don't limit your list to present constituents only. As your organization grows and develops, it will want to attract new people to it. You'll want future generations to take an active interest in what you want to accomplish, so consider their needs and values. Today's students are tomorrow's employees, customers, and investors. They may be the ones who actually help you to realize what you only dream of today. The point is this: identify those who have a stake today and will have a stake tomorrow in the outcomes of what you envision.

Then, once you've identified your constituents, conduct what the marketing folks call "focus groups" with your key constituencies. On a regular basis, ask your constituents to tell you about what they like and don't like about your product, services, programs, policies, leadership practices, and so on. The important points are that you value their opinions, and that you listen carefully to their opinions. What's more, in focus group or forum settings you benefit from the way people bounce ideas off one another. You also get a chance to test whether one person's or group's needs are idiosyncratic or commonly held. Everyone learns in this process about what it takes to work together to achieve common objectives.

At the Ritz-Carlton, the only hotel company to receive the coveted Malcolm Baldrige National Quality Award, they take this process one step further. Every morning at 9:00, about eighty of the company's top executives gather for The Daily Lineup, a ten-minute meeting in the hallway outside the president's office. Just as important, within twenty-four hours, at every hotel from Boston to Bali, the rest of the company's employees get the same concentrated dose of the Ritz credo at their daily shift meetings. The lineup is run by a volunteer facilitator, and the meeting is split into three parts. First, they introduce the topic of the week. Second, they revisit one of their "customer service basics." Finally, they run through operational issues that are specific to each department: anything from the specials on the menu to an upcoming meeting with an investor. Ten minutes after the meeting begins, everyone is back at work. Leonardo Inghilleri, senior vice president of human resources, explained that the lineup "establishes an emotional tie with rest of the company. For one critical moment every day, the entire organization is aligned behind the same issue."[15]

Your forum need not be as formal as that of the Ritz. You might simply devise a regular scheme of having a morning or afternoon break with a random group of people in your organization to talk about whatever they want to talk about. Barry Posner, does exactly that as dean at Santa Clara University's Leavey School of Business. One year Barry simply randomly divided the entire faculty into equal-size groups and took those people out to lunch (and conversation) during the month. The next year, he organized the groups by department or function; another year, by representative groups (relatively new and senior, tenured and untenured, assistant, associate, or full professors). As Posner says, "While there are lots of things that I hope my lunch guests, and constituents, get out of these conversations, but I know that I always come away with new ideas and insights. They remind me how easy it is to get out of touch with people, even in a relatively small organization."

• *Find the common ground.*

Finding common ground is ever more important with the increase in diversity, both in workforce and customers and with the influence of the Internet. Virtual isn't enough. To attract people from divergent backgrounds and interests, you must discover what aspirations, goals, needs, and dreams they have in common. People are bound to differ in much of what they value; you must work through the differences to find what can bring them together. Your ability to enlist people depends on how effective you are at detecting the tie that binds.

There are numerous ways you can find out what people want, from sophisticated market research techniques (including gathering customer information via the Internet) to simple surveys. Each has its usefulness. But no technique can substitute for face-to-face human interaction. The very best way to get to know what other people want is to sit down and talk with them on their turf. If you feel that you don't really understand people in the factory, move your desk onto the floor for the next few weeks. If you feel that you don't know much about the store owners who buy your packaged goods, ride the route trucks once a week for a year. Get out there and make contact. Ask one simple question: "What do you most want from this organization?"

Then, when you've gathered the data and have a true feel for your constituents, sit down and see what patterns and themes emerge. There are bound to be several. For example, Tom Melohn found out that customers of North American Tool and Die (NATD) wanted "quality, service, price"— in that order. At first, Tom was surprised by this. He had spent twenty-five years in the packaged goods industry, where a fraction of a cent made a major difference. So he kept on asking, and the customers kept on telling him: first quality, then service, then price. Not surprisingly, the focus of NATD today is first and foremost on quality.

One other hint about finding the common ground: avoid being too specific. Vision statements aren't job descriptions. They're not product or service specifications. To have the broadest appeal, visions must be encompassing. They should transcend the day-to-day work (voluntary or paid) and find expression in higher-order human needs. Visions should uplift and ennoble.

- *Draft a collective vision statement.*

Leadership is not a monologue, nor should the creation of a vision statement be done individually and without the active involvement of others who must attend to these operations. The process of finding common ground, often through the creation of a statement of shared values and vision, is as important as the content itself, and sometimes even more so. Soliciting people's ideas and listening to their concerns is critical at the early stages. Look for feedback through such questions as, What interests of yours are not well represented? In what respect is it not fair? How would you improve upon it? If people resist giving you their ideas or giving you feedback on yours, try to involve them by offering a choice or list of alternatives. Once an alternative is selected, it becomes their idea. Remembering the Chinese proverb is useful in this regard: "Tell me, I may listen. Teach me, I may remember. Involve me, I will do it."

Once you've elicited everyone's ideas, circulate draft versions of the vision statement incorporating those ideas. Revise the draft, and as necessary ask for more input or criticism. Gradually you will build consensus because as people get involved, they begin to think of the draft as their own. And it will be!

Yet the process of developing a common vision can seem overwhelming even in small organizations. In larger ones, it requires serious ongoing effort. Imagine the effort involved in aligning over thirteen thousand employees—simultaneously. Victoria Sandvig, vice president of the Event and Production Services Department of Corporate Communications at Charles Schwab & Co., Inc., spoke with us about the process used to align people and the long-term direction of Schwab. By 1999, nearly half of Schwab's employees were new since the vision and values had last been spread, company-wide. The beginnings of *VisionQuest* stirred when a group called Root Learning, Inc., started creating some maps of vision and values, originally for the executive committee. As Victoria puts it, "One of these maps addressed questions of who the company is, its vision, and values. The second one was very much about where we want to go, who our competition is, who our clients are, the profile of our customers." After the executive committee, the maps were presented to the senior management team, where their power became obvious to the larger group. Then began the process of involving the company at large. "We first thought of cascading it down through the organization. But," Victoria continues, "the idea of rolling it out to everyone at once took hold. We knew there was an incredible opportunity: we could create an event around it, and build in some elements that would touch the heart and the soul of every employee."

And so, across the United States and across the world, Schwab employees gathered on a Saturday in March 1999. The six-hour event kicked off in San Francisco's Moscone Center at 8:30 A.M., with six thousand people there. Other locations had fewer people—and they were all hooked up via satellite. "Whatever the locale," Victoria says, "everyone was seated in groups of ten, with a trained facilitator at each table. People were assigned seats so that they were mixed up by tenure, by enterprise, and by titles: we tried to get as much cross-pollenization as possible. The impact was incredible. It kept people renewed in the vision, committed to it, and absolutely aligned with who we are as a company and where we're going."

And, big as it was, *VisionQuest* was no one-shot deal. Schwab reenacted the event days later for the five hundred people in the crew that had kept the company up and running during the Saturday event. And it continued with a series of mini-*VisionQuests* for new employees who came on board subsequently.

As the people at Schwab understood, renewing community and commitment to shared values and common purpose is essential if we are to keep from being blinded by rigid adherence to a set of principles and aspirations that no longer make sense. Finding common ground is a dynamic rather than a stable process, and leaders are constantly vigilant in understanding how the ground beneath them may be shifting.

• *Expand your communication skills.*

If your communication abilities have room for improvement (and whose don't?), take advantage of training opportunities. Every leader ought to know how to paraphrase, summarize, express feelings, disclose personal information, admit mistakes, respond nondefensively, ask for clarification, solicit different views, and so on.

It is absolute that the higher you advance in an organization, the more presentations you will give to an ever-widening audience. A course in presentation skills will benefit you greatly. Don't wait until your next promotion to improve your communication skills. If you haven't taken a public speaking course yet, sign up for the next available class. Presentation workshops can help you learn effective techniques for getting your ideas across. They can also help you gain confidence in yourself. If giving a speech makes you nervous, you're neither unusual nor alone. According to research done by a nationwide communication training and consulting firm, many people are more afraid of having to give a speech than they are of dying.[16] Overcome the anxiety of public speaking and an enormous weight may be lifted from your shoulders.

Speak positively. When talking about mutual aspirations, don't say *try*, say *will* and *are*. There's no room for tentativeness or qualifiers in statements of vision. Sure, there are lots of contingencies and reasons why something might not happen. But citing eighty-three potential obstacles and thirty-three conditions that must be met will only discourage people from joining the cause. You need not be a Pollyanna: talk realistically about the hardships and difficult conditions—just don't dwell on them.

Reasonable people know that great achievements require hard work. Let people know that you have the utmost confidence in their ability to succeed. Tell them that you're certain that they'll prevail. Tell them that you have faith in them.

Furthermore, enthusiasm and emotions are catching, so let yours show. Smile. Use gestures and move your body. Speak clearly and quickly. Make eye contact. All of these signals are cues to others that you're personally excited about what you're saying. If you don't perceive yourself as an expressive person, begin to practice expressiveness by talking to a favorite friend about what most excites you in life. As you do this, pay attention to your verbal and nonverbal behavior. If possible, turn on a video camera so that you can watch yourself later. We bet that you'll discover that when you talk about things that excite you, you do a lot of the things we've just described.

- *Breathe life into your vision.*

Remember that vision statement you wrote at the end of the previous chapter? Critique it and look for places where you can breathe life into it (add inspiration) to make it come alive for your audience. Prepare yourself now to make the vision sing.

Because visions exist in the future, leaders have to get others in the present to imagine what that future will look like, feel like, sound like, even smell like. In short, just as attributes such as quality, service, and responsiveness don't exist in nature but must be defined in concrete terms, your vision—an intangible—must be made tangible. Use as many forms of expression as you can to transform the vision's intangibles into tangibles. Make any abstractions—such as freedom, service, respect, quality, or innovation—concrete so that others can recognize what you imagine. When it comes to visions, we're all from Missouri: we need to be shown. So enrich your language with stories, metaphors, analogies, and examples; use slogans, theme songs, poetry, quotations, and humor. Think of ways to incorporate symbols, banners, posters, and other visual aids in your presentations. Remember that symbols, not acronyms, capture the imagination. The eagle is a symbol of strength, the olive branch a symbol of peace, and the lion a symbol of courage. The Statue of Liberty is a symbol of America as the land of freedom of opportunity. Wells Fargo Bank uses the stagecoach to symbolize its pioneering spirit. Mary Kay Cosmetics uses the bumblebee as a symbol for doing what others say can't be done.

Think you can't give an inspiring speech? Remember that most famous speeches were not extemporaneous. They had been tested before, on other events and in other conversations. For example, Martin Luther King Jr. tried out versions of his famous "I Have a Dream" speech on several occasions, refining it before its seemingly spontaneous presentation before the crowd at the Lincoln Memorial. Be prepared to take your first draft (or latest draft, whatever its number) and continue to revise, hone, edit, and revise again until you think it expresses your ideas just right.

If you need some help in adding tangibility to your presentations, spend a little time studying advertising and the performing arts. Those in theater and advertising have to get their audiences to experience something vicariously. Both fields are rich sources of creative ideas on how to convey abstract concepts and how to appeal to human emotions.

• *Speak from the heart.*

None of these suggestions will be of any value whatsoever if you don't believe in what you're saying. If the vision is someone else's, and you don't own it, it will be very difficult for you to enlist others in it. If you have trouble imagining yourself actually living the future described in the vision, you'll certainly not be able to convince others that they ought to enlist in making it a reality. If you're not excited about the possibilities, how can you expect others to be? The prerequisite to enlisting others in a shared vision is genuineness. The first place to look before making that speech is in your heart.

When asked how she was able to lead the development team for the PCnet family of Advanced Micro Devices, breaking all barriers and launching this extremely successful family of products, Laila Razouk replied simply, "I believed. Believing is a very important part of the action. You have to have faith. If you don't have that, then you're lost even before you get started." It's easy to understand why people are eager to follow Laila: "If I believe in something badly enough, and if I have the conviction, then I start picturing and envisioning how it will look if we did this or if we did that. By sharing these thoughts with other people, the excitement grows and people become part of that picture. Without much effort—with energy, but not much effort—the *magic* starts to happen. People start to bounce ideas back and forth, they get involved, brainstorm, and share ideas. Then I know I don't have to worry about it."

How successful would the project have been if instead Laila had thought, "This project will never work. The person who thought this up doesn't understand the details. I'm doing this because I'm forced to, but I really think this project is a stupid idea!" For Laila, the net effect of speaking from the heart, as she explains, is that "by openly sharing what I saw, what I knew, and what I believed—not by dictating it, but by being willing to iterate and adjust things—I got other people involved."

- *Listen first—and often.*

Listening is one of the key characteristics of exemplary leaders. To truly hear what your constituents want—what they desperately hope to make you understand, appreciate, and include within the vision—requires that you periodically suspend your regular activity and spend time listening to others. Note the ratio between the number of your ears and your mouth, and make certain that you listen twice as often as you talk.

In listening we not only hear, but we are forced to pay attention. Leaders listen for more than just information; they listen to communicate how seriously they consider the feelings and thoughts of others. The *Journal of the American Medical Association* reported on a five-year investigation of why some doctors were sued, and others not, by parents who had all experienced the same tragedy (the death of their child during childbirth). The researchers report, "Physicians who had been sued frequently were perceived by their patients as unavailable, rushed, unconcerned, and poor communicators, while physicians with no malpractice claims were perceived as most available, interested, thorough, and willing to provide information and answer questions fully."[17] Clearly, listening deeply makes a difference.

And being a good listener has the side benefit of making you more flexible and capable of functioning in a wide range of cultures and environments. If you get feedback that you're too one-dimensional in your approach to situations, consider becoming a better listener. For example, if you're planning a trip to another country, be sure to study the culture. Read about that culture, its history, politics, and religion. Listen to the music and sounds of that people, group, or community. Watch films. Visit art galleries. Sample the food. Your international colleagues will feel more comfortable around you (and you around them). The same principles apply closer to home when you step outside your cultural experience. One way to become a more skillful listener is by seeking the assistance of an "interpreter," someone who can answer your questions and who can show you around and help you learn outside your realm of experience. In this interchange, both parties often learn more about each other's culture and gain insight into the subtleties and unexamined aspects of their own.

- *Hang out.*

Gretchen Kaffer, a human resource administrator with Honeywell-Measurex, had gotten so busy that she stopped spending time in the cafeteria and the patio chatting with her coworkers during lunch and started eating at her desk, instead. A reorganization brought her group into a refurbished building with a spacious new break room where, as Gretchen noticed, people began to hang out for lunch. So she decided to make lunch a regularly scheduled part of her day again and join her colleagues.

"The first couple of times I popped in," she reports, "everyone looked up at me as if I was coming to ask someone a work-related question. They were surprised that I was joining them for lunch. I think some people may have thought that I didn't want to spend time with them, or even didn't like them, since I had started eating lunch at my desk." It didn't take long before Gretchen learned all sorts of things about her colleagues, and the organization, things she'd been missing out on.

"It also opened up some good conversations about work and non-work-related issues and events," says Gretchen. "It has really allowed us to hash over some changes and procedures that we wouldn't normally get to discuss in such a large group, because we rarely have time to discuss even the big stuff in groups of more than two or three. I think this has allowed my coworkers access to what I am doing. It gives them the opportunity to ask me questions, make suggestions, and fill me in on the not-so-important, but interesting and possibly telling, employee relations and interactions that I have been missing while cooped up in my office."

There's another side benefit to the "lunch club thing," as they call it. Employees "from other departments seem pleasantly surprised by the laughter coming out of our break room. They walk by, or purposely seek us out. Sometimes they stop and ask if we're having a party. We often invite them to join us . . . I think this has definitely improved our image as a team, given us greater visibility and allowed us more contact with other employees in our building." And since the gang's gotten used to Gretchen's hanging out with them, they now expect to see her. "Around 12 or 12:15 there's usually a face in my doorway asking if I'm 'doing the lunch club thing.' "

Another way to hang out, get your ear to the ground, and be in a position to listen to others is to change places for some period of time with one of your key constituents or stakeholders. Many companies invite their employees to step into the shoes of their managers for a day and learn about the demands and responsibilities of management. But isn't what is good for the goose also useful for the gander? Why not have your management team take over the jobs of their nonmanagerial associates? That's the way they worked at the Florence, Kentucky, distribution center of Levi Strauss & Co. The plant's general manager told us that he learned a great deal about how hard people work in getting pants out the door. "Spending time on the plant floor actually packing jeans and carting boxes around gives me a much greater appreciation for the talents required and pressures we place on people than anything I learn from reading reports generated by our human resources department. I also get to meet lots of people on an informal and first-name basis. Of course, they get to meet me on the same basis." Learn about what other people do in your organization by periodically working alongside them for a day (or more).

Whether it's joining the lunch club or walking the plant floor, being present, paying attention, and listening to the concerns and accomplishments of others allows leaders to gather critical information about what people care about and how well they understand what's going on in the organization. You've got to be there to know what's happening. And when you hang out and spend time listening, people know you're interested in them, and they *want* to see and talk with you.

COMMITMENT NUMBER 4

ENLIST OTHERS IN A COMMON VISION BY APPEALING TO SHARED ASPIRATIONS

- *Get to know your constituents.*

- *Find the common ground.*

- *Draft a collective vision statement.*

- *Expand your communication skills.*

- *Breathe life into your vision.*

- *Speak from the heart.*

- *Listen first—and often.*

- *Hang out.*

Source: The Leadership Challenge by James M. Kouzes and Barry Z. Posner. Copyright © 2002.

PART FOUR

Challenge the Process

7 SEARCH FOR OPPORTUNITIES

We all have to ask ourselves, "How do I go to work today and do something that will move the enterprise and myself another step in the right direction?"

Elaine Fortier, New Focus

Challenge the process to the point of failure.

Dick Nettell, Bank of America

Early in the process of conducting our research we were given a recruitment poster from Operation Raleigh USA. At the top was printed, in big, bold letters, **"Venturers Wanted!"** Below the headline was a photograph of a group of people neck deep in a swamp, and in the lead was a young woman with an ear-to-ear grin on her face. The copy read

JOIN THE VOYAGE OF DISCOVERY

For 1500 young Americans between the ages of 17 and 24, it will be the adventure of a lifetime. Underwater archaeology on sunken ships, aerial walkways in tropical rainforests, medical relief for remote tribal villages—innovative, exciting, worthwhile projects. . . .

The selected applicants will join fellow venturers from many nations for three-month periods. They will work alongside an expert expedition staff under rigorous conditions in over 40 countries worldwide.

Science and service are the themes and leadership development is a primary goal. It is the pioneer spirit of Sir Walter Raleigh's day rekindled, and you are invited to apply.

These words and the image vividly portray the *conditions* that cultivate leadership. Leadership experiences are, indeed, voyages of discovery and adventures of a lifetime. They're challenging explorations under rigorous conditions, and they require pioneering spirits. You can see that spirit in the smiles on their faces.

Dick Nettell, corporate services executive for the Bank of America, might well have been one of the Operation Raleigh recruits if he'd had the opportunity. Dick is certainly no stranger to innovation and rigorous conditions. Whether he just happens to be caught in the middle of it, or whether he creates it, Dick greets challenge as if it were his best friend. He doesn't let circumstance overwhelm him, and he's never been intimidated by higher authority.

Talk about starting at the bottom. Dick started below ground level, in the garage. Literally. As an automobile fleet administrator, he ran several garages, bought and sold cars, and made sure they were all running. And when it comes to serving the customer, doing the right thing for his employees, or saving the bank some money Dick looks around every day for opportunities to improve—and he's constantly learning. "If you keep your eyes open and periodically actually shut your mouth," says Dick, "and you have the courage to turn the mirror around on yourself, it's amazing what you can learn and how you can change things."

But leaders don't always have the luxury of being the ones to challenge the status quo. Dick is no exception. When the Bank of America was acquired by NationsBank, creating the new Bank of America, there was a major restructuring, to put it mildly. Two huge organizations merged, and two very different cultures collided. There were sizable layoffs and wholesale changes at the top. Dick was asked to stick around and to help pick up the responsibilities of his former manager. The loss of a good colleague was personally devastating to Dick, but he remembered what his former mentor Warren Boero had told him: "'Professionals act as they must, not as they feel.' And it really hit home," says Dick, adding that he told himself, "I've got to shake this off. It's okay to grieve, but if I can't get through this and support it, then I need to go somewhere else. I knew that I needed to put a bounce back in my step and get us focused on the future."

Early on in the process of this painful transition, Dick's manager at the time came out to San Francisco from bank headquarters in Charlotte, North Carolina, to address Dick's group and talk about the cuts and all the changes. It was a bit of a risk, but Dick asked her if he could say a few words to the assembled group of about two hundred employees. In his familiar straightforward style Dick said, "Let's cut to the chase. David Lynch built this organization. He was here for thirty-five years, and he did an outstanding job. We're at a crossroads right now. We can sit here and moan and feel sorry for ourselves because it's not the same old bank. Or we can do what he would want us to do, which is build on the legacy he left behind and really show people what this organization is made of—its pride, its personal responsibility in delivering excellence. That doesn't change." You could feel the spirits lift and the attitudes shift that day.

When mergers first occur, there are typically a lot of redundancies that can be eliminated. Early in the process it's often easy to pick some low-hanging fruit, cut costs, and improve the bottom line. But as time goes on, the job gets tougher, so you have to be more innovative. Here again, Dick seems to have a knack for creating an environment where people are able to come up with creative ways to build value.

For instance, every large organization pays some invoices more than once, and recovering the twice-paid money can really add up. When Dick was given responsibility for this function, its scope was pretty narrow, with a goal of $1 million in recoveries a year. The woman who managed this unit saw a big opportunity to expand the scope. Her proposal to Dick centered on moving into areas that historically they had no responsibility over and implementing an innovative incentive program. Dick's response was, "I'd rather ask forgiveness than permission; go for it!" As a result, they began doing vendor payment reviews, researching escheated funds, and looking at unclaimed property. Bottom line? They recovered more than $12 million the first year, and the next year they committed to Dick another $10 million.

For Dick the challenge continues, and he knows that every day will present him with some wonderful chance to try something new. As he says, "In today's environment, if you want to be successful, doing things the same way just won't get it done, period. Expectations continue to be raised, by our shareholders, by our managers, and by our customers. And if we're not willing to be innovative and do things differently, we are going to have the competition pass us like we're sitting still on the freeway."

What Dick Nettell has done all his career is what all exemplary leaders do. When we first analyzed the initial set of personal-best cases, we discovered that the situations people chose to discuss were about *major change* that had a significant impact on their organizations. This remains true today; regardless of function, field, economic sector, organizational level, or national boundary, the leaders in our study talk about times when they turned around losing operations, started up new plants, developed new products or services, installed untested procedures, renewed operations threatened with closing, or released the creative spirit trapped inside stifling bureaucratic systems. The personal-best leadership cases were about radical departures from the past, about doing things that had never been done before, about going to places not yet discovered. In many cases, the magnitude of results was in the *hundreds* of percent.

What's significant about the emphasis on innovation in our leadership cases is that we don't ask people to tell us about change; we ask them to tell us about *personal-best leadership experiences.* They can discuss any leadership experience they choose—past or present, unofficial or official; in any functional area; in any community, voluntary, religious, health care, educational, public sector, or private sector organization. Our respondents elected to talk about times of change, underscoring the fact that leadership demands changing the business-as-usual environment.

When people think about their personal bests they automatically think about some kind of challenge. Why? The fact is that when times are stable and secure, we're not severely tested. We may perform well, get promoted, even achieve fame and fortune. But certainty and routine breed complacency. In contrast, personal and business hardships have a way of making us come face to face with who we really are and what we're capable of becoming. Thus the study of leadership is the study of how men and women guide us through adversity, uncertainty, hardship, disruption, transformation, transition, recovery, new beginnings, and other significant challenges. It's also the study of how men and women, in times of constancy and complacency, actively seek to disturb the status quo and awaken to new possibilities. They *search for opportunities* to change, grow, innovate, and improve.

If you want to create a climate that sustains personal-best leadership experiences, what situations would you look for? What context would most likely offer the right conditions? What leadership actions are required to establish a culture that is characterized by challenge, energy, excitement, determination, inspiration, and innovation? It's already clear that you need shared values and a shared vision. What else? To Search for Opportunities to get extraordinary things done, leaders make use of four *essentials:*

- Seize the initiative
- Make challenge meaningful
- Innovate and create
- Look outward for fresh ideas

Leaders take charge of change. They instill a sense of adventure in others, they look for ways to radically alter the status quo, and they continuously scan the outside environment for new and fresh ideas. Leaders always search for opportunities for ways to do what has never been done.

SEIZE THE INITIATIVE

In our research, we asked people, "What five or six words would you use to best describe the character—the feel, the spirit, the nature, the quality—of your personal-best leadership experience?" The words most frequently used have been *challenging, rewarding,* and *exciting.* Words signifying conviction—*dedication, intensity, commitment, determination, persistence*—and passion—*inspiring, uplifting, motivating, energizing*—also appeared regularly. *Unique, important, proud,* and *empowering* got their fair share. Fully 95 percent of the cases were described in these terms. No one ever used the word *boring.* Neither did anyone use *dull, unsatisfying, ordinary, indifferent, apathetic,* or *routine.* Humdrum situations simply aren't associated with award-winning performances.

The responses suggest a highly spirited outlook, one that views the white water of change as a personal challenge. All the descriptions are vibrant and full of life. Leaders seize the initiative with enthusiasm, determination, and a desire to make something happen. They embrace the challenge presented by the shifts in their industries or the new demands of the marketplace. They commit themselves to creating exciting new possibilities that make a meaningful difference.

Make no mistake about it. Leadership bests are filled with stress. Although people describe their projects as exciting, about 20 percent also call them frustrating, and approximately 15 percent say that their experiences aroused fear or anxiety. But instead of being debilitated by the stress of a difficult experience, they are challenged and energized by it. Stress always accompanies the pursuit of excellence, but when we're doing our best it never overtakes us. Disruptive change demands significant commitment and sacrifice, but the positive feelings associated with forward progress generate momentum that enables us to ride out the storm.

Make Something Happen

Legendary Hollywood superagent Irving ("Swifty") Lazar once said, "Sometimes I wake up in the morning and there's nothing doing, so I decide to *make something happen by lunch.*"[1] Lazar's philosophy is an elegantly simple and extraordinarily powerful view of life—and one that enabled him to outfox the competition. Like Lazar, leaders make something happen by lunch; they are proactive—and able to make something happen under conditions of extreme uncertainty and urgency. In fact, leadership is needed more during times of uncertainty than in times of stability. Leaders know that action and flexibility are required to bring people through these times, and they seize the imperative to act.

Notre Dame professor J. Michael Crant found, for example, that MBA students who rated high on proactivity were considered by their peers to be more transformational leaders, and were more engaged in extracurricular and civic activities targeted toward bringing about positive change.[2] And it's not just that proactive individuals make better leaders; Crant also found that real estate agents who score high on proactivity were likely to make significantly more sales and receive higher commissions than those who tended to score low on proactivity.[3] In a recent study, we found that proactive managers scored quite high on the leadership practice of challenging the process, and that this inclination was independent of both gender and national culture.[4] Indeed, it seems everyone performs better when they take charge of change.

Why? One reason is that proactive people tend to work harder at what they do. They persist in achieving their goals; others tend to give up, especially when faced with strong objection or great adversity. Just look at Jean Campbell, founder and CEO of Synergistic Systems, Inc. (SSI), a computer-based medical billing company. After a major earthquake rumbled through California's San Fernando Valley at 4:31 A.M. on Monday, January 17, 1994, Jean found her world shaken to its very foundation. But even this, the most serious crisis in her company's history, did not seem insurmountable to her.

As she worked her way toward the SSI building, located uncomfortably close to the hard-hit Northridge area, Jean was already formulating ways to keep clients apprised of the company's status. Her primary concerns were to keep the revenues flowing for her clients and to be operational within two weeks. She knew her employees would need money and didn't want anyone to go without a paycheck any longer than absolutely necessary. Yet as she inspected the SSI facility—its ceiling collapsed on the floor, its twenty-eight-foot-high south wall pulled ten inches off the concrete base, its desks overturned, its files scattered, and its ceiling pipes leaking—she saw that she had a "no-business business." Faced with such destruction, others might have thought her goal of being fully operational within two weeks utterly impossible. Not Jean: to her it became a mission.

Working closely with IBM Business Recovery Services, Jean organized, planned, listened, reassured, and motivated SSI employees and contractors to restore essential services within forty-eight hours and full services in less than ten business days. Jean and her team seized the initiative and energized a partnership of employees, suppliers, and customers so powerful that it overcame the forces of devastation unleashed by nature. She used her initiative and encouraged others to do the same; in so doing, she accomplished the extraordinary amid incredible chaos and change.

Encourage Initiative in Others

Like Jean Campbell, innovative leaders seize the initiative themselves and encourage initiative in others. They want people to speak up, to offer suggestions for improvement, and to be straightforward about their constructive criticism. Yet when it comes to situations that involve high uncertainty, high risk, and high challenge, many people feel reluctant to act, afraid they might make matters worse. The situation certainly doesn't have to be as dramatic as an earthquake. Economic recessions and the accompanying layoffs can just as easily cause people to freeze in place. So how do leaders create the conditions under which people will be ready and willing to seize the initiative in calm or calamitous times?

People who speak out and challenge the status quo have a belief in their ability to do something about the situation they face.[5] People who are high in self-efficacy—who consider themselves capable of taking action in a specific situation—are more likely to act than those who are not. The most important way leaders create this can-do attitude is by providing opportunities for people to gain mastery on a task one step at a time. Training is crucial to building self-efficacy and to encouraging initiative. During periods of rapid change it may seem as though there's no time to stop for training, but this short-term thinking is sure to doom the organization. The best leaders know that the investment in training will pay off in the long term. People can't deliver on what they don't know how to do, and short of firing everyone who doesn't come with all the skills intact—a virtual impossibility—you have to upgrade capabilities continuously.

Training is one form of preparation; another effective way is mental simulation.[6] Being able to imagine how things will be done before they need to be done is a powerful heuristic strategy for building people's confidence that they can act when the situation requires. It's much the same as practice fire drills, except you run them in your head. Playing a scenario through in your mind until you can picture it frame by frame is a terrific way to encourage and support initiative.

Leaders search for opportunities for people to exceed their previous levels of performance. They regularly set the bar higher. And the best leaders understand the importance of setting the bar at a level at which people feel they can succeed. Raise it too high, and people will fail; if they fail too often, they'll quit trying. Raise the bar a bit at a time and eventually more and more people master the situation. This awareness of the human need for challenge and sensitivity to the human need to succeed are among the critical balancing skills of any leader.

Exemplary leaders also provide positive role models of peers who are successful at meeting the new challenges. Seeing one of their own succeed in doing something new and different is an effective way to encourage others to do it, too. And the best leaders know that simply saying "I know you can do it; I know you can do it" actually works. When people hear those words they are more likely to try harder than if they hear nothing, or worse yet, hear those deflating words, "I'm not sure we're going to make it, but. . . ."

Lead Through Assigned Work

Leaders must be agents of change. They need not be entrepreneurs, if by that term we mean those who actually initiate and assume the risk for a new enterprise. Neither must they be "intrapreneurs"—entrepreneurs within a corporation. The majority of leadership in this world is neither entrepreneurial nor intrapreneurial.

When we asked people to tell us who initiated the projects that they selected as their personal bests, we assumed that the majority of people would name themselves. Instead, more than half the cases were initiated by someone other than the leader—usually the person's immediate manager. Yet if leaders seize the initiative, how can we call people leaders when they are assigned the jobs and tasks they undertake? Doesn't this finding fly in the face of all that we've said about how leaders behave?

As we see it, the fact that over half the cases were not self-initiated should be a relief to the leaders who thought they had to initiate all the change, and it should be encouragement to everyone in the organization that responsibility for innovation and improvement is everyone's business. If the only times people reported doing their best were when they got to be the founder, CEO, county supervisor, police chief, agency director, or other head honcho, the majority of leadership opportunities would evaporate— as would the majority of social and organizational change. The reality is that much of what people do is assigned; few of us get to start everything from scratch. That's just a fact of organizational life.

Stuff happens in organizations and in our lives. Sometimes we choose it; sometimes it chooses us. People who become leaders don't always seek the challenges they face. Challenges also seek leaders. It's not so important whether you find the challenges or they find you. What *is* important are the choices you make. The question is: When opportunity knocks are you prepared to open the door?

Seizing the initiative has absolutely nothing to do with position. It's about attitude and action. Innovation and excellence are the result of people at all levels making things happen by lunch. No surprise, then, to say that for nonstop innovation and for lasting change, everyone needs to believe that they can make something happen. It's your job to create the environment in which "Just do it!" isn't an advertising slogan, it's a fact of life.

MAKE CHALLENGE MEANINGFUL

In Chapter Three we reported that in our research we asked people to think of historical leaders they most admired—leaders who, if alive today, they would willingly follow. All of the nominated historical leaders were people with strong beliefs about matters of principle. And there's another consistent thread. They are all individuals who served during times of turbulence, conflict, innovation, and change. They're people who triumphed against overwhelming odds, who took initiative when there was inertia, who confronted the established order, who mobilized people and institutions in the face of strong resistance.

Leadership and challenge are inextricably linked. Leadership and principles are inextricably linked. The implication is very clear. The leaders people admire are ones who have the *courage of their convictions*. What's just as important to constituents as having leaders with values is having leaders who stand up for those beliefs during times of intense challenge and radical change.

Challenge with Purpose

What gets *you* going in the morning, eager to embrace whatever might be in store? What motivates *you* to do your best, day in and day out? Why do people push their own limits to get extraordinary things done? And for that matter, why do people do many things for nothing? Why do they volunteer to put out fires, raise money for worthy causes, or help children in need? Why do they risk their careers to start a new business or risk their security to change the social condition? Extrinsic rewards—the traditional organizational cliché of "what gets rewarded gets done"—certainly can't explain these actions. What's going on? How do people find satisfaction in efforts that don't pay a lot of money, options, perks, or prestige?

Just ask Arlene Blum. Arlene, who earned a doctorate in biophysical chemistry, has spent most of her adult life climbing mountains—literally and figuratively. She's had more than three hundred successful ascents. Her most significant challenge—and the one for which she is best known—was not the highest mountain she's ever climbed. It was the challenge of leading the first all-woman team up Annapurna I, the tenth-highest mountain in the world.[7]

"The question everyone asks mountain climbers is 'Why?' And when they learn about the lengthy and difficult preparation involved, they ask it even more insistently," says Arlene. "For us, the answer was much more than 'because it is there.' We all had experienced the exhilaration, the joy, and the warm camaraderie of the heights, and now we were on our way to an ultimate objective for a climber—the world's tenth-highest peak. But as women, we faced a challenge even greater than the mountain. We had to believe in ourselves enough to make the attempt in spite of social convention and two hundred years of climbing history in which women were usually relegated to the sidelines."[8] Arlene talks about how women had been told for years that they were not strong enough to carry heavy loads, that they didn't have the leadership experience and emotional stability necessary to climb the highest mountains. After a climb of Mount McKinley in 1970, her personal faith in the abilities of women climbers was confirmed.

"Our expedition would give ten women the chance to attempt one of the world's highest and most challenging peaks, as well as the experience necessary to plan future Himalayan climbs. If we succeeded, we would be the first Americans to climb Annapurna and the first American women to reach eight thousand meters (26,200 feet)."[9] At 3:29 P.M. on October 15, 1978, they succeeded. Two women and two Sherpas stood at 26,504 feet and celebrated a victory for women around the world.

In addition to her climbing adventures, for the past twenty years Arlene has been sharing with executives in her leadership seminars the lessons from her many expeditions. In talking about what separates those who make a successful ascent from those who don't, she says, "The real dividing line is passion. As long as you believe what you're doing is meaningful, you can cut through fear and exhaustion and take the next step."[10]

It wasn't just any old challenge that motivated Arlene to lead the Annapurna I expedition. It wasn't just any old challenge that motivated her to lead the Great Himalayan Traverse, a two-thousand-mile trek from Bhutan to Ladakh, India. It wasn't "because it was there." It was because it was *meaningful.* Leadership is not about challenge for challenge's sake. It's not about shaking things up just to keep people on their toes. It's about challenge with meaning and passion. It's about living life on purpose.

Meaning Comes from the Inside

As we were in the middle of writing this edition of our book, the Internet bubble burst. Suddenly instead of swimming in wealth, many were drowning in debt. Fear, uncertainty, and doubt began to creep in. Right in the center of the action was Elaine Fortier, vice president of human resources at New Focus, which designs and builds innovative fiber-optic products for telecommunications and other high-tech industries. She was personally dealing with the grueling job of handling the nitty-gritty of the profound impact that the shift in fortunes had on the people who worked in her company. In talking to her about how she and the other leaders in her company were handling this, we said, "It must be tough."

Elaine responded, "Yes, it's tough right here right now, but it's all part of the adventure. The pioneers crossed the Rocky Mountains in covered wagons, so this is really just a walk in the park, isn't it?" Realizing that hers is clearly a "Venturers Wanted!" leadership attitude, we asked her to tell us more. What she told us next makes a crucial connection between challenge and meaning.

Elaine said, "Most of my business philosophy really comes from my whole life philosophy—call it a set of values or a belief system, a philosophical approach, a spiritual approach, a construct." Her philosophy, as we've seen with so many other leaders, didn't just appear as a flash of light.

In Elaine's case it took ten years and an exhaustive process of addressing a series of personal challenges. But there did come a moment of clarity, and Elaine remembers the point at which she made her conscious choice. As she recalls:

> I realized that there was no magic that was going to happen. It was now up to me to decide, "What's my framework for living?" So I made a decision, and my decision was: love is the most powerful force in the universe. I believe that love and courage are the core elements of a fulfilling life and of most successful endeavors.
>
> You have to have an overarching sense of purpose larger than yourself so that you can say "This is why I'm coming into this place every day, this is what I'm doing." Every person ultimately has to ask, "Am I doing something that has meaning for me?" If I am, then that can get me through the day. And then the question I ask myself is, "Am I helping to provide an environment where it's possible to do what's important?

What gets Elaine through the tough times, the scary times, the times when you don't think you can even get up in the morning or take another step, is a sense of meaning and purpose. The motivation to deal with the challenges and uncertainties of life and work comes from the inside, and not from something that others hold out in front of you as some kind of carrot.[11]

It's evident from our research, and from studies by many others, that if people are going to do their best, they must be *internally* motivated.[12] The task or project in which they're engaged must be intrinsically engaging. We said this in prior chapters, and we'll be saying it again. When it comes to excellence, it's definitely *not* "what gets rewarded gets done," it's "What *is* rewarding gets done." You can never pay people enough to care—to care about their products, services, communities, families, or even the bottom line. True leaders tap into people's hearts and minds, not merely their hands and wallets.

But if external rewards and punishments are successful, and yours is a business, why concern yourself with intrinsic rewards? After all, people in the workplace *aren't* volunteers; they're getting paid. True, *and* it's precisely because people *are* getting paid, because people *are* eligible for bonuses and other awards, that a leader ought to be concerned. If work comes to be seen solely as a source of money and never as a source of fulfillment, organizations will totally ignore other human needs at work—needs involving such intangibles as learning, self-worth, pride, competence, and serving others. Employers will come to see people's enjoyment of their tasks as totally irrelevant, and they will structure work in a strictly utilitarian fashion. The results will be—and already have been—disastrous. Just take a look at the cost of living and the cost of retention in some of the celebrated New Economy companies. Have big stock option plans or huge signing bonuses really done much to make them successful? Have they done anything, in fact? There's very convincing evidence that reliance on extrinsic motivators can actually lower performance and create a culture of divisiveness and selfishness.[13]

Absolute dedication to extrinsic motivators severely limits an organization's ability to excel and to use the full potential of its employees. It wastes human talent and drains away organizational resources. Certainly, you should pay people fairly and provide equitable benefits; this isn't an argument for exploitation. However, reliance upon external incentives and pressures doesn't liberate people to perform their best, and it constrains leaders from ever learning why people *want* to excel. And those who don't learn that will never learn to lead.

Indeed, there are vast differences between a job and work. A job is about economics. As Matthew Fox explains, "work comes from the inside out; work is an expression of our soul, our inner being. It's unique to the individual; it's creative. Work is an expression of the Spirit at work in the world through us."[14] Without employing people's hearts, organizations lose precious return on their investment in people.

INNOVATE AND CREATE

When we're faced with new challenges—whether personal, organizational, economic, or technological—we live with a high degree of ambiguity. Change and the accompanying uncertainty throws off our equilibrium. Yet it's these fluctuations, disturbances, and imbalances in organizations that are the primary sources of creativity.[15]

Rosabeth Moss Kanter, a Harvard Business School professor, investigated the human resource practices and organizational designs of innovation-producing organizations, seeking to learn what fostered and what hindered innovation in the U.S. corporation. Our study and Rosabeth's were done quite independently of each other, in different regions and periods in time, and with different purposes. We were studying leadership; Rosabeth was studying innovation. Yet we and Rosabeth arrived at similar conclusions in analyzing our respective cases: leadership is inextricably connected with the process of innovation, of bringing new ideas, methods, or solutions into use. To Rosabeth, innovation means change, and "change requires leadership . . . a 'prime mover' to push for implementation of strategic decisions."[16] Like hers, our cases are evidence of that.

In a recent survey of senior managers in global companies in North America, Europe, and Japan, the Economist Intelligence Unit (EIU), in cooperation with Towers Perrin, found that the current focus on "improved profitability and cost management will give way by 2003 to an emphasis on innovation, new markets, new products, and e-commerce sales solutions." Innovation is seen as more critical than any other strategic lever. Furthermore, "receptivity to innovation/new ideas" is the third most influential work-environment characteristic in recruiting, retaining, engaging, and motivating employees—after "credible leadership" and "accessible leadership." (Notice how the finding that credible leadership is the most important ingredient in employee motivation supports our research on credibility as the foundation of leadership.) The EIU and Towers Perrin also found that being "Innovative" will be the number one critical employee skill attribute for delivering on the business strategy in 2003.[17]

It's quite clear that leaders must be innovators to navigate their organizations into and through the New Economy. This need is by no means limited to for-profit businesses. Luke Fennell exemplifies the leader who has a passion for innovation and is always ready to take on a new challenge with youthful vigor—and he's been in secondary education for over forty years. The difficulties Luke faced when he decided to become principal of Edison High School, a public school in Fairfax County, Virginia, were numerous and ran deep. Luke knew that he had to "breathe new life into an organization that was on hold."

Luke had to engage the students, parents, teachers, department chairs, administrators, and every employee in the organization, even the hierarchy of the central office, in a spirited effort to turn things around. Innovation was absolutely critical to success. So he flew in the face of the school system's somewhat top-down approach, and began to energize everyone to try new things. Luke continues,

> We were the only school in a large system of twenty-four high schools to take the risk of changing to a significantly different scheduling structure— what is called a "4 × 4" block schedule. Students take four courses each semester. Each course is ninety days in length and each block of instructional time is ninety minutes. Students earn four credits toward high school graduation each semester. Just think of the teacher in this model. Instead of teaching five or six classes of 25–30 students per day in blocks or class periods of fifty minutes with another fifty minutes for planning, we now had teachers teaching three classes of 25 students per day for ninety-minute blocks with 90 minutes for planning. From 150 students each day with fifty minutes for planning to 75 per day and almost double the planning time.

As if that wasn't radical enough, Luke relied on the curriculum department chairs for instructional decision making. He capitalized on the expertise of the teacher leaders. For instance, when the department chairs and other school personnel meet, the department chairs (officially, the "Instructional Leadership Team") sit at the table and "the rest of us (the administrators) sit around the outside and support the chairs in their decisions." He adds, "Notice the name of the group: *Instructional* (teaching and learning is our business), *Leadership* (sharing leadership is a key component to our success), and *Team* (teamwork is at the core of our actions). Not Task Force or committee, or group; not administrative or management team."

Maybe you'd expect an outpouring of support for Luke's efforts—but in fact he was encouraged to lie low, not challenge the top, and get back in line. There was even talk among central management of dropping the innovative schedule. Luke and his colleagues had to persevere, and their persistence paid off. As Luke reported, "We have had two straight years of tremendous gains on the outcomes of the Standards of Learning account-ability measures. . . . We had the highest overall improvement on the School-wide Achievement Index of the twenty-four high schools in the county." Record numbers of Edison students earned their International Baccalaure-ate (IB) diplomas, and more than three-quarters of those students scored well enough to be given college credit for their IB courses. These are remarkable results for a challenged public high school, and the district superintendent and leadership team recognized the school's achievement and Luke's positive deviance by naming him "Principal of the Year." As Luke says, "We were riding a new horse and it was a different day, and a different and renewed school." Whether in public schools or public companies, inno-vation pays off big time.

The real result of the work of all the leaders with whom we talked was that the organization was substantively improved. There was a significant difference that could be seen, felt, and measured. It wasn't just that a new system was installed but that the new system was in use and making a pos-itive difference for everyone.

Balance the Paradox of Routines

We've argued, on the basis of the personal-best cases, that the opportunity to change the business-as-usual environment is fertile soil for leadership. The challenge of creating a new way of life is intrinsically motivating to leaders and constituents alike. Routines, on the other hand, can be the ene-mies of change. They can stifle the very adventure that leaders seek to cre-ate. Indeed, as Warren Bennis, University of Southern California professor and leadership scholar, puts it:

> Routine work drives out nonroutine work and smothers to death all creative planning, all fundamental change in the university—or any institution.[18]

Situations and people do seem to conspire to make leaders into bureau-crats. Organizations do this through established procedures and demands—all those memoranda, telephone calls, reports, meetings, plans, speeches, letters. In today's "always on" world, where the mobile phone rings in the restaurant bathroom, it's all too easy to get caught up in the routine and the trivial, ensnared in an activity trap.

Leaders must destroy routines because routines get us into ruts, dull our senses, stifle our creativity, constrict our thinking, remove us from stimulation, and destroy our ability to compete. Once-useful routines can sap the vitality of an organization and cause it to atrophy. Yet there's a paradox: some routines are essential to a definable, consistent, measurable, and efficient operation. We get annoyed when we can't figure out who reports to whom. We get confused when our employers keep changing the strategy. We get absolutely livid when we're taken off one project and put on another just when we're beginning to get the hang of things. There are no economies in *always* changing; constant changes in direction and in the ways things are done are confusing and costly to everyone.

Progress with Discipline

So we can't live with routines and routine work—and we can't live without them. Established procedures annoy us, and yet we expect trains to run on time. Repetitious work is tedious. Yet if we never did anything the same way twice, how could we make any return on our investments or provide quality services and products? The issue isn't whether to have routines but which routines to have. Those few essential routines that serve the key values of the organization should be worshiped. Those that don't should be rooted out. Those routines that help the organization to change—routines such as customer satisfaction surveys—should be promoted. Those that are excuses—the "always done it that way around here" routines—should be exposed for the injury they do to the welfare of the organization and its people. If organizations and societies are to make progress, leaders must be able to detect when routines are becoming dysfunctional. They must be able to see when routines are smothering creative planning and blocking necessary advancement.

Dynamic change can increase stress on the system. We must balance it with extreme discipline; both are essential if we want to experiment and take risks. We'd better hope that a time of critical need brings out professionals and professionalism. Everyone must have mastered the job and must have a total sense of personal responsibility. True freedom is the result of first learning the discipline, and then being able to act with total spontaneity. This may seem paradoxical, but only those who master a way of doing things are liberated enough to improvise.

LOOK OUTWARD FOR FRESH IDEAS

Today's innovations can come from just about anywhere. Sometimes they come from the customers, sometimes from the lead users, sometimes from suppliers, and sometimes from the R&D labs. The environment is more uncertain, and recent research on the sources of innovation clearly indicates that the most disruptive and destructive innovations can wreak havoc on even the very best companies.[19] If innovation is crucial to leadership, what practical lessons can we draw from this unpredictable phenomenon? Perhaps none is more important than this: leaders must always be actively looking and listening to what's going on around them for even the fuzziest sign or weakest signal that there's something new on the horizon.

Innovation requires more listening and communication than does routine work. Leaders guiding a change must therefore establish more relationships, connect with more sources of information, and get out and walk around more frequently. Successful innovations don't spring from the fifty-second floor of the headquarters building or the back offices of City Hall. It's only by staying in touch with the world around them that leaders can ever expect to change the business-as-usual environment. Therefore, they stay in touch with trends in the marketplace, with the ideas and advice of people from a variety of backgrounds and disciplines, and with social, political, technological, economic, and artistic changes.

External and Internal Communication

Leaders can expect demand for change to come from both inside and outside the organization. But organizational leaders are likely to cut themselves off from critical information sources over time, often precisely because they're so busy trying to build an organization that'll be operationally efficient and sustain itself. And when the pressures for profit and efficiency are greatest, they may even mistakenly act to eliminate or severely limit the very things that provide the new ideas they need to weather the storms of uncertainty—by cutting the budgets for travel and training, for example. Unless external communication is actively encouraged, people interact with outsiders less and less frequently and new ideas are cut off.

If leaders are going to detect demands for change, they must use their *outsight*. They must stay sensitive to the external realities, especially in this networked, global world. They must go out and talk to their constituents, be they citizens, customers, employees, stockholders, students, suppliers, vendors, business partners, managers, or just interested parties. They must listen—in person, on the phone, via e-mail, via Web sites—and stay in touch.

Research by Ralph Katz and Tom Allen of the MIT Sloan School of Management supports the need for external and internal communication. As one aspect of their study of research and development teams, they examined the relationship between the length of time that people had been working together in a particular project area—what they called "group longevity"— and the level of communication of project groups at various stages of their lives. Three areas of interpersonal oral communication were examined for each team: intraproject communication, organizational communication, and professional communication. Each team's technical performance was also measured by department managers and laboratory directors.[20]

The higher-performing groups had significantly more communication with people outside their labs, whether with organizational units such as marketing and manufacturing or with outside professional associations. Groups with the highest longevity index reported lower levels of communications in all three areas and "were significantly more isolated from external sources of new ideas and technological advances and from information within other organizational divisions, especially marketing and manufacturing."[21] It seems the long-lived teams cut themselves off from the kind of information they needed the most to come up with new ideas, and thus reduced their performance.

There simply aren't enough good new ideas floating around the lab when people don't listen to the world outside. It's easy to understand how some workgroups and organizations become myopic and unimaginative. The people themselves aren't dull or slow-witted; they've just become too familiar with their routines and too isolated from outside influences.

When Randy Melville took over the operations of the Texoma Region of Frito-Lay, the region was ranked twenty-first out of twenty-two regions, and it was $2.5 million behind plan. He and his team needed to turn it around. After three years the region had moved up to number six and was $1 million ahead of plan. This dramatic shift was driven in part by the fact that Randy personally engaged in the field. He rode the trucks on their routes and visited the stores with delivery people. He made calls with sales associates. Randy was looking for ideas for improvement—and in the process, he convinced people that he was really "serious about changing this thing."

As Randy knew, to infuse fresh ideas into an organization, a leader needs to shake it up periodically. That can be done by adding new members to the group, sending people off on a tour, or holding a seminar. Whatever the technique, the leader must keep communication pathways open and vital.

Let Ideas Flow In from the Outside

On a visit to Northern California, we came across some important advice for leaders. Printed at the top of a pamphlet describing a particular stretch of coastline was this warning: "Never turn your back on the ocean." Why not turn and look inland to catch a view of the town? A rogue wave may come along when your back is turned and sweep you out to sea, as it has many an unsuspecting beachcomber. This warning holds good advice for travelers and leaders alike. When we take our eyes off the external realities, turning inward to admire the beauty of our own organization, we may be swept away by the swirling waters of change.

So too with innovation: we must always scan the external realities. Innovation requires the use of outsight, whether directed to pricing in the marketplace or diversity in the workforce. The sibling of *insight* (the ability to apprehend the inner nature of things), *outsight* (the awareness and understanding of outside forces) comes through openness. It's by keeping the doors open to the passage of ideas and information that we become knowledgeable about what goes on around us.

"Seeing and hearing things with your own eyes and ears is a critical first step in improving or creating a breakthrough product," says Tom Kelley, general manager of IDEO, the world's leading design consultancy specializing in new product development. "As IDEO human factors expert Leon Segal says, 'Innovation begins with an eye.'"[22]

At IDEO if you want to design a new shopping cart, you don't hold a focus group, you go down to the local grocery and watch people shop. If you want to know the right height for a keyboard and monitor, you watch people using them—and you see things like people propping their dangling feet on phone books, inspiring an adjustable footrest.[23]

If you want the level of innovation and creativity of an IDEO, then you need to destroy confining barriers. Keep your eyes and ears open for new ideas. Remain receptive and expose yourself to broader views. Remove the protective covering in which organizations often seal themselves. Be willing to hear, consider, and accept ideas from sources outside the company.

Whether you're an entrepreneur, an intrapreneur, a manager, a community activist, a volunteer, or an individual contributor, the leadership attitude is what makes the difference. That attitude is characterized by a posture of challenging the process—of wanting to change the business-as-usual environment. Enterprising situations contribute to a sense of personal achievement and self-worth. They promote leadership and high performance.

COMMITMENT NUMBER 5: SEARCH FOR OPPORTUNITIES BY SEEKING INNOVATIVE WAYS TO CHANGE, GROW, AND IMPROVE

In this chapter, we've emphasized how closely associated leadership is with change and innovation. When people talk about their personal-best leadership experiences, they talk about the challenge of change. When we look at leaders, we see that they're associated with transformations, whether small or large. Leaders don't have to change history, but they do have to make a change in "business as usual."

The quest for change is an adventure. It tests our skills and abilities. It brings forth talents that have been dormant. It's the training ground for leadership. The challenge of change is tough; it's also stimulating and enjoyable. For leaders to get the best from themselves and others, they must find their task intrinsically motivating. The pace of change has accelerated, and opportunities may come and go in a nanosecond. Exemplary leaders, therefore, are proactive: they actively seek and create new opportunities. They're always on the lookout for anything that lulls a group into a false sense of security; they constantly invite and create new initiatives. Leaders, by definition, are out in front of change, not behind it trying to catch up. Innovation and leadership are nearly synonymous. Leaders are innovators; innovators are leaders. The focus of a leader's attention should be less on the routine operations and much more on the untested and untried. Leaders should always be asking "What's new? What's next? What's better?" That's where the future is.

Leaders are open to receiving ideas from anyone and anywhere; they're porous people. They are net importers of ideas. Leaders use their outsight—their ability to perceive external realities—to constantly survey the landscape of technology, politics, economics, demographics, art, religion, and society.

Because projects that are fun, exciting, and challenging are often risky, leaders must balance innumerable benefits and risks. In the next chapter, we'll examine how leaders appreciate the risks involved in their experiments and innovations. But first, here are some action steps that you can take in searching for opportunities to challenge the status quo and move along the path of getting extraordinary things done.

• *Treat every job as an adventure.*

Even if you've been in your job for years, treat today as if it were your first day. Ask yourself, "If I were just starting this job, what would I do?" Begin doing those things now.

More young people have had the chance to be engaged in a start-up in the last several years than prior generations ever saw. If you have that chance, take it. But if you don't, at least approach every new assignment as a *start-over*. Stay alert to ways to constantly improve the organization. There's no magic to making a previously poor-performing unit a high-performing one. All you have to do is unlock the talent and resources for excellence. Often the critical difference is a leader who sees untapped energy and skill in the existing group and who assumes that excellence can be achieved. It's that old pioneering spirit reawakened.

Think of your leadership assignment as an exciting adventure through unexplored wilderness. Think of your constituents and colleagues as pioneers and discover new territory together. Identify those projects that you've always wanted to undertake but never have. Ask your team members to do the same. Pick one major project per quarter. Implement one smaller improvement every three weeks. Figure out how to do all of this within the budget you now have (or using the money you'll save or earn when your project succeeds). If you still need more money, go out and raise it from your supporters, as other adventurers do.

Be an adventurer, an explorer. Where in your organization have you not been? Where in the communities that you serve have you not been? Make a plan to explore those places. As kids we called it a field trip. Take a field trip to a factory, a warehouse, a distribution center, or a retail store. If you're in a school district, go sit in on the class that was once your favorite subject. How's it different today? If you're in city government, go to a department that really intrigues you. If you're in a professional services organization, go on a site visit with someone in a different practice. Field trips are more fun with other people. Take your team. Go on a bus or in a van so you can talk on the way there and the way back. Go!

Going to places that are brand new to us opens us to new possibilities. We're like kids at Disneyland—wide-eyed, giggly, in awe and wonderment. Wow! Look at *that!* Explorations are life's exclamation points. People need them frequently to stay energized, youthful, and fresh.

• *Seek meaningful challenges for yourself.*

Our research is very clear. People do better work when they feel challenged. If you're bored or doing routine work that doesn't use even your current level of skill, then the probability is that it's showing up in your performance and your team's performance. For people to excel, they must find what they do intrinsically motivating—and challenge is a major motivator, along with skill and interest.

Start by reviewing your answers to the questions about your values and vision in Chapters Three and Five. What do you care about? What inspires you? What's the legacy you want to leave? Which of your strengths are being underutilized? What can you do better than most anyone else? Where in your immediate organization is there an opportunity to do more right now that is personally meaningful and fulfills a greater purpose for you? Where is there a chance to stretch your strengths a bit so that you're succeeding and learning at the same time? The opportunities are there; you just need to *see* them.

Seek leadership opportunities to gain greater experience with the Five Practices. If you're in a staff job, get a line job. If you're in a line job, get a staff job. Take on a high-visibility staff assignment at headquarters. Lead a project team that is dealing with a crisis or business hardship. Ask for a really tough assignment. Outside of your immediate unit there's got to be something going on that you really want to be part of. Call up the manager; see how you can get involved. There's no better way to test your limits than to voluntarily place yourself in a difficult job.

What about your neighborhood or community? Where are there meaningful opportunities to be of service in a way that stretches you and appeals to one of your interests? Volunteer for leadership roles in your professional association or a community group. We believe that every leader should serve on at least one nonprofit board or be part of one community project. But don't do it only out of a sense of duty, or you'll make a lousy contributor. Do it because it serves an important need and it stimulates, challenges, and engages you. Enlightened self-interest has its place. Sure, it's time-consuming—and it keeps you fresh.

- *Find and create meaningful challenges for others.*

Leaders aren't the only ones who do their best when challenged. All of us do. Look for ways to add challenge to other people's work. Ask people to join you in solving problems or starting a new service or process, or try delegating more than just routine jobs to them. Ask for their creative ideas. The real magic in total quality management and total process reengineering was nothing more than a dedication to making what was once routine work more challenging and more meaningful. People who have never been asked for the time of day often thrive when given problem-solving tools and opportunities to contribute.

Typically, organizations assign their best-performing people to deal with problems—the main product line that's performing below expectations, the old technology that's being hammered by some new whiz-bang innovation—and no one is assigned to the "opportunities." But it's the opportunities that produce growth; problem solving is more like damage containment.[24] Allocate more resources and commitment to the opportunities than to the problems.

Draw up a list of the opportunities facing your organization. In that, you should be able to find creative and meaningful opportunities for others. First, however, be sure you know what motivates each of your team members and what they find challenging. Get to know their skill levels. What might be a stretch for one person is too easy for another. Aim to have everyone actively searching for opportunities to innovate, grow, and improve. Aim to provide each person with a way to see how they contribute to the overall success of the endeavor and to feel a real sense of urgency.

- *Add fun to everyone's work.*

Make the search for opportunities a fun adventure. If you—and others—aren't having fun doing what you're doing, chances are you're not doing your best. We aren't talking about a laugh-a-minute party, but the overall experience should be enjoyable. Appropriate humor can lead to cohesion and bonding among coworkers.

Fun is certainly one of the obvious characteristics at Southwest Airlines; in fact, having a sense of humor is an explicit hiring criterion. *Fortune* magazine even dubbed chairman Herb Kelleher the "High Priest of Ha Ha."[25] Walk through the halls of headquarters and you'll see walls and walls of Southwest family photos. Fly the airline and you may be entertained with a humorous song. And, oh my, how about those costume parties? At the open house for Southwest's corporate headquarters building at Love Field in Dallas, the dispatchers, who were the only ones who hadn't moved into the new facility, got there early and screened off part of the parking lot. They then provided valet parking—for dispatchers only! Everyone in the headquarters building retaliated by decorating the dispatchers' offices with wilted flowers, like a funeral parlor. There's much, much more—and there's also the very serious business side of Southwest—like having the most productive workforce in business—that goes hand-in-hand with fun.

Certainly if there are layoffs, throwing a party wouldn't be the right thing to do, but in other cases a little levity can help people through a tough time. Katherine Hudson, president and CEO of the Brady Corporation, tells of a time when she was head of the instant photography division and had been handed a "death sentence" involving a patent case with Polaroid. The division was forced to wind down the business. "At a luncheon of about 50 key people," she says, "one of my managers gave me a pair of air force combat boots as a symbol of the daunting leadership challenge I faced. People had placed bets on whether I'd don the boots on the spot (I did), and those boots became an icon of the division's grittiness in this dire time."[26]

Just for the fun of it, make a list of activities that are fun for you. Ask your colleagues at work to do the same. Then pick one and figure out a way to integrate it into the work of your organization. If you run short of ideas, consult Leslie Yerkes's book, *Fun Works: Creating Places Where People Love to Work*.[27] It's full of case examples from companies with fun as a central principle. Enjoy!

• *Question the status quo.*

Some standard practices, policies, and procedures are critical to productivity and quality assurance. On the other hand, many are simply matters of tradition. To divide them out, make a list of all the practices in your organization that are "the way we've always done it around here." For each one, ask yourself, "How useful is this in helping us become the best we can be? How useful is this for stimulating creativity and innovation?" If your answer is "absolutely essential," then keep it. If not, find a way to change it.

Review all the policies and procedures. For each one, ask yourself the same questions and take the same action. Vow to eliminate every stupid rule and every needless routine within the next month. At Wal-Mart they call this ETDT: "Eliminate the Dumb Things." Go find what needs fixing in your organization. Wander around the plant, the store, the branch, the halls, or the office. Look for things that don't seem right. Ask questions. Probe.

When Phil Turner moved from facilities manager to plant manager of the Wire and Cable Division of Raychem Corporation, he spent a lot of time getting accustomed to the sounds and smells of the place. At first it all seemed like indistinguishable noise; soon he was able to hear the special music of each machine. Phil discovered that the machines used to spool the wire weren't running at full speed. When he asked why, he was told that people didn't know how to fix them and were afraid that if the machines were run at capacity, they would wear down. Phil went into action and began an employee training program that got the machines up to speed and enabled the operators to fix them whenever they broke.

A new assignment is a perfect opportunity to use your naive understanding of the operation to your advantage. Everyone tolerates your dumb questions. By constantly asking, "Why do we do this, and why do we do that?" you'll uncover some needed improvements. Don't stop at what you can find on your own. Ask employees what really bugs them about the organization. Ask what gets in the way of doing the best job possible. Promise to look into everything they bring up and get back to them with answers in ten days. Commit yourself to removing three frequently mentioned organizational roadblocks that stand in the way of getting extraordinary things done.

Author and consultant Larry Downes has a process that will get the bureaucracy-busting innovation-inventing juices flowing. He often assigns what he calls the "Worst Nightmare" exercise to executives. "You separate the executives into a few small teams," instructs Downes, "and tell them that they have just left their jobs for a startup that will put their former company out of business. Absent the constraints for budget cycles, legacy systems, and broken human resource processes, it takes remarkably little time for the teams to come up with plausible ways to destroy businesses and entire industries that have been around for decades."[28]

Questioning the status quo is not only for leaders. Effective leaders create a climate in which others feel comfortable doing the same. If your organization is going to be the best it can be, everyone has to feel comfortable in speaking up and taking the initiative.

- *Renew your teams.*

Teams seem to go through life cycles, just as products do. Even the best teams get stale and need to be refreshed.[29] Never let teams get disconnected from outside information. Make sure members attend professional conferences, participate in training programs, and visit colleagues in other parts of the organization. It's tempting to slash the meeting, training, and travel budgets when times get tough, but beware: you could pay the price of falling further behind the competition. Staying ahead of the competition means staying ahead in your knowledge of the technology and the market.

Add a new member or two to the group every couple of years. Rotate some people out and others in. New people—especially those who haven't been socialized into your way of doing things—can help you get a new perspective. If you can't move people in or out and you have a long-tenure group to lead, be very directive in your insistence that they go out and locate a measurable number of process or product enhancements. Force them to interact with others, and send them as much information as you can about new developments in the field. Put everybody through a creativity course. Give people the knowledge, skills, and tools they need to contribute to the generation of new ideas.

- *Create an open-source approach to searching for opportunities.*

Proof of the power of intrinsic motivation can be found in the open-source movement in computer programming. Code listings for the Linux operating system and Apache HTTP server, for example, are open to any computer programmer who wants to contribute to improving them. Thousands of volunteers have contributed to their success, and today there are more than 12 million users of Linux worldwide. Linus Torvalds of Helsinki, Finland, could never have done that on his own.

Apply this concept to searching for opportunities, and instead of this being the task of a few hand-selected people, make it open-source innovation. Put the idea out there on the Web, and let anyone who wants to contribute take part in creation and innovation.

Baxter Healthcare's Renal Division needed to breathe life into the way new ideas got captured, turned into projects, and became profitable business. Harry Gill and his colleagues created, among other things, a "technovation room" to stimulate idea sharing and idea generation. They also created "idea hot lines"—Web sites and other accessible technologies—to make it easy to submit ideas and move new thoughts along.

To increase the probability that more ideas and better ideas will be contributed, consciously include people from diverse backgrounds, age cohorts, functional responsibilities, and levels. In the movie *Good Will Hunting*, the lead character, played by Matt Damon, was a pugnacious young mathematical genius who, as a janitor at MIT, would write solutions to complex mathematical problems on the math building's hall blackboards, much to the amazement and bewilderment of the faculty. Equally amazing things could happen at your organization if you provide the tools and the structure and allow all the minds to contribute.

• *Send everyone shopping for ideas.*

Make finding more ways to gather suggestions and innovations from constituents a priority. As one example, at Chef Allen's, an award-winning restaurant in North Miami Beach specializing in New Era cuisine, owner Allen Susser ran a "Chow Now" program. Allen gave servers and cooks $50 each to dine at any restaurant with cuisine similar to that of Chef Allen's. Employees returned with short written and oral reports on what they learned. One cook reported that he had sampled a competitor's fare and was dismayed to find elegant food being served on cold plates, ruining the meal. Nearly all staffers participated. "They like to laugh at the little mistakes and believe they wouldn't make them," said Allen. And there's no doubt they paid more attention to warming plates up—and the hundreds of other details that make a restaurant truly elegant.[30] As we were writing this edition, Chef Allen was running an online recipe contest. The grand prize was dinner for two at Chef Allen's. And more than likely the winning recipe will be served up online and on Chef Allen's dining tables. If you make shopping for ideas a part of the culture, it just keeps going and going and going.

Be on the lookout for new ideas, wherever you are. If you're serious about promoting innovation and getting others to listen to people outside the unit, make gathering new ideas a personal priority. Encourage others to open their eyes and ears to the world outside the boundaries of the organization. Choose among the abundant processes for collecting suggestions and make them fun for employees and customers. There are focus groups, advisory boards, suggestion boxes, breakfast meetings, brainstorming sessions, customer evaluation forms, mystery shoppers, mystery guests, visits to competitors, and scores more. The World Wide Web is a gold mine for this kind of thing. Chat rooms are great chances to swap ideas with those outside your field—anonymously, if you'd like. You can get a number of free online newsletters that are dedicated to innovation and include contributions from far and wide. At least once a day do a Web search for something related to what you do—and visit the site even if it's totally unrelated to your business. We're not in the restaurant business, but Chef Allen's gave us a great idea.

Make idea gathering part of your daily, weekly, and monthly schedule. Call three customers or clients who haven't used your services in a while and ask them why. Call three customers or clients who have made recent purchases and ask them why. Sure, we know about e-mail—the human voice is better for this sort of thing. Work the counter and ask people what they like and don't like about your organization. Shop at a competitor's store. Better yet, anonymously shop for your own product and see what the salespeople in the store say about it. Call your organization and see how the phones are answered and how questions are handled.

Make sure that you devote at least 25 percent of every weekly staff meeting to listening to *outside* ideas for improving processes and technologies and developing new products and services. Don't let staff meetings be simply status reports on routine, daily, inside stuff. Invite customers, suppliers, people from other departments, and other outsiders to your meetings to offer their suggestions on how your unit can improve.

Keep your antenna up, no matter where you are. You can never tell where or when you might find new ideas.

COMMITMENT NUMBER 5

SEARCH FOR OPPORTUNITIES BY SEEKING INNOVATIVE WAYS TO CHANGE, GROW, AND IMPROVE

- *Treat every job as an adventure.*

- *Seek meaningful challenges for yourself.*

- *Find and create meaningful challenges for others.*

- *Add fun to everyone's work.*

- *Question the status quo.*

- *Renew your teams.*

- *Create an open-source approach to searching for opportunities.*

- *Send everyone shopping for ideas.*

Source: The Leadership Challenge by James M. Kouzes and Barry Z. Posner. Copyright © 2002.

8 EXPERIMENT AND TAKE RISKS

Leadership is learning by doing, adapting to actual situations. Leaders are constantly learning from their errors and failures.

Claude Meyer, Swissair

It's amazing: once they get started, people always accomplish more than they originally thought they could.

Randi DuBois, Pro-Action Associates

Whenever leaders experiment with innovative ways of doing things, they put themselves and others at risk. To break out of the norms that box us in and restrict our thinking, to improve the way things are, we must be willing to take risks. Particularly in times when innovation is required, we must do the things we think we cannot. But how do we make that leap?

Reno Taini and Randi DuBois know about enabling people to make those leaps. Their organization, Pro-Action, sponsors executive development programs involving, among other things, outdoor challenges. Through these programs, participants learn about trust, risk taking, group problem solving, and teamwork.

Reno began experimenting with outdoor adventures while educating high school students. As a field biologist who felt that classroom learning was insufficient to give kids a true sense of the wonders of nature, he began taking students on field trips to climb mountains, cross deserts, and raft stretches of white water—a program he dubbed the Wilderness School. Reno also took his students into the urban wilderness—places in the inner city where students confronted the challenges of poverty and homelessness. They served holiday meals to seniors and gathered litter from public streets. In the process, the students did more than learn about nature, humanity, and survival; they also experienced themselves firsthand.

Reno then began working with Randi, a recreation specialist, to take the Wilderness School into the larger community, first to many of the parents and friends of his students, who wanted to have similar adventures. Reno and Randi created a Ropes Course on five acres in La Honda, California. It's a maze of ropes, cables, tires, logs, trees, platforms, ladders, and other gear collected from everything from ships to fire stations. Reno, Randi, and their staff have served over seventy-five thousand people. Executives from some of the country's largest corporations have learned about trust and risk taking through this unusually powerful form of education. Reno and Randi have also worked with Vietnam veterans in wheelchairs, Amerasians from Vietnam immigrating to the United States, abused women with emotional scars, children as young as five, and adults as old as seventy.

Reno and Randi encourage people to do things most have never done before, to experiment with themselves, to stretch and break their self-imposed limitations. For example, they invite people to walk a cable stretched thirty-five feet above the ground between two trees or leap for a ring from a platform at thirty feet. We use events like these in our leadership development programs as well, to provide leaders with the opportunity to personally experience what it feels like to try something new. It's the first time most participants have ever walked a tightrope or climbed a fifteen-foot-high wall. One lesson that emerges is that fear and apprehension are greater barriers to success than the actual difficulty or danger of the experiment itself. Randi puts it this way:

Consistently, we observe that the weakest muscle in the body is the one between the ears. Self-imposed limitations and beliefs hold most people back. When individuals feel the surge of adrenaline and the thump of their hearts growing louder, they frequently interpret that feeling as fear. We encourage them to explore and to push on their perceived limits. By translating that feeling into excitement, they then discover the elation of victory over crippling doubts—and the ways they link these feelings back to their workplace are enormous.

The key to Reno and Randi's success is in getting people to venture beyond the limitations that they normally place around themselves. They began by seeing the teaching of field biology as an outdoor adventure and recreation as an opportunity for personal growth; they now lead a creative enterprise that enables others to experience victory over doubt.

And this victory is key. Indeed, today's work climate for success demands a willingness to take risks and experiment with innovative ideas. True leaders foster risk taking, encouraging others to step out into the unknown rather than play it safe. Leaders get to know the skills and motivations of their constituents. They set goals that are higher than current levels, but not so high that people feel only frustration. Leaders raise the bar gradually and offer coaching and training to build skills that help people get over each new level.

The methods that Reno and Randi use appear far from gradual or step by step—yet each event is rigged for maximum safety, and no one has ever been injured. They challenge people, sometimes to their very cores—and participants come out changed and ready to take on new risks and experiments. In this endeavor, Reno and Randi demonstrate, as do all exemplary leaders, the need to:

- Initiate incremental steps and small wins
- Learn from mistakes
- Promote psychological hardiness

Leaders use these *essentials* to Experiment and Take Risks, to turn challenge, uncertainty, turmoil, change, and wonder into positive results.

INITIATE INCREMENTAL STEPS AND SMALL WINS

Why incremental steps? Why small wins? If we're talking about challenging the process, why not start big? Can you imagine solving the homelessness problem, the health care problem, or the world hunger problem? Unfortunately, problems conceived of too broadly are overwhelming because they defeat our capacity to even think about what might be done, let alone begin doing something.

Leaders face a similar challenge in trying to accomplish the extraordinary: that tightrope looks much too high to even contemplate taking the first steps. Getting ourselves and others to change old mindsets and habits and substitute new ones—and commit to them, long term—is daunting. Even with the best of intentions, people tend to revert to old and familiar patterns.

So how do leaders get people to *want* to change the way they're currently headed, to break out of existing behaviors, to tackle big problems, to attempt extraordinary performance? The answer: step by step! The most effective change processes are incremental; they break down big problems into small, doable steps and get a person to say yes numerous times, not just once. Successful leaders help others to see how progress can be made by breaking the journey down into measurable goals and milestones.

The scientific community has always understood that major break-throughs are likely to be the result of the work of hundreds of researchers, as countless contributions finally begin to add up to a solution. Advances in medicine or biophysics, for example, often involve many experiments focused on various pieces of the problem. Likewise, taking the sum total, all the "little" improvements in technology, regardless of the industry, have likely contributed to a greater increase in organizational productivity than all the great inventors and their inventions.[1] Indeed, researchers have found that rapid prototyping, and plenty of it, results in getting higher quality products to the marketplace more quickly.[2]

In contrast, the traditional management approach to carrying out an objective has been to start with strategic planning. Unfortunately, strategic planning simply doesn't capture the imagination. Strategic planning, it turns out, is *not* a magic potion. It's a process that detaches strategy from operations, thinking from doing. You certainly have to have plans. But if you rely on hammering out the perfect strategic plan or await a paradigm shift, you could be waiting decades. The world is simply moving too fast for that. Progress *today* is more likely to be the result of a focus on incremental improvements in tools and processes than of tectonic shifts of minds. Leaders keep the dream in mind; then they act and adapt on the move. And a focus on challenging the process step by step will enable more of us ordinary mortals to take part in the joys of transforming our schools, congregations, communities, agencies, hospitals, corporations, governments, or small businesses into high-performing organizations.

How Do Small Wins Work?

The small wins process enables leaders to build constituents' commitment to a course of action. Professional fundraisers do much the same thing when they begin by asking for a small or indeterminate contribution. They know that it's easier to go back and request more in the future from those who've made an initial contribution than to return to someone who's already said no. Leaders start with actions that are within their control, that are tangible, that are doable, and that can get the ball rolling. Leaders understand how hard it is to get anybody excited about just a vision; leaders know they must show something happening.

Consider, for instance, the experience of Melissa Poe. As a fourth grader at Percy Priest School in Nashville, Tennessee, she was fearful of the continued destruction of the earth's resources. Melissa wrote a letter to the president of the United States asking for his assistance in her campaign to save the environment for the enjoyment of future generations. After sending the letter, Melissa worried that it would never be brought to the president's attention. After all, she was only a child. So, with the urgency of the issue pressing on her mind, she decided to get the president's attention by putting her letter on a billboard. Through sheer diligence and hard work, the nine-year-old got her letter placed on one billboard free of charge and with this action launched Kids for a Clean Environment (Kids F.A.C.E.), an organization whose goal is to develop programs to clean up the environment.[3]

Almost immediately, Melissa began receiving letters from kids who were as concerned as she about the environment. They wanted to help. By the time Melissa finally did receive a response from the president, the disappointing form letter couldn't crush her dream. She no longer needed the help of someone famous to get her message across. Melissa had found in herself the person she needed—that powerful someone who could inspire others to get involved and make her dream a reality.

Within one year, more than 250 billboards across the country were displaying her letter free of charge, and Kids F.A.C.E. membership had swelled. As the organization grew, Melissa's first Kids F.A.C.E. project, a recycling program at her school, led to a manual full of ideas on how to clean up the environment. Melissa's impatience and zest motivated her to do something—and her work has paid off. Today there are more than 300,000 members and 2,000 chapters of Kids F.A.C.E.[4] Melissa is proof that small wins work—and for kids too.

The fact that small wins work isn't news to scholars of technological innovation. An extensive study involving five DuPont plants documented that minor technical changes (for example, introduction of forklift trucks)—rather than major changes (for example, introduction of new chemical processing technologies)—accounted for over two-thirds of the reductions in production costs over a thirty-year period.[5] The minor technical changes were small improvements, made by people familiar with current operations. Less time, skill, effort, and expense were required to produce them than to implement the major changes. Much of the improvement was really part of the process of learning by doing. Stanford University's Debra Meyerson calls people who engage in this sort of action "tempered radicals"—cautious catalysts whose small victories, won over time, lay the groundwork for something grander.[6]

The success of behavior-change programs such as Alcoholics Anonymous, Weight Watchers, and Smokenders is due in large part to their incremental change philosophies. None insists that participants become totally abstinent for the rest of their lives. Although this is the goal of the Alcoholics Anonymous program, alcoholics are told to stay sober one day at a time—or one hour at a time, if temptation is severe. The seeming impossibility of lifetime abstinence is scaled down to a workable task that drastically reduces the size of win necessary to maintain sobriety.

Small wins form the basis for a consistent pattern of winning that attracts people who want to be allied with a successful venture. Small wins build people's confidence and reinforce their natural desire to feel successful. Since additional resources tend to flow to winners, this means that slightly larger wins can be attempted next. A series of small wins therefore provides a foundation of stable building blocks. Each win preserves gains and makes it harder to return to preexisting conditions; each win also provides information that facilitates learning and adaptation.

Small wins also deter opposition for a simple reason: it's hard to argue against success. Thus small wins decrease resistance to subsequent proposals. In achieving a small win, leaders identify the place to get started. They make the project seem doable within existing skill and resource levels. This approach minimizes the cost of trying and reduces the risks of failing. Once a small win has been accomplished, natural forces are set in motion that favor stepping out toward another small win.

When leaders deliberately cultivate a strategy of small wins, they actively make people feel like winners and make it easier for people to want to go along with their requests. If people can see that a leader is asking them to do something that they're quite capable of doing, they feel some assurance that they can be successful at the task. If people aren't overwhelmed by a task, their energy goes into getting the job done, instead of wondering "how will we *ever* solve that problem?" They then have heightened interest in continuing with the journey.

This simple strategy of winning step by step succeeds while many massive overhauls and gigantic projects fail. Why? It's not just that it's easier. It's also because it builds personal and group commitment. By mobilizing for fast action—by working at finding all the little ways that people can succeed at doing things differently—effective leaders make people want to be involved and stay involved because they can see that what they are doing is making a difference.

Mobilize for Fast Action

Leaders ensure that people can take fast, responsive action. For example, they experiment continuously—setting up little tests (such as pilot studies, demonstration projects, laboratory tests, field experiments, and market trials) that continually help people learn something and that generate lots of possibilities. One of those possibilities just might catch on. Experimentation is key to challenging the process. "What have you improved lately?" is a wonderful question to ask to stimulate innovation. "What have you learned?" is another prod for getting things started.

Another important strategy is reducing items to their essence. Because the pace of managerial work is fast and relentless the average executive has less than nine minutes of uninterrupted time to spend on any one item. This forces leaders to act on their dreams in brief bursts. The beauty of a small win is that it's compact, it's simple, and it can catch the attention of people who have only a few minutes to listen to an idea or read a proposal. Small-win tasks make it easier to maintain an upbeat, noncontroversial atmosphere. The challenge is in keeping the long-term vision in mind and at the forefront of action over the long haul. It's critical to break problems down into small pieces, doable steps with milestones, so that they're more easily comprehended and accomplished.

The benefit of breaking major changes down into smaller, incremental changes is well demonstrated by the experience of LuAnn Sullivan, a branch office manager for Wells Fargo Bank. Although core deposits in her office hadn't grown for several years, they doubled in two years under her leadership. How? LuAnn broke her overall goal into smaller parts so that each person had individual monthly and weekly goals. Mary Delaney, a customer service representative, said that when LuAnn first told her of the broader goal, she thought that they would never be able to accomplish it. However, Mary explains, "Once I saw that I could achieve my weekly goals, the big goal didn't seem so crazy and it was easy to get motivated."[7]

Acting with a sense of urgency is another strategy leaders use to mobilize for fast action. Waiting for permission is *not* characteristic of people who get extraordinary things done, whether leaders or individual contributors. Acting with a sense of urgency *is*. Small wins allow for immediate action with near and clear success. LuAnn broke the long-term goals down into weekly goals and got everyone focused right away on making something happen. Moreover, she didn't wait to check with anyone else in the bank hierarchy before getting started.

Philip Diehl had been the chief of staff of the Senate Finance Committee, as well as chief of staff to the Secretary of the Treasury when he was appointed director of the U.S. Mint. Rather than spend his early days at the then $2.5 billion organization making big promises and bold declarations, he chose the small wins path. "I didn't rush the changes at the Mint," says Diehl: "I started small, with a few initiatives here and there. Then as the envelope was pushed or as roadblocks appeared, problems were tackled as they cropped up and progress continued. Big changes have been made over the past six years, but they've been made incrementally. You do big things by doing lots of small things."[8]

Consider the Mint's 50 State Quarters Program, one of the most successful consumer-product launches ever. It's a long-term project designed to rejuvenate the public's interest in coins and in coin collecting. The program honors each state with its own special quarter. The public gets involved, through the governor's office in each state, in the design process. Every ten weeks for ten years a new state quarter gets put into circulation, released in the order in which each state joined the Union. One step, or quarter, at a time. By early 2002, the U.S. Mint could describe itself as a $3.7 billion organization—and a near 50 percent increase is a major achievement at the billion-dollar-plus level.[9]

Small wins breed success and propel us down the path. Experiments, pilot projects, and market trials all facilitate the process of getting started. Breaking problems into manageable pieces keeps us from being overwhelmed. When our work and community lives are fast-paced and full of interruptions, to get extraordinary things done we must stay focused on what's essential. Above all, *leaders just do it*. Small victories attract constituents, create momentum, and get people to remain on the path.

We need those victories. Without them, the quest for the summit—for peak performance in ourselves and our organizations—can seem dauntingly difficult. Making a dent, let alone a difference, in the major problems we face can seem to require such overwhelming force that it's a challenge to set out on the journey. Leaders know that "the journey of a thousand miles begins with the first step." And they know that they must get started.

LEARN FROM MISTAKES

The risks involved in a ropes course are like the risks leaders must take when involved in learning and in mastering change: making a mistake—or worse yet, failing. To be sure, failure can be costly. For the individual who leads a failed project, it can mean a stalled career or even a lost job. For an adventurous leader, it can mean the loss of personal assets. For mountain climbers and other physical adventurers, it can mean injury or death.

It is, however, absolutely essential to take risks. Over and over again, people in our study tell us how important mistakes and failure have been to their success. Without those experiences, they would have been unable to achieve their aspirations. It may seem ironic, but many echo the thought that the overall quality of work improves when people have a chance to fail. Studies of the innovation process make the point: "Success does not breed success. It breeds failure. It is failure which breeds success."[10] If that advice seems patently absurd, think about the careers of many famous winners:

- Babe Ruth struck out 1,330 times. In between his strikeouts, he hit 714 home runs.
- Martina Navratilova lost twenty-one of her first twenty-four matches against arch-rival Chris Evert. She resolved to hit more freely on the big points and beat Evert thirty-nine out of their next fifty-seven matches. No woman tennis pro has ever won as many matches or as many tournaments, including a record nine Wimbledon singles titles, as Navratilova.
- R. H. Macy failed in retailing seven times before his store in New York became a success.
- Abraham Lincoln failed twice in business and was defeated in six state and national elections before being elected president of the United States.
- Theodor S. Geisel wrote a children's book that was rejected by twenty-three publishers. The twenty-fourth publisher sold six million copies of it—the first "Dr. Seuss" book—and that book and its successors are still staples of every children's library.
- Fred Astaire's first screen test assessment: "Losing hair. Can't sing. Can dance a little." RKO's head of production, David O. Selznick, also admitted to doubts about Astaire's "enormous ears and bad chin."[11]

- Paul Cézanne, now recognized as the father of modern painting, was refused admission to the all-powerful Paris art school, the École des Beaux-Arts.

Consider the times when you tried to learn a new game or a new sport. Maybe it was skiing, snowboarding, tennis, bridge, golf, hockey, inline skating, or the latest video game. Did you get it perfect the very first day? Not likely. Yet Urban E. Hilger Jr. once reported to us that he did get one sport right the first time he tried it. Naturally, we asked Urban to tell us about that experience, and this is what he said:

It was the first day of skiing classes. I skied all day long, and I didn't fall down once. I was so elated; I felt so good. So I skied up to the ski instructor, and I told him of my great day. You know what the ski instructor said? He told me, "Personally, Urban, I think you had a lousy day." I was stunned. "What do you mean, lousy day? I thought the objective was to stand up on these boards, not fall down." The ski instructor looked me straight in the eye and replied, "Urban, if you're not falling, you're not learning."

Urban's ski instructor understood that if you can stand up on your skis all day long the first time out, you're doing only what you already know how to do, not pushing yourself to try anything new or difficult. If your objective is to stay upright, you aren't going to improve yourself, because when you try to do something you don't know how to do, you'll fall down. That's guaranteed, as anyone who has ever learned to ski knows very well.

Nothing is ever done perfectly the first time someone tries it—not in sports, not in games, not in school, and most certainly not in organizations. Our point isn't to promote failure for failure's sake, of course. We don't advocate for a moment that failure ought to be the *objective* of any endeavor. Instead, we advocate learning. Leaders don't look for someone to blame when mistakes are made in the name of innovation. Instead, they ask, "What can be learned from the experience?" Consider the very shape of most learning curves: they invariably show performance going down before it goes up. Learning doesn't take place in the absence of mistakes.

Leaders are simply great learners. They have, to begin with, a great sense of humility about their own sense of skills and abilities, and many leaders, despite what may objectively be "extraordinary" achievements are loath to attribute them to some extraordinary competency on their part. Think about which people in your organization are the most likely to voluntarily sign up and participate in leadership development programs. Chances are they are already high, rather than low, on this set of abilities as demonstrated by their track record. Similarly, church services are populated not by sinners seeking redemption, but by ordinary souls who know that life is full of struggles, temptations, and challenges.

The only way that people can learn is by doing things they've never done before. Those who do only what they already know how to do never learn anything new. Promoting learning requires building in a tolerance for error and a framework for forgiveness. "Learning requires tolerating people who make mistakes," says Agile Software's senior vice president of product development, Joe Hage, "and it requires tolerating some inefficiencies and failures. Learning requires letting people try things they've never done before; things that they probably won't be all that good at the first time around." It means accepting the necessary trade-off between proficiency and learning.

When projects or programs don't pan out as intended at Xilinx, the conclusion is always that the project or concept failed, *not* the individuals or the group involved. Otherwise, there would be little support for innovation and experimentation, explains Clay Johnson, vice president and business development manager: "We never go first to 'Who screwed up?' but always focus on 'What was the problem, and how can we solve it or learn from it." This perspective is explained further by the company's senior HR manager, Chris Taylor: "We're not about finger-pointing. Everyone is going to make mistakes, the issue is what you do with this experience, how you grow and learn from it." Taylor explains how one product was canned ("failed"), and, in fact, the team involved with the project itself determined that it wasn't worth pursuing, even after years of intensive development. They could make that recommendation because they knew they themselves wouldn't be blamed. This same group subsequently came up with the most significant new product ever for the company—out of this so-called failure. Leaders at companies like Xilinx appreciate that learning always comes with a cost, but that the price is worth it.

We've recently discovered ways in which learning and leadership are directly related. In a series of empirical studies we found that managers could be differentiated by the range and depth of learning tactics they employ when facing a new or unfamiliar experience. For example, they may learn by "taking action" (preferring to learn by trial and error), by "thinking" (reading articles or books or going online to gain knowledge and background), by "feeling" (confronting themselves on what they are worrying about), and by "accessing others" (bouncing hopes and fears off someone they trust). We found that managers who were *more* rather than less engaged in each of these learning tactics were also *more* engaged in the Five Practices of Exemplary Leadership.[12] (See Table 8.1, which sets forth the mean scores of low and high groups on learning tactics and each leadership

Table 8.1. Learning Tactics and Leadership Practices.

Learning Tactics	Leadership Practices				
	Model	Inspire	Challenge	Enable	Encourage
Action					
Low (153)	45.7	37.0	41.4	47.9	43.8
High (159)	47.7**	40.0***	44.9***	49.1**	45.1
Thinking					
Low (148)	45.5	36.3	40.8	46.9	43.3
High (164)	47.9***	40.7***	45.2***	49.9***	45.5**
Feeling					
Low (135)	45.4	36.2	41.6	47.9	42.9
High (177)	47.8***	40.4***	44.4***	48.9	45.7***
Accessing Others					
Low (155)	45.9	36.8	42.0	47.9	42.9
High (157)	47.5	40.3***	44.4***	49.0	46.0***

Note: Numbers in parentheses refer to sample sizes, which vary as a result of median splits.
** p <.02 *** p <.001
Source: Lillas M. Brown and Barry Z. Posner, "Exploring the Relationship Between Learning and Leadership," *Leadership & Organization Development Journal,* 22(6), 274–280.

practice.) Others have shown that people more engaged in these various learning tactics were more likely to have started something from scratch, played a significant role in an acquisition, turned around an organizational unit, negotiated a major contract, and the like.[13]

There's no simple test for determining the best tactic for learning. But it is clear that leaders approach each new and unfamiliar experience with a willingness to learn, an appreciation for the importance of learning, and a recognition that learning necessarily involves making some mistakes. Neither is there a simple test for ascertaining the appropriate level of risk in a new venture. Costs and benefits, potential losses and potential gains must all be weighed. Knowing that one person's risk is another's routine activity, we must factor in the present skills of the team members and the demands of the task. But even if we could compute risk to the fifth decimal place, every innovation would still expose us to some peril. Perhaps the healthiest thing we can do is determine whether what we can learn is worth the cost. And it turns out that the ability to grow and learn under stressful, risk-abundant situations is highly dependent on how we view change.

PROMOTE PSYCHOLOGICAL HARDINESS

Uncertainty, risk, and mistakes are part of the price we pay for innovation, change, and ultimately learning. But how do we learn to accept the inevitable failures and accompanying stress of innovation, and how do we help others to handle the stress of change?

Many of us associate stress with illness. We've been led to believe that if we experience seriously stressful events, we'll become ill. If we adopt this point of view, we might as well sit back in our overstuffed easy chairs, surf through the television channels, and never venture into the world. But the reports of illness resulting from stress are misleading. Stress—even at its most strenuous—doesn't necessarily contribute to severe illness. After all, many people have experienced life-threatening, even torturous, circumstances and remained healthy. Indeed, some stress even energizes us. The personal bests shared with us by the leaders in our study are clear examples of difficult, stressful projects that generated enthusiasm and enjoyment. It isn't stress that makes us ill but how we respond to stressful events.

Approach Stress Positively

Intrigued by people who'd experienced a high degree of stress yet had a relatively low degree of illness, psychologists have hypothesized that such individuals must have a distinctive attitude toward stress.[14] Studies of psychological hardiness began with a twelve-year longitudinal study of executives at Illinois Bell Telephone as that organization experienced the firestorm of changes produced by the federal antitrust case against the Bell System and the resulting breakup of the company. Some executives were undermined by the mounting stresses of this upheaval: they had high stress scores along with high rates of illness. Yet another group of executives with equally high stress scores thrived and were below average on incidence of illness.

As the researchers had predicted, there was a clear attitudinal difference between the high-stress/high-illness group and the high-stress/low-illness group—a difference they called *psychological hardiness*. High-stress/low-illness executives made these assumptions about themselves in interaction with the world:

- They felt a strong sense of *control*, believing that they could beneficially influence the direction and outcome of what was going on around them through their own efforts. Lapsing into powerlessness, feeling like a victim of circumstances, and passivity seemed like a waste of time to them.
- They were strong in *commitment*, believing that they could find something in whatever they were doing that seemed interesting, important, or worthwhile. They were curious about what was going on around them, and this led them to find interactions with people and situations stimulating and meaningful. They were unlikely to engage in denial or feel disengaged, bored, and empty.

- They felt strong in *challenge,* believing that personal improvement and fulfillment came through the continual process of learning from both negative and positive experiences. They felt that it was not only unrealistic but also stultifying to simply expect, or even wish for, easy comfort and security.

What we found is that leaders are psychologically hardy, as expressed in their personal best case studies. They believe that, whatever is going on (successful or unsuccessful), there is value in being involved in it and learning from the experience.

There are over 650 hardiness references in the literature. Such diverse groups as armed forces personnel on peacekeeping or combat missions, officer candidates in the military, health care processionals, high school and college students, elderly people, immigrants to the United States, American civilians working overseas, those with chronic illness, police officers, basketball players, working women, and city bus drivers report consistent differences between psychologically hardy and nonhardy individuals as well.[15]

Researchers continue to find that psychological hardiness is a more important source of resistance to stress than are personal constitution, health practices, or social support. Often investigated are the effects on illness levels of various combinations of hardiness, physical exercise, and work support. Scrutiny of the role played by the particular buffers suggests a synergistic effect—and shows that hardiness, both singly and in combination with other buffers, is the most effective protector of health.[16]

People with a hardy attitude take change, risk, turmoil, and the strains of life in stride. When they encounter a stressful event—whether positive or negative—they react predictably. They consider the event engaging, they feel that they can influence the outcome, and they see it as an opportunity for development. This hardy way of framing events has been called by researchers a "learning and challenge mindset" and has been shown as crucial to executive success.[17] Managers with a "learning mindset" are characterized by a continuous sense of ongoing learning and transformation and receive the highest job performance ratings of all those studied. The next-highest performers are those with a "challenge mindset," characterized by an overwhelming sense of challenge and adventure.

These managers "were natural questioners. They reported learning early on or learning over time that it is often more important to ask questions than to seek answers. They tended to see their job as a process, not just a series of activities and tasks. . . . They used information from a variety of sources."[18] Managers with this attitude also reported more transformational events—events that altered the very fabric of their lives. These events became catalysts for change, opening up new possibilities for learning and advancement.

Apparently, it isn't just innovation and challenge that play important roles in our personal progress; it's also the way we view the challenges that come our way. If we see them as learning opportunities, we're much more likely to succeed than if we see them simply as check marks on a report card. Thus our view of events contributes to our ability to cope with change and stress: with a positive view, we can transform stressful events into manageable or desirable situations rather than regressing, ignoring, or avoiding issues and situations.

Foster Hardiness

How do we develop the hardy personality? Is it wired in our genes? Do we learn it in school? In the neighborhood? Just how do people come to have the attitudes of commitment, control, and challenge? It turns out that the family atmosphere is the most important breeding ground for a hardy attitude. When there's a varied environment, many tasks involving moderate difficulty, and family support, then hardiness flourishes, regardless of socioeconomic background. But we shouldn't resign ourselves to a life of illness or unresolved stress if we didn't grow up in the right environment. Hardiness can be learned and cultivated at any time in life.[19]

Leaders can help their constituents cope more effectively by creating a climate that develops hardiness; they can

- Build a sense of control by choosing tasks that are challenging but within the person's skill level.

- Build commitment by offering more rewards than punishments.
- Build an attitude of challenge by encouraging people to see change as full of possibilities.

This situation has two important implications for leaders. First, people can't lead if they aren't psychologically hardy. No one will follow someone who avoids stressful events and won't take decisive action. Second, even if leaders are personally very hardy, they can't enlist and retain others if they don't create an atmosphere that promotes psychological hardiness. People won't remain long with a cause that distresses them. They need to believe that they can overcome adversity if they're to accept the challenge of change. Leaders must create the conditions that make all of that possible.

The personal-best examples involved change and stressful events in the lives of leaders; they involved significant personal and organizational change. And nearly all of these cases were described in terms consistent with the conditions for psychological hardiness. Participants experienced commitment rather than alienation, control rather than powerlessness, and challenge rather than threat.

Although our cases represent a sample of only the best of times, it's instructive to know that people associate doing their best with feelings of meaningfulness, mastery, and stimulation, that people are biased in the direction of hardiness when thinking about their best. It's equally helpful to know that people don't produce excellence when feeling uninvolved, insignificant, and threatened. Furthermore, feelings of commitment, control, and challenge provide internal cues for recognizing when we're excelling and when we're only getting through the day. They tell leaders what signs to look for when assessing the capacity of their constituents to get extraordinary things done and give them guidelines to use when creating an environment for success. The relationship of risk and uncertainty to psychological hardiness is illustrated graphically in Figure 8.1; when these two forces are balanced, people feel in charge of change.

The vast majority of us can feel in charge of change at least some of the time. As the personal-best cases demonstrate, people have an intuitive sense of what makes them strong and what makes them weak. The challenge is to apply these lessons to daily life at work. As leaders, we have a responsibility

Figure 8.1. Balancing Forces in Change.

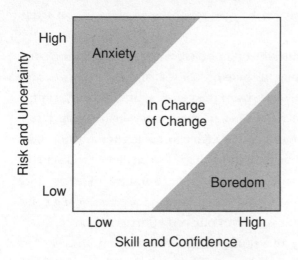

Source: Based on the work of M. Csikszentmihalyi and I. S. Csikszentmihalyi, *Optimal Experience: Psychological Studies of Flow in Consciousness* (Cambridge, U.K.: Cambridge University Press, 1988), 74; and S. R. Maddi and S. C. Kobasa, *The Hardy Executive: Health Under Stress* (Chicago: Dow Jones-Irwin, 1984).

to create an environment that breeds hardiness on a regular, not an occasional, basis. From this foundation, leaders Enable Others to Act, as the next chapters describe.

COMMITMENT NUMBER 6: EXPERIMENT AND TAKE RISKS BY CONSTANTLY GENERATING SMALL WINS AND LEARNING FROM MISTAKES

Leaders are experimenters: they experiment with new approaches to all problems. A major leadership task involves identifying and removing self-imposed constraints and organizational conventions that block innovation and creativity. Yet innovation is always risky—and leaders recognize failure as a necessary fact of the innovative life. Instead of punishing it, they encourage it; instead of trying to fix blame for mistakes, they learn from them; instead of adding rules, they encourage flexibility.

Leaders have a hardy attitude about change. They venture outside the constraints of normal routine and experiment with creative and risky solutions. They create climates in which organizational members can also accept the challenge of change.

Leaders guide and channel the often frenetic human motion of change toward some end. When things seem to be falling apart, leaders show us the exciting new world we can create from the pieces. Out of the uncertainty and chaos of change, leaders rise up and articulate a new image of the future that pulls the organization together. Through efforts such as the action steps that follow, leaders show how accepting the present challenge will actually help shape a better tomorrow. This is critical to commitment levels, since we need to believe that we're dedicating ourselves to the creation of a noble and meaningful future that is worthy of our best efforts.

By having and fostering an attitude of psychological hardiness, leaders can turn the potential turmoil and stress of innovation and change into an adventure. By getting started, taking the first step, creating small wins, leaders set the stage, creating a climate and the conditions for turning their constituents into leaders themselves.

- *Set up little experiments and develop models.*

If you're uncertain about the effect of a new idea, experiment with it first. Remember that consumer product companies try out new products in select locations before launching them in all markets. Given how quickly the window of opportunity can close, don't wait until you have a perfect product or process before trying it out. Better to run trials at the early stages of innovation than to wait until thousands, or even millions, of dollars have been spent and possibly wasted.

Evaluate your process innovations. After you've completed alpha (or first) tests, select a few beta (or second) test sites. Establish ways of quantifying the outcomes, select comparison groups, conduct pretests with your experimental and control groups, run the experiment, and measure the results. While the costs of research evaluation are often as great as the costs of the intervention itself, the learnings are usually worth the expense.

Another variation on "little experiments" is to try out lots of ideas. For example, Joe Jenkins, business manager for Jenkins Diesel Power Company

(Springfield, Missouri) asked the ten people working in the Parts Department to each generate fifteen ideas about how productivity could be boosted: five ideas about what each individual could do, five ideas about what the department could do, and five ideas about what the organization could do. He paid each person $50 for the resulting list. Joe then took all these ideas and circulated them back among all the parts department personnel and with others in the organization, asking people to select the ones they thought were most important and feasible. In a second round, he circulated the best ideas and asked folks to again pick out the "best of the best" ideas. Working with this prioritized list of ideas, the parts department improved its productivity 64.9 percent within the next twelve months.

Another very effective way to get started is to select one site or program with which to experiment and use it as a model of what you'd like to do in other programs or locations. The turnaround at the car dealerships within the Whites Group in London began with recruiting volunteers to get started on doing anything that they thought would make the customer experience more delightful. Cross-functional teams were formed and empowered to spend up to £500 (about $800) on improvements without specific management approval. Because Whites allowed teams free rein to decide what they wanted to achieve, many of the early processes were focused on their headaches—such as redoing the kitchen and cleaning up the workshop—and not necessarily on things that would have an immediate impact on customers. Managing Director Lindsay Levin understood that the more fulfilled and satisfied employees were, the more they would tend to deliver better service. The teams rapidly moved onto projects that would directly benefit the customer.

For example, parking had been a problem for customers and staff alike. A team at Camberley completely reorganized the parking lot and managed to create twenty new spaces. Flowerbeds had to be moved, concrete dividers had to be torn up, and the whole area repainted. It may sound simple but it was a major achievement, not least because it was a problem that had been talked about for years and no one had done anything about it. This experience became an example (a model, if you will) to show people what could be done. This success uplifted people's spirits, and they wanted to show how they could make a difference in their locations. Thus the parking lot became a showcase for Lindsay's dream.

When you make a model, don't require that every subsequent project or facility track it exactly. People's commitment is increased if they sense that what they're doing has its own distinctive image and is unique. If people are forced to copy the model, they won't develop a feeling of ownership of their project. Instead, use the model as a visual aid in teaching people about the principles of achieving excellence and then challenge them to improve on it and adapt it to their environment.

Models are experiments, really. As such, they can serve as laboratories for trying, failing, and learning. Challenge one of your teams to go off and experiment with something. If your organization is a small-town store whose sales per square foot need improving, team members might change the floor layout, widen the aisles, reorganize the shelves, or visit a successful competitor in the area for good ideas. Whatever team members do, your job is to encourage them to test and learn.

• *Make it safe for others to experiment.*

How do Reno Taini and Randi DuBois get people to go beyond their physical and psychological comfort levels at Pro-Action? They do it the same way that leaders make it easy for people to experiment: by doing whatever it takes to make people feel safe and secure. Reno and Randi go to great lengths to demonstrate how the safety systems work, the experience of the spotter, and the strength of the rope; this reassurance helps allay anxiety. As a leader, you must make your constituents feel equally safe if you expect them to venture out and take chances.

In the aptly titled book *Highwire Management,* Gene Calvert offers a number of specific actions that leaders can take to make others feel safe.[20] For example, he suggests verifying whether people feel ready for the new or challenging assignment, asking them how best to support their management of the risks involved, and encouraging them to ask for help whenever they need it. Calvert also suggests holding informal, face-to-face update sessions and implores, "Resist the well-meaning tendency to snoop." Another valuable suggestion he offers is to provide others the flexibility to handle any risk in their own way—unless this sets them up to fail in ways you find unaffordable or that are detrimental to them. It's also important to keep your word about not punishing people when they've done their best under the circumstances, regardless of how the situation turns out.

In making it safe for people to experiment, you must also make sure it's safe for them to challenge authority. Be aware of certain "boss" behaviors that create a sense of fear and apprehension. Abrasive and abusive conduct—such as glaring eye contact ("the Look"), silence, brevity or abruptness, snubbing or ignoring people, insults and put-downs, blaming, discrediting or discounting, aggressive mannerisms, job threats, yelling and shouting, angry outbursts, and physical threats—whether these behaviors are intentional or not—erect very thick walls of antagonism and resentment. You also generate tension by creating ambiguity—by, for example, making decisions behind closed doors or failing to acknowledge or respond to people's input and suggestions.[21] People simply won't share ideas unless they feel there's a safe, open place for them to do so.

And safety is not simply a "boss" issue. Everyone must be involved in generating this feeling of safety. Too often, people cling to the familiar and put down new ideas: "It's not in the budget." "It'll never work." "We've never done that before." When confronted with change, some tend to respond like firefighters hosing down a fire—they douse ideas before they can flare up—and thereby extinguish enthusiasm and spirit.[22] To move us out of our comfort zones, leaders should be on the lookout for ways to eliminate firehosing.

Maureen Fries, administrator of Los Olivos Women's Medical Group, knew that before she could motivate the staff to find and implement more cost-effective processes, she would have to break the atmosphere of negativism hanging over the department. Discussing how negativism was draining the department of the energy needed to actively meet new challenges, Maureen introduced the staff to the idea of firehosing at a meeting. One staff member suggested that anyone heard firehosing should be required to contribute 25 cents to a fund. Everyone agreed, and the policy went into effect immediately.

As this meeting (and subsequent meetings) progressed, Maureen listened with amazement as staff members began to think more carefully about what they were saying in order not to be—or sound—negative. Team members policed each other on a daily basis. "You owe me a quarter!" could be overheard across the department; collection jars could be found everywhere.

Morale improved noticeably, as did the number of innovative ideas. The jars were a physical reminder of the importance of keeping a positive attitude about new possibilities.

• *Break mindsets.*

Mired down in a numbing daily routine, people often behave automatically, stop thinking for themselves, and just form unquestioning attitudes, or mindsets, based on the first information they hear.[23] Yet organizations—and the worlds in which they operate—are constantly undergoing internal and external change. As the ancient saying goes, "You can never step into the same river twice, because the water is always flowing."

Leaders encourage people to break out of mindsets by questioning routines, challenging assumptions, and, with respect to appreciating diversity, continually looking at what is going on from variously changing perspectives. Don't let success lead to mindsets or get in the way of learning. Toyota's chief of personnel, Iwao Isomura, put it this way: "Our current success is the best reason to change things."[24]

How we get into mindsets is well illustrated in one experiment where a collection of objects was introduced to one group of people by saying, "This is a hair dryer," and "This is a dog's chew toy," and so on. Another group was introduced to the same objects but were told "This *could be* a hair dryer," and "This *could be* a dog's chew toy," and so on. Later, the experimenters for both groups invented a need for an eraser—and only those people who had been conditionally introduced to the objects thought to use the dog's toy in this new way.[25] The intuitive understanding that a single thing is, or could be, many things, depending upon how you look at it, is central to the learning climate created by leaders.

At United Electric Controls Company they worked hard at pushing people out of preconceived ideas and mindsets.[26] Everywhere you looked, people were using devices that they themselves invented—to work faster or test more accurately or track materials more closely. Operations vice president Bruce Hamilton explained: "It's the process of arriving at those ideas—even thinking about them—that we want to reward, not just the result. A person may come up with nine ideas that save a dollar apiece, then the tenth saves

$50,000. People hate rejection. If you reject the first few, you don't get the last one." United Electric Controls learned this lesson the hard way.

Over the previous twenty years, employees had slipped a mere two dozen or so ideas into the company's suggestion box. Not only was the procedure drawn out and intimidating but management had a reputation for implementing employees' ideas without giving them credit. These days almost everyone contributes ideas via one forum or another. Their initiative, among other rewards, earns them chances in monthly, quarterly, and annual drawings for such prizes as sports tickets, getaway weekends, and even a week-long cruise. About two-thirds of all ideas are implemented.

One big reason for this turnaround was that employees thought about things that they could do, rather than pointing out what other people were doing wrong (and needed to get right). That explains the aquarium test that Harry Moumdjian came up with to ensure that his parts were watertight, Cheryl O'Connell's rolling pegboard for storing inventory labels, and Bob Comeau's spool rack (born out of Bob's desire to relieve the pain of lifting spools of wire). Just day-to-day improvements, fostered by involved and liberated people. The benefits to the company? Over a four-year period inventories were cut by 60 percent, work-in-progress reduced 90 percent, on-time deliveries increased from 65 percent to a consistent 95 percent, and sales expanded by over 30 percent.

• *Break it up and break it down.*

Try this exercise. Take a hundred cards and count them one at a time. Now count again, this time stacking the cards in ten piles of ten. Which was easier and faster? We bet it was the ten piles of ten. Why? Because—as with most of life's tasks—you were probably interrupted (even if only by a thought), losing your place and having to start all over again. Breaking things into smaller tasks is a smart tactic. South Africa's Archbishop Desmond Tutu appreciated this perspective in dealing with the consequences of apartheid. The process of reconciliation, he explained, would require understanding that "you can't eat an elephant in one bite."

Once you've set your sights, move forward incrementally. Don't attempt to accomplish too much at once, especially in the beginning. Break large groups and goals into small, cohesive teams and doable tasks. Provide orientation and training at the start of every new project, even if members of the team are experienced. Every new project has a shakedown period: group members may not have worked together before, and the project is likely to be unique.

Make sure you include a few early successes in your plan. There's nothing more discouraging than being confronted initially with tasks that you don't know how to do and at which you know you'll fail. Assigning tasks that team members are unequipped to handle is like sending a group of novices to the top of the expert ski slope. Instead, let people start on the beginners' slope and work their way up to the advanced. Identify a doable project that people feel they can accomplish with existing skills and resources.

That's just what Rayona Sharpnack did when she was coaching her eight-year-old daughter's softball team. Rayona certainly knew the game: she was the first player-manager in the 1980s of the most profitable franchise of the International Women's Professional Softball League. Before that, she set a Junior Olympic record by throwing a softball 189 feet. On one of the first days of practice for her daughter's team, she had everyone try to do some batting. As she explains:

I take a really soft, spongy ball, and I toss it to the first girl. She's standing maybe 10 feet away, I'm throwing baby tosses, and she screams and hides her head. So I say, "Hey, no problem, Suzy. Go to the back of the line. That's fine. Betsy, you step up." Next girl in line. She does the same thing—buries her head and screams. So I'm realizing that this is going to be a really long practice if we don't do something different.

I go out to my car where I have my handy whiteboard markers in my briefcase. I take the bag of practice balls and draw four smiley faces—red, black, blue, and green—on each ball. When you look at a ball, all you see is one smiley face. I go back out and call the girls back over: "Okay. We're going to play a different game this time," I say. "This time, your job is to name the color of the smiley face. That's all you have to do."

So little Suzy stands up, and I toss a ball by her. She watches it all the way and goes, "Red." Next girl, Betsy, gets up there. Betsy goes, "Green."

They're all just chirping with excitement because they can identify the color of the smiley face, so I say, "Okay. Now I want you to do the same thing, only this time I want you to hold the bat on your shoulder when the ball goes by." Same level of success. Excitement builds. The third time through, I ask them to touch the smiley face with the bat.

We beat our opponents 27 to 1 in the first game.[27]

Do as Rayona did and keep people focused on the meaning and significance of the vision, and remind them to take it one day at a time (or one hour at a time, if necessary). Implement things in small, planned increments. As most college students who've pulled an all-nighter before a final exam come to realize, it's a lot more productive to make a little progress daily than to attempt to do the whole task all at once.

• *Give people choices.*

Give people a *choice* about being part of what's happening, and they're much more likely to be committed. Choice builds commitment and creates ownership, and making people feel like owners is key. Unless people feel like owners, unless they have choices to make, they can't truly exercise personal responsibility.

Choice can be as simple as talking over a change with your team. What needs to be done? Who's going to do what? What decisions will people have to make along the way? If you already have established a clear vision, built a team consensus, and shared strong feelings about the right way to do things in your organization, you have an opportunity for "guided autonomy." Your team can autonomously determine how to reach the summit, with team members guided by the agreed-upon direction. Although choice is always bounded, people have varying amounts of space within which to operate. The larger the space, the greater the maneuvering room. The art of leadership lies in knowing how to create a sense of spaciousness while staying focused on the horizon.

That's just what Andy Hodges did as district manager for the U.S. Postal Service in Atlanta, Georgia. When he was transferred to Atlanta (from the highly successful district based in Albany, New York), his new district, with over thirteen thousand employees, was near the bottom rung, among eighty-seven districts, on nearly every metric used by the USPS. By first "spending lots of time listening," Andy found out what people felt was good and bad about their operations. Then he gave his senior management team a choice by saying: "Let's find something we can be the best at." Andy explained that he didn't care what they wanted to select; the important thing was that they would all agree on a metric, an aspect of their operation, that they all believed they were capable of showing some significant improvement, possibly even being one of the best in the nation. From experience, Andy knew that whatever metric they selected, achieving significant improvement in that area would necessarily require significant improvements in a number of other areas as well. (He also knew that they didn't have to consciously choose all of these at the start, because to do so might be too overwhelming.)

After one year, they were not yet the best in the nation on their chosen metric. But they had achieved the single biggest improvement from one year to the next of any operation in the country, and with that achievement they were poised for the future.

• *Accumulate yeses.*

Yes is a magical word and a powerful tool for bringing people closer. Be on the lookout for opportunities to say yes: "Yes, you have a point there." "Yes, I can understand that." Say yes as often as possible and try to *get* as many yeses from others as you can. When people say yes to one another their relationship changes, transforming a potential argument into the beginning of a reasoned dialogue.

In addition, don't say *but,* say "yes, *and.*" When people hear a but they think you disagree with them and that you are about to try to prove them wrong. Unfortunately, an all-too-common reaction is to stop listening. People will be more receptive if you first acknowledge their views with a *yes* and then preface your own with an *and.* In this way, your views can be seen as an addition, not a contradiction, to their own point of view.[28]

If reaching agreement on the whole idea or package of shared values seems impossible at first, try breaking up the agreement into steps. Each partial agreement can open up opportunities that were not evident at the outset. Start where people are, with the easiest issue for them to agree with.

By moving progressively from the easier to the more difficult issues, you can get people in the habit of saying yes and showing them that agreement is possible. If people are reluctant to make even a small agreement, then you don't have to press for an immediate concession. Set people at ease by reassuring them that they need not make a final commitment until the very end when they can see exactly what they will get in return.

• *Admit your mistakes.*

What happens when there is a screw-up? It may be an innovation, a bad decision, or a dropped ball—someone didn't do what they said they would do. Then what?

When someone provides you with poor service, what do you expect? Well, at a minimum, most people expect an apology, an acknowledgment that a mistake was made and that it will be rectified. If leadership is viewed as a service, then shouldn't leaders hold themselves as leaders to the same standards? We believe that leaders should apologize and atone for their mistakes. After all, their mistakes may cause inconvenience, loss, and possibly injury.

But doesn't admitting mistakes damage credibility? If clients and colleagues know the leader has failed, won't they be more likely to think the leader is incompetent? Our evidence suggests that acting in ways to hide mistakes will be much more damaging and will, in fact, erode credibility. When asked to explain how they know if someone is honest, the most frequent response people give is, "They tell the truth." When probed further, people say that an honest person "admits making mistakes." By admitting you were wrong, you can build credibility rather than destroy it. If someone makes too many mistakes, of course, that could damage credibility on the dimension of competence. But early recognition and admission of mistakes promotes learning, which in turn prevents similar errors in the future.

The point is that leaders are human, too. They are saying: "Look, I don't know everything about how to do this. I am a humble servant just like you. Together we'll figure it out if we all dedicate ourselves to the same set of values and common purpose. My job is to let you know that we are serious about this and to do my best to live up to our collective beliefs. Don't expect perfection; do expect dedication. If I don't show you dedication, then judge me not to be credible. If I make a few mistakes along the way, though, make sure you tell me so that you and I can learn."

We spent a lot of time in our interviews exploring whether or not it was possible for people to make a mistake and not lose their credibility. People told us that making a mistake (even now and then) doesn't have to destroy credibility. First, it depends upon overall track record. It's hard to break through this Catch-22 of needing experience to develop a track record, which requires making some mistakes but not enough that your place on the track is taken over by someone else. Second, it depends upon whether there is evidence that you have learned from your experience. That is, do you make this same mistake again?

The logic is easy to understand in terms of product reliability or customer service; it also applies to each of us as individuals. To use a typically American metaphor, we tend to give people "three strikes and you're out!" The first time someone makes a mistake, we say, "He's still learning." The second time, we say, "Slow learner." The third time, it's "He'll never learn!"

This perspective is echoed by Bob Phillips, president and CEO at Guide Dogs for the Blind: "Let's say a new program doesn't make its projections the first year. Well, everyone's disappointed. But this 'mistake' doesn't really affect credibility so long as the process was one in which everyone was involved, we challenged assumptions, we examined alternatives, feelings were expressed openly, and people listened and heard one another's ideas and apprehensions, and then we made a collective decision." What this involves, Bob goes on to explain, "is making leadership (and innovation) not just an individual issue but using the process to enhance the leadership and imagination of everyone in the group." Certainly these are goals worth the risk.

• Conduct pre- and postmortems for every project.

No matter what your position or location, learning from mistakes—yours and others'—is key. Indeed, we sometimes suggest that participants in our training programs write a case on their personal-worst leadership experience. Although it's tempting to let painful memories fade, the lessons from failure are too precious to go unrecorded.

At the completion of a project (or at periodic intervals during it) take the team through a review retreat. Build the agenda around four questions:

- What did we do well? Or, what are we doing well at the moment?
- What did we do poorly? Or, what are we doing poorly?
- What did we learn from this? Or, what are we learning from this project?
- How can we do better the next time? Or, how can we be doing better than we are currently?

Make sure that everyone contributes. Record all the ideas visibly on chart paper and then type up the notes and make them available to everyone. Take immediate action as needed when you return, and begin the next project with a review of any lessons learned. Says Xilinx's director of product development, Steve Douglass: "We hold informal postmortem sessions so we can look at the issues we ran into and discuss what we can do differently to avoid them on the next project." On a more general level, the lessons learned are communicated to project teams around the company, "so that we can develop best practices based on everyone's cumulative experiences."

Another idea is to fix problems before they happen. At Klein Associates, work groups conduct a "pre-mortem" to discover the possibly hidden flaws and mine fields in any new projects. It works like this: When a team gathers to kick off a new project, people conclude that meeting by pretending to gaze into a crystal ball: "Look six months into the future. The news is not good. Despite our hopes, the project has failed. How did this happen?" Then team members take three minutes to run a mental simulation: They write down why they think their work derailed. All sorts of reasons emerge. For example: "There were too many distractions." "The project was overly ambitious." "We pushed the project too much in our own self-interests, without considering those of our partners."

Gary Klein, the company's founder and its chief scientist, finds that the group's comments are unusually candid, and that's because the context of this conversation is very different from a critique. The entire focus is on trying to understand why the project failed. By looking six months into the future, people feel secure enough to say what they really think. Each comment is recorded, so that everyone knows the potential speed bumps before they go forward. Pre-mortems help people work smarter and keep them from being overly confident at the start.[29]

At the Whites Group, they use a similar technique, which they call the "worse case scenario." They imagine what it could be like if things don't quite go the way they expect them to. For example:

- Your management team think it's the wrong way to go.
- People throughout the organization don't seem to buy in.
- It's demanding far more of your time than you thought it would.
- Things are progressing really slowly.
- The bottom line is going to suffer in the short term.
- People have bought into the vision now, but don't seem to want to take the first step and make any changes today.
- Things seem to be progressing well—but small, careless comments by people in leadership positions really undermine all the efforts.
- You try to communicate—you know you communicate—but still people say they haven't been informed.
- You can see the improvements and you know that others can too, but you don't have the right measures and facts to illustrate this.
- Improvements have been made, but everyone's expectations have also gone up, so people still complain!

This sounds like a very negative list, but Managing Director Lindsay Levin says that all of these things happened, and more, in the process of her personal best leadership experience. Any of them could happen to you! What are you going to do to ensure that if they do happen, you can cope with them? Use a list like this one, stressing that it's a worse case scenario, and get everyone's ideas about how to avoid or minimize these risks, and deal effectively with them—as they (inevitably) arise.

COMMITMENT NUMBER 6

EXPERIMENT AND TAKE RISKS BY CONSTANTLY GENERATING SMALL WINS AND LEARNING FROM MISTAKES

- *Set up little experiments and develop models.*

- *Make it safe for others to experiment.*

- *Break mindsets.*

- *Break it up and break it down.*

- *Give people choices.*

- *Accumulate yeses.*

- *Admit your mistakes.*

- *Conduct pre- and postmortems for every project.*

Source: The Leadership Challenge by James M. Kouzes and Barry Z. Posner. Copyright © 2002.

PART FIVE

Enable Others to Act

9 FOSTER COLLABORATION

Do not think that you are the best and that you can do everything all by yourself—only teamwork brings the best results.

Hans-Ulrich Schaer, The Information Management Group (Switzerland)

Even higher levels of skill in working with others are required because nothing is staying the same.

Claudio Fernández-Aráoz, Egon Zehnder International

Early in our research, we asked Bill Flanagan, then director of manufacturing of Amdahl Corporation, to describe his personal best. After a few moments, Bill said that he couldn't do it. We were startled by his response—until he explained: "It wasn't *my* personal best. It was *our* personal best. It wasn't *me*. It was *us*."

In the thousands of cases we've studied, we've yet to encounter a single example of extraordinary achievement that's occurred without the active involvement and support of many people. We've yet to find a single instance in which one talented person—leader or individual contributor—accounted for most, let alone 100 percent, of the success. Throughout the years, leaders from all professions, from all economic sectors, and from around the globe continue to tell us, "You can't do it alone." Leadership is not a solo act, it's a team effort.

In the personal-best cases there were also no reports that creating competition between group members was the way to achieve the highest levels of performance. Quite the contrary. People spoke passionately about teamwork and cooperation as the interpersonal route to success, particularly when the conditions were extremely challenging and urgent.

Turbulence in the marketplace, it turns out, requires more collaboration, not less.[1] A quick online search of the Library of Congress for works related to collaboration, for example, yields more than 10,000 titles. The increasing emphasis on networks, business-to-business and peer-to-peer e-commerce, strategic acquisitions, and knowledge work, along with the surging number of global alliances and local partnerships, is testimony to the fact that in an ever more complex, wired world, the winning strategies will be based upon the *"we* not *I"* philosophy. Collaboration is a social imperative.[2] Without it we can't get extraordinary things done in organizations.

COLLABORATION IMPROVES PERFORMANCE

Collaboration is *the* critical competency for achieving and sustaining high performance—especially in the Internet Age![3] It won't be the ability to fiercely compete but the ability to lovingly cooperate that will determine success.

Jim Kouzes writes,

This was made glaringly obvious when I first had DSL (Digital Subscriber Line) service installed in my home office. The experience seemed never-ending: It took at least six different vendors before the service was functioning, and those were just the ones with whom I was in direct contact. There was my ISP, the DSL provider, the supplier of the router, the local phone company for the outside wiring, the company that connected the phone line to the router, and a tech support person I hired once it got too weird, too technical, and too time-consuming for me to coordinate. At one point, with three of us on a conference line trying to figure out why the router wouldn't route, I overheard one vendor scold another. "And these folks," I thought to myself, "are supposed to make my life easier? If that's going to happen, first they need to learn how to get along."

Then after less than a year, my DSL provider declared bankruptcy and disconnected 100,000 customers. I waited three weeks for the new DSL provider to install the service—and it didn't work. It took at least six separate visits from the voice people and the data people—who were in different divisions in the same company and wouldn't talk to each other—before it worked properly!

Broadband may be key to speed and performance on the Internet, but unless high-tech companies—or low-tech companies, for that matter—get their acts together, a lot more will go broke. It won't be because of a failure of technology. It'll be a failure of relationships. In the Old, New, or Next Economy learning to work well together was, is, and always will be a critical success factor.

Rather than focusing on stomping the competition into the ground, exemplary leaders focus on creating value for their customers, intelligence and skill in their students, wellness in their patients, and pride in their citizens. In a world that's trying to do more with less, competitive strategies naturally lose to strategies that promote collaboration. Maybe that's why we're seeing so many strategic alliances these days: cooperation and collaboration make good business sense.[4] For leaders, the message is clear: *collaborate to succeed!*

Indeed, world-class performances aren't possible unless there's a strong sense of shared creation and shared responsibility. To Foster Collaboration, leaders are essential who can skillfully:

- Create a climate of trust
- Facilitate positive interdependence
- Support face-to-face interactions

With multiple constituencies come diverse and frequently conflicting interests—and these *essentials* become particularly key. As paradoxical as it might seem, leadership is *more* essential—not less—when collaboration is required.

CREATE A CLIMATE OF TRUST

At the heart of collaboration is trust. It's *the* central issue in human relationships within and outside organizations. Without trust you cannot lead. Without trust you cannot get extraordinary things done. Individuals who are unable to trust others fail to become leaders, precisely because they can't bear to be dependent on the words and work of others. So they either end up doing all the work themselves or they supervise work so closely that they become overcontrolling. Their obvious lack of trust in others results in others' lack of trust in them.

Carolyn Borne is program director of the Women's Health Initiative (WHI) in the Department of Obstetrics and Gynecology in the School of Medicine at the University of California, Los Angeles (UCLA). The WHI, a National Institutes of Health (NIH) study begun in 1991, is one of the largest and most ambitious longitudinal studies of postmenopausal women's health concerns ever undertaken, involving some forty-five centers across the United States and over 165,000 women. It requires careful planning, analytical ability, and meticulous attention to detail, and, because of the sensitivity, significance, and collaborative nature of the study, it also requires a high degree of trust. But that wasn't how Carolyn found it. When she first joined as program director, during the recruitment phase of the study, the WHI group lacked collaboration, respect, and trust for each other. People did not socialize; there was a lack of trust and support. The emphasis seemed to be competition rather than cooperation. Hard as they were working, they were not at the expected national study goal for recruitment. Productivity and morale were low.

Carolyn took immediate steps to create a different kind of climate, a climate of trust and respect. She did a needs assessment, in which she interviewed each staff member, and "found the group was enthusiastic about the study but frustrated because of a lack of systems, organization, and teamwork. Each member of the team was a talented professional, but ready to quit. They all liked their jobs, but did not feel supported." Having identified the sources of frustration, Carolyn's goal then became increasing group cohesion through improved communication among each other. As Carolyn put it: "We started creating a team environment with a day-long retreat in which we began to identify our values, philosophy, and mission. We shared stories about families and loved ones and began to feel a sense of trust and respect for each other."

She understood that to create a climate of trust she needed to determine what the group needed and build the team around purpose and respect. Just as Carolyn did, leaders put trust on the agenda; they don't leave it to chance. As a leader, you have to make a conscious effort to create and sustain trust.

Trusting Others Pays Off

Several major research studies support the trust-building actions taken by exemplary leaders.[5] For example, in a PricewaterhouseCoopers study on corporate innovation in companies listed on the Financial Times 100, trust was "the number one differentiator" between the top 20 percent of companies surveyed and the bottom 20 percent. The top performers' trust empowered individuals to turn strategic aims into reality.[6] The more trusted we feel, the better we innovate.

Psychologists have also found that people who are trusting are more likely to be happy and psychologically adjusted than are those who view the world with suspicion and disrespect.[7] We like people who are trusting and seek them out as friends. We listen to people we trust and accept their influence. Thus the most effective leadership situations are those in which each member of the team trusts the others.

In another study, several groups of business executives in a role-playing exercise were given identical factual information about a difficult manufacturing-marketing policy decision and then asked to solve a problem related to that information as a group. Half of the groups were briefed to expect trusting behavior ("You have learned from your past experiences that you can trust the other members of top management and can openly express feelings and differences with them"); the other half, to expect untrusting behavior.

After thirty minutes of discussion, each team member completed a brief questionnaire. Other executives, who had been observing the team meetings, also completed the questionnaire. The responses of team members and observers were quite consistent: the group members who'd been told that their role-playing peers and manager could be trusted reported their discussion and decisions to be significantly more positive than did the members of the low-trust group on *every* factor measured. In the high-trust group,

- Members were more open about feelings.
- Members experienced greater clarity about the group's basic problems and goals.
- Members searched more for alternative courses of action.
- Members reported greater levels of mutual influence on outcomes, satisfaction with the meeting, motivation to implement decisions, and closeness as a management team as a result of the meeting.

In the group whose participants were told that their manager wasn't to be trusted, genuine attempts by the manager to be open and honest were ignored or distorted. Distrust was so strong that members viewed the manager's candor as a clever attempt to deceive them, and generally reacted by sabotaging the manager's efforts even further. Managers who experienced rejection of their attempts to be trusting and open responded in kind. Said one who played the manager role, "If I had my way I would have fired the entire group. What a bunch of turkeys. I was trying to be honest with them but they wouldn't cooperate. Everything I suggested they shot down; and they wouldn't give me any ideas on how to solve the problem."[8]

The responses of the other members were no less hostile. Said one, "Frankly, I was looking forward to your being fired. I was sick of working with you—and we had only been together for ten minutes."[9] Not surprisingly, more than two-thirds of the participants in the low-trust group said that they would give serious consideration to looking for another position. People don't want to stay very long in organizations devoid of trust.

It's crucial to keep in mind that this was *a simulation;* participants were executives from various organizations attending an executive development program. They behaved and responded as they did simply because they'd been told that they couldn't trust their role-playing manager. Their actions showed that trust or distrust can come with a mere suggestion—and in mere minutes.

After this simulation, participants were asked to think about what factors might have accounted for the differences between the outcomes and feelings reported by the various groups in the experiment. Not one person perceived that trust had been the overriding variable. One executive in the study reported this insight: "I never knew that a lack of trust was our problem (at work) until that exercise. I knew that things weren't going well, but I never really could quite understand why we couldn't work well together. After that experience, things fell into place."[10]

To put it quite simply, trust is the most significant predictor of individuals' satisfaction with their organizations.[11] When leaders create a climate of trust, they take away the controls and allow people to be free to innovate and contribute. Trusting leaders nurture openness, involvement, personal satisfaction, and high levels of commitment to excellence.

Be Open to Influence

Brian Coughlin was an outsider when he took on the challenge of managing director of Brown Brothers Harriman Fund Administration Services Ireland. But, as he tells it, "I just jumped in. I wanted to know what all the aspects of the business were doing. I wanted to get to know the individuals involved, to understand who they were, what motivated them, and how we could work collectively to achieve things. I attempted to be open, honest, and consistent. I made a conscious effort to listen and learn from them—the local experts."

Brian knew that especially early on with a new group he needed to build trust. He also knew that he couldn't mandate changes, especially when he didn't yet know the people or the organization. Instead he had to listen and learn. His openness to influence from the "local experts" quickly earned Brian the respect of his new colleagues, and enabled all of them to significantly improve the quality of their services.

Knowing that trust is key, exemplary leaders make sure that they consider alternative viewpoints, and they make use of other people's expertise and abilities. Because they're more trusting of their groups, they're also more willing to let others exercise influence over group decisions. It's a reciprocal process. By demonstrating an openness to influence, leaders contribute to building the trust that enables their constituents to be more open to their influence. Trust begets trust.

In contrast, managers who create distrustful environments often take self-protective postures. They're directive and hold tight to the reins of power. Those who work for such managers are likely to pass the distrust on by withholding and distorting information.[12]

Brian sums up the success of his own openness to influence this way: "We had people from all levels of the organization talking to each other about ways of doing things differently and better. We had tremendous amounts of success identifying opportunities for improvement. We were able to mobilize people because they all had a sense of ownership and commitment." Isn't this exactly what all leaders want?

Make Yourself Vulnerable

Trust is built when we make ourselves vulnerable to others whose subsequent behavior we can't control.[13] If neither person in a relationship takes the risk of trusting at least a little, the relationship is inhibited by caution and suspicion. If leaders want the higher levels of performance that come with trust and collaboration, they must demonstrate their trust *in* others before asking for trust *from* others. Leaders go first, as the word implies. That includes going first in the area of trust.

Going first to trust is akin to what psychologists refer to as "self-disclosure." Letting others know what we stand for, what we value, what we want, what we hope for, what we're willing (and not willing) to do means disclosing information about ourselves. That can be risky. We can't be certain that other people will appreciate our candor, agree with our aspirations, want to enroll, or interpret our words and actions in the way we intend. But once leaders take the risk of being open, others are more likely to take a similar risk—and thereby take the next step necessary to build interpersonal trust.

Imagine the following scenario: Your work group is at an offsite meeting, participating in some team-building exercises, one of which is the "trust fall." Team members stand in two rows of six people each, about two feet apart, and facing each other. At the head of the rows is a step ladder. Each team member is going to be invited to step onto the top of the four-foot ladder, turn to face away from the group, cross both arms, remain straight and stiff, and then fall over backward. The team's common goal is to catch each person by putting their arms up at exactly the same time, making a safe cradle for each falling colleague.

Pretend you're the third person in line. The first person climbs the ladder, and on cue falls over backward. Every member of the team reaches out and catches the person. They lower her safely to the ground. "Way to go!" everyone shouts. "Great teamwork!" The faller heaves a big sigh of relief, and thanks everyone for doing their jobs. The second person now goes up to the top of the ladder. On cue, he falls over backward. But a few members of the team aren't paying attention, and don't put their arms up. The group can't catch him. He falls to the ground, getting the wind knocked out of him. And you're next! How are you feeling? In addition to being concerned for the welfare of your colleague, are you more or less trusting of the group members? Are you more or less willing to take a personal risk? Our guess is that you're less trusting as well as less willing to risk.

It doesn't take an offsite to experience this: variations of the trust fall occur at work all the time. Trust is built as people get to know each other and their leaders. Personally sharing your weaknesses as well as your strengths is one way to do that. Of course there are risks. You might end up looking off-the-wall, weak, or incompetent. But the risks are well worth it in creating a trustworthy system.

Listen, Listen, Listen

Sensitivity to people's needs and interests is a key ingredient in building trust. The simple act of listening to what other people have to say and appreciating their unique points of view demonstrates your respect for others and their ideas.

People listen more attentively to those who listen to them. For instance, in one management simulation, whenever the person assuming the role of chief executive officer was informed that the financial vice president was a "friend," the latter's influence was far more readily accepted than when their relationship was merely professional—even though in all cases the "information" presented was adequate to solve the company's problem.[14] Friends and family are the most important sources of believable information about everything from health care to restaurants, and leaders who listen are more likely to become accepted as members of the family than those who don't.

Harry Cleberg certainly acted like one of the family, though you might not assume it from his title. When we interviewed Harry, he was CEO of Farmland Industries, then the largest farmer-owned cooperative in North America. Farmland had sales in all fifty U.S. states and nearly sixty countries and was one of the top two hundred Fortune 500 companies. Despite his position in a huge global enterprise, more often than not you'd find Harry in his Ford pickup heading out to a farm cooperative, not on Wall Street or at the company's headquarters. About two hundred days a year, Harry traveled to meet with the cooperative members and Farmland employees. His purpose was getting to know the people and listening; in fact, he called the small-group sessions his "listening posts." Harry didn't let long distances get in his way, nor did he listen passively. Instead, he was likely to be helping out as well. Typical was his behavior as he strode into the Farmland Feed Mill in Muncie on one occasion, calling, "Anybody home? Got anything around here I can do?"[15]

By attitude and action, Harry was earning the trust of his constituents. High-tech and low-tech leaders take note: when someone of Harry's stature and success spends over two-thirds of his time listening and offering a helping hand, you may want to reassess how you allocate your time. How many of your days are spent out in the field listening to your colleagues? How does your devotion to listening stack up?

FACILITATE POSITIVE INTERDEPENDENCE

At the beginning of the new millennium, millions tuned in to watch *Survivor*, the latest rage in "reality-TV." With its competitive games, petty rivalries, back-stabbing betrayals, tribal councils, a modest tease of sex and romance, and cliff-hanger endings the show was a hit. During the peak weeks of the show, we'd find some of our clients using *Survivor* as a case study in how to be successful in the world of business. A carefully staged and edited production had become an entertainment phenomenon—and a classroom for the corporate world. To us, this was troubling. Riveting or not, *Survivor* teaches all the wrong lessons about how to survive in the "real world." In the real world, if people were to behave as these players on television did, they'd all be dead. As the acclaimed anthropologist Lionel Tiger put it when commenting on the first *Survivor* series, "The contest format distorted savagely what would have otherwise been a very different outcome involving ongoing cooperation. The behavior on the island is also not a reflection of corporate America, as has been suggested. It is a reflection of the nature of the prize, and what winning it demanded. The goal of human survival has always been to endure for another day, and in the group."[16]

Survivor lacked all the elements of a cooperative effort. While the alliance-building gave an appearance of working together, these alliances were nothing more than transparent means of beating the other players. Everything was structured to support the victory of only one person in the end. Exemplary leaders recognize that such self-serving behavior is the path to organizational suicide, and that successful leaders and team members subordinate their own goals to the service of a greater good.

One of the most significant ingredients to cooperation and collaboration missing from *Survivor* was a sense of interdependence, a condition where everyone knows that they cannot succeed unless everyone else succeeds, or at least that they can't succeed unless they coordinate their efforts. If there's no sense that "we're all in this together," that the success of one depends on the success of the other, then it's virtually impossible to create the conditions for positive teamwork. To get extraordinary things done, we have to rely on each other. We need to have a sense of mutual dependence—a community of people each of whom knows that they need the others to be successful.

Director Sidney Lumet, whose films include such cinematic greats as *12 Angry Men* and *Network,* understands what it takes to be successful as a leader of a group of highly talented and very demanding people. In talking about his role as a director, he says:[17]

But how much in charge am I? *Is* the movie *un Film de Sidney Lumet?* I'm dependent on weather, budget, what the leading lady had for breakfast, who the leading man is in love with. I'm dependent on the talents and idiosyncrasies, the moods and egos, the politics and personalities, of more than a hundred different people. And that's just in the making of the movie. At this point I won't even begin to discuss the studio, financing, distribution, marketing, and so on.

So how independent am I? Like all bosses—and on the set, I'm the boss—I'm the boss only up to a point. And to me that's what's so exciting. I'm in charge of a community that I need desperately and that needs me just as badly. That's where the joy lies, in the shared experience. Anyone in the community can help me or hurt me.

Lumet has captured the essence of the second condition for cooperation and collaboration. Leaders have to take an active role in creating a positive context and structure for cooperation and collaboration. Among the most important actions a leader can undertake to create conditions in which people know they can count on each other are to develop cooperative goals and roles, support norms of reciprocity, and reward joint effort.

Develop Cooperative Goals and Roles

Mike Ricci is the alternate captain of the San Jose Sharks, a team in the National Hockey League. An experienced player with the distinction of being on a Stanley Cup winning team, and a leader on all the teams on which he's played, Mike knows a thing or two about teamwork. When we talked to him about the lessons from hockey that might apply to business, here's one of the things he told us:

> If everything around you is falling apart . . . no one person's going to make a difference, but if everyone makes a little bit of a difference, you can get to where you want to go. That's what happens when the hockey team struggles. One guy's not going to pull you out of it, or two guys. If everyone pulls a little harder on the rope, then you're going to do what you've got to do by the end of the day.

Whether it's hockey or health care, education or financial services, for a team of people to have a positive experience together, they must have shared goals that provide a specific reason for being together. No one person can completely teach a child, build a quality car, connect a customer to the Internet, or treat a patient. Even in hockey, where one person shoots the puck into the net, more often than not someone else gets an assist. No one can do it alone. A focus on a collective purpose binds people into cooperative efforts. Shared values and visions serve this function for the long term, and group goals provide this same common focus for the shorter term.

Similarly, tasks must be structured so that each person's job makes a contribution to the end result. Certainly individuals within the group each have distinct roles, but on world-class teams everyone knows they can't achieve the group goals unless they all play their individual parts. After all, if you could do it alone, why would you need a team? Soccer isn't a one-on-eleven sport, hockey isn't one-on-six. They require team effort—as do all organizations. For cooperation to succeed, tasks must be designed so that every person contributes something unique and independent to the final outcome. All the individuals must clearly understand that unless they each contribute whatever they can, the team fails. It's like putting together a jigsaw puzzle. We each have a piece, and if even one piece is missing the picture is impossible to complete.

Support Norms of Reciprocity

When we first met Antonio Zárate, he was in the process of leading a successful turnaround of Metalsa, an automotive metal stamping company in Mexico. Antonio knew that Mexican people shared values that were hospitable to quality service—and they were somehow inhibited from expressing them at work. He suspected that the bureaucratic and autocratic nature of traditional Mexican business practices prevented tapping into the best efforts and the will of the people. This would have to change if Metalsa was to become competitive in world markets.

Antonio believed that people at all levels were expected to treat others with mutual respect and fairness. "We say that people have to live to serve instead of living to be served," he says. Antonio was equally adamant about solidarity, asking rhetorically, "When you want to conquer your enemy, you try to divide them; so why divide our own company?"

One of the methods that Antonio used to foster a sense of mutual benefit was to create a unique approach to departmental budgeting. At the beginning of each month, every department received the total amount of its monthly operating budget as a lump-sum payment—in the form of play money. How the money was "spent" was entirely up to the department's discretion. (Training and maintenance budgets weren't affected by this exercise.) At the end of the year, Metalsa exchanged 50 percent of any play money a department had remaining for an equivalent amount of real currency, which was then distributed equally among all the members of the department. It was simple and it worked: all personnel knew that if they helped their department keep its expenses below budget, they'd be rewarded at the end of the year in proportion to their cooperative success.

In any effective long-term relationship, there must be a sense of mutuality. If one partner always gives and the other always takes, the one who gives will feel taken advantage of and the one who takes will feel superior. In that climate, cooperation is virtually impossible. To develop cooperative relationships, leaders must quickly establish norms of reciprocity within teams and among partners.

Political scientist Robert Axelrod dramatically demonstrated the power of reciprocity in the best-known study of the situation known as the "Prisoner's Dilemma."[18] Axelrod invited scientists from around the world to submit their strategies for winning in a computer simulation of this test of win-win versus win-lose strategies. In the predicament, two parties (individuals or groups) are confronted with a series of situations in which they must decide whether or not to cooperate. They don't know in advance what the other party will do. There are two basic strategies—cooperate or compete—and four possible outcomes based on the choices players make—win-lose, lose-win, lose-lose, and win-win.

The maximum individual payoff comes when the first player selects a noncooperative strategy and the second player chooses to cooperate in good faith. In this "I win but you lose" approach, one party gains at the other's expense. Although this might seem to be the most successful strategy—at least for the first player—it rarely proves to be successful in the long run, largely because the second player won't continue to cooperate in the face of the first player's noncooperative strategy. If both parties choose not to cooperate and attempt to maximize individual payoffs, then both lose. If both parties choose to cooperate, both win, though the individual payoff for a cooperative move is less than for a competitive one (in the short run).

"Amazingly enough," says Axelrod, "the winner was the simplest of all strategies submitted: Cooperate on the first move and then do whatever the other player did on the previous move. This strategy succeeded by eliciting cooperation from others, not by defeating them."[19] Simply put, people who reciprocate are more likely to be successful than those who try to maximize individual advantage.

The dilemmas that can be successfully solved by this strategy are by no means restricted to theoretical research. We all face similar dilemmas in our everyday lives:

- Should I try to maximize my own personal gain?
- What price might I pay for this action?
- Should I give up a little for the sake of others?
- Will others take advantage of me if I'm cooperative?

Reciprocity turns out to be the most successful approach for such daily decisions, because it demonstrates both a willingness to be cooperative and an unwillingness to be taken advantage of. As a long-term strategy, reciprocity minimizes the risk of escalation: if people know that you'll respond in kind, why would they start trouble? And if people know that you'll reciprocate, they know that the best way to deal with you is to cooperate and become recipients of your cooperation.

Reciprocity leads to predictability and stability in relationships, which can keep relationships and negotiations from breaking down.[20] Why? Part of the reason is that the knowledge that we share goals and will reciprocate in their attainment makes working together less stressful. Improved relationships and decreased stress: fine goals under any circumstances.

It's absolutely essential that every leader keep the norms of reciprocity and fairness in mind. Robert Putnam, Harvard professor of public policy and author of *Bowling Alone,* a recent and influential book on community, tells us: "The norm of generalized reciprocity is so fundamental to civilized life that all prominent moral codes contain some equivalent of the Golden Rule."[21]

Whether the rewards of cooperation are monetary or not, when people understand that they have something to gain by cooperating, they're inclined to recognize the legitimacy of others' interests in an effort to promote their own welfare. The leader's job is to make sure that all parties understand each other's interests and how each can gain from collaboration.

Reward Joint Effort

Egon Zehnder, founder of Egon Zehnder International (EZI), Europe's largest global search firm, knows very well that if you want people to cooperate you have to reward joint effort. That's no small feat when you're in an industry with norms of paying the most to those who sell the most. It's even more difficult when your entire population is a group of high-achieving professionals who each have at least two university degrees and trade on their connections and intelligence. But that's not how Egon sees it. To him the unique compensation system at EZI is in the best interests of the clients, the firm, its consultants, and its partners.

The system is quite simple, actually. After people make partner, they each get a base salary and an equal share of the profit of the firm. That's right: *an equal share.* Partners also receive another set of profit shares based solely on the length of time they've been partner. That means that even if a five-year partner breaks records and bills twice what a ten-year partner bills, the ten-year partner will make more money than the five-year partner.

How can that possibly work? How can they retain professionals and pay like that? It does and they do. In an industry that averages a 30 percent turnover among partners, EZI averages 2 percent. As Egon explains:

> The reasons are simple, really. First, our approach to compensation forces us to hire consultants who have little interest in self-aggrandizement. We must hire people who are team players, people who get more pleasure from the group's success than their own advancement. These individuals by nature tend to be highly collaborative. They eagerly share information and ideas about existing and potential clients. Similarly, they pass around information about the executives who might best meet a client's needs. After all, if a consultant in Hamburg is paid according to

overall firm performance, not her own billings, she will happily pick up the phone, and call a colleague in New York to say, "I just met a candidate who isn't ideal for my client here. But he might be just perfect for your client's open position."

Second, our seniority-based system requires us to find people who want to stay with a company for the long haul, for whatever reasons. . . . Nothing benefits a client and its executive search firm more than a consultant with a well-developed network of executive contacts and a finely honed intuition.[22]

Egon himself readily admits that this system may not be right for even a majority of companies, but in the professional services world, it reinforces shared values and builds a sense of community. EZI's consistently increasing profits do a lot to recommend a more collaborative approach to rewards.

People are more likely to cooperate, whether in the classroom or the corporation, if their joint efforts are rewarded. Yet growing up in a culture that rewards individualistic or competitive achievement leaves many with the perception that they'll do better if they are each rewarded solely based on their individual accomplishments. They're wrong. The fact is that cooperation pays bigger bonuses.

Another benefit of the reward system at EZI is that it also emphasizes long-term payoffs—that is, it makes certain that the long-term rewards and benefits of mutual cooperation are greater than the short-term benefits of taking advantage of the other party (or simply not cooperating). Leaders who align constituents with a common vision of the future are much more likely to gain their cooperation than those who focus on short-term victories. Here you can see the necessary relationship between the practices of inspiring a shared vision and enabling others to act.

Emphasizing the long term is also effective in helping people deal with short-term setbacks. Leaders reframe any such incidents as learning experiences that will help the team meet more difficult challenges in the future. By emphasizing the ultimate goal, leaders strengthen team members' resolve.

SUPPORT FACE-TO-FACE INTERACTIONS

Group goals, reciprocity, and rewarding joint efforts are all essential for collaboration to occur, but what has the most powerful influence on whether those goals get achieved? Positive face-to-face interaction.[23] And this need for face-to-face communication increases with the complexity of the issues.[24] Leaders must therefore provide frequent and lasting opportunities for team members to associate and intermingle across disciplines and between departments. Handy as virtual tools are for staying in touch, they are no substitute for positive face-to-face interactions.

Sustain Ongoing Interaction

People who expect durable and frequent face-to-face interactions in the future are more likely to cooperate in the present. Knowing that we'll have to deal with someone in the future ensures that we won't easily forget about how we've treated, and been treated by, them. When durable interactions are frequent, the consequences of today's actions on tomorrow's dealings are that much more pronounced. In addition, frequent interactions between people promote positive feelings on the part of each for the other.[25]

We recognize, in this global economic environment where speed is a comparative advantage and loyalty is no longer a strong virtue, that durable interactions may seem quaint and anachronistic. But that doesn't make the facts disappear. Sure, it's more difficult. That's a reality of the New Economy. Knowing that sustaining durable and face-to-face interactions is likely to make you more effective, you have to make it one of your leadership imperatives.

One of the most troubling developments during the 1990s was the growing selfish "brand-meism" and mutual disloyalty between employee and employer. This lack of a sense that there was value in long-term relationships is mirrored in a number of other social phenomena, such as the divorce rate and declining membership in community associations. There appeared to be a short-term benefit to individuals and to the economy for this self-centric perspective and its human disposability counterpart in organizations. But the longer term tells another story. It's one thing to venture out and take a risk to be part of a new enterprise. It's another to hop from start-up to start-up in search of personal wealth, or to use people as disposable assets. In the end, durable relationships are more likely to produce collaboration than short-term ones.

There is one important amendment to this. The reality is that people don't stay in one job forever, nor should they. Marriages do fall apart, and abusive ones should end. Companies do fail, sometimes because of bad management and sometimes because the marketplace isn't buying. The point is that every significant relationship should be treated *as if* it'll last a lifetime, and *as if* it will be important to all parties' mutual success in the future. Universities and many successful consulting and executive search firms trade on this attitude about alumni, every one of whom is a potential source of goodwill and good business. Begin with the assumption that in the future you'll be interacting with this person in some way, and both you and the whole society will all be better served.

Link to the Human Network

To whom would you turn to get something done? Someone who is strongly connected to two people or to fifty people? Any doubts? Human networks make things happen, and the leaders who get extraordinary things done are right there in the middle of them.

Dick Nettell, the Bank of America corporate services executive we introduced in Chapter Seven, knows all about the importance of networks. Describing himself as "the epitome of the old operating guy," he says, "It makes no difference what level in the organization it is, it's how you grease it to get it done." But when San Francisco-based Bank of America merged with Charlotte-based NationsBank, his network got blown to bits. Dick had to rebuild his network before he could get on with his new job.

For family reasons, Dick chose to remain in the San Francisco Bay Area, but he needed close relations with people at the Charlotte headquarters. That meant spending one week a month in North Carolina, as well as constant talking on the phone. It took him about a year to develop relationships with the thirty-five or so key individuals he relies upon to make things happen. "It's important to nurture those relationships," says Dick, "and to make a conscious effort to continue them. You need to make sure you're always doing the right things and people want to deal with you." Dick knows that without personally investing time and effort in building his web of relationships, he would be unable to do his job. Every leader should know as much.

We are, in fact, all connected to each other through the people we know. The "six degrees of separation" phenomenon plays out continually, reminding us that it is indeed a small world we live in.[26] Networking has value, value that goes far beyond anything monetary. It has to do with what really counts in our daily lives. We're helpless if left to ourselves. Socially and professionally, we need other people.

Connect Others to Sources of Power

There's extraordinary value being placed on what people know—their intellectual capital. There's no doubt that brains are essential to success in the New Economy, but knowing stuff doesn't necessarily translate into action. This emphasis on intellectual capital is only marginally advanced from the prior emphasis on physical capital. Brains count, sure, but what about the rest? Making something happen is not only a function of what we know. It's also a function of who we are and who we know.

Sadly, there has been increasing disconnection from family, friends, civic groups, and other social institutions. Even with the advances in technology that enable us to be more connected electronically, people have been feeling less connected emotionally over the years. A silver lining to wrenching political and economic changes is that this trend may shift in the other direction.

The new currency of the Internet Age isn't simply intellectual capital, it's *social capital*—the collective value of the people we know and what we'll do for each other. When social connections are strong and numerous there's more trust, reciprocity, information flow, collective action, happiness—and, by the way, greater wealth.[27] Leaders, therefore, must make it a part of their personal agenda to get connected to the sources of information, resources, and influence they need to get extraordinary things done. They must also make sure that they connect their associates to each other and to those on the outside who are central to key networks. It'll make them more effective, more engaged in critical tasks, and more satisfied with their lives and work.

When you look more deeply into the value of social capital and social connections, you learn two other very important lessons. The first is that six degrees of separation doesn't hold for all of us. Some people are farther away from almost everyone, and some people are closer. A few people are *very* well connected and very close to the center of the network. These are the people that others call when they want to reach someone. This is where you want to be as a leader—fewer than three steps away from the people who influence change in your world.

That leads to the second lesson. The most well-connected individuals are those who have played the greatest variety of roles in their lives. They haven't been typecast in one function, company, industry, or community.[28] They've moved in and out of a range of assignments, experiences, and cultures. They know people from a wide range of places and have made connections in more and different domains. They've honed their functional skills and knowledge so that they're credible to their constituents, and they've not dug themselves into a rut. Much as our complex world requires specialists, when it comes to being a leader, you have to draw on your connections. If those connections are only in your specialty, it's likely that you'll be less influential than you can be if your connections cross a lot of boundaries. There's real long-term payoff in mining deep and wide when it comes to social connections.

In a world that is becoming more and more dependent on virtual connections, there's a temptation to believe that these connections automatically lead to greater trust. If we can reach across boundaries with the stroke of a key and the click of a mouse, we can more easily establish the foundation for better relationships. The hitch is, there really is no such thing as *virtual* trust.[29]

Virtual trust, like virtual reality, is one step removed from the real thing. We are social animals, it's in our nature to want to interact face to face. If we didn't, we might as well abandon travel altogether and let our wireless personal digital assistants do all the talking. But bits and bytes make for a very weak social foundation. This may sound heretical in a world driving itself more and more to depend on electronic connections, but somehow we have to figure out how to combine and balance the benefits of technology with the social imperative of human contact.

To build and sustain social connections, you have to be able to trust others and others have to trust you. It's not just what's in your mind, it's also what's in your heart. Funny, isn't it, how the old saws about "trust" and "who you know" are beginning to have a contemporary ring to them? It turns out that the New New Thing is neither new nor a thing. It's trust in people that will make the difference between the new winners and losers.

Share Information and Resources

In our workshops, we put five people to work on a project that requires them to build five squares of equal size from a variety of puzzle pieces.[30] Each person is given a different set of pieces. Some can put a square together with their own pieces (and generally set about doing so immediately); others can't. But the only way the *group* can build five squares is by sharing resources. Group members who build squares with the pieces they receive must break up those squares and give pieces to other members, trusting that they'll get the pieces they need from someone else. As participants soon learn, they must each understand and be committed to their common goal—*and* be willing to share resources—to achieve success.

People realize that they can achieve cooperative goals when day-to-day organizational norms of reciprocity encourage them to share information, listen to each other's ideas, exchange resources, and respond to each other's requests through positive interdependence. As in the puzzle-assembly experience, people will collaborate when they can actively contribute to the goal of making a whole from their separate pieces.

Maggie Hammid knows the importance of this firsthand. She also knows how frustrating it can be to get people to share information. Maggie joined Lam Research Corporation as a senior program manager for Lam's Customer Report Card Program—the company's only vehicle for understanding the customers' perspective and what improvements were needed to build and sustain customer loyalty. The challenge Maggie faced was immense: she had about sixty people reporting dotted line to her, in jobs scattered all over the world. None of them worked in Fremont, California, where she was based. She knew none of them—and she was 100 percent dependent on their support. "My job," Maggie says, "was to find out from the field reps what the customers felt were Lam's barriers to success and work with the reps to remove those barriers. In essence, I was to serve as the glue that connected the field reps to the Fremont factory, a practice, that—as I soon discovered—had been fought by the field for a long time."

Among the many initiatives that Maggie undertook was a sustained campaign of information sharing. She gathered, analyzed, and shared all the data that had been collected in the preceding year—which, prior to her arrival, had never even been looked at. She shared the collective goals and objectives for the next year and told the reps that they were in control of their own destiny. Yet Maggie knew that information sharing had to be in all directions, not just from her to the reps. They had to exchange information with her and with each other. So she shared her desire to hear from every one of the reps, and she told them that she was there to support them.

"But the problem I had," Maggie reports, "was that initially some of the reps resisted sharing their knowledge with other reps, claiming that they were in competition with each other. I very quickly sent out an e-mail to all the reps and explained that there was absolutely no competition among any of us. If one of us failed, then we all failed. By helping each other gain customer loyalty with each customer, we were working for the good of the organization, and ultimately, ourselves, since we were each stockholders and had a stake in the company's success. We would sink or swim together. After that, they started experimenting on their own and sharing their knowledge with me and their peers. This freed me up a lot to focus on other aspects of the program."

Maggie modeled the value of collaboration by sharing information herself. She made very effective use of electronic communications in a situation in which very little communication had existed. But hers is not a case of just sending messages. It's one of leadership: she made good on her own promises to the group, and established the fact that sharing information was to everyone's benefit. It's these kinds of actions that can begin to create the climate of trust and collaboration so critical to success.

By consulting with others and getting them to share information, leaders make certain that people feel involved in making decisions that affect them. This is no guarantee that a particular final decision will be accepted, but it's certain to decrease resistance. By seeking diverse inputs, leaders also help to get people's cards out on the table; they provide a more open forum for competing viewpoints to be aired and discussed. Knowing how other people feel about issues enables the leader to incorporate aspects of all the relevant viewpoints into a project and demonstrate to others how their ideas have been heard and included.

Develop Social Awareness and Social Skills

Leaders at all levels must be socially competent. Daniel Goleman has generated widespread awareness of this set of abilities, which he and others refer to as *emotional intelligence*. Goleman has extensively studied this subject since his doctoral days at Harvard, and consults to organizations around the world on how to develop this skill set. Goleman describes it this way: "Emotional Intelligence—the ability to manage ourselves and our relationships effectively—consists of four fundamental capabilities: self-awareness, self-management, social awareness, and social skill."[31] In the context of this chapter's discussion, we're speaking primarily to the abilities that are involved in social awareness and social skills. It's important to note that our research also indicates that self-awareness and self-management—which we discussed in the chapters on credibility and modeling—are absolutely essential to authentic leadership. The skills of emotional intelligence are particularly central to leadership. For one reason, as Goleman reports, "Interpersonal ineptitude in leaders lowers everyone's performance: It wastes time, creates acrimony, corrodes motivation and commitment, builds hostility and apathy."[32]

Emotional intelligence is no passing fad. Those at Egon Zehnder International see its relevance to executive success and have become leaders in applying emotional intelligence to the world of work. That effort has been spearheaded by Claudio Fernández-Aráoz, a partner and a member of EZI's Executive Committee. "During the past fifteen years," says Claudio, "I have personally conducted over two hundred senior executive search projects. As the leader of Professional Development for the fifty-eight offices of our firm worldwide, I have also been exposed to the results of several thousand cases of hiring senior executives all around the world. This experience has left me with no doubts about the relevance of emotional intelligence to senior management success." Claudio adds that he "had the opportunity to conduct research that . . . clearly demonstrated that the classic profile organizations look for in hiring a senior executive (relevant experience and outstanding IQ) is much more a predictor of failure than success, unless the relevant emotional intelligence competencies are also present. In fact, serious weaknesses in the domain of emotional intelligence predict failure at senior levels with amazing accuracy."[33]

This is serious stuff. Senior executives can graduate at the top of the best business schools in the world, reason circles around their brightest peers, solve technical problems with wizardlike powers, have the relevant situational, functional, and industry experience, and *still* be more likely to fail than succeed—unless they also possess the requisite personal and social skills. Boards of directors beware! Do not hire that brilliant turnaround artist with decades of experience in your industry and three degrees from the most elite universities—and a track record of not working and playing well with others. The appointment is likely to get you into more trouble than you were in in the first place.

The mandate is very clear. Build your own and your constituents' abilities to recognize and manage your emotions and build your collective abilities to work with each other. How well you do this will have a direct impact on your personal and organizational success.

There's one other significant contributor to collaboration that we have yet to mention: personal accountability and responsibility. In enabling others to act, leaders have to skillfully balance creating a climate of teamwork and trust while holding each single person accountable for his or her actions. A leader must build and sustain a culture in which people know and believe that "We each have to do our part—and do it very well." That's the subject of our next chapter—how leaders strengthen others so that they feel fully capable and are eager to take ownership for the process and the outcome.

COMMITMENT NUMBER 7:
FOSTER COLLABORATION BY PROMOTING COOPERATIVE GOALS AND BUILDING TRUST

"You can't do it alone," is the mantra of exemplary leaders—and for good reason. You simply can't get extraordinary things done by yourself. Collaboration is the master skill that enables teams, partnerships, and other alliances to function effectively. Collaboration can be sustained only when leaders promote a sense of mutual reliance—the feeling that we're all in this together. Mutual goals and roles contribute to mutual reliance, and the best incentive for others to help you in achieving your goals is knowing that you'll reciprocate, helping them in return. Help begets help just as trust begets trust. Focusing on what's to be gained fosters agreement in what might otherwise be divisive issues.

Leaders understand that there's no substitute for positive face-to-face interactions. Leaders help to create a trusting climate by the example they set and through listening. Leaders also make sure that key constituents are able to make human contact, and they connect people to the right sources of influence and information.

In this commitment, we offer steps that you can take to foster collaboration and create positive interactions among all your constituents. With trusting relationships, the capacity to rely on each other, and frequent face-to-face interactions, your organization can get extraordinary things done.

• *Conduct a collaboration audit.*

We can't stress enough the power of collaboration. The old American myth that competition is the path to business heaven has died a slow death. Now we need to bury it. We must all recognize that collaboration—whether in school, business, sports, health care, or government—produces more gains than trying to beat the stuffing out of someone or something.

Just how collaborative is your organization? To find out, conduct a collaboration audit, using the form shown in Exhibit 9.1. First, clarify who you will be including in your "organization." It could be only you and your direct reports—but in this age of networks, alliances, and partnerships we'd encourage you to think more broadly. Your "organization" might include all those interested parties with whom you must interact to get your work done—for example, you, your peers from other units, anyone who reports directly to you, suppliers, and internal clients. Then, with a clear focus on this organization, respond to each item.

If you rate any items in the exhibit below a 4, take a look at what you can do to develop a more collaborative approach among your constituents.

Exhibit 9.1. Collaboration Audit.

Rate the extent to which you agree or disagree that each statement describes the actions of people of your organization. Use the following scale to indicate your level of agreement or disagreement.

Strongly Disagree	Disagree	Neither Disagree nor Agree	Agree	Strongly Agree
1	2	3	4	5

Around here, people . . .

_____ 1. Act in a trustworthy and trusting manner.

_____ 2. Ask others for help and assistance when needed.

_____ 3. Treat others with dignity and respect.

_____ 4. Talk openly about their feelings.

_____ 5. Listen attentively to the opinions of others.

_____ 6. Express clarity about the group's goals.

_____ 7. Make personal sacrifices to meet a larger group goal.

_____ 8. Can rely on each other.

_____ 9. Pitch in to help when others are busy or running behind.

_____ 10. Give credit to others for their contributions.

_____ 11. Interact with each other on a regular basis.

_____ 12. Treat every relationship as if it will last for a lifetime, even if it won't.

_____ 13. Make it their business to introduce their colleagues to people who can help them succeed.

_____ 14. Freely pass along information that might be useful to others.

_____ 15. Relate well to people of diverse backgrounds and interests.

Source: The Leadership Challenge by James M. Kouzes and Barry Z. Posner. Copyright © 2002.

- *Be the first to trust.*

If we could offer you only one bit of advice on how to start the process of creating a climate of trust it would be this: *be the first to trust.* Building trust is a process that begins when one party is willing to risk being the first to open up, being the first to show vulnerability, and being the first to let go of control. Going first requires considerable self-confidence. If you, as the leader, show a willingness to trust others with information (both personal and professional), constituents will be more inclined to overcome any doubts they might have about sharing information. Trust is contagious. And distrust is equally contagious. If you exhibit distrust, others will hesitate to place their trust in you and in their colleagues. It's up to you to set the example. To promote trust throughout the organization, *be the first to*

- Disclose information about who you are and what you believe.
- Admit mistakes.
- Acknowledge the need for personal improvement.
- Ask for feedback—positive and negative.
- Listen attentively to what others are saying.
- Invite interested parties to important meetings.
- Share information that's useful to others.
- Openly acknowledge the contributions of others.
- Show that you're willing to change your mind when someone else comes up with a good idea.
- Avoid talking negatively about others.
- Say, "We can trust them," and mean it!

Trust can't be forced. If someone is bent on misunderstanding people and refuses to perceive them as either well-intentioned or competent, there may be little you can do to change that perception. If you find yourself in a climate of fear and distrust created by someone else, recognize that it's quite natural for the people involved to be reluctant to trust others. Give them time, but don't give up.

People must feel safe and secure to develop trust. Defensive communication strategies are an indication that the participants don't feel secure in some way, at some level. You can moderate a defensive climate by taking these steps whenever possible:

- Provide descriptive rather than evaluative comments.
- Paraphrase others' ideas.
- Ask questions for clarification.
- Express genuine feelings of caring.

Being willing to actively seek out, listen to, understand, and use other people's perspectives builds trust. You must take the initiative by demonstrating your trust in others and have faith that they'll respond in kind. Doing so involves risk—a risk that leaders find well worth taking.

- *Ask questions, listen, and take advice.*

If you want people to trust you, and if you want to build a climate of trust in your organization, the listening-to-talk ratio has to be in favor of listening. People need to feel that their voice matters and that their vote counts. The best way to get the conversation going so that you can listen is to ask a question. (Of course, people will stop giving you advice if you never take it, and they'll see your listening as a human relations technique.) If you truly listen to the advice people give you in response to your questions, extraordinary things can happen.

Whether it's a traveling "listening post" like the one Harry Cleberg had or a regular town hall meeting, you've got to have a routine for asking questions, listening, taking advice, losing arguments, and following up. Practice these two things at the next two team meetings you have. At the first meeting, ask more questions than you give information. But first, ask someone to monitor your actions and record your questioning-to-informing ratio. See how you did. The ratio should be at least 2:1.

At the second team meeting, practice listening. Remember that listening doesn't mean not speaking. It may mean asking questions for clarification or paraphrasing what someone else said. Your job is not to give advice and win arguments; it's to pay attention to what others want and need. Once again, have someone monitor you and make note of your listening-to-informing ratio. See how you did. If it's not at least 2:1, then try again.

- *Always say* we.

Because no one ever accomplishes anything significant alone, your approach can never be one of imposing *your* plan on others. It's not, "Here's what I plan for us to do"; instead, it's "Here's what we've agreed we'll do together." This inclusive language reinforces the fact that goals are truly collaborative, not exploitative. When talking about what is planned or what has been accomplished, it's essential that you talk in terms of *our* vision, *our* values, *our* goals, *our* plans, *our* actions, and *our* achievements. Your task as a leader is to help other people reach *mutual* goals, not *your* goals, and to get there with a sense that *we* did it together. None of this is to say that *you* don't have individual goals or individual tasks. It's just that as the leader *your* job is to make sure that *we* get extraordinary things done. You're a part of the larger mission, and your language needs to reflect that sense of being part of the team.

So, conduct an I/We language audit. Ask someone to observe the meetings you hold, whether one-on-one or large group, and count the number of times you say *I* and the number of times you say *We*. On balance, there ought to be more references worded in first-person plural than first-person singular. Do the same with your memos and e-mail.

You can also use this technique when interviewing candidates for roles in which leadership is required. Candidates who use *I* more than *We* will make poor leaders, and the organization will suffer from their attempts to push their own agenda on the group or claim credit for themselves.

- *Create jigsaw groups.*

Elliot Aronson, professor of social psychology at the University of California, Santa Cruz, has won wide acclaim for his seminal research on the benefits and applications of cooperative approaches to learning. Among his highly innovative methods is "The Jigsaw Classroom."[34] As the image implies, students are organized in a way that gives each a "piece of the puzzle." Every person is essential to the accomplishment of the final result, whether the outcome is a tangible product or a bit of knowledge. Each is an "expert" individual contributor and, at the same time, an interdependent team member.

In the Jigsaw Classroom, students typically are divided into five or six groups of five or six students each. A subject is divided into five or six specific and essential parts, and each student in each small group is assigned one of those specific topics. It now becomes that student's job to become expert in that area and to teach the rest of the group about that topic. However, the subject matter experts don't have to learn alone, as is the case in most classrooms. To help the experts develop their knowledge and their presentations to their "jigsaw groups," topic area groups are formed by pulling together the five or six students assigned to that topic. They assist each other in becoming experts. The experts return to their jigsaw groups and present what they've learned.

The results of this approach—now in its fourth decade of use—are dramatic. Not only do all students do as well or better in their knowledge, the lowest-performing students do significantly better than students in classes that use traditional instruction. More important, the levels of cooperation, self-esteem, compassion, and tolerance increase. In other words, in a situation structured so that they are at once experts *and* interdependent team members, people become much better team players and much better learners and producers.

Think about how you can apply the Jigsaw Classroom to your organization. Are there critical projects that require learning or the transfer and application of several different disciplines? Let's say you're trying to figure out how to serve a younger market. Think of what you need to learn about this market—their values, fashion trends, what TV programs and films are hot, what technology is cool, what music rocks. Then select a few people for diverse jigsaw groups. You could choose from five or six of your own functional groups—marketing, general and administrative, sales, manufacturing, development, and so on—or choose based on gender, ethnicity, and skill level. Bear in mind that the purpose of jigsaw groups is to build cooperation, not just a product. Assign only one topic to each member, and make sure that each focuses only on that topic. Form temporary "expert groups" around each topic area, and have those assigned the topic come together to learn. Then have them return to their jigsaw groups to pass along their knowledge and produce a set of recommendations.

While this process has been used extensively in education, it's not yet widely used in business. The folks at IDEO, the highly acclaimed new product design firm, use a variation of this approach. Their "hot groups" or "hot teams" are intentionally made up of widely divergent individuals.[35] Since leaders are innovators, why not be among the first to try it?

- *Focus on gains, not losses.*

Begin a problem-solving session by asking the involved parties to state their areas of agreement first, rather than their differences. This is a simple, extremely powerful technique to keep people focused on gains instead of losses. This focus is important to cooperative solutions, as leaders understand. Leaders must also communicate clearly to each party how gains can happen *only* if they work together. The emphasis today must be on forming alliances that benefit all parties, and not host-parasite relationships that produce more for some and less (or none) for others.

This idea finds support in research showing that people respond differently depending upon how problems are framed; when the focus is on profits to be achieved rather than on possible costs, people are more willing to make concessions. When trying to get others to cooperate, leaders should frame suggestions to show what both sides will gain.[36] Whether in outside negotiations with customers and vendors or inside negotiations with colleagues, you can increase the number of win-win solutions by stating aloud how your goals and others' goals are aligned. This is one of the most effective techniques for creating a sense of mutuality.

Another simple technique for keeping interactions focused on gains rather than losses is to delete the word *but* from your vocabulary. As noted in Chapter Eight, *but* stimulates disagreement; it inspires an either-or mentality and is antithetical to integrative and possibility thinking. Eliminating *but* from your vocabulary will free you from focusing on constraints and force you to consider the alternatives about how to make things happen.

- *Make a list of alternative currencies.*

To gain specific support for a cooperative project or proposal, leaders must also be able to satisfy the concerns and needs of various constituents. That requires a very different perspective on rewards from the traditional monetary one. Some people might be seeking financial gain; others, something else— more discretionary time, for instance. Leaders must generate alternative currencies, customizing rewards to the needs of the different parties involved.

The search for alternative currencies that satisfy diverse needs requires that we see differences as creative opportunities. If viewed creatively, differences can generate more alternatives than similarities do. Effective leaders are masters of finding appropriate alternative currencies by asking lots of questions and listening intently to the needs and problems thus exposed.[37]

Think about a current situation that requires negotiation between you and another party. Now divide a piece of paper into four sections. In the upper-left quadrant, write down your needs. In the lower-left quadrant, write down the other party's needs. In the upper-right quadrant, make a list of the alternative currencies—tangible and intangible resources—that the other party controls that might satisfy your needs. In the lower-right quadrant, record the alternative currencies that you control that might satisfy the other party's needs. For an example of a chart in progress, see Exhibit 9.2.

Review your entire chart before entering the negotiation. Then, in the course of the discussion, ask a lot of questions and listen hard for needs and currencies that you hadn't thought of. Instead of making demands and proposing offers, search for the best fit between needs and alternative currencies. You'll be pleasantly surprised at the creativity of the negotiation and the collaborative result.[38]

• *Take a lot of human moments.*

We all need "human moments"—face-to-face conversations—in our lives. Yet, as Edward M. Hallowell, a psychiatrist and instructor at Harvard Medical School, is uncovering, in this virtual world people are losing the ability to listen and interact.[39] Hallowell says there are only two prerequisites to a "human moment": physical presence and attention. All of us must make sure we have more human moments in our day; it's your job as a leader to create them and set the example.

Meet one-on-one with your key colleagues at least once a week. Meet one-on-one with your top hundred at least once a year. Start at the beginning of the alphabet, and once you're done start over. Worthwhile in and of itself, such face-to-face communication also improves the likelihood that you will develop understanding with team members even when opposition or criticism is expected. Additionally, it decreases the chance that you'll be surprised by another's arguments or concerns.

Exhibit 9.2. Sample Alternative Currencies Chart.

My Needs	Other's Currencies
• To have colleagues take more ownership of the success of the business.	• Spending time studying the business • Asking more questions about how the department is doing • Listening with understanding to discussion of margins • Submitting timely and accurate expense reports • Contributing cost-saving ideas • Learning other parts of the business—cross-training
Other's Needs	**My Currencies**
• To feel equitably rewarded for efforts to increase business success	• Instituting flextime • Converting to a four-day work week • Providing for employee participation in the bonus plan • Offering cafeteria benefits • Sharing financial information about the company • Showing more respect • Providing opportunities for telecommuting

The most genuine way to demonstrate that you care and are concerned about other people as human beings is to spend time with them. This time shouldn't be yet another business meeting; instead, plan on unstructured time to joke and kid and learn more about each other as parents, athletes, musicians, artists, or volunteers. Forget the chain of command: strike up conversations with colleagues, customers, suppliers, shareholders, and the person next to you in the elevator. Five or ten minutes at a time is sufficient, if done regularly. Take some kind of action *daily* that forces you to interact with people you know (and want to know better) and with people you don't know (and need to). Don't wait for someone else to make the connections; take charge and make it happen. Over the long haul, your network will prove to be the most valuable career asset you have.[40] Never, ever, neglect it.

To further increase interactions among people, take it a step further and *triangulate.* Why? Consider this: While standing on a street corner listening to a musician, have you ever talked to someone you'd never met before? Of course you have. Yet the probability of your stopping that person on the street, introducing yourself, and starting a conversation is about zero—without the street musician. The fact that you *both* stopped to listen made that moment possible. Our advice to you is to triangulate as much as you can. Increase those interactions!

• *Create places and opportunities for informal interactions.*

What do Main Street, the English pub, the French café, the Italian taverna, the Japanese teahouse, the American coffeehouse, the German beer garden, and some bookstores and hair salons all have in common? They are what sociologist Ray Oldenburg calls "third places" or "great good places."[41] These are neutral ground—places that include diverse people, where conversation is the main function and playfulness and enjoyment is the norm. They're not the big entertainment centers and malls that make the masses anonymous; they're places that enable small groups of regulars to gather in a home-away-from-home environment. They provide us all with a way of interacting with others informally without regard to status or role. There we have casual conversations, catch up on community news, relax, and make and meet friends. They serve a vital role in creating social bonds of community trust.

You might think this is not something that work organizations should pay attention to, but that wasn't Paul O'Neill's feeling when he was CEO of Alcoa. In planning new headquarters, O'Neill wanted to make some radical departures from the old, cold, stuffy, status-oriented, lifeless office tower of the past. He replaced private offices and hallways with open plan offices, including the one for the CEO. He, like everyone else in the building, worked in a 9-foot-square cubicle. A football field-length skylit atrium with open escalators encouraged visibility and communication. Interaction was also encouraged by the Isabella Street Café, the Isabella Newstand, and cafeteria facilities on each of the six floors.[42] These design features were not installed for purely aesthetic reasons or to win architectural awards. They're there because Alcoa began the design process with business and organizational goals in mind. One of those was to increase the connections and interactions among employees.

Similarly, at Yhtyneet Kuvalehdet Oy (United Magazines Ltd.), a large magazine publisher in Finland, there's a lounge on each floor where writers, editors, and other personnel can gather to watch CNN. There people quickly get into discussions of the late-breaking news stories. A central courtyard inside the building is open to all floors; it includes a stage for lunchtime announcements and afternoon concerts. Everyone must pass through that courtyard to get to the elevator and stairs. Balconies on each floor extend the courtyard by allowing people to lean out and observe the "street scenes." People working in this building couldn't avoid interaction if they wanted to.

To make certain that people aren't working in isolation from one another, leaders must create opportunities for informal interaction. Even if you can't design a brand new building, you certainly can take steps to create the sense of a "third place" for conversation. Here are some possibilities:

- Put a couple of chairs outside your cubicle or office. Encourage people who pass by to sit down for a conversation. Have some of your own informal one-on-ones out in the open.
- Be sure that the coffee, refrigerator, and other shared resources are in a central place where everyone walks by, not in some corner or basement hideaway.
- Hold ten-minute stand-up meetings at the start of every morning in an open area. Move the meeting around the workplace so that you tour the facility.
- If you don't yet hold regular group meetings at established times so people get used to coming together, get started. There's more to meetings than disseminating information and solving problems. They're also ways of building connections.
- Start your formal meetings with five or ten minutes of community building before you get down to business. Ask a question as simple as, "So what did everyone do over the holiday weekend? Stephanie, would you mind starting?"
- Make sure there's food in the middle of the table during meetings.

- Hold small celebrations in very public places—like on the plant floor—instead of in distant, secluded conference rooms.
- Intentionally move your office—sorry, cubicle—to the furthest spot from the restroom so you have to walk by everyone's desk before you get there.
- Rotate team meeting leadership so everyone gets a turn.

Some leaders may see these ideas as gimmicky and a waste of time and resources. Those who have used them disagree. The reality is that we can't all be in this together unless we're face to face on both a personal and professional basis. We need opportunities to socialize, exchange information, and solve problems informally.

COMMITMENT NUMBER 7

FOSTER COLLABORATION BY PROMOTING COOPERATIVE GOALS AND BUILDING TRUST

- *Conduct a collaboration audit.*
- *Be the first to trust.*
- *Ask questions, listen, and take advice.*
- *Always say* we.
- *Create jigsaw groups.*
- *Focus on gains, not losses.*
- *Make a list of alternative currencies.*
- *Take a lot of human moments.*
- *Create places and opportunities for informal interactions.*

Source: The Leadership Challenge by James M. Kouzes and Barry Z. Posner. Copyright © 2002.

10 STRENGTHEN OTHERS

Team members felt strong and capable because their input made a difference. Support others, and they are more likely to support you.

Marianne Hane, Applied Biosystems

Taking the time to work with the staff as individuals and understanding their motivation helped me assign tasks that complemented their interest and ability.

Sanjay Bali, Indian Navy

When Sanjay Bali was assigned as officer-in-charge, his department was not up to standards—neither his nor those of the fleet. "It was clear to me," he explains, "that while the staff members were talented, they lacked the leadership that was necessary to bring them together as a team. My challenge was to instill confidence in them and help them recognize their abilities."

While the Indian navy, like armed services around the globe, is largely hierarchically structured, within his unit Sanjay created an organization that was greatly influenced by individual personalities and aspirations, areas of competence, career paths and interests, resources, and, of course, "military mandates." Sanjay felt strongly that it was important to recognize each individual's area of interest and skill in assigning them a task and responsibility:

To understand what each person aspired to and enjoyed doing, I sat down and discussed these things with them individually. By doing this I was able to avoid assigning people to roles with which they were not comfortable. We used honest, disciplined, and respectful communications and fostered mutually beneficial relationships with people. They were willing to help out and cooperate with me and with one another because they were confident that we would do the same for them.

Sanjay often asked group members to share their ideas and suggestions, and to "think outside of the box" because "the regimented life of the service kills one's creativity. My being open to their thoughts made them more willing to think of solutions and alternate courses of action instead of waiting to be told what to do." Sanjay made sure that making suggestions was always a positive experience—even if someone's idea wasn't implemented: "I appreciated the fact that they were putting forth the effort of coming up with ideas. How were they going to get stronger without practice?" This is an approach, Sanjay says, "that is not often seen in the Indian navy, but I believe it made the group members feel empowered."

Sanjay felt that mutual respect and accountability were key components to the team's success. "I emphasized that no one in the group was smarter or better than anyone else," he explains, "and the key was to share knowledge and information rather than hoard it. We needed to recognize that every individual in the group brought value to the whole team. Rather than dwelling on areas in which they lacked skills, I pointed out the importance of them playing complementary roles . . . so they, as well as the entire group, would benefit."

While lack of experience was unavoidable, lack of knowledge or enthusiasm were not acceptable to Sanjay. If someone did not have knowledge in an essential area, they were responsible for gaining that knowledge. To make this possible, Sanjay set up a buddy system where a younger, less knowledgeable individual was paired up with someone who had more experience and expertise. This way, one gained knowledge while the other reinforced knowledge (even gaining wisdom) by helping someone else learn. An additional benefit to this system was cross-training, so that more than one person was able to perform a particular task. Sanjay later expanded this idea to a peer instruction program in which individuals would share past experiences with the group, explaining situations that had arisen and how they were dealt with. They also did research within their areas of expertise, which they would then share with the group. Everyone had something to contribute. By the end of his tour, the sailors in Sanjay's tanker were rated first among the more than forty fleet ships, even higher than the aircraft carrier, which had five times the number of people and had traditionally achieved the number one ranking. The tanker subsequently instituted an internal award in the name of Sanjay Bali to honor the best department on the ship.

GENERATE POWER ALL AROUND

Like Sanjay, exemplary leaders make other people feel strong. They enable others to take ownership of and responsibility for their group's success by enhancing their competence and their confidence in their abilities, by listening to their ideas and acting upon them, by involving them in important decisions, and by acknowledging and giving credit for their contributions. Long before *empowerment* was written into the popular vocabulary, exemplary leaders understood how important it was that their constituents felt strong, capable, and efficacious. Constituents who feel weak, incompetent, and insignificant consistently underperform; they want to flee the organization, and they're ripe for disenchantment, even revolution.

People who feel powerless, be they managers or individual contributors, tend to hoard whatever shreds of power they have. Powerless managers, for example, tend to adopt petty and dictatorial styles. Powerlessness creates organizational systems in which political skills are essential and "covering yourself" and "passing the buck" are the preferred modes of handling interdepartmental differences.[1]

To get a better sense of how it feels to be powerless as well as enabled, we often ask people to clarify their own experiences. We've asked them what actions or situational conditions contributed to their feelings of powerlessness, of feeling weak, insignificant, like a pawn in someone else's chess game. Here are some representative statements:

- I had no input into a hiring decision of someone who was to report directly to me. I didn't even get to speak to the candidate.

- People picked me apart while I was making a presentation, and the champion of the project didn't support me.
- I was told I couldn't ask questions because I lacked the appropriate educational level.
- They treated us like mushrooms. They fed us horse manure and kept us in the dark.
- I worked extremely hard—long hours and late nights—on an urgent project, and then my manager took full credit for it.
- No one would answer my questions.

When people felt powerful—strong, efficacious, like the creators of their own experience, they said:

- I was able to make a large financial decision on my own. I got to write a large check without being questioned.
- I was asked to take on a project for which I didn't have the experience. My manager said, "I'm confident you'll be successful."
- My president supported my idea without question.
- After having received a memo that said, "Cut travel," I made my case about why it was necessary to travel for business reasons; and I was told to go ahead.
- I was five years old, and my dad said, "You'll make a great mechanic one day." He planted the seed. Now I'm an engineer.
- All the financial data were shared with me.

As we examine powerless and powerful times, we're struck by one clear and consistent message: *feeling powerful—literally feeling "able"—comes from a deep sense of being in control of life*. People everywhere seem to share this: when we feel able to determine our own destiny, when we believe we're able to mobilize the resources and support necessary to complete a task, then we persist in our efforts to achieve. But when we feel we're controlled by others, when we believe that we lack support or resources, we show no commitment to excel (although we may comply). Thus any leadership practice that increases another's sense of self-confidence, self-determination, and personal effectiveness makes that person more powerful and greatly enhances the possibility of success.[2]

Gallup surveys involving more than 1.5 million employees, from over 87,000 work units, clearly show that the extent to which people feel powerful and engaged in their work is directly linked to positive business outcomes (sales growth, productivity, customer loyalty, and so forth).[3] Those who can answer questions like these affirmatively feel powerfully engaged:

- Do you know what is expected of you at work?
- At work, do you have the opportunity to do what you do best every day?
- Does your supervisor, or someone at work, seem to care about you as a person?
- At work, do your opinions seem to count?
- In the last six months, has someone at work talked to you about your progress?
- In the last year, have you had opportunities at work to learn and grow?[4]

Leaders who can strengthen others can boost worker performance. At the core, it's all about how people are made to feel. Paying attention to these factors may seem obvious. Yet nearly 19 percent of all U.S. workers (that's 24.7 million people aged eighteen or older), feel powerless and are actively disengaged from their workplaces—at an estimated cost of $300 billion in economic performance. Actively disengaged workers report nearly 120 million days missed from work each year, more than three times the number of days missed annually by their more engaged peers.[5]

A key factor in why people stay in organizations is their managers. It's equally important in why people leave organizations. People, in fact, don't generally quit companies, they quit managers.[6] Sharon Winston, senior vice president for the outplacement firm Lee Hecht Harrison, has found that the most politically correct answer given by people in company exit interviews, on their last day at work, is money. But wait another six to eight weeks, and far and away the most important reason people will report for why they left the company was the "poor quality of my manager" and the fact that the individual did not feel respected or appreciated.[7]

Creating a climate where people are involved and important is at the heart of strengthening others. People must have the latitude to make decisions based on what they believe should be done. They must work in an environment that both builds their ability to perform a task or complete an assignment and promotes a sense of self-confidence in their judgment. People must experience a sense of personal accountability so that they can feel ownership for their achievements. We've identified four leadership *essentials* to Strengthen Others:

- Ensure self-leadership
- Provide choice
- Develop competence and confidence
- Foster accountability

By using these essentials, leaders significantly increase people's belief in their own ability to make a difference. In a sense the leader acts as a coach and an educator, helping others to learn and develop their skills, and providing the institutional supports required for ongoing, experiential learning and maturation. In the final analysis, what leaders are doing is turning their constituents into leaders themselves.

ENSURE SELF-LEADERSHIP

Leaders accept and act on the paradox of power: *we become most powerful when we give our own power away.* For example, the late Major General John Stanford told us that "we don't get our power from our stars and our bars. We get our power from the people we lead." It's not exactly what you'd expect to hear from a two-star Army general, yet John's observation is precisely the attitude required of leaders who hope to strengthen others. It's also what Karyn DeMartini told us in her personal best leadership experience, which arose when her sixty-one-year-old aunt was diagnosed with cancer. Lala (Genovese for *aunt*) was a woman who loved her family very deeply; she never married and had lived with Karyn's eighty-three-year-old grandmother her entire life. Lala's illness would affect all fourteen members of the extended family, a family that Karyn described as "not dealing very well with crisis. We're stubborn, hotheaded, set in our ways, resistant to change—far from the 'poster child' of how to communicate in a healthy fashion." Dealing with Lala's illness was going to require the family to pull together as they had never had before.

Beyond the normal routines of life and work, there were many tasks and details that needed attending to, including driving Lala to various doctors' appointments, cooking meals, talking with health care specialists, communicating information about Lala's condition to other family members—in nine different locations—enlisting in support groups, paying bills, and working with insurance providers. And there was unexpected cataract surgery for Nonie (Genovese for *grandmother*). Karyn soon learned the importance of giving power away. As she explains:

> I've historically tried to control most facets of any project I have worked on. In this situation, however, I truly learned the importance of looking at leadership as a relationship. The task of giving my power away and asking certain relatives to take charge of specific projects (for example, a particular doctor appointment) was easier than I expected. Putting them in charge made members of my family feel needed and empowered. They felt they were making a positive impact on a terrible situation. I always thought people hated receiving more work, but I now realize that assignments are valued and welcomed if the work is important to the receiver.
>
> Many of my family members had important insights and creative ideas that I had not seen. Encouraging others to act as leaders helped our family to deal with these issues in a new and beneficial manner. Now that I see the benefits of giving my power away, I do this even sooner—in my family and in my workplace. As new dilemmas and challenges surface, I make more of a conscious effort to encourage people to get involved and to carry out ideas they develop.

Traditional thinking promotes the archaic idea that power is a fixed sum: if I have more, then you have less. Naturally, people with this view hold tightly to the power that they perceive is theirs and are extremely reluctant to share it with anyone. This notion is wrongheaded and clearly inconsistent with all the evidence on high-performing organizations. And families!

Give Power to Get Power

For more than a quarter-century, researchers have shown that the more people believe that they can influence and control the organization, the greater organizational effectiveness and member satisfaction will be. Shared power results in higher job fulfillment and performance throughout the organization.[8]

We discovered this ourselves when we investigated why some branch offices of a nationwide insurance company were more effective than others.[9] Senior home-office management, familiar with the performance of the branches, identified ten branch offices as high performers and another ten as low performers. These designations were highly correlated with various financial variables (for example, profit, growth, and expense control) and with self-ratings by people within the branch offices. After careful consideration of financial factors, environmental factors (for example, location), and managerial factors, we found that employee power—the sense of being able to influence what was going on in their own offices—was the most significant factor in explaining differences between high- and low-performing branch offices.

All the people in that study recognized the authority that comes with position. Power in the various branch offices was still distributed across hierarchical levels in a typical fashion: people at every level of the organization had more total power than did the people at the level below them. Despite the uniformity of this hierarchy, the total amount of perceived power in the high-performing branch offices was greater *at every level* than it was in the low-performing offices.

The leaders in the more successful branch offices understood, and acted on, the concept that power is an expandable pie. They knew that the more everyone in the organization felt a sense of power and influence, the greater the members' ownership of and investment in the success of the organization would be. They knew that when leaders and constituents are willing to be mutually influenced by one another, everyone's level of influence increases.

When leaders share power with others, they're demonstrating profound trust in and respect for others' abilities. When leaders help others to grow and develop, that help is reciprocated. People who feel capable of influencing their leaders are more strongly attached to those leaders and more committed to effectively carrying out their responsibilities. They *own* their jobs.

Which was precisely the experience of Don Foley when he was assistant manager for the California State Automobile Association. "Office management was trying to think of something to let employees know that they are important to productivity," says Don, "and to tell them that their work was appreciated. That's when we came up with the idea of wearing buttons that say 'I Make A Difference.'" Don and then office manager Harry Rasmussen personally handed out the buttons and told each employee *individually* that management appreciated their hard work and that each person's contribution mattered to overall productivity. "When we were handing out the buttons, we encouraged them to accentuate the positive in their work, to think of all the ways that they contribute to productivity," explains Harry.

And how do the employees feel? "It makes us realize how important each of us is to our company," says cashier Irene McManus. "It's nice to know that management recognizes us for our contribution. The buttons were a really nice surprise. I either wear mine or display it where I can see it, so even on those hard days, I can look at it and know that I'm contributing something important."

That knowledge is important. When he was working with mechanics, service technicians, and parts and inventory personnel, Bruce Collins, state manager for Detroit Engine & Turbine Company, simply told them that they were responsible for making their customers happy, period. "Eliminate the word 'NO' from your vocabulary," he urged. Their motto? "Yes, I Can." "When someone wants something from us," says Peter Croswell, parts manager, "we tell them (regardless of whether they are outside or inside the company): YES. Nobody's problem is somebody else's problem."

People Are Already Empowered

People who say "Yes, I Can" and realize that "I Make A Difference" in their organizations know that what they do matters. This feeling of personal effectiveness leads them to take it upon themselves to do whatever is needed to bolster organizational vitality. These *can-do* attitudes also sustain people's efforts through difficult and challenging situations.

Putting people in charge and in control of their own lives is a key factor in liberating the leader within each person. Yet we do not mean to suggest that this is something leaders magically give or do for others. People already have tremendous power. It is not a matter of giving people power—it's liberating people to use the power and skills they already have. It's a matter of setting them free, of expanding their opportunities to use themselves in service of a common and meaningful purpose. What is often called empowerment is really just letting people loose, liberating them to use their power.

Listen to how people feel when working with the leaders they most admire: alive, valued, turned-on, enthusiastic, respected, significant, capable, and proud! What do leaders do to make us feel this way? They respect and listen to us, they support and encourage us, they follow through on their commitments to us, they coach and mentor us, and they make us believe that we can make a difference. We all want our ideas to be solicited, listened to, and acted on. We all want to know that we—you, me, the fellow next door, the woman at the next desk—make a difference. Leaders heed the voice within each of us that cries out for acknowledgment that we are neither invisible nor inconsequential.

Leadership scholars have shown how "performance beyond expectations" results when the leader is able to intellectually and emotionally stimulate people, and how so-called super leaders lead others to lead themselves.[10] Leaders are transformational in that they enable people to transcend their own self-interests for the good of the group or organization. As Alan Daddow, regional manager with Australia's Elders Limited explains: "My personal best as a leader simply involved being able to maximize my staff's potential." Organizational effectiveness depends upon the sharing or distribution, not the hoarding, of power and influence.

PROVIDE CHOICE

"What made this experience so significant," explains John Zhang, who was just starting out his career at Dalin International Trading Corporation, "was that my manager listened carefully to me and then asked me what I thought we should do." After John presented several alternatives, his manager asked again what he thought should be done. "It's your decision," he said. They talked some more about the alternatives and John recommended a particular strategy. John says of his manager: "He backed me up completely. I did everything I could to ensure our success. There was no way I was going to let us not be successful." Choice builds commitment.

Many have written about how choice is required for organizations and their employees to provide exceptional customer service.[11] Responsive service and extra employee efforts emerge when employees have *latitude,* or the necessary leeway to meet customer needs, and *discretion,* or sufficient authority to serve customer wants. These ideas don't just apply with frontline service personnel. Consider a study of the Fortune 200. Over a period of two decades, 13 of the top 200 companies outperformed the other 187 organizations. Only a few factors separated the top 13 from the rest of the pack. One of the key factors was a much higher spending authority at the divisional level. For example, divisional managers in the most successful firms could spend up to $20 million on their own signature (ten times the amount at the other organizations).[12]

Resources, Responsibility—and Results

When Joseph Sensenbrenner was mayor of Madison, Wisconsin, he was convinced that providing choice (greater latitude and discretion) was essential for enabling people to apply such concepts as "continuous improvement" to the government or public sector. He decided to begin where the rubber literally met the road—with the city garage.[13] Performance and service complaints were rampant, especially about how long it took to make repairs. The problem was painfully apparent: They didn't stock the right parts! But who had responsibility?

The fleet included 440 different types, makes, models, and years of equipment. Why the bewildering variety? The parts manager explained that it was city policy to buy whatever vehicle had the lowest sticker price on the day of purchase. Joseph looked into this further. A mechanic explained to him: "It doesn't make any sense. When you look at all the equipment downtime, the warranty work that weak suppliers don't cover, the unreliability of cheaper machines, and the lower resale value, buying what's cheapest doesn't save us anything." The parts purchaser agreed: "It would certainly make my job easier to have fewer parts to stock from a few reliable suppliers. But central purchasing won't let me do it." What did central purchasing have to say? "I understand what you are saying because I hear it from all over the organization. But there's no way we can change the policy. The comptroller wouldn't let us do it." And the controller? "You make a very strong case, however, I can't let you do it because the city attorney won't let me approve such a thing." The city attorney's reply: "Why, of course you can do that. All you need to do is write the specifications so they include the warranty, the ease of maintenance, the availability of parts, and the resale value over time. Make sure that's clear in advance, and there's no problem." In fact, he admitted: "I assumed you were doing this all along."

For Joseph this was a stunning disclosure. The problem was not flawed workers but a flawed system that kept people from using their experience and judgment to make the necessary decisions. Subsequently, involving frontline employees in problem solving, rather than blaming or ignoring them, brought about huge improvements in productivity and morale. The twenty-four-step purchasing policy, with its multiple levels of control, was cut to just three steps. This change gave people latitude and discretion, enabling them to get involved and to provide good service.

People can't lead and can't make a difference unless they have a choice. If someone has no freedom of choice and can only act in ways prescribed by the organization, then how can they respond when the customer or another employee behaves in ways that are not in the script? They will have to ask the "boss" what to do—even if they think they know what needs to be done and feel they could do it! And a boss who doesn't know will have to ask the next higher boss. And up the ladder it goes.

This same need for choice applies to all aspects of life. In one study, Connecticut residents in a state-run nursing home were given the responsibility for making seemingly trivial environmental choices, such as when to see a movie or how to arrange their rooms. General health and psychological well-being improved, and death rates were 50 percent lower than for a comparison group that had been informed that it was management's responsibility to make such decisions.[14] This outcome suggests that the energy that can be unleashed as a result of giving people choices is life-sustaining: *control over your destiny can save your life!* In the long run, it can also save the life of your organization. As we've seen time and again, a sure way to sink an organization in the turbulent seas of the changing economy is to centrally control the resources.

Design in Alternatives

If leaders want higher levels of performance and greater initiative, they must be proactive in designing work that allows people discretion and choice. In other words, alternatives: being able to take nonroutine action, exercise independent judgment, and make decisions that affect how we do our work without having to check with someone else. It means being creative and flexible—liberated from a standard set of rules, procedures, or schedules. It means having more broadly defined jobs. Narrow job categories confine choices, broader ones permit increased flexibility and discretion. Those who hold broadly defined jobs have more choice about *how* to accomplish the assigned objectives. The shift to fewer job classifications in large organizations is a clear sign that breadth is essential to rapid response. In fact, the old notion of work as a collection of "jobs" is being replaced by the more expansive concept of work as a series of "projects." This restructuring allows people more freedom of movement and contact. Get rid of multiple managerial layers and sign-offs; those requirements are disabling and wasteful of time, money, talent, and motivation. They also lose customers. And increase contact among the people who make the product or provide the service and those whose resources or support they need—that will also increase capacity and responsiveness.

In the dynamic contemporary environment, only adaptive individuals and organizations will thrive. To create increasingly adaptive systems, leaders must support more and more discretion to meet the changing demands of customers, clients, suppliers, and other stakeholders. With this increased discretion comes an increased ability to use and expand our talents, training, and experience. The payoff is improved performance.

Choice fuels our sense of power and control over our lives. Yet as necessary as choice is, it's insufficient. Without the knowledge, skills, information, and resources to do a job expertly, without feeling competent to skillfully execute the choices that it requires, people feel overwhelmed and disabled. Even if we have the resources, there may be times in which we don't have the confidence that we're allowed to utilize them, or that we'll be backed up if things don't go as well as expected. To achieve the extraordinary, leaders need to provide choice—and more.

DEVELOP COMPETENCE AND CONFIDENCE

Strengthening others requires up-front investments in initiatives that develop people's competencies and foster their confidence. These investments in training and development produce profits: companies that spend more than the average amount on training have a higher return on investment (ROI) than companies that are below average spenders.[15] Organizations that have invested more than the average amount of money on training enjoy higher levels of employee involvement and commitment and better levels of customer service, along with greater understanding of and alignment with company visions and values.

A study of the U.S. navy's best ships revealed that their commanding officers give top priority to the development of their sailors.[16] (This is no surprise to Sanjay Bali, of the Indian navy, whose personal best leadership story opened this chapter.) For leaders, developing the competence and confidence of their constituents (so that they might be more competent, more capable, more effective, and leaders in their own right) is a personal and hands-on affair. Leaders are genuinely interested in those they coach, having empathy for and an understanding of each of their constituents.[17] Among sales managers, for example, developing others has been shown to be the competency most frequently found among those at the top of their field.[18] In today's world, if you're not growing and learning in a job, you'd better find a new one.

Share the Data

Leaders know that if people are to feel strong, they must be honing and developing their skills and competencies. Leaders know they need to share information and resources with constituents. "You can't ever know exactly what a person needs to know and doesn't need to know. We simply made sure that people had access to as much information as possible," is how

Warren Anderson, founder of Anderson Soft-Teach, explains his enabling strategy to us. Since retiring he's been taking this same philosophy down to elementary schools where he teaches "Money for Kids."

Tradition suggests that only people with at least a master's degree in business administration or people in specialized roles can talk and think in the following terms:

"Cash flow is projected to increase by $20,000 this month."
"If we watch our material usage variance we could very well end the month making a profit large enough to qualify everyone for a bonus!"
"Operating income for the month was $88,000, which represents a 3.4 percent return on sales."[19]

But at SRC Holdings Corporation, these comments were made by *frontline employees* (not the CFO or the treasurer) after having played SRC's "Great Game of Business."

Jack Stack, CEO of SRC Holdings, writes: "THE best, most efficient, most profitable way to operate a business is to give everybody in the company a voice in saying how the company is run *and* a stake in the financial outcome, good or bad. . . . Financial education of the workforce—we call it open-book management—is the key to extraordinary and sustained success. . . . Everyone at SRC . . . understands how they personally affect the income and profitability of the company."[20] At SRC, 86 percent of the training budget is spent on educating everyone to be a businessperson. Jack believes that when everyone has the same information about what's happening in the business, then everyone starts thinking and acting like a CEO—regardless of their organizational position.

Practice Problem Solving

Leaders know that if people don't have important opportunities to put their talents to good use, they'll wind up frustrated. To strengthen others, leaders place their constituents, not themselves, at the center of solving critical problems and contributing to key goals. This is not always easy to do; leaders must deliberately back off, so that others can figure out for themselves what needs to be done. As Gabrielle Mariscal found out, to let others move ahead, to get extraordinary things done, leaders must let go.

Gabrielle headed up part of the team that was to divide up the real estate worldwide for Hewlett-Packard when it spun off a new independent company (Agilent Technologies). The job's previous manager had been very controlling, which had resulted in poor morale and a decidedly unenthusiastic attitude toward the project. Gabrielle decided to allow the team total autonomy, giving them the necessary data and resources to do their jobs. She didn't abdicate responsibility, but she made certain that others exercised their own judgment. Gabrielle explains:

> This was difficult at first because I had to learn to trust that they would do the right thing. My role was to make sure that the team was well organized, that we were all moving in the right direction, and meeting our deadlines. I was constantly involved and interacted with team members on a daily basis, providing guidance, support, and feedback as they moved along. I noticed that by standing aside—being there to listen and encourage them to come up with solutions instead of finding answers for them—you get people to be more involved and committed.

Gabrielle understood that if she gave specific instructions on how to do something, she would, in a sense, stifle people's creativity and minimize their learning, and she was very careful not to do that. "Instead, I constantly encouraged the team to work together and come up with ideas, brainstorm alternative approaches, develop action plans, and so on. We would review them as a team and implement them." In this way, she worked to make them individually, and collectively, more capable of working on their own, with a strong sense of ownership and accountability.

One of the important tasks in the project was to gather sensitive information about the two companies from senior management. Not everyone on the team was comfortable or had experience in dealing with senior management, yet, Gabrielle realized, "We could not complete the task without getting everyone involved." She coached each team member on how to conduct the meetings with senior management. Gabrielle struggled a bit with giving power away—and found the effort well worth it. As she recalls, "I learned that if you challenge and empower people, they will produce incredible results. It gives them a sense of pride, authority, and the confidence to do well."

Confidence Provides a Way

The confidence to do well, as Gabrielle notes, is critical in the process of strengthening others. Just because individuals know *how* to do something, that doesn't necessarily mean that they *will* do it. Enabling others to act is not just a practice or technique. It's a key step in a psychological process that affects individuals' intrinsic needs for self-determination. Each of us has an internal need to influence other people and life's events so as to experience some sense of order and stability in our lives. Feeling confident that we can adequately cope with events, situations, and people we confront puts us in a position to exercise leadership. Leaders, like Gabrielle, take actions and create conditions that strengthen their constituents' self-esteem and internal sense of effectiveness.

Without sufficient self-confidence, people lack the conviction for taking on tough challenges. The lack of self-confidence manifests itself in feelings of helplessness, powerlessness, and crippling self-doubt. Building self-confidence is building people's inner strength to plunge ahead in uncharted terrain, to make tough choices, to face opposition and the like because they believe in their skills and in their decision-making abilities.[21]

Empirical studies document how self-confidence can affect people's performance. In one study, managers were told that decision making was a skill developed through practice. The more one worked at it, the more capable one became. Another group of managers were told that decision making reflected their basic intellectual aptitude. The higher the underlying cognitive capacities, the better their decision-making ability. Working with a simulated organization, both groups of managers dealt with a series of production orders, requiring various staffing decisions and establishing different performance targets. When faced with difficult performance standards, those managers who believed that decision making was an acquirable skill continued to set challenging goals for themselves, used good problem-solving strategies, and fostered organizational productivity. Their counterparts, who believed that decision-making ability was latent (that is, you either have it or you don't), lost confidence in themselves as they encountered difficulties. They lowered their aspirations for the organization, their problem solving deteriorated, and organizational productivity declined.[22]

In a related set of studies, one group of managers were told that organizations and people are easily changeable or predictable. Another group was told, "Work habits of employees are not that easily changeable, even by good guidance. Small changes do not necessarily improve overall outcomes." Those managers with the confidence that they could influence organizational outcomes by their actions maintained a higher level of performance than those who felt they could do little to change things.[23] A study of entry-level accountants revealed that those with the highest self-confidence were rated ten months later by their supervisors as having the best job performance. Their level of self-confidence was a stronger predictor of job performance than the actual level of skill or training they had received before being hired.[24]

As these studies—and experience—underscore, having confidence and believing in your ability to handle the job, no matter how difficult, is essential in promoting and sustaining consistent efforts. Fostering self-confidence is not a warmed-over version of the power of positive thinking. By communicating to constituents that we believe that we and they can be successful, leaders help people to extend themselves and to persevere.

Leaders Coach

Leaders actively seek out ways to increase choice, providing greater decision-making authority and responsibility for their constituents. They also develop the capabilities of their team and foster self-confidence through the faith they demonstrate in letting other people lead. In taking these actions, leaders act as coaches, helping others learn how to use their skills and talents, as well as learn from their experiences.[25] And in this relationship, leaders make a lasting difference. After all, as we've said before, it really is all about relationships. In case you're not yet convinced, take this short quiz:

1. Name the five wealthiest people in the world.
2. Name the last five people named as *Time* magazine's person of the year.

3. Name ten people who have won the Nobel or Pulitzer prize.
4. Name the last decade's worth of Olympic Gold medalists in your favorite sport.

How did you do? The point is, few of us remember yesterday's headliners. The applause dies, awards tarnish, achievements are forgotten.

Here's another quiz. See how you do on this one:

1. List five teachers who aided your journey through school.
2. Name six friends who have helped you through a difficult time.
3. Name five people who have taught you something worthwhile.
4. Think of six people who have made you feel appreciated and special.

Easier? The lesson? The people who make a difference in our lives are not the ones with the most credentials, the most money, or the most awards. They are the ones who care. That's why this relationship between leaders and their constituents is so crucial.

Brian Baker, family-practice physician and colonel in the U.S. Army, understood this relationship and how important it is for leaders to coach. Upon his arrival as hospital commander he was told that the Raymond Bliss Army Community Hospital (located on Fort Huachuca near Tucson, Arizona) was the "most problematic hospital in the army." Brian found a group of talented people in disarray and an organization with low morale, a set of rigidly followed institutional rules, and a high degree of conflict between doctors and nurses. He also found a stunningly unfavorable accreditation report by the Joint Commission for the Accreditation of Hospital Organizations, a report that threatened to harm the military career of nearly everyone on staff. There was neither vision nor camaraderie—only fear, hostility, and conflict. Yet within two years, under Brian's leadership, the hospital came "within inches" of receiving an exemplary rating—*all without a single change in personnel*. Brian didn't fire anyone, nor did he reassign anyone or significantly change anyone's job.

What Brian *did* do was coach. He listened, mentored, and fundamentally changed the culture and the decision-making process. Restoring his staff's sense of self-confidence was the first challenge. To that end, Brian held a series of meetings in rapid succession designed to allow him to meet and communicate openly with all of his constituents. No one's supervisor was allowed at these meetings because he wanted to ensure open and honest discussion. Brian promised that he would take no direct action as a result of the meetings, nor would he discuss what was said with anyone. He explained his philosophy of participatory and supportive (versus directive) management. These meetings set a tone of openness, genuine concern, and trust that was key to ultimately restoring people's belief in their ability to succeed.

From Brian's perspective, his leadership challenge was just a matter of educating an already very bright and capable staff that wasn't fulfilling their potential:

> All I had to do was point them toward the data and explain how important it was that we did what the accreditation agency required. We're here not to tell people *what* to do but to make sure they *understand* what needs to be done and understand *how* to do it.
>
> You can't just tell them to go out and do a monumental task if you aren't sure they really know what exactly needs to be done. So you ask lots of questions to guide their thinking—you ask, "How are you going to do this and such"—but you never assume control of the issue. They own it, not you. You coach and you mentor, but you make them decide and act. If it's their plan, they're more likely to make it happen. I helped add what I consider the most important ingredient: mutual respect and a feeling of togetherness. After that, everything just came together.

Brian believed in others, and they in turn came to believe in themselves.

A synergistic and circular process (as Brian demonstrated) is created as power and responsibility are extended to others and as people respond successfully. As constituents increase their competencies, even further amounts of power and discretion can be extended. As more responsibility is assumed by constituents, leaders can expend more energy in other areas, enhancing their own sphere of influence and bringing additional resources back to their units to be distributed once again among the group members.

FOSTER ACCOUNTABILITY

A final key in strengthening others is making certain that people recognize their interdependency through fostering accountability. The more we believe that everyone else is competent and taking responsibility for their own part of the job, the more trusting and the more cooperative we're going to be. It's also true that we'll be more confident in knowing that if we do our part, others will do theirs. This interconnectedness takes on increasing importance in a virtual-connected global workplace.

Unless people take personal responsibility and unless they are held accountable for their own actions, we're not very inclined to want to work with them nor much inclined to cooperate in general. Individual accountability is a critical element of every collaborative effort. Everyone has to do their part for a group to function effectively. Structuring the situation so that people have to work collaboratively can actually increase personal accountability. Why? Because we know that our peers are expecting us to be prepared and to do our jobs, and peer expectations are a powerful force in motivating us to do well. The feeling of not wanting to let the rest of the group down strengthens people's resolve to do their best.

Some people believe that teams and other cooperative endeavors minimize individual accountability. They believe that if we encourage people to work collectively, somehow they'll take less responsibility for their own actions than if we encourage them to compete or to do things on their own. It's true that some people become social loafers when in groups, slacking off while others do their jobs for them. But this doesn't last for long, because their team members quickly tire of carrying the extra load. The slacker either steps up to the responsibility, or the team wants that person out. Leaders know that part of their job is to set up conditions that enable each and every team member to feel a sense of ownership for the whole job.

When Andy Gere was appointed to the new position of water treatment supervisor at San Jose Water Company, an investor-owned water utility serving approximately one million people in Silicon Valley, his challenge was to transform a fragmented, feuding group of individuals into a cohesive, cooperative workforce. In the end, this group developed a set of guidelines for communicating, problem solving, interacting, and performing critical functions as a team. The guidelines were published in a manual (called *An Operator's Guide to Making Teamwork Work*) and each person signed an agreement that made the guidelines a contract for the way they would work with one another. Water quality improved dramatically, production increased by 8 percent, and plant-related overtime decreased by 12 percent.

This didn't happen instantly. Andy began by making the operators accountable. He gave them the authority to make plant process changes, including plant shutdowns, without first checking with a supervisor. "It took them awhile," Andy admits, "to get used to the idea that as a licensed water treatment plant operator they not only had the authority but the responsibility to optimize the plant processes to the best of their ability, all the time." He made the operators own the new procedures by letting them establish their specific intergroup work rules (such as the protocol for deciding when to turn on a creek intake after a storm) rather than dictating them from management. Similarly, the operators developed working rules, relationship rules, and getting-along rules as a way to get beyond years of rivalry, grudges, and sour relationships.

After Andy first brought the various individuals together for a discussion, he was terrified. That meeting quickly got out of control and turned into a free-for-all gripe session laced with personal attacks. Later on, however, Andy says he realized that "giving them all the opportunity to speak their minds without penalty was probably a good thing." When the operators learned that they had a say in the program, and were treated as stakeholders instead of peasants, they were eager to participate.

Accountability was pushed by reminding the operators to "focus on the problem, not the person." And making each operator accountable was critical to the success of Andy's initiative. As Andy explains, "Asking the operators to write their own mission statements and goals gave them a new sense of purpose and created an opportunity for them to see an end product that went beyond the end of their shift. They could see how they were interconnected and how by working together they could accomplish more than by working alone." One of the ways that Andy reinforced who was accountable for what was by pointing out individuals' success in the presence of their peers. Not only did this reinforce team members' existing feelings of personal strength and capability but, Andy found, it "helped them to recognize just how competent their counterparts in other areas were." Accountability results in feelings of ownership, that we—not someone else—have the responsibility for what's going on around us.

Employees at the General Electric plant in Durham, North Carolina, build some of the world's most powerful jet engines. It turns out that jet-engine assembly is indeed "rocket science." In an engine that weighs 8.5 tons and has 10,000 parts, even a nut that weighs less than an ounce must be installed to a very specific tightness. And after each step, a technician takes responsibility, becomes accountable, by initialing the step on a computer terminal. Duane Williams, tech-3, explains that in this plant, team members always have the power to change things that don't work out. Says Duane, "All the things you normally fuss and moan about to yourself and your buddies—well, we have a chance to do something about them. I can't say, 'They don't know what's going on.' or 'They made a bad decision.' I am 'they.' "[26]

When there is no "they," then no one has to be told what to do or why it is important. We can all figure it out for ourselves. Leaders have created real owners en route to the extraordinary.

COMMITMENT NUMBER 8: STRENGTHEN OTHERS BY SHARING POWER AND DISCRETION

Strengthening others is essentially the process of turning constituents into leaders—making people capable of acting on their own initiative. Leaders strengthen others when they give their own power away to them, when they make it possible for constituents to exercise choice and discretion, when they develop in others the competence and confidence to act and to excel, and when they foster the accountability and responsibility that compels action. Exemplary leaders use their power in service of others because they know that capable and confident people perform better. In this commitment, we offer specific actions you can take to strengthen your constituents. Then, in the chapters that follow, we address the need to encourage the heart, in asking people to climb higher and higher.

- *Offer visible support.*

Power doesn't flow to unknown people; becoming powerful requires getting noticed. Visibility is a precursor to access and recognition and is key to forming strategic alliances. Major General John Stanford demonstrated his dedication to increasing the visibility of his colleagues when he spoke at one of our workshops. Before his speech, we noticed that John had picked up someone else's name tag and put it on his uniform. At the end of his one-hour presentation, as he was about to step down from the podium, he pointed to the name tag and said, "My aide-de-camp, Albert A. A. Cartenuto III, couldn't be with me today. I hope I represented him well." John had intentionally picked up Cartenuto's name tag so that he could give him visibility and acknowledge Cartenuto's contributions. John's was a conscious leadership act, requiring caring and attention.

It's no wonder that Cartenuto said of John, "He's the greatest."

In strengthening your constituents ensure that they're highly visible and that individual and group efforts get noticed and recognized. Visibility is also enhanced when you keep team members in contact with people outside their department—for example, by placing people on task forces and committees whose members come from across the organization or by encouraging active participation in professional and community groups. By providing others with access to senior executives, fostering outside contacts, and developing and promoting people with promise, you help build those critical relational networks.

- *Assign critical tasks.*

People who are most central to solving the organization's crucial problems and ensuring the company's long-term viability have the most power. This is especially true when their particular resources are critical and in short supply. In our case studies of personal bests, people talked of confronting critical organizational issues—whether improving quality, reducing manufacturing start-up times, changing customer perceptions, raising literacy rates, reengineering core agency processes, or mobilizing legislative initiatives. Although it may seem obvious that people do their best when the work is critical to success, this principle is often lost in the day-to-day design of work.

How do you know if everyone on your team or in your department even understands the critical issues and tasks of the business you are in and why? Try this: Get a cross-section of people together and see if they can answer these questions, as they relate to your company or business unit:

- How do we make money (profit)?
- Who are our toughest competitors?
- What have our annual profits and revenues been over the past five years?
- What do our customers see as our differential advantages in the marketplace?
- Who are the five senior officers in our organization?
- What new products or services will we initiate in the next six months?

Many other questions could be asked; pick the ones that make most sense in your context. The point? If your constituents can't answer relevant business questions such as these, how can they work together to transform shared values and common purposes into reality? How can they know how their performance affects other parts of the business, and ultimately the success of the entire enterprise or endeavor? How can they feel very strong or capable if they don't know the answers to the same questions every "owner" would know?

What's critical to an organization—and what the owners should know—is dynamic and ever-changing. What's central this year may be peripheral the next. To stay ahead of the curve, you ought to ask the following questions:

- How can I give people more control over the resources they need to do their work?
- How can I make sure people are connected to the information they need?
- How can I make sure that I personally offer or acquire the support that people need to do the very best that they can?

Act on your answers to make others more powerful and effective. Be on the lookout for situations to induce people to assume responsibility by giving them experience in making decisions.

• *Enrich people's jobs.*

The content of the jobs at such companies as SRC Holdings Corporation and Madison, Wisconsin's city garage are not particularly glamorous. Yet these companies, and others like them, have been able to augment people's jobs so that they feel important and connected to the big picture. You can best liberate the leader within your constituents by understanding how the contextual factors of their jobs play out. Do people perceive themselves as lacking control over their immediate situation, or lacking the required capability, resources, or discretion needed to accomplish a task? If so, the most common reasons are excessive bureaucracy, authoritarian supervisory styles, non–merit-based reward systems, and rigid or limiting job design.[27] The latter area may be one over which you can have the most direct influence.

Here's what to do: Make certain that peoples' jobs are designed so that they know what is expected of them. Provide sufficient training and technical support so people can complete their assignments successfully. Enrich their responsibilities so that they experience variety in their task assignments and opportunities to make meaningful decisions about how their work gets accomplished. Create occasions for them to network with others in the organization (including peers and senior managers). Involve them in programs, meetings, and decisions that have a direct impact on their job performance. Take a careful look at what your constituents are doing in their jobs and determine—best to include them—where you could be enriching their positions and consequently fostering greater self-confidence.

If you haven't already, make certain that everyone in your organization, no matter the task, has a customer: another person or group that they are serving through their efforts. Having a customer enlarges most people's understanding of what they do and what the company overall does. It also typically puts each person in direct contact with other parts of the business. And it makes people feel important and significant. "I really like it," an auto mechanic for Western Australia's Total Nissan told us, "when customers come back and ask for me personally. They say they really liked the way I fixed their car and they want me to work on it again. That makes me feel great. Proud. I really want to make sure they keep asking for me." Do artists leave their work unsigned? Why should anyone else?

• *Use modeling to develop competencies.*

Modeling as a learning and developmental practice is being used in a wide variety of settings to develop intellectual, social, and behavioral competencies. The method that produces the best results includes three major elements:

- The appropriate skills are modeled to convey the basic competencies.
- People receive guided practice under simulated conditions so they can perfect the skills they are endeavoring to master.
- People are helped to apply their newly learned skills in work conditions in ways that will bring them success.[28]

Determine first which competencies you want to develop. Break complex skills down into subskills. Demonstrate, generally via videotape, an illustration of the desired skill (or behavior) using many brief examples. Use "models" that are similar to your audience—having respected peers as teachers is especially effective. Provide informational feedback on how people are doing. Focus on the corrective changes that need to be made, rather than emphasizing what was wrong or flawed. Keep in mind that feedback should be given so as to *build* self-confidence in one's capabilities. This is achieved by calling attention to successes and improvements, while correcting deficiencies. Finally, give people the opportunity to practice new skills, especially in situations where they are likely to produce good results. Sufficient success using what they have learned is necessary so that they believe in both themselves and in the value of the new ways.

• *Stop talking and start building at staff meetings.*

We've mentioned the importance of listening. Have you really heard it? How much do you talk at your own staff meetings? If you dominate communications there, you are implying that you don't value other people's contributions, that they have little to offer. If that's the case, stop having the meetings; write a memo instead! Staff meetings should be an opportunity for people to see the big picture, learn about what others are doing, and how they can help one another. They are also important opportunities to develop capacity.

Gary Miocevich demonstrated this when he was managing director of VEEM Engineering Group, a hundred-person, high-quality customized engineering firm in Western Australia. No one thought it was such a great idea when he said that the "chair" responsibilities for the weekly staff meetings would be rotated. And in fact, for the first several months, it was a disaster. Some people were good at chairing the meeting, others used it as a chance to dominate, many lost control, and a few just had no interest. See, they told him, this really was a dumb idea.

So Gary took another try at it. He knew that he hadn't ever really trained the other managers about how to chair an effective meeting—and he worried that they behaved as they did having learned from his example! He realized that in simply rotating this responsibility he hadn't provided any learning opportunities—that is, no one got any informational feedback about what they did well or areas they could improve. Moreover, by the time anyone's turn came around again, whatever vicarious learning might have taken place was forgotten and lost.

So Gary had each person chair the meetings for a month. One person was formally assigned to give feedback to the individual chairing the meeting and this responsibility rotated at each session. Special attention was focused on noticing improvements from one week to the next. In the process, each person at the meeting began picking up ideas about what worked and what didn't. Gary noticed that after a while most people began recognizing the meeting behaviors in themselves that made the chair's job so demanding and often unrewarding, and began shaping up. These managers also improved the way they ran their sessions with their own staffs; several have begun rotating the chair's position.

- *Enlarge people's sphere of influence.*

At the Ritz-Carlton Hotels, a two-time winner of the Malcolm Baldrige National Quality Award, associates have the latitude and authority to spend up to $2,000 to correct an error or satisfy or impress a guest—without checking with a manager. We know many *managers* who don't have that kind of signature authority.

If you really want people to feel more powerful (and personally responsible), try these steps:

- Substantially increase signature authority at all levels.
- Remove or reduce unnecessary approval steps.
- Eliminate as many rules as possible.
- Decrease the amount of routine work.
- Assign nonroutine jobs.
- Support the exercise of independent judgment.
- Encourage creative solutions to problems.
- Define jobs more broadly—as projects, not tasks.
- Provide more freedom of access, vertically and horizontally, inside and outside.

Remember to provide the necessary resources—materials, money, time, people, and information—to perform autonomously. There's nothing more disempowering than to have lots of responsibility for doing something but nothing to do it with.

People's increased sphere of influence ought to be over something relevant to the pressing concerns and core technology of the business. Choosing the color of the paint may be a place to start, but you'd better give people influence over more substantive issues as well. For example, if quality is top priority, find ways to expand people's influence and discretion over issues of quality control. If innovation is a priority, increase people's influence over the development of new products, processes, or services.

Assess the critical tasks and issues in your organization and then make sure that your constituents are well represented on the task forces, committees, teams, and problem-solving groups dealing with them. If you're on one, make sure you take a key constituent or two with you to meetings.

• *Educate, educate, educate.*

When you increase the latitude and discretion of your constituents, you also have to increase expenditures on training and development. Successful quality programs, for example, all have in common the fact that the group members receive training in basic statistical measurement methods, group communication skills, and problem-solving techniques. Without education and coaching, people are reluctant to exercise their authority, in part because they don't know how to perform the critical tasks and in part out of fear of being punished for making mistakes.

You don't have to spend megabucks to have good training. In the early days at Solectron, the high-technology service manufacturer, we were on the road early to make a seven o'clock gathering of company managers. The first half-hour of the meeting was for reporting the quality numbers from the day before; the second, for learning something about management, finance, marketing, quality, communications, or other relevant topics. Solectron's first CEO, Winston Chen, was dedicated to education and information sharing—and years later, the efforts paid off for this (two-time!) winner of the Malcolm Baldrige National Quality Award.

Education is important because it enables people to face the often uncomfortable feelings that any change produces. In Chapter Eight, Rayona Sharpnack described the way she introduced her daughter's teammates to the skills needed for batting. As founder of the Institute for Women's Leadership, she tackles the issues of competence and confidence head-on:

> I'll go around the room and ask people how many of them would like to have more confidence as a result of being in the class. Almost all of the hands go up. I say, "Okay, I'm going to make you a counteroffer. I'm not going to promise to give you more confidence. I'm going to promise to give you more competence. And I'm going to ask you to look and see where confidence comes from." Then I ask how many of them think of confidence as a prerequisite—how many of them will do something if they feel confidence enough to attempt it. All of the hands go up. Then I ask them what they are confident about in their lives and how they got to be confident about those things. Whether it's horseback riding or shipping products or developing software code, they all got confidence by doing something over and over again. Oh, so then confidence is an aftermath, not a prerequisite. Bing, bing, bing, bing!
>
> Then it hits them: They've been spending their whole lives waiting to be confident before trying to do something new, when they couldn't pos-

sibly be confident until they're competent. That's transformational, because it suddenly sheds light on whole arenas of restriction and impediment that have nothing to do with anything other than the context from which they're viewing the situation or their lives or themselves.[29]

And be sure to tap the teachers in your midst. Schoolteachers have long realized that the learning of older children can be enhanced by having them tutor younger students. In this process, the learning by both parties is strengthened. So too in the organization (or the navy, as Sanjay Bali knew). Peter Drucker has observed that "knowledge workers and service workers learn most when they teach."[30] He says that the best way to improve a star salesperson's productivity is to ask for a presentation of "the secret of my success" at the company's sales conference, or have your top surgeon give a talk at the country medical society, or your top volunteer speak to the board.

Keep in mind that sometimes the so-called teaching can be informal. A study by Xerox's Palo Alto Research Center revealed that service personnel learn most about fixing copiers not from company manuals but from hanging around swapping stories.[31] Instead of busting up the gang by the water cooler, make opportunities for learning at informal get-togethers and loosely organized offsite meetings.

- *Create a learning climate.*

Strengthening others requires that leaders provide a climate conducive to learning. As we described in Chapter Eight, a prime requirement for people to be capable of learning—changing and developing new skills—is that they feel safe; they must feel able to trust the system and the people involved. Without that level of comfort (safety) people are generally unwilling to be vulnerable, to take in information that might seem threatening, or to develop new skills. The typical reaction is defensiveness, screening out criticism, and putting the blame on anyone and everyone else.

Our own research reveals that a learning climate, characterized by trust and openness, is a critical precursor for any successful organizational change efforts.[32] With trust and openness comes greater willingness to communicate about feelings and about problems. As people are listened to, more information becomes available, and they experience greater common ground and reasons to engage in cooperative behavior. They have less motivation to defend either themselves or the status quo, and are ready to take on the leadership challenges associated with, for example, customer service and continuous quality improvement.

To further bolster a learning climate, schedule a once-a-month one-on-one dialogue with each of your direct reports. Marshall Goldsmith, founding director of A4SL—the Alliance for Strategic Leadership—shared this tested and effective method for one-on-ones. He recommends always starting the first session by thanking the person for previous feedback. As appropriate, he says to tell the person: "I'm sorry I haven't listened before. I'd like you to help me so I can get better in the future." Then have a conversation based on six discussion questions. We recommend that *you* start each conversation so that the other person doesn't feel set up or playing "guess what the leader wants." Here are the six questions, with follow-up statements.

1. Where are *we* going?
   - I'll tell you where I think we're going.
   - You tell me where you think we're going.
2. Where are *you* going?
   - I'll tell you where I see you and your group going.
   - You tell me where you see you and your group going.
3. What are *you* doing well?
   - I'll give you my sense of what you're doing well.
   - You give me your sense of what you're doing well.
4. What suggestions for improvement do you have for *yourself*?
   - I'll tell you the suggestions I have.
   - You tell me what suggestions you have.
5. How can I help you?
   - I'll add anything else I think I can do.
   - You tell me what I can do to help and support you.
6. What suggestions do you have for *me*?
   - I'll tell you what I think I need to do.
   - You tell me what you think I need to do.

In this discussion, both parties learn how they can be doing better than they have been. Do this every quarter and you'll be sure to notice "continuous" improvements as people become stronger and more capable as a result of being encouraged to learn from their experiences. The difference may well be extraordinary.

COMMITMENT NUMBER 8

STRENGTHEN OTHERS BY SHARING POWER AND DISCRETION

- *Offer visible support.*

- *Assign critical tasks.*

- *Enrich people's jobs.*

- *Use modeling to develop competencies.*

- *Stop talking and start building at staff meetings.*

- *Enlarge people's sphere of influence.*

- *Educate, educate, educate.*

- *Create a learning climate.*

Source: The Leadership Challenge by James M. Kouzes and Barry Z. Posner. Copyright © 2002.

PART SIX

Encourage the Heart

RECOGNIZE CONTRIBUTIONS

Would people value having a colleague say "Thank You"

and "Good Job"? I thought about how I would feel—

and I realized the incredible power of recognizing and

appreciating others.

Andris Ramans, Intuitive Surgical

Never underrate the importance of visibly appreciating

others and their efforts.

Joan Nicolo, Computing Resources, Inc.

Almost midway through her career, Joan Nicolo found that the leadership skill of encouraging the heart remained particularly challenging. She was uncomfortable praising people in public and started asking herself what was holding her back. On the surface, it seemed such a simple task. So what was the big deal?

After considerable soul-searching, she came up with some theories. She was afraid that if she praised one person, others would think she was playing favorites. She also felt that praising and encouraging activities took too much time, time that—with her already burgeoning list of responsibilities—was in short supply. Recognition, she worried, was for warm-and-fuzzy types, not for serious and performance-oriented managers. And maybe providing recognition would play into stereotypes of women as "nurturing."

The more she thought about it, however, the more she realized that her associates really did deserve to be recognized, and it was high time for her to give it a try.

Shortly thereafter, during a presentation, she made a special point of thanking people publicly for fostering a collaborative spirit in the project they were working on. It felt great—to her and to others! She said, "I found that my spirit was lifted. They felt appreciated, and I felt that they had received the credit they deserved." Joan knew beyond a shadow of a doubt that she'd established a human connection with her colleagues that hadn't been there before. Communication became more open, and she felt far less guarded. This was a real turning point for her.

In the weeks ahead she brought much more of herself to her work relationships, and people responded with a new level of enthusiasm for her leadership. Indeed, she began to see her coworkers in a different light. She could focus on getting the job done and enjoy a human bond with everyone around her. Contrary to her worst fears, nobody got jealous when she praised one person or another, and the time it took to show her appreciation was well worth it. Coming to work in the morning, she felt more energetic than ever, and when she went home in the evening she increasingly felt deep satisfaction with what she'd accomplished. At first it wasn't clear how these changes were going to affect productivity. Would they translate into anything that would benefit the company? In a short time she saw that this new way of relating brought her group together as never before, fueling an esprit de corps that spurred everyone on to give their personal best whenever an extraordinary effort was required.

Joan, like other leaders we talked with, came to understand that recognition is about acknowledging good results and reinforcing positive performance. It's about shaping an environment in which everyone's contributions are noticed and appreciated.

Andy Pearson, as CEO of PepsiCo, was named one of the ten toughest bosses in America. More than twenty years later, now at Tricon (the world's second-largest fast-food chain, a $22 billion retail operation with more than 30,000 restaurants and 725,000 employees), Andy has discovered, like Joan, that the human heart drives a company's success, and that this kind of success must be kindled through attention, awareness, recognition, and reward. Says Andy:

> If the need for recognition and approval is a fundamental human drive, then the willingness to give it is not a sign of weakness. . . . Great leaders find a balance between getting results and how they get them. A lot of people make the mistake of thinking that getting results is all there is to the job. They go after results without building a team or without building an organization that has the capacity to change. Your real job is to get results and to do it in a way that makes your organization a great place to work—a place where people enjoy coming to work, instead of just taking orders and hitting this month's numbers.[1]

Andy is right in tune with what we found. In our personal-best case studies, people reported working very intensely and very long hours—and enjoying it. Yet to persist for months at such a pace, people need encouragement. Literally, they need the heart to continue with the journey. One important way that leaders give heart to others is by recognizing individual contributions. That praise is important, too—most people rate "having a caring boss" even higher than they value money or fringe benefits. In fact, how long employees stay at a company, and how productive they are there, is determined by the relationship they have with their immediate supervisor.[2]

Exemplary leaders understand this need to Recognize Contributions and are constantly engaged in these *essentials:*

- Focus on clear standards
- Expect the best
- Pay attention
- Personalize recognition

By putting these four essentials into practice and recognizing contributions, leaders stimulate and motivate the internal drive within each individual.

FOCUS ON CLEAR STANDARDS

When you were a kid you might have read Lewis Carroll's *Alice in Wonderland*. Remember the croquet match? The flamingos were the mallets, the playing card soldiers were the wickets, and the hedgehogs were the balls. Everyone kept moving and the rules kept changing all the time. Poor Alice. There was no way of knowing how to play the game to win. Besides, it was all rigged in favor of the Queen.

You needn't have gone down the rabbit hole to know how Alice felt: we've all been Alice at one time or another in our lives. We've all been at a place where we're not sure where we're supposed to be going, what the ground rules are that govern how we behave, or how we're doing along the way. And just when we think we get the hang of it, the organization comes along and changes everything. This is a recipe for maddening frustration and pitiful performance. Our hearts just aren't in it.

If leaders want us to give our all, to put our hearts into it, leaders must first focus on clear standards. Here we're using *standards* to mean both goals and values. They both have to do with what's expected. Goals connote something shorter-term than values (or principles), which connote something more enduring. Typically, values and principles serve as the basis for goals. They define the arena in which goals and metrics must be set.

Standards Concentrate Us

Values set the stage for action. Goals release the energy. The ideal state—on the job, in sports, in other areas of life—is often called *flow*. "Flow experiences" are those times when we feel pure enjoyment and effortlessness in what we do.[3] To experience flow, it helps to have clear goals—because goals help us concentrate and avoid distractions. By having an intention to do something that is meaningful to us, by setting a goal, we take action, action with a purpose.

Goals help us keep our eye on the prize. Way back in the late 1990s, the average employee received 180 different messages a day.[4] Imagine what it is today! Voice mail, e-mail, fax, phone calls, internal memos, instant messages, pagers, shouts over the cubicle wall all disrupt our work constantly. How do we know what needs attention? How do we know how to respond?

Goals and intentions keep us on track. They help us put the phone in do-not-disturb mode, shut out the noise, and schedule our time. Goal-setting affirms the person, and, whether we realize it or not, contributes to what people think about themselves.

Now is it better that individuals set their own goals, or should leaders set the goals for others? In the best of all worlds, people would set their own. Vast amounts of research show that people feel best about themselves and what they do when they voluntarily do something. People feel worst "when what they do is motivated by not having anything else to do."[5] The lesson for leaders is to make sure that whenever people engage in something they know why it's important and what end it's serving. This knowledge helps people feel more alive, more in charge, and more significant.

Feedback Keeps Us Engaged

People need to know if they're making progress toward the goal or simply marking time. Standards help to serve that function. But standards and goals are not enough. People's motivation to increase their productivity on a task increases *only* when they have a challenging goal *and* receive feedback on their progress.[6] As shown in Figure 11.1, goals without feedback, and feedback without goals, have little effect on motivation.

So just announcing that the idea is to reach the summit is not enough to get people to put forth more effort. People will ask, "The summit? What summit? Why are you giving me feedback about that? I didn't know that was our goal!" We need to know if we're still climbing, or if we're sliding downhill. With clear goals and detailed feedback, people can become self-correcting and can more easily understand their place in the big picture. With feedback they can also determine what help they need from others and who might be able to benefit from their assistance. Under these conditions they will be willing to put forth more productive effort.

The importance of feedback was demonstrated in an empirical study involving soldiers who, after several weeks of intensive training, were competing for places in special units. The soldiers were divided into four groups, which were unable to communicate with one another. All the men marched twenty kilometers (about twelve-and-a-half miles) over the same terrain on

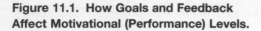
Figure 11.1. How Goals and Feedback
Affect Motivational (Performance) Levels.

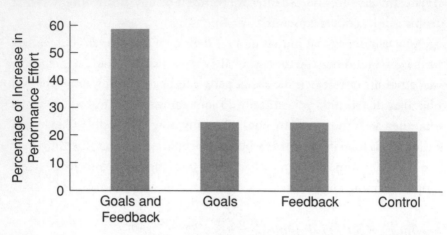

Source: A. Bandura and D. Cervone, "Self-Evaluative and Self-Efficacy Mechanisms Governing the Motivational Effects of Goal Systems," *Journal of Personality and Social Psychology* 45 (1983): 1017-1028.

the same day. The first group was told how far they were expected to go and were kept informed of their progress along the way. The second group was told only that "this is the long march you hear about." These soldiers never received any information about the total distance they were expected to travel, nor were they told how far they had marched. The third group was told to march fifteen kilometers, but when they had gone fourteen kilometers, they were told that they had to go six kilometers farther. The fourth group was told that they had to march twenty-five kilometers, but when they reached the fourteen-kilometer mark, they were told that they had only six more kilometers to go.

The groups were assessed as to which had the best performance and which endured the most stress. The results indicated that the soldiers who knew exactly how far they had to go and where they were during the march were much better off than the soldiers who didn't get this information. The next-best group was the soldiers who thought that they were marching only fifteen kilometers. Third best was the group told to march a longer distance, then given the good news at the fourteen-kilometer mark. Those who performed worst were the soldiers who received no information about the goal (total distance) or the distance that they had already traveled (feedback).[7]

We can draw numerous conclusions from this and similar research. Certainly the type of leadership that even highly motivated, achievement-oriented people receive can make a difference in the level of stress and success they experience. When leaders provide a clear sense of direction and feedback along the way, they encourage people to reach inside and do their best. Information about goals and about progress toward those goals strongly influences our abilities to achieve—and influences how well and how long we live.[8] Talk about encouraging the heart!

Encouragement Is Feedback

Encouragement is a form of feedback: wonderful, personal feedback. It's positive information that tells us that we're making progress, that we're on the right track, that we're living up to the standards. Giving encouragement requires us to get close to people and show that we care. And because it's more personal and positive than other forms of feedback, it's more likely to accomplish something that other forms cannot: strengthening trust between leaders and constituents.

In a study of the effects of feedback on self-confidence, MBA students were praised, criticized, or received no feedback on their performance in a simulation of creative problem solving. They had been told that their efforts would be compared with how well hundreds of others had done on the same task. Those who heard nothing about how well they did suffered as great a blow to their self-confidence as those who were criticized.[9] People hunger for feedback. They really do prefer to know how they are doing, and clearly no news has the same impact as bad news.

To ensure that people achieve their best, leaders have to take steps to bring forth the best from others. This begins with an expectation of high standards, which then becomes a self-fulfilling prophecy.

EXPECT THE BEST

Successful leaders have high expectations, both of themselves and of their constituents. These expectations are powerful because they are the frames into which people fit reality. People are much more likely to see what they expect to see even when it differs from what may be actually occurring. Social psychologists have referred to this as the "Pygmalion effect," based on the Greek myth about Pygmalion, a sculptor who carved a statue of a beautiful woman, fell in love with the statue, and brought it to life by the strength of his perceptions. Leaders play Pygmalion-like roles in developing people. Research on the phenomenon of self-fulfilling prophecies provides ample evidence that other people act in ways that are consistent with our expectations of them.[10] If we expect others to fail, they probably will. If we expect them to succeed, they probably will.

Our expectations also shape our own behavior. Much of this has to do with how we behave toward others. The high expectations that leaders have of others are based in large part on their expectations of themselves. This is one reason why leaders model the way. What gives their expectations for others credibility is their own record of achievement and dedication, and daily demonstrations of what and how things need to be done. What's more, leaders tend not to give up on people, because doing so means giving up on themselves, their judgment, and their ability to encourage others to accomplish their best.

One of the clearest and most often mentioned responses to the question "What is so special about leaders?" is that they bring out the best in us. Leaders recognize the impact of self-fulfilling prophecies. Leaders treat people in a way that bolsters their self-confidence, making it possible for them to achieve more than they may have initially believed possible of themselves. Feeling appreciated by others increases a person's sense of self-worth, which in turn, precipitates success at school, home, and work. Research and everyday experience confirms that men and women with high self-esteem, of all ages and levels of education and socioeconomic backgrounds, "feel unique, competent, secure, empowered, and connected to the people around them."[11] If we have someone in our life who believes in us, and who constantly reinforces that belief through their interactions with us, we are strongly influenced by that support. If the potential exists within us, it will come out when a leader takes the time to bring us along.

No right-thinking manager would do anything that would not help people to succeed, right? Surprisingly, European researchers' meticulous studies show "that bosses—albeit accidentally and usually with the best intentions—

are often complicit in an employee's lack of success. How? By creating and reinforcing a dynamic that essentially sets up perceived under-performers to fail. If the Pygmalion effect describes the dynamic in which an individual lives up to great expectations, the set-up-to-fail syndrome explains the opposite."[12]

The set-up-to-fail syndrome may begin quite innocently. An employee seems to have a performance problem—a missed deadline, a lost account. Or it can even start when a manager is distant (figuratively or literally) from the direct report for personal reasons. This triggers an increase in the manager's supervision and control of the direct report, who then begins to believe that the manager lacks trust and confidence. Eventually, because of low expectations the direct report withdraws, stops making independent decisions or taking initiative—and the problem intensifies.

The leader's expectations have their strongest and most powerful influence in times of uncertainty and turbulence. When accepted ways of doing things are not working well enough, then a leader's strong expectations about the destination, the processes to follow, and the capabilities of the team serve to make dreams come true. There is no doubt, expectations—high or low—influence other people's performance. But only high expectations have a positive impact—on actions and on feelings about oneself. Only high expectations can encourage the heart.

High Expectations Lead to High Performance

The high expectations of leaders aren't just fluff that they hold in their minds to keep a positive outlook or to psych themselves up. Another person's belief in our abilities accomplishes much more than that. The expectations that successful leaders hold provide the framework into which people fit their own realities. Just as with Pygmalion, these frameworks play an important role in developing people. Maybe you can't turn a marble statue into a real person but you can draw out the highest potential of your constituents.

Nancy Tivol, executive director of Sunnyvale Community Services (SCS), demonstrates this principle in action. She believes strongly in her own ability and in the abilities of every staff member and volunteer at SCS. Before Nancy, administrators and paid staff had made certain assumptions about volunteers. They assumed that volunteers would not be motivated, skilled, or experienced enough to take on the responsibility of some of the tasks, including interactions with clients and corporate contacts. As a result, volunteers were given only minimal responsibilities and did not have opportunities to explore or demonstrate their own capacities beyond these menial tasks. In contrast, Nancy encouraged the same group of people to excel. She placed volunteers in responsible positions, gave them the training and direction they required, and encouraged them to do their best. And they did just that!

Today, SCS has over two hundred volunteers year-round doing things that only staff members did previously; indeed, three major operations are run by volunteers, mostly over sixty-five years of age. Though programs have exploded in terms of clients served and amount of aid distributed, these volunteers' efforts and dedication have enabled SCS to reduce its payroll costs by over one-third.

Under Nancy's leadership, SCS became the county's only emergency assistance agency that doesn't turn people away for lack of funds. Over an eight-year period, SCA increased its funding for the prevention of evictions and utility disconnections and for paying for medical, prescription, and other critical services from $34,000 a year to $450,000—despite recessions and significantly reduced government and corporate contributions. During the same period the number of families served by its food program skyrocketed, climbing by 80 each month to more than 650.

The SCS picture changed so radically because Nancy had very high *expectations* of her volunteers, and these higher expectations breathed new life into the people around her. She prophesied their success. Listen to what one of those volunteers, Carol Schweizer, has to say: "I think you always rise to expectations. If somebody thinks that you can't do something, then you can't do it. But when they ask me around here to do some things I've never done before . . . I think, gosh, I can try it. I bet I could do that. And I can."[13]

Our own research has shown that people are often anxious or nervous when they are encouraged by people in leadership positions to go out and deliver their personal best. Yet those same people marched in and did what was expected of them. They were all willing; they were all excited by the challenges they faced. Spurred on by their leaders' high expectations, they developed the self-confidence, courage, and volition to live up to their leaders' expectations.

Positive Images Create Positive Possibilities

Positive expectations yield positive results. They also begin to create positive images in our minds and generate other positive possibilities. Positive futures for self and others are first constructed in our minds. "We see," say researchers, "what our imaginative horizon allows us to see."[14] Seeing is believing, and the results can be life-affirming and life-enhancing.

Athletes have known for a long time that stored mental pictures influence performance. Unless we can see ourselves as being successful, it is very difficult to produce the behavior that leads to success. Experiment after experiment shows that positive images make groups more effective, relieve symptoms of illness, and enhance achievement in school, the military, and business.[15]

One rather intriguing experiment demonstrates the power of positive images on performance. Divided into different groups, people were first instructed in effective bowling methods. Following these lessons, the bowlers practiced. Some of those who practiced were videotaped. One group of the videotaped bowlers saw only the positive things they did, and the other group saw only the negative. Those who saw only their positive moves improved significantly more than any of the other bowlers.[16]

Consider how this principle was put into practice by Kyle Von Raesfeld, a Santa Clara University freshman, who told us about coaching a football team at an elementary school while he was only in high school himself:

My first year there I was an assistant coach. The head coach knew a lot about football. He probably would have been a good coach for older kids, but he did not stay very positive with the kids, which is essential for any team, especially a younger team. He would always point out their mistakes, and very seldom point out their successes.

It didn't take very long for the kids to start getting down on themselves. The coach seemed to be constantly shouting. Soon enough, attendance at practices started to drop. The kids had lost all of their desire to play the game, and they clearly were not having fun. When it came my turn to talk at the end of a game or practice, I would try to encourage them and lift their spirits, but they were already defeated by the coach's comments. Needless to say, we did not have a very successful season, not only in terms of win-loss record, but also in accomplishing the primary goal, providing a good time for the kids.

The next year, I was the head coach with a friend from high school as an assistant. I had the same kids, we played the same teams, ran the same plays—and this year we went undefeated. Even better than that, each kid improved greatly and had a great time playing football. After we were a few weeks into the season I began to ponder why this team had basically done a 180-degree turnaround from the previous season. The first thing I noticed was that each kid had a big smile on his face as he came running out to practice. The kids were very enthusiastic about practice and always showed up. Why? I always made sure to keep a positive attitude. Where the previous coach would say, "Here's what you did wrong," I would say, "Here's what you guys did right," and then, "Here are two or three things you can improve upon." I also required the kids to stay positive with each other. I had the players tell each other when they did something good, and encourage each other when they make a mistake. Instead of hearing shouts of, "Why didn't you catch it? That was an easy catch," a player would be greeted by, "You'll get it next time." More often than not, he would catch the next pass!

Kyle had learned how high expectations lead to high performance. By focusing on positive images, he was able to noticeably change the way the kids felt about themselves and about others on the team. As he puts it, "If people feel like they've been defeated, whether it be from not receiving any praise, having a pessimistic leader, or comments from teammates, they will act and perform like they are defeated. But if you encourage and motivate them, more often than not, they will excel."

What do we learn from all this? Clearly, before we can lead, we have to believe in others, and we have to believe in ourselves. This has positive benefits for individual leaders, positive benefits for their constituents, and positive benefits for the organizations they serve. High expectations matter—and they matter a lot. To hold the belief that we and others can change and can develop new skills and abilities not only works its magic on the constituents but on the leader that holds this perception. Exemplary leaders know this and know how to purposefully hold in their minds high expectations for themselves and for other people.

With the attitude that people will live up to high expectations and with clear standards, leaders have to pay attention to what's happening around them so they can find those positive examples to recognize.

PAY ATTENTION

Leaders are out and about all the time. They're attending meetings, visiting customers, touring the plants or service centers, dropping in on the lab, making presentations at association gatherings, recruiting at local universities, holding roundtable discussions, speaking to analysts, or just dropping by employees' cubicles to say "Hello." Being mobile goes with the territory. In fact, at its root the word *lead* comes from an Old English word that means "go, travel, guide."

This is not purposeless wandering. Leaders are out there for a reason. One of the reasons, we would maintain, is to show that you care. One way of showing you care is to *pay attention* to people, to what they are doing, and to how they are feeling. And if you are clear about the standards you're looking for and you believe and expect that people will perform like winners, then you're going to notice lots of examples of people doing things right and doing the right things.

In contrast, what happens in organizations where managers are constantly on the lookout for problems? Three things: managers get a distorted view of reality; over time, production declines; and the managers' personal credibility hits bottom. Wandering around with an eye for trouble is likely to get you just that. More trouble.

Put yourself in the situation. If you knew someone was coming around to check up on you, how would you behave? Conventional wisdom holds that as soon as we spot the boss coming we put on our best behavior. Wrong. We may put on different behavior, but it's not our best. In fact, it can be our worst because we get nervous and tense. Plus, when we know that people are coming around to look for problems, we're more likely to hide them than to reveal them. People who work for more controlling managers are more likely to keep information to themselves, not reveal the truth, not be honest about what is going on. They know that little good comes from telling the truth.

No surprise then, that controlling managers have low credibility. Highly controlling behaviors—inspecting, correcting, checking up—signal lack of trust. How do you respond to people who don't trust you? You don't trust them. And since trustworthiness is a key element of personal credibility, credibility diminishes. We are just much less likely to believe someone who does not exhibit trust in us.[17] So when we're walking around our organizations paying attention, we need to have on our Pygmalion glasses and fully expect to find the best.

Release the Positive

It's human nature: when we're being watched by a person who is looking for our faults, we act very differently than we do in a supportive environment in which there's an opportunity to be rewarded for special achievements. When we know someone is looking for positive examples we'll make an effort to reveal them. Pygmalions don't so much carve a statue from the stone as release the beauty that's already in it.

When you see yourself as a caring leader, you act differently than you do when you see yourself as a controller. You begin to behave like a person who is genuinely interested in seeing others succeed, someone who is a cheerleader and coach much more than a militant authority figure out patrolling the neighborhood. People soon begin relating to you differently, they open up. They no longer dread seeing you coming down the hallway.

If people know there's a caring leader in their midst, in search of achievements to recognize, they'll want to show the best of themselves. That translates into increased productivity. This positive focus on behavior and performance, linked to goals and values, significantly improves morale as it moves the company toward higher levels of performance. In a supportive climate people are also much more likely to help each other succeed. They teach and coach each other. In this more open environment people are more likely to let you know when problems are brewing and to lend a hand in solving them before they escalate.

Listen with Your Eyes and Your Heart

Learning to understand and see things from another's perspective—to walk in their shoes—is absolutely crucial to building trusting relations and to career success.[18]

Comedian and actor Michael Pritchard told us a story that we'll never forget. He was making a presentation at a local elementary school (at the time he was a probation officer), and he got to talking with a third grader. When he asked her what she'd been learning, she responded that she'd been learning sign language. Michael was, as we were, intrigued. Sign language? Kids don't typically learn sign language in third grade. So he asked how she got started on that educational adventure.

The young girl explained that her best friend since first grade couldn't speak and couldn't hear. So she asked her mom if she could learn sign language to communicate with her friend. Her mom agreed. Now, the young girl said, "I listen with my eyes and my heart, not just my ears and my brain." All leaders can learn from this third grader. Listening with the eyes and the heart, not just the ears and the brain, requires a deeper level of paying attention and understanding. It requires that we hear the heart and see the soul.

Eyes-and-heart-listening can't be from a distance, reading reports or hearing things second hand. Our constituents want to know who we are, how we feel, and whether we really care. They want to see us in living color. Since proximity is the single best predictor of whether two people will talk to one another, you have to get close to people if you're going to communicate. It means regularly walking the halls and plant floors, meeting often with small groups, and hitting the road for frequent visits with associates, key suppliers, and customers. It may even mean learning another language if a large portion of your workforce or customer base speak it.

The third grader in Michael's story learned the language of another to strengthen their relationship. "Well," you might say, "she had to if she wanted to be her friend." Precisely! Learning another's language, literally or figuratively, is essential to leadership, and absolutely critical in this era of global leadership.[19] Unfortunately, listening is not well practiced. Research by the Hay Group, covering a million employees in over two thousand organizations, reveals that only about one in three people respond favorably when asked how well their company listens to them.[20] Yet it's only by learning what others value, what others enjoy, what others treasure, that we can expect to reach their hearts.

When you're out there paying attention to the positive, you're highly visible and you also make yourself known to others. While you're getting to know them, they're getting to know you. And who do you trust more, someone you know or someone you don't know? In general we're all much more likely to trust friends than strangers. Paying attention and actively appreciating others increases their trust in you. This kind of relationship is becoming more and more critical as we become increasingly global and diverse in our workforce. If others know we genuinely care about them, they're more likely to care about us. This is how we bridge cultural divides.

Be a Friend

As Daniela Maeder, of the Department of Economics and Labor, Switzerland, said to us: "Organizational diagrams don't matter at all. Be sure to treat employees as human beings and not as functional workers." Yet managerial myth says we shouldn't get too close to our associates, we can't be friends with people at work. Well, set this myth aside. Over a five-year period, researchers observed groups of friends and groups of acquaintances—people who knew each other only vaguely—performing motor skill and decision making tasks. The results were unequivocal. The groups composed of friends completed, on average, more than three times as many projects as the groups composed merely of acquaintances. In terms of decision-making assignments, groups of friends were over 20 percent more effective than groups of acquaintances were.[21]

There is an important caveat, however. Friends have to be strongly committed to the group's goals. If not, then friends may not do better. This is precisely why we said earlier that it is absolutely necessary for leaders to be clear about standards and to create a condition of shared goals and values. When it comes to performance, commitment to standards and good relations between people go together.

People are just more willing to follow someone they like and trust. To become fully trusted we must trust. And that means being open: open to others, open *with* others. An open door is a physical demonstration of a willingness to let others in. So is an open heart. This means disclosing things about yourself. We don't mean tabloid-style disclosures. We mean talking about your hopes and dreams, your family and friends, your interests and your pursuits. We mean telling others the same things you'd like to know about them.

When we're open we make ourselves vulnerable—and this vulnerability makes us more human and more trusted. If neither person in a relationship takes the risk of trusting, at least a little, the relationship remains stalled at a low level of caution and suspicion. If leaders want the higher levels of performance that come with trust and collaboration, then they must demonstrate their trust *in* others before asking for trust *from* others. As discussed in Chapter Nine, when it comes to trust, leaders ante up first.

Certainly, disclosing information about ourselves can be risky. We can't be certain that other people will like us, will appreciate our candor, will agree with our aspirations, will buy into our plans, or will interpret our words and actions in the way we intend. But by demonstrating the willingness to take such risks, leaders encourage others to take a similar risk—and thereby take the first steps necessary to build mutual trust. Disclosing information about yourself is a start, as is asking for and encouraging feedback. When you're out there attending to what's happening, noticing the positive contributions people are making, stop and ask for feedback yourself. It's a demonstration that you appreciate your associates and a way to encourage people to provide more information.[22]

Often, on the basis of this information, leaders are able to learn more about other people, their colleagues as well as their constituents, and in this process better understand how to personalize their recognition. We can only genuinely honor someone when we know who they are, what they like, and what they've done. We have to have the person in mind to make it special.

PERSONALIZE RECOGNITION

One of the more familiar complaints that we've heard about recognition is that it's too often highly predictable, routine, and impersonal. A one-size-fits-all approach to recognition feels disingenuous, forced, and thoughtless. Over time it can even increase cynicism and actually damage credibility.

That's why it's so important for leaders to pay attention to the likes and dislikes of each and every individual. To make recognition personally meaningful, you first have to get to know your constituents. By personalizing recognition, leaders send the message that someone took the time to notice the achievement, seek out the responsible individual, and personally deliver praise in a timely manner.

Linda Lewis of Charles Schwab & Company understands that timeliness and personalization count. About a month after Linda arrived as senior vice president of learning and education, she initiated the Giraffe Award (given, naturally enough, for sticking your neck out, going above and beyond normal responsibilities and duties). Linda told the first person who received the award to select another deserving person and present the award at the next meeting.

The Giraffe Award is given monthly; everyone within Schwab is eligible. Winners receive custody of a stuffed giraffe, plus a colored poster to commemorate the event. Cute but maybe a bit predictable? Not so—and that's the beauty of it. Schwab University associates found a way to take the predictable and make it a surprise. They found a way to take something that might be impersonal and make it a personal, one-to-one experience. Somewhere along the way, Paul Oknaian decided he'd add a little something extra, and he put a lei around the stuffed giraffe's neck. Pretty soon the giraffe had a cowboy hat, some shoes, and a shoulder bag. Then came the navel piercing that Linda Chan gave the giraffe before she passed it on to Denise Green, who'd jumped in above and beyond the call to assist Chan in facilitating some classes.

Along with the stuffed giraffe, which gets passed from person to person each month, there's a small poster. The prior recipient personalizes the poster, which is then proudly displayed in each recipient's cubicle or office area for everyone to see. What Linda started was a process that enabled everyone to get involved and to make every recognition special. She created a climate of personalization; which when you think about it, is one of things that Schwab values.

Ann Cessaris of Key Communication reminds us all of another reason why it's essential to personalize, or "culturalize," recognition. "I had a client," she reports, "who was born in Asia, came to this country at age twelve, and was very well acclimated to life in the United States. However, when his boss rewarded him for exceptional contribution on a team project by giving him a delightful corner office, the client was horrified. He felt it destroyed the feeling of teamwork and his future relations with his team members."

"Culture values run deep," says Ann, and she's absolutely correct. Personalizing requires knowing what's appropriate individually and culturally. It's pretty arrogant for someone to assume that they naturally know what's right for others without even bothering to inquire or observe. Leaders know that uncomfortable or embarrassing as it may seem at first to recognize someone's efforts, it's really not difficult to do. And it's well worth the effort to make a connection with each person. Leaders learn from many small and often casual acts of appreciation what works for each of their constituents and how best to personalize recognition.

Use a Variety of Rewards

Leaders don't rely exclusively on the organization's formal reward system, which offers only a limited range of options. After all, promotions and raises are scarce resources. So don't make the mistake of assuming that individuals respond only to money. Although salary increases or bonuses are certainly appreciated, individual needs for and appreciation of rewards extend much further. Verbal recognition of performance in front of one's peers and visible awards, such as certificates, plaques, and other tangible gifts, are powerful indeed and almost unlimited.

Spontaneous and unexpected rewards are often more meaningful than the expected formal rewards. "The form of recognition that has the most positive influence on us, and that is used most often, is on-the-spot recognition," says HR manager Michelle Carlson.

"When something fantastic happens, I comment on it right away and to whomever may be close enough to hear. In a group setting, when one person really goes the extra mile to make sure the company delivers on its promises, we all really try to give that person public recognition."

In contrast, relying upon an organization's formal reward system typically requires considerable effort. For example, we found that the time lapse between performance and promotion is often more than six months.[23] So instead of relying only or even primarily on formal rewards, effective leaders make tremendous use of *intrinsic* rewards—rewards that are built into the work itself, including such factors as a sense of accomplishment, a chance to be creative, and the challenge of the work—immediate outcomes of an individual's effort. These rewards are far more important than salary and fringe benefits in improving job satisfaction, commitment, retention, and performance.[24] Often it's the simple, personal gestures that are the most powerful rewards. It's true that money may get people to do the job but it doesn't get them to do a *good* job.

Praise and coaching are significant forms of recognition. Not enough people make enough use of one powerful but inexpensive two-word reward—"thank you." Personal congratulations rank at the top of the most powerful nonfinancial motivators identified by employees.[25] There are few if any more basic needs than to be noticed, recognized, and appreciated for our efforts. And that's as true for volunteers, teachers, doctors, priests, and politicians as it is for the maintenance staff and those in the executive suite. There's little wonder, then, that a greater volume of thanks is reported in highly innovative companies than in low-innovation firms.[26] Extraordinary achievements do not come easily and seldom bloom in barren and unappreciative settings.

Leaders are constantly on the lookout for ways to spread the psychological benefits of making people feel like winners, because winners contribute in important ways to the success of their projects. Leaders often serve as a mirror for the team. They reflect back to others what a job well done looks like, make certain that the members of the team know that they have done well, and ensure that others in the organization are aware of the group's effort and contributions. To that end, when he was vice president of business development for Comerica Bank, Sam Bhaumik hung a large bell on the wall. Every time an associate booked a new deal or signed up a new client, that person got to ring the bell. The individual was instantly recognized, and others were stimulated to make a sale so that they, too, could ring the bell. Simple, but satisfying. That also describes something that Naomi Boyd did during her very first leadership experience, as the senior QA analyst for Visa International. Boyd explains:

Because I knew everyone was working hard and long hours, I would often bring in breakfast or dinner, depending on the shift. The team members viewed it as a sign that I appreciated the hard work and the sacrifices they were making working such long hours and not spending time with their families. Saying thank you and showing appreciation will get you a long way.

Naomi understood that rewards—especially rewards that are made personal—do make a difference.

What happens when you provide both intrinsic and extrinsic rewards? The idea of an additive effect is intuitively appealing—but it does not always occur. In fact, there is some evidence that intrinsic and extrinsic rewards are negatively related and may actually work against one another. For example, in a situation that is already intrinsically rewarding, the addition of extrinsic rewards may reduce the effectiveness of the intrinsic rewards.[27] On the other hand, some studies show that while achievement-oriented people do find success rewarding in and of itself, money and fame are also important rewards, serving as symbols of that success.[28] One executive referred to this as the "fun being in playing the game down on the field, while the results are posted on the scoreboard." What we found among leaders was not so much an either-or mentality as a both-and type of thinking. Leaders are remarkably skillful in using these types of rewards in complementary ways.

The extent to which recognition and rewards are applied to each individual in a personal (rather than an impersonal) manner also explains a lot about how leaders and their organizations get a motivational bang for their buck (or not) from recognizing people's contributions. After all, leaders get the best from others not by building fires under people but by building the fire within them. As U.S. Postal Service District Manager Mike Matuzek observes: "There is a fire that already burns inside of each person. My job is to simply stoke it." This explains Mike's own motivation in sending out *personally* addressed and *personally* signed birthday cards to all 13,567 postal employees in his district each year (that's thirty-seven a day, seven days a week!). This human touch and the few minutes it takes to establish some personal connection with each person in the organization is certainly a factor in why Mike's district is consistently at the top in the United States.

Be Thoughtful

What personalized recognition comes down to is *thoughtfulness*. It means taking those observations you've made about an individual and asking: "What would really make this special and unique for this person? What could I do to make this a memorable experience so that he always remembers how important his contributions are?" This kind of thoughtfulness was evident in how Wayne Bennett gave personalized recognition—and did so in a manner that reinforced clear standards, acknowledged high expectations, and indicated that he had been paying attention. Wayne was the founder and president of Glenn Valley Homes, a unique company set up to build computer-designed, precision-crafted custom homes in a plant in Orland, California, a small town northeast of Sacramento.

As a start-up, the company was so successful that its new factory was faced with a backlog of home orders. When Wayne needed a highly skilled production manager to meet this extraordinary challenge, he selected Ray Freer, a veteran with fifteen years in the industry. Ray was an eager and energetic worker whose talents and expertise had not been fully used in previous jobs. Wayne believed in Ray and entrusted him with full responsibility to lead the crew.

Wayne's confidence in Ray was well placed. After several six- and seven-day weeks, they were ready to begin regular production. The plant was state-of-the-art, the previously inexperienced crew well-trained, and Ray had personally built and installed additional buffer stations to augment production during unexpected delays. The first house was successfully cut, sized, and shipped within three days of the start of production.

Wayne wanted to acknowledge Ray's accomplishments, so—during a barbecue party he was holding for all the workers and their families—he called the group over to one side of the factory and asked Ray to show how one of the buffer stations worked. When Ray threw the lever to operate the skate-wheel conveyor that he had designed and constructed, an automotive radio antenna popped up, displaying a flag with an envelope attached. Ray looked inside the envelope, and found a $1,000 check and a personal letter from Wayne thanking him for his outstanding work. Wayne read the letter out loud to everyone else in the company (and their spouses and families) acknowledging the importance of Ray's innovativeness, dedication, and tireless work. Ray was clearly moved by Wayne's public display of appreciation, and the loud clapping and cheers of his coworkers and crew demonstrated their mutual support for his well-earned award.

Wayne obviously put some *thought* into this recognition. He closely observed what Ray had done to contribute to the success of the factory, and he used equipment that Ray had constructed as an integral part of the celebration. Wayne could have just handed a check to Ray in private without all the ceremony. Not Wayne. He knew that personalizing recognition was essential. He also knew that telling the story in public would create more meaning, go a long way toward thanking everyone for their hard work, and help build a strong sense of community. This is exactly what leaders do when they celebrate values and victories, as we explain in the next chapter.

COMMITMENT NUMBER 9:
RECOGNIZE CONTRIBUTIONS BY SHOWING APPRECIATION FOR INDIVIDUAL EXCELLENCE

Leaders have high expectations of themselves and of their constituents. Their standards are clear and help people focus on what needs to be done. Leaders provide clear directions, feedback, and encouragement. They expect the best of people and create self-fulfilling prophecies about how ordinary people can produce extraordinary actions and results. By paying attention, offering encouragement, personalizing appreciation, and maintaining a positive outlook leaders stimulate, rekindle, and focus people's energies and drive.

Leaders make people winners, and winning people like to up the ante, raise the standards, and explore uncharted territory. Leaders recognize and reward what individuals do to contribute to vision and values. And leaders express their appreciation far beyond the limits of the organization's formal performance appraisal system. Leaders enjoy being spontaneous and creative in saying thank you, whether by sending notes, handing out personalized prizes, listening without interrupting, or trying any of the myriad other forms of recognition. In this commitment, we provide a variety of strategies that you can adapt to your situation for help in using recognition as a leadership process and linking rewards with performance.

- *Be creative about rewards.*

People respond to all kinds of rewards. A shop foreman presents employees who achieve their production objectives with a new chair for the workplace. The comfortable chairs are a good reward in themselves, but a major part of the reward comes with the presentation. The employee is called into the foreman's office and presented with the new chair. Then, amid the cheers of coworkers, the foreman wheels the honored employee in the chair—all the way back to the work station. One of our university colleagues takes his highest-performing students out for lunch and bowling each term to show his appreciation for their hard work. There's no limit—except your imagination—to creative rewards.

Remember the DeMartini family from Chapter Ten? When Karyn DeMartini wondered how she was going to bring laughter and fun to her family as they dealt with life-threatening illness, she thought outside the box and planned an awards night to celebrate getting through surgery:

Lala was awarded for her courageousness as the CEO of the family. Nonie was dubbed Vice President of Internal Affairs and received an award for her excellence in preparing Lala's meals, distributing her medications, and taking care of anything else that happened at home. My Auntie Paula was named Vice President of Transportation since she was one of the main drivers to all of the appointments. Everyone received an award for something positive they had done—and a senseless, but meaningful, title. This whimsical ritual brought a smile to everyone's face—something we hadn't seen in a number of weeks.

This worked for the DeMartini family. To get a sense of what will work for your organization, discuss with your team members what they find encouraging, and ways they can encourage others. Here are some questions to get you started:

- *What types of encouragement make the most difference for you?* Think of a time when you felt encouraged, supported, or cared about by this team. What happened? Who helped? Think about the best recognition you ever received. What happened? Who helped?
- *What talents do you use in encouraging people?* Name two talents you use most often in recognizing others. (For example, writing and singing.) How do you use them? How do they affect what you find encouraging? Think about two talents of your teammates in recognizing you or others. How can you make use or tap into these talents?

You can also brainstorm about what you and your teammates could do to better support one another. Consider "Super person of the month" awards, employee photographs with the president, verbal encouragement, pictures in annual reports and company newsletters, published thank-yous, contributions to employees' favorite charities, gift certificates and merchandise credits, embossed business cards, gifts for spouses and families, and banners displayed in the cafeteria.[29] There are many, many ways to show you care, and to encourage colleagues—just use your imagination.

• *Make recognition public.*

Maybe, like Joan Nicolo once was, you're reluctant to recognize people in public, fearing that to do so might cause jealousy or resentment. But private rewards do little to set an example—and often the recipient, not wanting to brag or appear conceited, has no opportunity to share the story with others. So tell your workers and colleagues that they've done well as soon as you find out about it, and let other people know about the accomplishment too. When recognition is public, the individual's self-esteem is bolstered, the behavior being recognized serves as a model to others, and people see that doing the right things will be noticed and rewarded. While all recognition encourages others to continue their good work, public recognition portrays the recipient as a role model, conveying to everyone the message, "Here's someone just like you. You too can do this."

Public recognition builds commitment, because it makes people's actions visible to their peers and therefore difficult to deny or revoke. It also helps to strengthen recipients by increasing their visibility. Military organizations make tremendous use of medals and insignias, which are almost always handed out at ceremonies. Awards serve the same purpose.

But what do you do about people who do not get recognized? Someone, for example, whose performance is not specifically acknowledged in a meeting or did not receive an award for top performance? The question suggests that this person who is left out is somehow equally deserving of recognition and so is likely to feel hurt, offended, or slighted at the oversight. If you are doing recognition well, you are including everyone who is deserving. So the concern is really, What do you do about people who are not deserving of recognition, public or otherwise? The answer is relatively simple: Don't recognize them. Don't thank them for simply showing up to work when others have been working hard to get the results needed. Don't make them the super-person-of-the-month just because they've been around longer than anyone else who has received this recognition. To do so undermines your credibility and that of the role of recognition in your organization.

So, what should you do? Here's what Bob Nelson, author of *1001 Ways to Reward Employees* suggests:

If an employee who works for me ever comes to ask or complain why they did not receive recognition for an achievement for which I praised someone else in the department, I react in one of two ways: (1) I made a mistake and need to correct it. *"Tell me, Sally, what you did and if I overlooked that achievement I apologize and will reference you in the next staff meeting."* . . .

Or, (2) The employee has not warranted a praising and I now have a chance to talk to him openly about the topic. *"I'm really glad you came to talk with me about this, Tom. Frankly, I haven't seen where your performance merits recognition. I would like to be able to recognize you and would like to discuss what would need to be different in your performance for that to happen—and how I can be of help to you."* For some employees, such a discussion might be the first spark of interest in wanting to be a higher performer and the start of an entirely new level of contribution to the department. It gives you a chance to start over with new performance goals for the employee and a plan to attain those goals.[30]

• *Provide feedback en route.*

People produce best when they're given feedback about how they're progressing. Without feedback, production will be less efficient and will exact a significant toll in the form of increased levels of stress and anxiety. Recognition signals successful accomplishment, reinforcing both the employee's "I can do it" attitude and the leader's expectations: "I knew you could do it." This certainly happened for Katie Hasserd, associate director of clinical operations. Five years after she was given the opportunity to put together a cardiovascular advisory panel meeting for Connetics, what she remembers most vividly from that project is "not all of my hard work, organizing and planning, nor the long hours preparing slides and presentations, nor handling all the logistics and coordination. It was the call from the CEO who took the time to personally congratulate me and thank me."

A study of the winningest high school and college athletic coaches reveals that they pay great attention to providing real-time feedback on their players' performance and will, as appropriate, recognize and reward outstanding contributions. Players—regardless of fame or fortune—need to hear when they do well and when they don't. As the coaches explained, ongoing feedback "is a highly effective way to shape the behavior of the athletes so as to increase the team's ability to continue winning. Without immediate and precise feedback, the learning process ends and mediocrity is sure to emerge. Ongoing evaluation of the players' ability to play your game, to your expectations, is critical given the constant need to restock the team with younger athletes."[31] What works for athletes also applies to those on the factory floor, behind the counter, in city hall, and in the corner office.

• *Be a Pygmalion.*

Realize that your behavior toward people is based on your expectations about them. Treating people in a friendly, pleasant, and positive fashion and being attentive to their needs—behavior that reflects your high expectations of them—produces increased performance, because that behavior has a favorable effect on their motivation. Likewise, when you have high expectations of others, you tend to give them more input—suggestions, helpful hints, and responsive answers to their questions—and more feedback about the results of their efforts. Both of these factors enhance people's learning and increase the likelihood that they'll achieve competence and mastery rather than repeat mistakes or let ineffective habits become ingrained.

If you have any doubt about the power of expectations, think of Antonio Zárate. As described in Chapter Nine, he led a dramatic turnaround of Metalsa into an award-winning, world-class company—all with the same local Mexican workforce that had staffed the company when he took on the challenge. Antonio believed in the workers—and the company blossomed.

The standards of performance (or "output levels") that you set communicate your expectations of others, and these in turn affect others' levels of aspiration. Therefore, make sure that these standards are high and that they're linked directly to what's important to the success of your organization. Make sure, too, that your performance standards include what's important to constituents as well as what's important to management, stockholders, or the larger organization and community.

Being a Pygmalion entails developing a winner's attitude in those around you. This means paying considerable attention to your constituents' successes, since only those who envision themselves as winners are likely to work hard, try new actions, and become leaders in their own right. If they stumble or fall, discuss this result with them as only a temporary lack of success. If criticism is necessary, comments should be restricted to behavior rather than character. Similarly, feedback—preferably extensive—should stress continuous progress rather than comparisons with other people.[32] When the goal is reached, leaders make certain that constituents understand that it happened because of what they did.

• *Foster positive expectations.*

One way to promote positive expectations is to let others take the lead in setting their own goals, rather than dictating the terms and manner of their development. This communicates your belief that people have the capacity to be the pilots of their destiny, which is a core tenet held by those who take initiative.

Another technique that cultivates positive expectations is to point to problems without offering a solution. Outstanding tutors use this strategy with their students, initiating what amounts to a Socratic dialogue, leading the person through a series of questions. This allows people to find their own way to the answers and bolsters their confidence in decision making.

Fostering positive expectations is also an important deterrent to "stereotype threat," a term coined by Stanford University psychologist Claude Steele.[33] To be successful on a job people need to feel they belong there, are accepted and valued, and have the skills and inner resources needed to be successful. When negative stereotypes undermine these assumptions, they hamper performance.

In one set of studies, Steele recruited men and women who were strong in math to solve problems from the qualifying exam for graduate school. They took the test in two groups. The first group was told that the test usually showed differences in ability between men and women. The women in this group scored appreciably lower than the men. Gender differences were not mentioned to the second group—and these women and men scored equally well. This same performance-lowering effect occurred when black test takers were given a similarly threatening message. The active ingredient in lowering women's scores, or those of black test takers, was debilitating anxiety, triggered by the threatening stereotype.

Those most likely to feel the effects of stereotype threats are those at the vanguard of a group; for example, the first women to become jet pilots or the first minority group members to enter a brokerage house. At this point, Steele argues, people are particularly vulnerable to doubting their own abilities, questioning their talents and skills and thus undermining their own sense of capability. Their anxiety acts as a spotlight, both for themselves and (at least in their minds) those who are watching to see how well, or how poorly, they will do.

Positive expectations generally reflect a meritocracy in the minds of leaders, and a strong respect and appreciation for people from different backgrounds. You need to envision the possibilities for greatness within each of the people on your team. Recognize that extraordinary achievements require the commitment and cooperation of other (and often many) people. Value the insights brought to work by people of diverse backgrounds and bring positive expectations to each and every workplace site.[34]

• *Make the recognition presentation meaningful.*

An effective presentation makes a significant impression. In fact, according to an O.C. Tanner survey of more than thirty-three thousand award recipients in the United States and Canada, the presentation of an award affects employees' perceptions of the entire recognition program, even their perceptions of the company as a whole.[35] When surveyed employees called their award presentation "excellent," 97 percent of them said their "contribution was acknowledged." In contrast, when employees said their presentation was "poor" or even "non-existent," only 39 percent felt their contribution to the company was acknowledged. This even though they had indeed received an acknowledgment. Talk about losing the proverbial bang for the buck!

Where does cash fit in? Just ask yourself: Do you remember the amount of your last cash bonus? Do you remember what bill, credit card, or loan you paid off with it? And if you did buy yourself (or your family) something, isn't that what you remember and not the cash? On the other hand, you can probably list almost every award you ever won in high school or college, even if it's been ten, twenty, thirty years or more. Why? Because it was tangible, and probably given in a formal (public) awards ceremony.

Any time Dick Nettel awards someone a new title, he makes it an event. When Charlene Nichols, who had been with the bank for twenty-five years, made senior vice president, Dick had an idea. He had Charlene's assistant get ten or fifteen people—including Charlene's mother, in North Dakota—on a conference call, secretly hooked up to the intercom. Then, with all the staff gathered, Dick said: "I really want to recognize someone with a passion behind making customer service a reality—someone who is so devoted that if you looked up customer service in the dictionary, this person's picture would be there." At that point, he brought Charlene in front of the group and told her she was getting the title. She got tears in her eyes, and prepared to talk. That's when Dick said, "Charlene, This is your life! We're going to have a contest for you right now to see how many people you can remember over your career." Then all those memorable people from past and present spoke in turn about the fantastic, sometimes funny moments they'd shared with her. Of course, she knew exactly who they were! It was simple—and something she will remember the rest of her life.

As Dick knew, an effective presentation does not mean holding an elaborate banquet, shutting down the plant, or other costly events. It does require some thought and time to prepare in advance. For example, the right person to make the presentation often isn't the highest-ranking officer in the firm. To ensure sincerity and meaning, the presenter should be the highest-ranking individual who personally knows the recipient's accomplishment and contributions. Make sure that whoever makes the presentation knows exactly what is being recognized and can talk about specific contributions that have affected the company. Be certain that the actions can be linked and tied to the company's vision and values. Invite peers and colleagues to attend the presentation, and ask coworkers to comment on the difference that the recipient's actions have made on them and their own work. This helps everyone to understand and better appreciate the contribution being recognized, how it is related to the company's goals, and how it can be emulated.

Also, give the recipient an opportunity to make a few comments. Not everyone will want to, but everyone should be asked. Recipients often want to thank others who have helped them, and to talk about their emotional attachment to the goals and the company. By their example, they provide direction to others in the audience about how aspirations can be achieved and reinforce the sense of common purpose. Finally, wrap up the presentation by offering a sincere thank-you, not just to the recipient, but to everyone in attendance. Let them know that you're on the lookout for people doing things right, and you plan to catch them at it!

- *Find people who are doing things right.*

Rewards are most effective when they're highly specific and in close proximity to the appropriate behavior. One of the most important results of being out and about as a leader is that you can personally observe people doing things right and then reward them either on the spot or at the next public gathering.

Once you've selected people for recognition, be sure to tell them—and everyone else—*why* they've been chosen. Tell the story of why the person is being recognized, and make it specific. Merely saying "Hey, you did a great job in that meeting last week" may sound nice, but in practical terms, it is a fairly worthless remark. The person you're praising has no idea what action impressed you or how it made a difference. Give as much information as you can about why you're pleased and what effect the person's actions have had on the larger picture. Remember that stories describing valued actions are very powerful ways to communicate what behaviors are expected and will be rewarded. Walk employees through the specific actions that contributed to goal attainment and explain why they were consistent with the shared values.

You might say something along these lines: "Sue was selected as the employee of the month because she called five different stores to locate an item that a customer requested but that we didn't have in stock. And she picked it up on her way home from work so that the customer could have it in time for an important event. That's the kind of behavior that makes us so highly valued by our customers. Thank you, Sue. We make this award to you in appreciation of your contribution to our organization's goal of delighting every customer."

This kind of positive example can be particularly useful when you're trying to get people to understand the right things to do to achieve a high standard. It provides a behavioral map that people can store in their minds and rely on when a similar situation arises in the future.

To broaden the net for recognition, set up systems that make it possible for people to be recognized by their constituents—be they peers, customers, or suppliers—not just managers. This encourages everyone in the organization to be on the lookout for good behaviors—and to be mindful that others are observing their actions as well. Weekly breakfast meetings are perfect opportunities to ask for such incidents. Add to your agenda the question, "Who have you seen doing something special this week that's really helped our organization?"

After just two weeks focused on encouraging the heart through recognition and celebration of values, Sam Bhaumik of Comerica Bank reported improved productivity, more interaction among employees, improved relationships between employees and senior management, and increased motivation and self-confidence. "The next challenge," Sam says, "will be to remain consistent and to maintain and improve the benefits from encouraging the heart."

- ### *Don't be stingy about saying thank you.*

Who among us thinks that they have been thanked enough, appreciated enough, recognized enough for what they do and who they are? Indeed, it might be easy to trivialize thanking people by taking it to an extreme, but we're quite far from reaching that point on the continuum.

Bob Greene, a syndicated columnist for the *Chicago Tribune,* describes talking with a group of people about a particular manager. Some of them liked the person, some didn't. But everyone agreed about one thing: he never said thank you. Greene concluded that for some managers the reluctance to say thank you is a device used to maintain a symbolic distance between themselves and their constituents.[36] The unfortunate result is a real loss of trust.

Less than half of all managers indicate that they give recognition for high performance. Why? They say they're dealing with professionals and professionals don't need it. Wrong on many counts. First, who among us is not a professional? Second, when we ask people if they *need* encouragement to perform at their best, their responses are all over the board. But when we ask people if getting encouragement *helps them* to perform at a higher level and sustain that level of performance longer, the answer is a resounding yes. In other words, if we want high sustained levels of performance, encouragement is key.

When John Schallau was a sales engineer at Centigram Communications Corporation, he wanted to be sure to recognize people and he wanted to be reminded of it daily. So he created a screen saver that popped up every time he turned on his computer and when it was idle for more than seven minutes. It listed some of the ways he might say thank you, including possible rewards for individuals, ways to acknowledge group milestones, and even ideas for theme days to encourage camaraderie. He told us that as he discovered new ways to encourage the heart, he would add them to the list. Every day, the screen saver helped get John started, helped him encourage the heart and cheer on others in the organization.

Look up the word *cheerleader* in the dictionary. It exists. Try looking up *cheer-manager* and you'll find it doesn't exist. We can't manage cheers. The fire already burns in people, and leaders must stoke it, whether that means personally signing a birthday card for each individual in the organization, giving an unexpected note of appreciation and a movie pass, or passing on a compliment. Whatever the method, it needs to be genuine and be praise that matters.[37]

Joan Carter discovered the powerful effect of publicly giving thanks when she was general manager and executive chef of the Faculty Club at Santa Clara University. Following her extremely successful but difficult first year at the club (in which revenues increased by 35 percent and costs decreased by 5 percent, ending a period of deficits that had threatened the club's continued existence), she sent a letter to all club members, university departments, and members of the club's staff. In this "Open Letter of Thanks" she described in glowing detail the recent party the club had thrown to celebrate its dramatic turnaround. She also took the opportunity to describe the contributions of those on her staff and within the university community who had made that night, and that past year, so successful. As she recalls:

So many people had come up to me during that party to thank *me* for the changes that had occurred at the club. All I could think about was that it was *my staff* whose efforts and willingness to make changes had made us successful; *they* were the ones who needed to be thanked. So I wrote the letter. As I wrote it, I realized that the list of people who needed to be thanked was endless and I began feeling very humble. Not only did I need to thank each staff member by name and contribution, but also so many others on campus who helped every day and our customers who were excited about our changes and supported us through their patronage and referrals, I wanted them all to know that I knew we couldn't have done it without them.

The response was totally unexpected. "I received dozens of phone calls and personal notes echoing the mutual admiration that had grown between the club and the university community. Those notes were posted on the bulletin board in the kitchen for the staff, further reinforcing the staff's commitment to their customers. It was incredible. I never dreamed saying 'Thank You' would make *me* feel so good or be so good for our business."

What makes a *thank-you* work is the leader's genuine care and respect for those who are doing the work. Exemplary leaders recognize that they can't do it alone and that it is only when constituents feel appreciated by their leaders that they put forth extraordinary effort.

COMMITMENT NUMBER 9

RECOGNIZE CONTRIBUTIONS BY SHOWING APPRECIATION FOR INDIVIDUAL EXCELLENCE

- *Be creative about rewards.*

- *Make recognition public.*

- *Provide feedback en route.*

- *Be a Pygmalion.*

- *Foster positive expectations.*

- *Make the recognition presentation meaningful.*

- *Find people who are doing things right.*

- *Don't be stingy about saying thank you.*

Source: The Leadership Challenge by James M. Kouzes and Barry Z. Posner. Copyright © 2002.

12 CELEBRATE THE VALUES AND VICTORIES

Ceremonies, celebrations, and rituals are not about the event. They're about touching the hearts and souls of every employee.

Victoria Sandvig, Charles Schwab & Co., Inc.

If you can create a community that supports itself, you can really achieve wonderful things.

Keith Sonberg, Roche Bioscience

All over the world, in every country, in every culture, people stop working on certain days during the year and take the time to celebrate. We hold elaborate parades to shower the hometown championship team with cheers of appreciation. We set off fireworks to commemorate great historic victories. We convene impromptu ceremonies in the company conference room to rejoice in the award of a new contract. We attend banquets to show our respect for individuals and groups who've accomplished the extraordinary. We get together with colleagues at the end of a grueling work session and give each other high-fives for a job well done. Even in tragic times we come together in remembrance and song to honor those before us and to reaffirm our commitment.

Why? Why do we take time away from working to come together, tell stories, and raise our spirits? Sure, we all need a break from the hectic pace of our jobs, but celebrations are not trivial excuses to goof off. Celebrations are among the most significant ways we have to proclaim our respect and gratitude, to renew our sense of community, and to remind ourselves of the values and history that bind us together. Celebrations serve as important a purpose in the long-term health of our organizations as does the daily performance of tasks.

Besides, who really *wants* to work for a place that has no ritual or ceremony—a boring place that celebrates nothing? David Campbell, senior fellow with the Center for Creative Leadership, says it well: "A leader who ignores or impedes organizational ceremonies and considers them as frivolous or 'not cost-effective,' is ignoring the rhythms of history and our collective conditioning. [Celebrations] are the punctuation marks that make sense of the passage of time; without them, there are no beginnings and endings. Life becomes an endless series of Wednesdays."[1]

Keith Sonberg, director of site operations for Roche Bioscience in Palo Alto, California, definitely doesn't think organizational gatherings are frivolous. He loves to find ways to bring people together to have some fun, build a spirit of camaraderie, and enjoy each other's company. He's very creative about it—and he even boasts that he does a lot of things that are little crazy.

For example, several years back Keith got the idea that it'd be fun to have a camp out on the company grounds. The facility has an expansive, campus-like setting, with trees and green lawns and rolling hills. When he went to his staff with the idea, at first they responded, "What are you talking about, a camp out?" He launched into his idea, saying, "We'll do it like we used to when we were kids. We'll just build it like a fair, and use all homemade stuff." It didn't take too much persuading to convince his staff—who're very handy with tools and materials—to give this "gift" to the company's employees and their families.

Now, over one weekend every summer, 300 to 350 children and adults show up for a weekend of great fun and celebration. There's a water slide built from giant sheets of plastic and PVC pipe. There're tractor rides with hay bales, a pony ride, a pitch and putt area with some driving nets, volleyball and horseshoe courts, and races with little electric Barbie and Jeep cars. At night they pitch tents, play music and sing around the camp fire. They string together four king-sized bed sheets to make a giant screen like a drive-in movie, and everyone sits around in lawn chairs and watches the flicks. The evening meal is cooked by the employees, potluck style, and in the morning everyone awakens to enjoy a pancake breakfast in the company cafeteria. It's a special event—and a wonderful environment. As Keith says, "I strive for a community spirit where people can go out and raise a barn together. That's the kind of human interaction that I'm looking for and want to build." This spirit of community, one that builds and strengthens relationships, is one of the most significant contributors to a strong and resilient workforce, and one that, in the long run, can get extraordinary things done. It's a value that Keith holds dear, and his barn-raising–style celebrations are ways of paying tribute to it.

To some a camp out on a corporate campus may seem like a wasteful distraction. You can hear the critics in their Scrooge-like tones saying, "We haven't got time for fun and games. After all, this is a business." Well, pharmaceuticals is a scientifically complex business and a money-making enterprise. But Sonberg knows that promoting a culture of celebration fuels the sense of unity and mission essential for retaining and motivating today's workforce.

What leaders like Keith know from practice is confirmed in our research. Performance improves when leaders bring people together to rejoice in their achievements and to reinforce their shared principles. If leaders are to effectively Celebrate the Values and Victories, they must master these three *essentials:*

- Create a spirit of community
- Tell the story
- Set the example

By bringing people together, sharing the lessons from success, and getting personally involved, leaders reinforce in others the courage required to get extraordinary things done in organizations.

CREATE A SPIRIT OF COMMUNITY

Individual recognition increases the recipient's sense of worth, and it improves performance. Public celebrations have this effect and more: they add other significant and lasting contributions to the welfare of individuals and the organization. It's this added benefit that makes celebrating together so powerful.

Professors Terrence Deal and M. K. Key express it this way: "Celebrations infuse life with passion and purpose. . . . They bond people together and connect us to shared values and myths. Ceremonies and rituals create community, fusing individual souls with the corporate spirit. When everything is going well, ritual occasions allow us to revel in our glory. When times are tough, ceremonies draw us together, kindling hope and faith that better times lie ahead."[2]

Public ceremonies serve as a collective reminder of why we are here, of the values and visions that we share. In acknowledging the "common unity" that we share with one another, leaders create a sense of community and team spirit, and they build and maintain the social support we need to thrive, especially in the most stressful times.

Reinforce Shared Values and Outcomes

There's definitely a unique feeling of community among the employees at Charles Schwab. A pioneer in the industry, Schwab has weathered the ups and downs of the markets and the uncertainties of international crises as much because of its culture as anything else. To build and sustain that strong culture, Schwab engages in periodic events that renew its sense of community. Every year Schwab holds a Senior Management Team offsite. Attended by the approximately 180 senior vice presidents, these offsites have solid business objectives, and another purpose as well. As Victoria Sandvig, vice president of Schwab's Event and Production Services Department, told us, "We're asked to create a ritual during these meetings that really brings the group together, allows people to get to know each other better, and builds upon the culture of our company."

At the October 2000 senior management team meeting, for instance, the theme was *Picture This*. The entire agenda was focused on the future. For one evening of the three-day event, Victoria and her team planned a dinner on the beach. This was no ordinary picnic but a celebration of communal spirit and purpose. After some casual conversation over refreshments, David Pottruck, co-CEO of Schwab, invited all the senior vice presidents to join him and gather around a large firepit dug in the sand. Dave then told the group:

> Craft-making was a communal effort in which all participated. It was believed that the strength of all would be infused into the final outcome. We've asked you here this evening to participate in a communal effort, as well. I now invite you to join me in lighting this fire as a symbol of our common character and purpose.

A torch was passed, and the group lit the fire. Dave continued.

> This is our fire. It represents the passion, the determination, and the soul of Schwab. All of you here tonight are what keeps this fire going. All of you make this fire grow stronger every day. Thank you all for being the heart and soul of this company, for energizing us, for fueling us.

This may not be the stuff of ordinary organizations, but it is the stuff of great ones, ones with strong cultures. The best leaders know that every gathering of a group is a chance to renew commitment. They never let pass any opportunity to make sure that everyone knows why they're all there and how they're going to act in service of that purpose. Whether it's in honor of an individual, group, or organizational achievement, celebrations offer leaders the perfect opportunity to explicitly communicate and reinforce the actions and behaviors that are important in realizing shared values and shared goals.

Celebrations are much more than parties; they're ceremonies and rituals that create meaning. Public ceremonies can serve to crystallize personal commitments. And because celebrations are so visible, it's vitally important to be clear about the statements you're making and the behaviors you're reinforcing. You should be fully aware that people are going to leave the event remembering and repeating what you say and what they see. You should always be personally prepared, as Dave was in this instance, with the key messages you want to send. Constantly ask yourself, "What values do we hold dear, what visions do we aspire to realize, and what behaviors do we want to reinforce?" Be prepared for every public opportunity to reinforce the culture and the meaning you want to create.

If being fast and flexible is what's expected, leaders make sure that the individuals who got a customized product to market quickly are publicly acknowledged and rewarded. If an important agency objective is to obtain new sources of funding, leaders celebrate when grants are signed. If an organization values loyalty, leaders celebrate tenure with years-of-service dinners and recognition pins. If personalized service is what makes the business profitable, then leaders make a big deal of publishing that special letter from a customer who expresses appreciation to the people who turned a potential nightmare into a delightful experience. If innovation is valued, then whenever a new patent is granted leaders give out awards to those involved in creating new technology.

Everything about a celebration should be matched to its purposes. From the setting to the speeches, from the music to the mood, every little detail can have an impact on the lasting influence of the event. For organizational values to have an impact, leaders must make explicit connections between shared values and the actions that exemplify those values. Celebrations are magnificent opportunities for leaders to expressly link principles to practices in a way that's memorable, motivating, and uplifting. Celebrations are to the culture of an organization "what the movie is to the script or the concert is to the score—they provide expression of values that are difficult to express in any other way."[3]

What leaders preach and what leaders celebrate must be one and the same. If they aren't, the celebration will come off as insincere and phony—and the leader's credibility will suffer. The celebration must be an honest expression of commitment to certain key values and to the hard work and dedication of those people who have lived the values. It's authenticity that makes conscious celebrations work.

Provide Social Support

Ceremonies and celebrations are opportunities to build healthier groups, to enable members of the organization to know and care about each other. And supportive relationships at work—relationships characterized by a genuine belief in and advocacy for the interests of others—are critically important to maintaining personal and organizational vitality.[4]

One of the significant lessons learned from an extensive ten-year study of service quality is that social support networks are essential for sustaining the motivation to serve. Service-performance shortfalls are highly correlated with the absence of social support and teamwork. As the researchers point out, "Coworkers who support each other and achieve together can be an antidote to service burnout. . . . Working with others should be rejuvenating, inspirational, and fun."[5]

This is just what Bob Branchi, managing director of Western Australia's largest network of automobile dealerships, imparted to one of the parts delivery drivers. When Bob attended a celebration at a large parts supply facility and mingled with those attending, he came across a fellow who held himself in low esteem. The man said that he was just a delivery driver and didn't feel that he had made any real contribution. Bob replied that if this was the criterion, then he (Bob) shouldn't have been there himself, but "each of us makes an important contribution, and in doing our best makes this company a success. We're in this together. It's important that you get involved in these celebrations so people know that you can be counted as part of this team." Bob made it a point to introduce the delivery driver to others at the celebration "as an important contributor to our team and to our success."

A similar situation existed at the Conferences and Catering department at the University of California at Los Angeles (UCLA). The department was preparing for its summer season—its busiest time—when it became aware that members of other departments on campus (such as physical plant, central receiving, and scheduling and facilities) were upset that they'd have to put out a great deal of effort to help Conferences and Catering be successful but would receive very little in the way of rewards themselves. Mary Pat Hanker, director of Conference Services, knew that the department's success depended on these other units, and that she needed to gain their support, commitment, and involvement. She realized that the intervention had to be pleasant, playful, and humorous so that people would want to participate wholeheartedly (rather than feeling threatened—and hence reluctant to participate).

So the Conferences and Catering department staged a celebration—its employees held a barbecue for the people they were calling on for help. Unlike most office parties, at this event the managers—the people responsible for generating the heavy summer business traffic—were the ones who cooked and served the food. This symbolic reversal of roles did indeed foster a spirit of cooperation.[6]

Investigations from a wide variety of disciplines consistently demonstrate that this kind of social support enhances productivity, psychological well-being, and physical health. The California Department of Mental Health has stated the point strongly: "friends can be good medicine."[7] Studies have found that social support not only enhances wellness but also buffers against disease, particularly during times of high stress. This latter finding was true irrespective of an individual's age, gender, or ethnic group. Even after adjusting for such factors as smoking and histories of major illness, people with few close contacts were two to three times more likely to die during the study period than those who regularly had friends to turn to.[8]

Our files are full of personal-best leadership cases in which strong human connections produced spectacular results.[9] Extraordinary accomplishments are achieved when everyone—leader and constituent alike—gets personally involved with the task and with other people. When people feel a strong sense of affiliation and attachment to their colleagues they're much more likely to have a higher sense of personal well-being, to feel more committed to the organization, and to perform at higher levels. When they feel distant and detached they're unlikely to get anything done at all.[10]

Leaders understand that what makes us most miserable is being alone. Celebrations create positive interactions among people, providing concrete evidence that people generally care about each other. Knowing that we aren't alone in our efforts and that we can count on others if necessary helps build the courage to continue in times of turmoil and stress. The case for social support is also bolstered by the fact that information exchange is more likely to be facilitated by formal and informal interactions.[11] Even in the age of the Internet, people are just more likely to share things when they're in a gathering with other people than when they're sitting alone at their work stations. When celebrations cut across functional and hierarchical boundaries, as they frequently do, people get a chance to exchange ideas with and be stimulated by people outside their own specialties.

Without group celebrations, we might all come to believe that the organization revolves around our individual work and that we're independent and not responsible to others. Social interactions remind us that we're all in this together, that we need each other, that our work gets done because we're connected and caught up in each other's lives. They bring more joy to people's work lives. Celebrations reinforce the fact that it always takes a group of people working together with a common purpose in an atmosphere of trust and collaboration to get extraordinary things done. By making achievements public, leaders build a culture in which people know that what they do is not taken for granted and clearly feel that their efforts are appreciated and applauded. As Martin Zeder, of the European energy company Axpo, told us, "Appreciating the work and good results of people involved" was a key ingredient in his own personal-best leadership experience.

TELL THE STORY

Stories by their nature are public forms of communication. As we've discussed in Chapter Four, storytelling is how we pass along lessons from generation to generation, culture to culture. Stories aren't meant to be kept private; they're meant to be *told*. And because they're public, they're tailor-made for celebrations. In fact, stories are celebrations, and celebrations are stories.

Stories exist in all organizations. They are, as Dave Snowden, Europe/Middle East/Asia director of IBM's Institute for Knowledge Management, puts it, "an integral part of defining what that organization is and what it means to work for it. Stories show, for example, whether employees are rewarded or punished for speaking up. A lack of stories may indicate heavy-handed controlling management."[12] Indeed, much about the culture of a company can be learned as a result of listening to and understanding the stories it tells about itself. The same can be said at an individual level as well. When Bob Phillips became CEO of Guide Dogs for the Blind he knew very little about the actual workings of the organization. To find out, he asked people to tell him a story about some important organizational event or experience. He followed that up by asking the person for one of their own personal stories, a time that they felt proud about what they had accomplished in the organization. Bob understood the importance of learning what has, and is, going on with people and their organizations; as he puts it, you have to "say *hi* to the *story*, and that's how you find out about the *history*."

David Armstrong, chief operating officer of Armstrong International, is the most prolific corporate storyteller we've ever met. He's the only COO we know who's published three books, a boxed CD set, and produced three videos of stories about real things that go on in his company. By our count there are 285 stories in this amazing collection, organized around themes such as "stories that kick start urgency," "stories to make people brave and wise," "stories about core values," "stories to inspire innovation." Each story is about a page or two in length, and every one explicitly concludes with "The Moral of the Story." Each story portrays the real-life Armstrong men and women who exemplify the actions that are most valued at the company. While the business press is overflowing with heroic stories about well-known CEOs of multibillion-dollar corporations, David is sitting around the campfire telling corporate tales about the true heroes and heroines of the workplace.

David started telling stories around 1987 after his minister's sermon one Sunday morning. He noticed how alert and attentive the congregation was when Rev. Kent told stories, and he thought stories could work just as well in business. "Right there in church, I decided we would tell stories in our company. We'd tell stories about our goals and objectives, stories that would explain our core values and our vision of the future, and stories that would celebrate our victories."[13] David goes on to say, "Storytelling has turned out to be an amazingly effective form of communication. Rules, either in policy manuals or on signs, can be inhibiting. But the morals in stories are invariably inviting, fun and inspiring. Through storytelling, our people can know very clearly what the company believes in, and what needs to be done."[14]

David's biography says of him, "He flies slightly out of formation because he firmly believes it breeds curiosity, builds new relationships, and encourages innovation." Yet, David is flying tightly in formation when it comes to the power of storytelling. Telling great stories is one of the most effective ways leaders can model the values and beliefs essential to organizational success. Armstrong has mastered that technique.

Teach, Mobilize, and Motivate

Stories put a human face on success. They tell us that someone just like us can make it happen. They create organizational role models that everyone can relate to. They put the behavior in a real context. They make standards more than statistics; they make standards come alive. By telling a story in detail, leaders illustrate what everyone needs to do to live by the organizational standards. Take, for example, this story about Joe Costello.

Joe once volunteered to be fired if he couldn't, within three months, turn around the sales situation of the company for which he was director of operations. Joe had no previous sales experience, yet in this—his personal-best leadership experience—he completely altered the psychology of the company by increasing sales quickly and significantly. A large thermometer-type chart was put in the main lobby to track the daily progress of sales activity. The overall push was to get everyone in the company focused on these sales goals: no decrease in the first month, $250,000 increase in the second month, and $1 million increase in the final month.

To capture people's attention and get everyone involved, Joe used what he called the "closing coat" ceremony. Whenever they made a sale, the sales force would select someone from the company to wear the "closing coat"— a bright yellow polyester jacket that carried the huckster image to the extreme. The coat-wearer would then walk around the company with Joe and tell colleagues the details of that particular sale. When people saw someone wearing the "closing coat," they knew they were one step closer to their goal. Joe's idea was "to make sure everyone had fun." The final monthly goal of $1 million in sales was exceeded by $400,000, and an $800,000 backlog was carried into the next quarter!

Not only does this story illustrate how a leader can personally and publicly recognize someone for contributing to success, it also shows the motivational and educational power of stories. Joe could have just exhorted people to meet their sales goals, given out a few sales incentives, and let it go at that. But having the wearer of the "closing coat" walk around with

Joe and tell the story of how the sale was made was miles more effective. It made the achievement very public and enabled others to share in the lessons learned.

By publishing a story in the company newsletter, holding a ceremony to give out an award, or making a video and broadcasting it on the internal television network, leaders shine the spotlight on someone who's lived out an organizational value—*and* provide others in the organization with an example they can emulate. They make sure people see that efforts to go the extra mile really are appreciated and recognized.

Make It Memorable

The world of business loves to talk in numbers: financial statements, income statements, balance sheets, stock tables, and bulleted overhead presentations. Numbers are so prevalent that we have come to accept them as *real*. But numbers aren't real. Numbers are abstractions from reality; bullet points are summaries of history and projections. The story is the reality.

Information really is more quickly and accurately remembered when it is first presented in the form of an example or story.[15] Kathi Vian, director of technology forecasting at the Institute for the Future in Menlo Park, used stories to teach students and teachers about possible scenarios in wireless technology. As she says, "It was the stories they remembered. Storytelling provides a framework for sharing information, meaning and knowledge."[16] Other researchers have found that when American history textbooks were translated into the story-based style of *Time* and *Newsweek* the students were able to recall up to three times more information than they were after reading a more typical school text.[17]

The Math Works, Inc., is a Massachusetts-based developer of engineering software. Despite the company's high-tech focus, leaders at all levels of the organization use stories to communicate organizational values and practices. As CEO Jack Little explains, "Storytelling is more compelling than just giving rules, guidelines, and policies. It gives you an actual example that people can remember a lot better. Storytelling can be tied to people and names and events that are much more relevant." Telling the story can be particularly helpful in providing inspiration to individuals facing challenging situations. Allison Babb of The Math Works points out that "telling the story gives the details and it helps people to be there, even though they weren't there. It's real easy to find stories that are just like what somebody else is now encountering." The story can highlight "roadblocks that somebody else has had . . . people who've really struggled with the exact same issues, and here's what they did to get over it."

A story is not only easier to remember and recall than a set of facts, it translates more quickly into action. Since 1985 scientist Gary Klein has been studying and writing about how people make decisions under conditions of extreme emergency. He's taken a look at professionals in high-stakes environments where a decision could mean life or death—people like firefighters, critical care nurses, paramedics, pilots, nuclear plant operators, and battle planners. Klein has discovered that in an emergency, the rational model of decision making is *not* how people make decisions. Instead they use a more nonlinear approach that involves intuition, mental simulation, metaphors, analogies, stories, and other less rational means. In discussing his research, Klein says, "The method we found most powerful for eliciting knowledge is to use stories."[18] Klein believes that storytelling is an essential skill for passing along the lessons that we learn from highly complex, challenging situations.

Stories are better able to accomplish the objectives of teaching, mobilizing, and motivating than bullet points on an overhead. Well-told stories reach inside us and pull us along. They give us the actual experience of being there and of learning what is really important about the experience. This explains why Nike has a corporate storytelling program. Begun with an hour-long lesson given to new employees in the late 1970s, the program today lasts two days, and the story of Nike's heritage is the first item on the agenda. When Nike employees think of their own company, they think of a retired university track coach (Bill Bowerman), an Olympic runner whose career ended tragically in a 1975 car crash (Steve Prefontaine), and a so-so athlete (Phil Knight) whose achievements as an entrepreneur far outpaced his accomplishments as a runner. Storytelling isn't just for new hires. Each tech rep, or "Ekin" (that's Nike spelled backwards), undergoes a nine-day Rookie Camp at Nike Headquarters. A full day is spent in Eugene, where Ekins run at the Hayward field track (where Bill Bowerman coached Phil Knight) and visit the site of Prefontaine's fatal car crash. (Prefontaine was also coached by Bowerman; his passion for better equipment inspired both Bowerman and Knight to build the Nike empire.) Nike has made understanding its heritage an intrinsic part of its corporate culture. "Our stories are not about extraordinary business plans or financial manipulations," explains Nike's director of corporate education and chief storyteller Nelson Farris, "they're about people getting things done." Like all great stories, the ones about Nike offer crystal clear illustrations that people can learn from. When Nike's leaders tell the story of how Coach Bowerman, after deciding that his team needed better running shoes, went out to his workshop and poured rubber into the family waffle iron, they're not just talking about how Nike's famous "waffle shoe" was born. They're talking about the spirit of innovation.[19]

SET THE EXAMPLE

"I was a cheerleader," is how Ted Avery, general manager for the Houghton Winery in Western Australia, began describing his personal best: "I would see the great things that were going on in marketing, for example, and I'd tell them, 'Way to go!' I'd hear about a new development in operations and I'd go into the plant and tell them, 'Fantastic!' If they figured out a more efficient process in the fields, I'd go out and find those responsible and let them know how much we appreciated their hard work."

Over and over again, it's the same story. Wherever you find a strong culture built around strong values—whether the values are about superior quality, innovation, customer service, distinctiveness in design, respect for others, or just plain fun—you'll also find endless examples of leaders who personally live the values. It's the same with encouraging the heart, whether through individual recognition or group celebration. The leader has to set the example.

The health care system in the United States has been badly bruised over the last decade. Increasing demand for quality services and increasing costs of providing those services have rammed head-on into cost containment pressures from insurers and employers. And while demand is growing, fewer and fewer individuals want to join the ranks of health-care professionals just to battle for long hours and modest pay. Tensions have increased between medical professionals and their health-care institutions and insurers. Plans for reform are fought over in the halls of Congress, but they seem to die on the operating table. Some hospitals are in critical condition and others are on life support.

Dick Pettingill, president and chief executive officer, California Division, Kaiser Foundation Health Plans and Hospitals, finds himself squarely in the middle of all of this. He joined the organization as a general manager in 1996. In 1997–98 the organization lost over $300 million. Dick was promoted to the chief operating officer role the next year, with the specific charter of turning around the California Division. He hired a chief turnaround officer (CTO), a singular role for the institution and one that was explicitly limited to the length of the turnaround. Dick partnered with the CTO to begin a program to control operating losses and boost margins. He set some very specific goals for himself and his colleagues, which he referred to as 2–4–6: operating margins of 2 percent in 1999, 4 percent in 2000, and 6 percent in 2001.

When the program first started in 1999, the California Division had three straight quarters of success. Its staff were on target to beat their goal of 2 percent operating margins. Dick wanted to make sure that the momentum was maintained so that they would make it, and he wanted to do something personally to rally the team. In talking it over with his CTO, she told him that every once in a while, people hosting MTV jump in a bus and drive around. She suggested that Dick get in a bus and go out to facilities located all over California and cheer the group on and get them pumped up for the fourth quarter. Dick liked the idea, hopped onto a bus in San Diego and drove north through California visiting Kaiser staff. Things didn't exactly go as Dick expected. They went even better! As he says:

> When I started out with this, it was really a talking tour. I expected to talk up the great success that we'd had and talk about what we had to do in the fourth quarter. It became very apparent to me (probably by mid-morning in the first day of the bus trip) that this wasn't about talking, it was about listening. It was about me listening to our employees and physicians talk about what was important to them, about what they wanted me to hear.

When we asked Dick the lessons he learned from this bus tour, he answered:

> One is that you have to believe it has value . . . that there's going to be a good return on the investment of time.
>
> Another is that you have to make yourself vulnerable. You have to have a willingness and a desire to be connected with the people of the organization. . . . I knew before I left that when we took our "people pulse," our employee opinion survey, 70 percent of the people didn't trust leadership. So I'm out there, trying to get people to have a sense of believability in what we're all about, recognizing that, again, it's not what I say, it's what I do that's going to make a difference.

For Dick, as well as for all the other leaders we've studied, the only way to truly show people you care and that you appreciate their efforts is to be out there with them. You've got to ride the bus, walk the halls, stroll the streets, eat in the cafeteria, listen to their complaints, and tell stories about their successes. This visibility makes the leader vulnerable. It also makes the leader more real and more genuine. Believability goes up when you get personally involved.

By being personally involved, Dick learned the following story. It's one that still chokes him up, even having told it many times.

> A mother wrote a letter about her son, and we acknowledged the two physicians and the nurse who, through their exceptional clinical judgment, figured out this kid needed a liver transplant and sent him off to the University of California. As he was leaving our medical center up in Santa Rosa, the nurse took her karma bracelet off her wrist and put it on the young boy's wrist. This was in April. By June, he was doing fine. He was well enough to return to his high school senior prom. It's those types of stories that are the heartbeat of what this company is all about.

Dick and his team heard and felt the power of the people in the organization. Wonderful, isn't it, that when you go out to encourage the hearts of others, your heart is encouraged as well.

Make It Genuine—Let It Come from Your Heart

Dick's story supports one other lesson about recognition and celebration: recognition and awards don't work unless they come from a credible source. As many people pointed out to us, "I don't need recognition from someone I don't respect." It's a theme we've repeated over and over again—*credibility is the foundation of leadership*—and when it comes to celebrating values and victories, it's even more critical.

Sonya Lopes was a school reform coordinator at Turnbull Learning Academy, a public elementary school in San Mateo, California. She managed the organization development and change process in the school. As she puts it, "I'm an adviser-critic-listener-reflective partner-confidante to the principal." Inspired by the book *301 Ways to Have Fun at Work,*[20] Sonya decided that she didn't want any more opportunities for fun to pass her by. So she started by putting the word "fun" in a few key places. She put it on a sign that she hung by her office door so she could see it whenever she walked out. She put it in her daily planner as a bookmark. "It helped me," she says, "become more proactive in the search for 'fun' opportunities." For example, one week she had people turn in their "regular old staff meeting questionnaires" by making them into paper airplanes and flying them to her. Sonya reports, "For the first time ever, *everyone* turned in the questionnaire!"

Sonya started talking to everyone about having fun at work. She left positive notes, muffins, and tea bags in staff mailboxes. During Teacher Appreciation Week, she got the PTA involved in creating a more lively school environment. PTA members decorated the staff bathrooms with tables, potpourri, wall hangings, and color, color, color. "Teachers," she says, "talked about it for *days.*"

Sonya reports that she received smiles, hugs, and notes for the actions she took. She also saw the environment change. But most important, Sonya learned a lesson that everyone who begins this journey learns. "Encouraging the heart of others encouraged *my* heart. As I was going around smiling, looking at people and saying their names, I became uplifted! I felt *excited* while making muffins and attaching notes to them as spirit-lifters for teachers. And simply telling people that the retreat will have *fun* as one of its top five priorities has led to curiosity from teachers as to what we will be doing and their desire to be there."

As Sonya discovered, when you *feel* genuinely excited and encouraged yourself, other people know it's for real. And, as her experience demonstrates, recognizing individuals and celebrating accomplishments is mostly about the little things. It doesn't take a grand plan to begin to set the example for encouraging the heart. It doesn't take a huge budget, it doesn't take psychotherapy, and it doesn't take the boss's permission. What it does take is initiative.

The Circle of Leadership—Modeling Is Encouraging

Remember: leadership is a relationship, and people are much more likely to enlist in initiatives led by those with whom they feel a personal affiliation. It's precisely the human connection between leaders and constituents that ensures more commitment and more support. Saying thank you—and genuinely meaning it—is a very concrete way of showing respect and enhancing personal credibility.

As we approach the end of our Five Practices story we've come full circle. We started our discussion of personal-best leadership with Model the Way—and here we are again. If you want others to believe in something and behave according to those beliefs, you have to set the example. You have to practice what you preach, put your money where your mouth is, and walk the talk. If you want people to stay true to shared values, you have to stay true to them as well. If you want people to aspire to be the best, you have to live and breathe that vision. If you want people to innovate, you have to innovate. If you want people to collaborate, you have to collaborate. If you want to build and maintain a culture of excellence and distinction, then you have to recognize, reward, reinforce and celebrate exceptional efforts and successes. You have to get personally involved in celebrating the actions that contribute to and sustain the culture. And if you want people to have the courage to continue the quest in the face of great adversity, you have to encourage them yourself.

When it comes to sending a message throughout the organization, nothing communicates more clearly than what the leaders *do*. You don't have to ride site-to-site on a bus, publish a CD-ROM of corporate tales, bake muffins, make a bonfire on the beach, hold a camp out, or copy any particular method from our leadership stories. You might want to adopt a few of these inventive ideas for yourself, but the specific technique is not the point. The point is that by directly and visibly showing others that you're there to cheer them along, you're sending a positive signal. You're more likely to see others do it if you do it. It's that simple.

You can't delegate any of these practices—though you can expect that everyone should perform them. What you can do is model them. Indeed, you have to be a model people can point to and say, "If you want to know how to lead people in getting extraordinary things done, just follow her. If you want to know what credible leadership is, just watch him." When you set the example that communicates the message "Around here we say thanks, show appreciation, and have fun," others will follow your lead. The organization will develop a culture of celebration and recognition. *Everyone becomes a leader,* everyone sets the example, everyone takes the time to celebrate accomplishments.

When leaders model encouragement and others follow their example, organizations develop a reputation for being great places to work. They're magnetic, attracting and retaining employees and customers far better than their competitors can. People form a strong bond with these institutions. They're proud to be affiliated. Employees *want to* excel, business partners *want to* delight, and customers *want to* stay loyal for a lifetime. You can influence all of that when you encourage the heart.

COMMITMENT NUMBER 10:
CELEBRATE THE VALUES AND VICTORIES
BY CREATING A SPIRIT OF COMMUNITY

Celebrating values and victories together reinforces the fact that extraordinary performance is the result of many people's efforts. By celebrating people's accomplishments visibly and in group settings, leaders create and sustain team spirit; by basing celebrations on the accomplishment of key values and milestones, they sustain people's focus.

Public ceremonies provide opportunities to reiterate key values and to make heroes and heroines of individuals with whom everyone can identify. Telling stories about individuals who have made exceptional efforts and achieved phenomenal successes provides role models for others to emulate.

Social interaction increases people's commitments to the standards of the group, and has a profound effect on people's well-being. Intimacy heals; loneliness depresses. When people are asked to go beyond their comfort zones, the support and encouragement of their colleagues enhance their resistance to the possible debilitating effects of stress.

Leaders who set the example by getting personally involved in celebration and recognition let everyone know that encouraging the heart is something everyone should do. Making personal connections with people in a culture of celebration also builds and sustains credibility. It reduces any we-they demarcations between leaders and constituents.

Adding vitality and a sense of appreciation to the workplace is what encouraging the heart is all about. In this final commitment, we provide several action steps you can take to celebrate values and victories together.

• *Schedule celebrations.*

At Roche Bioscience the camp out is on the calendar. At Schwab, each senior management offsite includes a ceremony of some sort. These scheduled celebrations are no different from other similar gatherings around the globe that pay homage to a common history and common culture. As a leader you need to put celebrations on your organization's calendar so that people come to expect that they'll be getting together to share in the values and the victories.

Celebrations should always serve a dual purpose: one is to honor a principle or an achievement, and the other is to create a spirit of community. In setting up your celebrations, therefore, your first task is to decide which organizational values, events of historical significance, or specific successes are of such importance that they warrant a special ritual, ceremony, or festivity. Perhaps you want to honor the group or team of people who created the year's important innovations, praise those who gave extraordinary customer service, or thank the families of your constituents for their support. Whatever you wish to celebrate, formalize it, announce it, and tell people how they become eligible to participate. At a minimum, you ought to have at least one celebration each year that involves everyone, though not necessarily at the same site, and one that draws attention to each of the key values of your organization.

Bring celebration into as many critical events as you can. In *Corporate Celebration*, Terrence Deal and M. K. Key provide a detailed framework to schedule or anticipate celebrations that will serve your purposes.[21] Here's a brief glimpse:

- *Cyclical Celebrations.* Seasonal themes, key milestones, corporate anniversaries, individual birthdays, marriages, reunions, and other recurring events.
- *Recognition Ceremonies.* Public applause and acknowledgment for a job well done, being best-in-class, attaining specific goals, achieving a special rank, getting a promotion, and other achievements that deserve broad attention.
- *Celebrations of Triumph.* Special occasions for accentuating collective accomplishments, such as winning a championship, beating forecasts, beating the competition, launching a new product or strategy, founding a new company, and opening a new office, plant, or store.
- *Rituals for Comfort and Letting Go.* Not all of organization life is about victory; sometimes there's calamity and loss. There's the loss of a contract, layoffs of employees, death of a colleague, an experiment that failed, and site closings. These occasions can be marked by ceremony and ritual to help people let go and move on.
- *Personal Transitions.* People come and go in organizations, and there need to be ways to celebrate entrances and exits, initiations, separations, and other life passages.
- *Workplace Altruism.* Celebrations of doing good for others, pulling together to help others, promoting social change, showing appreciation to customers and clients.
- *Events.* A company's anniversary, opening day, holidays, articulation of an organization's vision.
- *Play.* Energizing meetings and conventions, spoofing and poking fun, games and sporting events.

Add to this list all the ways you can think of to bring more ceremony, ritual, commemoration, observance, and convivial good times into your organization. If your organization doesn't do much celebrating, start an informal celebration task force. Make it your job to liven up the place, borrowing where you can from the inventiveness of others and creating your own fun and games at work.

A word of caution: don't make *everything* that people accomplish a reason for celebrating. You don't want to replace people's intrinsic motivation with external motivators or justifications, nor do you want to trivialize recognition so that it's taken for granted. However, in our studies, *over*doing recognition and celebration was not a problem; more typically, the concern was about how to increase encouragement and recognition.

• *Install a public "Bragging Board."*

Our friend, author Hal Zina Bennett tells the story of a recognition in his parents' small furniture factory. During the Christmas rush, his father always hired extra workers, and since they were temporary hires motivation was often a problem. One day Hal's dad installed what he called a "Bragging Board" at the entrance where employees hung up their coats. Whenever he wanted to acknowledge an employee for an achievement he wrote a quick thank-you note and pinned it to the "Bragging Board" for all to see.

People appreciated the notes, and they left them pinned to the board in public view rather than taking them down and storing them in a private place. Then they started attaching their own notes to the board, announcing achievements and even family events outside of work that they wanted to brag about. Pretty soon notes such as "I'm a Grandma! First one!" began to appear on the board, usually with a photo of the new baby. One proud parent even pinned up her son's perfect report card. The "Bragging Board" helped to create a sense of community and camaraderie; it reinforced the fact that people's humanness mattered. The success of the "Bragging Board" also demonstrates that people love to *participate* in the recognition of achievements and special milestones in their lives.

• *Create a commemorative award honoring exemplary actions.*

In Vincent J. Russo's office hangs a plaque for the "Vincent J. Russo Leadership Award." There's a story behind its creation that illustrates the dual power of commemorative awards.

For about ten years, from 1988 until 1998, Vincent was director of the Materials and Manufacturing Directorate of the Air Force Research Laboratory, which is recognized nationally and internationally as the premier aerospace materials research laboratory in the world. The Directorate has about five hundred government and another five hundred contractor employees, and each year it holds an annual luncheon during which it acknowledges the contributions of its most outstanding people. For many years, the Directorate had awards for science, engineering, and support, each named after previous outstanding members of the organization. Then in the early 1990s the Directorate established a Leadership Award—with no personal name attached—based on its desire to instill a culture of leadership within the organization.

Vincent left the Directorate in 1998 to become executive director of the Aeronautical Systems Center at the Wright-Patterson Air Force Base in Dayton, Ohio. As part of his going-away ceremony, the organization honored and thanked him for his service by renaming the Leadership Award in his honor. Given annually to the employee who best demonstrates the principles of leadership on the job, the Vincent J. Russo Leadership Award is special to its recipients, and particularly meaningful to Vincent himself. Here's what he says about it:

To this date, it is the single most significant recognition I have had. Other awards such as large monetary awards, performance recognition awards, election as a Fellow to a national society, etc., are all well behind in significance to me personally. The naming of an award for leadership excellence by the employees you served for ten years was a tremendous highlight of my career and needless to say, it was a very moving experience for me. Each year, I get to attend the luncheon and personally present the award to the recipient.

Commemorative awards create a unique opportunity for organizations. These awards reinforce important values and contributions—such as leadership or innovation—and provide a role model for the actions being recognized. When we receive awards named in the honor of a highly credible individual we ourselves are honored to receive it and we are honored to be in the company of all those who have been recognized before us. We know we're in good company. Create a couple of these distinctive and special awards in your organization and call attention to the values and contributions you hold most dear.

- *Demonstrate caring by walking around.*

When Tom Melohn was head sweeper of North American Tool and Die—actually he was the owner, but he called himself "head sweeper"—he used to do what he called caring by walking around (CBWA). It was his way of talking about how he would always go around the shop looking for people doing things right. Then, in a regular shop floor meeting, he'd present the Super Person of the Month award. It'd go to the person who best exemplified one of the NATD values. Tom wouldn't just hand out the award and say thanks, though, he'd always make it fun and engaging, sometimes actually recreating the scene, and he'd always tell the story behind the action that deserved the award because he'd observed it firsthand on one of his visits.

Thomas Mueller understood this point about caring by walking around. When he was head of the components engineering group in the Business Area Electronics of Mettler-Toledo in Europe, he told us that "personal meetings are essential, even in the age of electronic communication, and cannot be replaced by phone calls and e-mail. People often think it's too expensive to travel around the globe for a workshop of one or two days. In a global organization you have to deal with different cultures, mentalities, and ways things are done. The best way to overcome these hurdles is to meet, watch, listen and discuss." In being out and about, Thomas explains, he was able to "appreciate verbally whenever an important step was taken or an individual task was completed with success."

By increasing human interaction, you increase optimism and you increase credibility. So make a commitment to start your day by chatting with your constituents. Stop by your colleagues' offices or cubicles and ask them how they are doing. Ask what they did last night, or what good news they might have to share or what problems you might be able to help them with. With each person, find out something you didn't know before. Be self-disclosing yourself and let others know about the things that bring joy to your life.

Let's say you have fifty constituents you ought to see each week. That's ten each work day. At five minutes each, that's just under one hour each day. If strengthening credibility is the goal, there is no more productive way to spend that hour than talking one-on-one. Fit some form of CBWA into your daily routine. Reach out. Whether by foot, bus, plane, or train, reaching out sends a message that you're personally involved. It has the added benefit of giving you a better sense of what's happening outside the walls of your office and building.

- *Show passion and compassion.*

Emotions are contagious. Literally. Moods are social viruses, and you can catch a bad mood as easily as a bad cold. You can also catch a good mood.[22] So make a conscious effort to avoid the nay-sayers and to seek out the can-doers.

Try playing Gail Wilson's "Passion-Compassion" game. We had the opportunity to do this in an executive seminar of Square D Company's Vision College, a two-day seminar on the company's vision and values. Over a two-year period, this seminar was attended by all of Square D's twenty thousand employees, in groups of twenty-five.

Here's how the game works: People get into pairs. One person chooses to be the presenter and selects a topic about which he or she feels passionately. The other member of the team plays the compassionate role, encouraging expressiveness, listening actively, showing interest or concern, and drawing forth enthusiasm. In this session, seminar leader Gail Wilson—an actress, acting teacher, and executive educator—modeled the compassionate role for us. A soft-spoken senior executive who had difficulty expressing himself with enthusiasm volunteered to be her passionate partner. As the executive spoke about something he loved to do, Gail would laugh, or touch, or slap her thighs, or say "Uh huh" or "Tell me more about that," or open her eyes wide, or gesture encouragingly. Like a dancer, she moved with her partner as he gradually became more animated, energetic, expressive, and uplifting. He slashed the air with his hands, rose up on his toes, spoke with varying intonations and inflections, bounced up and down, and smiled with joy.

In the span of a minute, through her expressiveness and her empathy, Gail had enabled another human being to intensely display his passion for something he loved. Her compassion—and yes, her love—enabled him to become passionate. By sympathizing deeply, she enabled her partner to give her a gift of energy and excitement. Her ability to struggle with that executive as he attempted to be more expressive gave him the courage and encouragement to show more passion. In those brief moments, we saw how readily compassion can benefit both sides of a relationship, in all aspects of our lives.

• *Be a cheerleader—your way.*

You can cheerlead for your group better than anyone else. Yet if your ideas of what it means to cheerlead are based upon traditional views of school cheerleaders, you may find this task difficult. There's much more to cheerleading than standard cheers, acrobatics, and flashy shows.

As with individual recognition, all kinds of rewards can be used for cheerleading. Use your imagination—and, most important—be authentic. If you're comfortable giving out plaques, flowers, T-shirts, and the like, do it! If you can't think of anything to celebrate, try a thank-goodness-it's-Monday party or a we-blew-the-roof-off-this-week get-together. These work in tough times and in good times. One design group at Apple Computer celebrated every milestone achieved with champagne or sparkling cider. They had lots of milestones *and* lots of milestones *achieved.*

Tim Hendrix, project manager for LSI Logic, used cheerleading to help his team members feel strong and capable. He gave them progressively stretching goals and then was around to help them succeed, "ensuring that I gave them positive reinforcement individually and to the team as a whole." They had critical milestones that had to be met for the project to move from one phase to the next. Completion of each milestone was monitored closely by corporate and then followed up with celebrations. Several of the celebrations were luncheons, some were dinners, and at the end of the project a banquet (with spouses) was held. Each member received a cash award and saw their accomplishments noted both through the corporate e-mail system and through features in the company's internal newsletters. At each stage along the way, Tim was there to cheer his troops forward. Celebrations such as this are excellent ways to acknowledge progress and small wins.

As the leader, your job is to create a culture of celebration, but you don't have to be the one to do all the organizing and cheering. In fact, if you are, you're not doing your job. You can facilitate everyone's participation in coming together to celebrate spontaneously and openly. Make it easy for everyone to find ways to celebrate successes that are informal, inclusive, and fun. For example, Dick Pettingill didn't stop with the first bus trip we described earlier in the chapter. Because everyone at Kaiser felt so positive about that trip, he and his team decided to go on another during the second year of the turnaround. Before this trip, they asked people in the organization to nominate "Extra Mile Heroes"—people who had gone the extra mile in service of the organization's goals. By the time they got on the bus, they had sixteen hundred people sharing stories about their colleagues who do extraordinary things in the organization every day. You can bet those stories got retold loud and clear across the company.

- *Have fun.*

Fun isn't a luxury, even at work. Most personal-best leadership experiences were a combination of hard work and fun. In fact, most people we spoke with agreed that without the fun and the pleasure that they experienced with one another on the team, they wouldn't have been able to sustain the level of intensity and hard work required. Anna Dushine understood this point intuitively. As a high school student she was teaching dance at a summer camp for seventh and eighth graders. What did she do to bring out the best in these kids? "I made it fun! There was no way they were going to work hard, practice, and come back for another day unless they were enjoying being with one another and having fun."

Empirical research has found a significant relationship between fun and productivity under the perspective of "subjective well-being." Knowing about the quality of people's work, whether they enjoy a supportive network of close relationships and knowing whether a person has a faith that encompasses social support, purpose, and hope are key components.[23] And we can see the importance of this relationship in even everyday mundane affairs. Consider, for example, the experience of Doug Podzilni, president of Gourmet Source Food Brokers, who bought a box of candy suckers and placed them out in a common area of the office. Very quickly, "everyone had a sucker sticking out of their mouth and a smile on their face," he says. Later that afternoon, during the break in a particularly tedious and combative meeting, he put another bunch of suckers in the middle of the table. Before he knew it, Doug says, people were reaching for their favorite flavors, and the tone of the meeting got noticeably friendlier: "It's hard to be too combative or in a bad mood when you have a sucker in your mouth!"

Having fun sustains productivity, but don't take Doug's word for it. Listen to Nancy Tivol, executive director of Sunnyvale Community Services, who makes it a habit to have fun with people. She explains, "If you talk to each other only when there's a problem, it doesn't work. We have to stress looking for the good; not just knowing it's there, but *doing* something— celebrating!" And celebrate she does. As one way, Nancy creates personalized songs. Whether it's a tribute to Charlie for faithfully organizing the food program, or an Irish jig on St. Patrick's Day honoring volunteers for their efforts, Nancy finds ways to let people know that they matter.

Go visit an organization that you know has a reputation for being a really fun place to work—places such as The Math Works, Disney, Eureka!Ranch, or Southwest Airlines, for example. Find out what makes them so inventive when it comes to celebration. Be a good observer—there and everywhere. When you're at a wedding or other celebratory event, or buying birthday party supplies at a local store, make mental notes on what you like and what really inspires you. You'll be amazed at the possibilities. See if you can incorporate some of these ideas into your plans to encourage the heart.

Show up in a costume at your next group celebration. If Sam Walton, at one time the richest man in America, could put on a hula skirt and hula on Wall Street when his associates achieved a milestone over daunting odds, we all have permission to dress in a clown suit for a special event. Besides, people love it when they can laugh with the boss. More than a few CEOs, including Herb Kelleher of Southwest Airlines and Harry Quadracci of Quad/Graphics, have made big successes out of their public displays of playfulness.

- *Set the example—plan a celebration right now.*

We often conclude our leadership workshops by asking participants in small groups to plan and perform a celebration for the rest of their colleagues. People have performed rap songs and poems, led us in sing-alongs, roasted the trainers, played Leadership Jeopardy, taken us on walks on the beach, and sent us on scavenger hunts. You name it; we've done it.

So we conclude our action steps for this chapter—and for all the commitments in this book—by asking you to set the example for celebrating by planning a celebration right now. You've got a meeting that's coming up. How can you use that opportunity to celebrate a milestone? Is there a regularly scheduled quarterly review on the books? How can you include in it a ceremony that calls attention to a special part of your culture? Perhaps you've got a training session at which you're going to give a presentation. How can you include a story about real people in your organization who exemplify one or more of your values?

Anytime people gather there's the opportunity to create a spirit of community, to tell a story that reinforces a cultural standard, or to model the behavior you expect of others. Exemplary leaders use every opportunity to celebrate the values and the victories. Do the same: View every occasion your constituents gather as a chance for some kind of celebration, big or small.

Encouraging the heart doesn't have to come at the end of a seminar or the conclusion of a project. It also doesn't have to come after you've done everything else a leader does. It's not the end of the process; it's a continuous part of the leadership journey. You can celebrate at any time, anywhere. So do it! Give courage, spread joy, and care about people, product, and process all along the way.

COMMITMENT NUMBER 10

CELEBRATE THE VALUES AND VICTORIES BY CREATING A SPIRIT OF COMMUNITY

- *Schedule celebrations.*

- *Install a public "Bragging Board."*

- *Create a commemorative award honoring exemplary actions.*

- *Demonstrate caring by walking around.*

- *Show passion and compassion.*

- *Be a cheerleader—your way.*

- *Have fun.*

- *Set the example—plan a celebration right now.*

Source: The Leadership Challenge by James M. Kouzes and Barry Z. Posner. Copyright © 2002.

PART SEVEN

Leadership for Everyone

13 LEADERSHIP IS EVERYONE'S BUSINESS

Leadership requires learning on the job. With the willpower—and the heart—to continue, you can lead the way.

Christian Fux, International Committee of the Red Cross in Kenya

There are no shortages of opportunities for people to do great things. They can, and they must.

Mary Beth Cahill-Phillips, TrustLine

Throughout this book we've told stories of ordinary people who've gotten extraordinary things done. We've talked about men and women, young and old, from a variety of organizations, public and private, government and third sector, high-tech and low-tech, small and large, schools and professional services. Chances are you haven't heard of most of them. They're not famous people or mega-stars. They're people who might live next door or work in the next cubicle over. We've focused on everyday leaders because we firmly believe that leadership is not about position or title. It's about relationships, credibility, and what you *do.*

Beyond the practices, beyond the action steps, there's another fundamental truth about leadership: *leadership is everyone's business.*

Sometimes leadership becomes your business unexpectedly, as it did for Mary Beth Cahill-Phillips, years ago. Her morning began like any other, with the family scurrying to get up and about. She left her six-month-old daughter, Elizabeth, at a friend's home, to share services of a child-care provider (their own having just moved away), and made her way to graduate school classes. Two hours later, Mary Beth and her husband were paged to come to the emergency room at Alta Bates Hospital. Elizabeth was in a coma. Over the next few days, weeks, and years they learned that Elizabeth had been shaken so severely by her child-care provider as to suffer brain damage and be permanently blinded. Subsequent events revealed aspects of that child-care provider's background that made her quite unsuitable, even dangerous. "Had anyone known, none of us would have left our loved ones in this monster's hands," Mary Beth explains.

How could this have happened? How could it have been prevented and avoided? What needed to happen so that no other parents, or their children, would experience this nightmare? Mary Beth certainly did not choose this experience, but she took on the questions and led a battle with the State of California so that parents could have background checks done on the men and women to whom they were entrusting their children. More than 85 percent of those providing child care in California are unlicensed; the percentages are generally even higher in other states and countries around the globe. Mary Beth saw the need and established TrustLine.

It wasn't easy and it wasn't quick: the journey from Elizabeth's tragedy to the governor's signature, State Assembly's funding, and implementation by the departments of Social Services and Justice took more than a decade. Mary Beth did it without benefit of any existing organizational launching pad, formal position, authority, or initial expertise in child welfare. She was driven in her quest—and she was not alone. She involved and mobilized thousands of others—she modeled, inspired, challenged, enabled, and encouraged—all along the way. Mary Beth found her voice and the leader within her to make certain that no other family would suffer her family's experience.

Even while Mary Beth was leading the TrustLine effort, she wondered how much her reaction to her family nightmare resembled how other parents dealt with, made sense of, and even found some purpose in cruel twists of fate. For her doctoral dissertation, she focused on a sample of women, each of whom had, like her, suffered through the death or serious injury to her child.[1]

They had all become leaders, creating organizations (Vanished Children's Alliance and the Head Trauma Clinic at Children's Hospital San Diego) and galvanizing people and special interests. Their efforts resulted in new product standards and recalls (new safety requirements for pool covers by the U.S. Consumer Product Safety Commission), social movements (Mothers Against Drunk Driving—MADD), and government legislation (California's TrustLine).

Based upon a priori criteria, none of these "ordinary" women would have been singled out from the population for their leadership potential. They were mostly young or middle-aged, many were single parents, less than half had graduated from college, many worked at home, and all lacked substantial years of work experience, unique professional talents, and prestigious organizational positions. They hadn't had any formal (or perhaps even informal) training or special preparation to be leaders. Yet each suffered the death or serious injury of her child and determined that this situation would not—*must not*—happen again for another parent or another child. These women got extraordinary things done because they cared. There's no denying the leadership within them.

Like Mary Beth and the women featured in her dissertation, many of the leaders we studied didn't initiate the personal-best leadership projects that they wrote and talked about, yet they rose to the occasion. Some got angry and caught fire. Some saw an opportunity where others didn't. Others simply believed they could make something better than it was or had been. And still others accepted an assignment and then found something within themselves that they hadn't known they had. None of us knows our true strength until challenged to bring it forth.

LEADERSHIP IS LEARNED

There still persists, even in this new millennium, a pernicious myth that leadership is reserved for only a very few of us. That myth is perpetuated daily every time someone asks, "Are leaders born or made?" Whenever we're asked this question—which is almost every time we give a speech or conduct a class or workshop—our answer, always offered with a smile, is this: "Yes, of course, *all* leaders are born. We've never met a leader who wasn't. So are all accountants, artists, athletes, parents, zoologists, you name it." We're all born. What we do with what we have before we die is up to us.

There's another leadership myth that stands in the way of personal and organizational success. It's the myth that leadership is associated with position. It's an assumption that leadership starts with a capital "L," and that when you're on top you're automatically a leader. It's part of a larger hero myth that inhibits us from seizing the initiative. "It's not my job," we say, and we wait for someone to ride in and save us.

Well, forget it! It's just pure myth that only a lucky few can ever understand the intricacies of leadership. Leadership is not a place, it's not a gene, and it's not a secret code that can't be deciphered by ordinary people. The truth is that leadership is an observable set of skills and abilities that are useful whether one is in the executive suite or on the front line, on Wall Street or Main Street, in any campus, community, or corporation. And any skill can be strengthened, honed, and enhanced, given the motivation and desire, the practice and feedback, and the role models and coaching.

It's very curious—and revealing—that no one has ever asked us, "Can *management* be taught? Are *managers* born or made?" Why is it that management is viewed as a set of skills and abilities, while leadership is typically seen as a set of innate personality characteristics? It's simple. People *assume* management can be taught. Because they do, hundreds of business schools have been established, and each year thousands of management courses are taught. By assuming that people can learn the attitudes, skills, and knowledge associated with good management practices, schools and companies have raised the caliber of managers. They've also contributed to the idea that good management skills are attainable.

The same can be said for leadership. In over twenty years of research, we've been fortunate to have heard and read the stories of thousands of ordinary people who've led others to get extraordinary things done. And there are millions more. It's not the absence of leadership potential that inhibits the development of more leaders; it's the persistence of the myth that leadership can't be learned. This haunting myth is a far more powerful deterrent to leadership development than is the nature of the person or the basics of the leadership process.

It's our collective task to liberate the leader within each and every one of us. Rather than view leadership as an innate set of character traits—a self-fulfilling prophecy that dooms society to having only a few good leaders—it's far healthier and more productive to assume that it's possible for *everyone* to learn to lead. By assuming that leadership is learnable, we can discover how many good leaders there really are. Somewhere, sometime, the leader within each of us may get the call to step forward—for the school, the congregation, the community, the agency, the company, the union, or the family. By believing in yourself and your capacity to learn to lead, you make sure you'll be prepared when that call comes.

We wouldn't have written this book if we didn't know that it's possible for ordinary people to learn how to get extraordinary things done. We wouldn't have written this book if we didn't know that ordinary people can become extraordinary leaders. We cast our votes on the side of optimism and hope. Chances are good that you do, too.

Certainly, we shouldn't mislead people into believing that they can attain unrealistic goals. However, neither should we assume that only a few would ever attain excellence in leadership (or in any other human endeavor). We do know that those who are most successful at bringing out the best in others are those who set achievable "stretch" goals and believe that they have the ability to develop the talents of others. We do know that effective leaders are constantly learning. They see *all* experiences as *learning* experiences, not just those sessions in a formal classroom or workshop. They're constantly looking for ways to improve themselves and their organizations. By reading this book and engaging in other personal development activities, you're demonstrating a predisposition to lead. Even if some people think that they're not able to learn to lead, you must believe that you can. That's where it all starts—with your own belief in yourself.

Jim Whittaker, REI's first employee and the first American to climb Mount Everest, once observed, "You never conquer the mountain. You conquer yourself—your doubts and your fears." We would say the same for leadership. You don't conquer your organization. You don't conquer leadership. You conquer your own doubts and fears about leading.

LEADERS MAKE A DIFFERENCE

By now, you know that we believe there's a lot to be learned from leaders—both the famous, whose biographies line the shelves, and the everyday leaders. You know that we regularly ask people in our classes and workshops to share a story about a leader they admire and whose direction they would willingly follow. From this exercise, we hope they'll discover for themselves what it takes to have an influence on others. We have another objective as well: we want them to discover the power that lies within each one of us to make a difference.

Virtually everyone we've asked has been able to name at least one leader whose genuine influence they've felt. Sometimes it's a well-known figure—perhaps someone out of the past who changed the course of history. Sometimes it's a contemporary role model who serves as an example of success. Most often, however, it's someone personally close to them who's helped them learn—a parent, friend, member of the clergy, coach, teacher, manager.

Verónica Guerrero's story underscored for us just how extraordinary those around us can be. Verónica selected her father, José Luis Guerrero, as the leader she admired. She told the story of her father's leadership in the Unión Nacional Sinarquista (UNS) back in the early 1940s. (UNS later became part of another political party—Partido Democrata Mexicano [PDM], or Mexican Democratic Party.) She related in detail what her father did and then summed up his influence with this remembered observation from José Luis: "I think the work that I did back then helped me extend myself and others to levels that I didn't know I could reach. . . . If you feel strongly about anything, and it's something that will ultimately benefit your community and your country, don't hold back. Fear of failing or fear of what might happen doesn't help anyone. . . . Don't let anyone or anything push you back."

Verónica Guerrero closed her description of her father (who was then dying of pancreatic cancer) with this observation: "As I heard his story and I saw a sick, tired, and weak man, I couldn't help thinking that our strength as humans and as leaders has nothing to do with what we look like. Rather, it has everything to do with what we feel, what we think of ourselves. . . . Leadership is applicable to all facets of life." That's precisely the point. If *we* are to become leaders, we must believe that we, too, can be a positive force in the world. Leadership *does* have everything to do with what we think of ourselves.

And does that make a difference? Historian Arthur M. Schlesinger Jr. observed that "the very concept of leadership implies the proposition that individuals make a difference to history."[2] Yet there has never been universal acceptance of this proposition. Determinism and fatalism govern the minds of many. Some management scholars claim, in fact, that leaders have little impact on organizations, that other forces—internal or external to the organization—are the determinants of success.[3] Others claim the role of the leader is largely symbolic, even romantic, but not substantive.[4] Our evidence suggests quite the contrary. Managers, individual contributors, volunteers, pastors, government administrators, teachers, school principals, students, and other leaders who use the Five Practices of Exemplary Leadership more frequently are seen by others as better leaders.[5] Here are a few particulars:

- They're more effective in meeting job-related demands.
- They're more successful in representing their units to upper management.
- They create higher-performing teams.
- They foster renewed loyalty and commitment.
- They increase motivational levels and the willingness to work hard.
- They promote higher levels of involvement in schools.
- They enlarge the size of their congregations.
- They raise more money and expand gift-giving levels.
- They extend the range of their agency's services.
- They reduce absenteeism, turnover, and dropout rates.
- They possess high degrees of personal credibility.

Additionally, people working with leaders who demonstrate the Five Practices of Exemplary Leadership are significantly more satisfied with the actions and strategies of their leaders, and they feel more committed, excited, energized, influential, and powerful. In other words, the more you engage in the practices of exemplary leaders, the more likely it is that you'll have a positive influence on others in the organization.

Other researchers have also found that leaders can have a significant impact on their organizations. Leadership has been shown to account for improved performance as measured by a variety of factors: net income; sales, profits, and net assets; employee commitment, job satisfaction, and role clarity; and employee turnover, achievement of company goals, and teamwork.[6]

Reaching the top of *Fortune*'s annual list of the world's most admired companies isn't easy. To make it, a company needs innovative products, financial stamina, global reach, empowered employees, and a devotion to shareholders. And if getting to the top of the list is hard, staying there is even tougher. Every year business moves just a bit faster, the competition gets a little more menacing, and the world seems slightly smaller. The answer to how some companies manage to stay ahead year in and year out isn't luck. No, say the editors at *Fortune,* "Try the other L word. Try leadership. Leadership is what *Fortune*'s all-star ranking is all about." Mel Stark, a Hay Group vice president who co-led this research, says the findings confirm the importance of aligning the behavior of leaders with the values and culture of their organization. "In today's environment," he says, "leaders must do far more than merely meet the numbers. To effectively implement strategy, they must put people first and continually connect with and motivate their human capital."[7]

Leaders make connections—between people and between the present and the future. Person to person and over time, leaders do make a difference. If you want to have a significant impact on people, on communities, and on organizations, you'd be wise to invest in learning to become the very best leader you can. But first you too must believe that a leader lives within each of us.

FIRST LEAD YOURSELF

Leadership development is self-development. Engineers have computers; painters, canvas and brushes; musicians, instruments. Leaders have only themselves. The instrument of leadership is the self, and mastery of the art of leadership comes from mastery of the self. Self-development is not about stuffing in a whole bunch of new information or trying out the latest technique. It's about leading out of what is already in your soul. It's about liberating the leader within you. It's about setting yourself free.

There's a scene in the film adaptation of Muriel Spark's classic, *The Prime of Miss Jean Brodie,* during which Headmistress MacKay calls Miss Brodie to her office to chastise Miss Brodie for her somewhat unorthodox teaching methods.[8] Headmistress MacKay comments on the precocity of Miss Brodie's students. Miss Brodie accepts this as a compliment, not a criticism and says:

"To me education is a leading out. The word education comes from the root 'ex,' meaning 'out,' and 'duco,' 'I lead.' To me education is simply a leading out of what is already there."

To this Headmistress MacKay responds rather haughtily, saying, "I had hoped there might also be a certain amount of putting in."

Miss Brodie laughs at this notion and replies, "That would not be education, but intrusion."

We agree. The process of development should never be intrusive. It should never be about just filling someone full of facts or skills. It won't work. Education should always be liberating. It should be about releasing what is already inside.

The quest for leadership is first an inner quest to discover who you are. Through self-development comes the confidence needed to lead. Self-confidence is really awareness of and faith in your own powers. These powers become clear and strong only as you work to identify and develop them.

Learning to lead is about discovering what *you* care about and value. About what inspires *you*. About what challenges *you*. About what gives *you* power and competence. About what encourages *you*. When you discover these things about yourself, you'll know what it takes to lead those qualities out of others.

Sure, we've said already that every leader has to learn the fundamentals and the discipline, and to a certain extent there's some period during which you're trying out a lot of new things. It's a necessary stage in your development as a leader. The point is you have to take what's been acquired and reshape into your own expression of yourself.

Sometimes liberation is as uncomfortable as intrusion, but in the end when you discover it for yourself you know that what's inside is what you found there and what belongs there. It's not something put inside you by someone else; it's what you discover for yourself.

LEADING QUESTIONS

As you begin this quest toward leadership, you must wrestle with some difficult questions:

- How certain am I of my own conviction about the vision and values?
- What gives me the courage to continue in the face of uncertainty and adversity?
- How will I handle disappointments, mistakes, and setbacks?
- What are my strengths and weaknesses?
- What do I need to do to improve my abilities to move the organization forward?
- How solid is my relationship with my constituents?
- How can I keep myself motivated and encouraged?
- What keeps me from giving up?
- Am I the right one to be leading at this very moment? Why?
- How much do I understand about what is going on in the organization and the world in which it operates?
- How prepared am I to handle the complex problems that now confront my organization?
- What are my beliefs about how people ought to conduct the affairs of our organization?
- Where do I think the organization ought to be headed over the next ten years?

Honest answers to these questions (and to those that arise from them) tell you that you must open yourself to a more global view. The leader, being in the forefront, is usually the first to encounter the world outside the boundaries of the organization. The more you know about the world, the easier it is to approach it with assurance. Thus you should seek to learn as much as possible about the forces—political, economic, social, moral, or artistic—that affect the organization.

Honest answers tell you that to become as effective as possible, you must improve your understanding of others and build your skills to mobilize people's energies toward higher purposes. To be a leader, you must be interpersonally competent, and you must be able to develop the trust and respect of others.

MORAL LEADERSHIP

Leadership practices per se are amoral. But leaders—the men and women who use the practices—are moral or immoral. There's an ethical dimension to leadership that neither leaders nor constituents should take lightly. This is why we began our discussion of leadership practices with a focus on finding your voice—your authentic self grounded in a set of values and ideals.

These, you have to find for yourself and test against others. There are, according to the late John Gardner, Stanford professor, secretary of Health, Education, and Welfare in the Johnson administration, and founder of Common Cause, four moral goals of leadership:[9]

- Releasing human potential
- Balancing the needs of the individual and the community
- Defending the fundamental values of the community
- Instilling in individuals a sense of initiative and responsibility

Attending to these goals will always direct your eyes to higher purposes. As you work to become all you can be, you can start to let go of your petty self-interests. As you give back some of what you've been given, you can reconstruct your community. As you serve the values of freedom, justice, equality, caring, and dignity, you can constantly renew the foundations of democracy. As each of us takes individual responsibility for creating the world of our dreams, we can all participate in leading.

All great leaders have wrestled with their souls. For instance, while attending Crozer Seminary, Martin Luther King Jr. read extensively in history. The more he read, the more he questioned whether Christian love could be a potent force in the world. He doubted his own capacity to be a pacifist. His faith in love was deeply shaken by Nietzsche's writings glorifying war and power and proclaiming the coming of a master race to control the masses. It wasn't until he was introduced to the teachings of Gandhi that King was inspired to live by the discipline of nonviolent resistance. And it was through reading Gandhi's biography that King also learned that the Indian lawyer himself had struggled to overcome his own tendencies toward hatred, anger, and violence. Only after resolving his internal conflicts was King able to enthusiastically embrace the philosophy of nonviolence.[10]

Such personal searching is essential in the development of leaders. Like King, you must resolve those dissonant internal chords. Extensive knowledge of history and the outside world increases your awareness of competing value systems, of the many principles by which individuals, organizations, and states can choose to function. You can't lead others until you've first led yourself through a struggle with opposing values.

When you clarify the principles that will govern your life and the ends that you will seek, you give purpose to your daily decisions. A personal creed gives you a point of reference for navigating the sometimes-stormy seas of organizational life. Without such a set of beliefs, your life has no rudder, and you're easily blown about by the winds of fashion. A credo that resolves competing beliefs also leads to personal integrity. A leader with integrity has one self, at home and at work, with family and with colleagues. Leaders without integrity are putting on an act.

Leaders take us to places we've never been before. But there are no freeways to the future, no paved highways to unknown, unexplored destinations. There's only wilderness. To step out into the unknown, begin with the exploration of the inner territory. With that as a base, you can then discover and unleash the leader within everyone. We'll find in the years to come that the most critical knowledge for all of us—and for leaders especially—will turn out to be self-knowledge.

CONTRASTS AND CONTRADICTIONS

In our research we identified Five Practices of Exemplary Leadership. We learned that in performing at their personal bests leaders Model the Way, Inspire a Shared Vision, Challenge the Process, Enable Others to Act, and

Encourage the Heart. And we found that leaders who more frequently engage in the Five Practices are significantly more likely to achieve extraordinary results than leaders who make use of these practices less often. Exemplary leadership and credible leaders make a difference in the world.

But there's a catch. *You can do all of this perfectly and still get fired!* Maybe we should have told you this sooner, but no doubt you knew it already. There's absolutely no way that we can say that it will always work all the time with all people. We know for certain that there's a much greater probability that it will, but there's no ironclad, money-back guarantee. And if any gurus ever stand in front of you and claim—or if any authors, including us, ever write—that they have *the* three-, five-, seven-, or nine-factor theory that's 100 percent certain to get you results and rewards, then grab your wallet and run. There's no get-rich-quick, instant-weight-loss program for leadership.

Remember film director Sidney Lumet's comment we quoted earlier? He said that he was "dependent on the talents and idiosyncrasies, the moods and egos, the politics and personalities, of more than a hundred different people."[11] That was just in making the movie, and didn't include all the other aspects of the business. Leadership in all settings is just like that. You will never, ever find, in historic or present times, even one example of a leader who controlled every aspect of the environment. And you'll never find an example of a leader who enlisted 100 percent of the constituents in even the most compelling of future possibilities. Not only is this realistic, it's fortunate. We should all be grateful for the forces we can't control and the voices we can't enlist. We need the cynics, skeptics, and alternative voices to keep our freedom. We need the challenges, surprises, and adversities to strengthen our courage.

There's another catch. Any leadership practice *can* become destructive. Virtues can become vices. There's a point at which each of the Five Practices, taken to extremes, can lead you astray.

Finding your voice and setting an example are essential to credibility and accomplishment—but an obsession with being seen as a role model can lead to being too focused on your own values and your way of doing things. It can cause you to discount others' views and be closed to feedback. It can push you into isolation for fear of losing privacy or being "found out"; it can also cause you to be more concerned with style than substance.

Being forward-looking and communicating a clear and common vision of the future are what set leaders apart from other credible people. Yet a singular focus on one vision of the future can blind you to other possibilities as well as to the realities of the present. It can cause you to miss the exciting possibilities that are just out of your sight or make you hang on just a little too long to an old, tired, and out-of-date technology. Exploiting your powers of inspiration can cause others to surrender their will. Your own energy, enthusiasm, and charm may be so magnetic that others don't think for themselves.

Challenging the process is essential to promoting innovation and progressive change. Seizing the initiative and taking risks are necessary for learning and continuous improvement. But take this to extremes and you can create needless turmoil, confusion, and paranoia. Routines are important, and if you seldom give people opportunity to gain confidence and competence they'll lose their motivation to try new things. Change for change's sake can be just as demoralizing as complacency.

Collaboration and teamwork are essential to getting extraordinary things done in today's turbulent world. Innovation depends on high degrees of trust. And people must be given the power to be in control of their own lives if they are to accomplish great things. But an overreliance on collaboration and trust may reflect an avoidance of critical decisions or cause errors in judgment. It may be a way of *not* taking charge when the situation requires. Delegating power and responsibility can become a way of dumping too much on others when they're not fully prepared to handle it.

And people do perform at higher levels when they're encouraged. Personal recognition and group celebration create the spirit and momentum that can carry a group forward even during the toughest of challenges. At the same time a constant focus on who should be recognized and when we should celebrate can turn us into gregarious minstrels. We can lose sight of the mission because we're having so much fun. Don't become consumed by all the perks and pleasures and forget the purpose of it all.

Far more insidious than all of these potential problems, however, is the treachery of hubris. It's fun to be a leader, gratifying to have influence, and exhilarating to have scores of people cheering your every word. In many all-too-subtle ways, it's easy to be seduced by power and importance. All evil leaders have been infected with the disease of hubris, becoming bloated with an exaggerated sense of self and pursuing their own sinister ends. How then to avoid it?

Humility is the only way to resolve the conflicts and contradictions of leadership.[12] You can avoid excessive pride only if you recognize that you're human and need the help of others. As Egon Zehnder, chairman emeritus of Egon Zehnder International, told us: "Listen to what your colleagues have to say. They know more than you do. Have the humility to step back and correct yourself." Humility. It comes up time and again. In fact, in their research on companies that transition from mediocrity (or worse) to long-term superiority, Jim Collins and his team found a remarkable pattern of humility among the chief executives of what they categorize as "good-to-great" companies. "In contrast to the *I*-centric style of the comparison leaders, we were struck by how the good-to-great leaders *didn't* talk about themselves. During interviews with the good-to-great leaders they'd talk about the company and the contributions of other executives as long as we'd like but would deflect discussion about their own contributions."[13] Their compelling modesty is perhaps why most of these executives were not the ones to grab the headlines of the press or gain rock-star status in the popular leader-as-hero culture. Instead, they focused their attention and will on their company and on others.

Jim Collins's observation is consistent with our own findings. As we've discussed, exemplary leaders know that "you can't do it alone" and they act accordingly. They lack the pride and pretense displayed by many leaders who succeed in the short term but leave behind a weak organization that fails to remain strong after their departure. Instead, with self-effacing humor and generous and sincere credit to others they get higher and higher levels of performance; they get extraordinary things done.

There's another way to avoid the temptations of power that lead to becoming overbearing and presumptuous. You can avoid this arrogance by refusing to become one-dimensional, focused narrowly on your work. Do not allow work to consume you. Get involved in the world that surrounds you. The very best leaders have numerous pursuits and interests—arts, literature, science, technology, entertainment, sports, politics, law, religion, and family and friends.

There's one other important lesson here. Nothing in our research even hints that leaders should be perfect. Leaders aren't saints. They're human beings, full of the flaws and failings of the rest of us. They make mistakes. Perhaps the very best advice we can give all aspiring leaders is to remain humble and unassuming—to always remain open and full of wonder. The best leaders are the best learners.

THE SECRET TO SUCCESS IN LIFE

Constituents look for leaders who demonstrate an enthusiastic and genuine belief in the capacity of others, who strengthen people's will, who supply the means to achieve, and who express optimism for the future. Constituents want leaders who remain passionate despite obstacles and setbacks. In uncertain times, leaders with a positive, confident, can-do approach to life and business are desperately needed.

Leaders must keep hope alive, even in the most difficult of times. They must strengthen their constituents' belief that life's struggle will produce a more promising future. Such faith results from an intimate and supportive relationship, a relationship based on mutual participation in the process of renewal. In keeping hope alive, credible leaders demonstrate their faith and confidence by first accepting responsibility for the quality of the lives of their constituents. Even when everything goes wrong or when they suffer resounding defeats, leaders display constancy and unwavering commitment to the cause.

Without hope there can be no courage—and this is not the time or place for the timid. This is the time and place for optimism, imagination, and enthusiasm. Leaders must summon their will if they are to mobilize the personal and organizational resources to triumph against the odds. Hope is essential to achieving the highest levels of performance.[14] Hope enables people to transcend the difficulties of today and envision the potentialities of tomorrow. Hope enables people to bounce back even after being stressed, stretched, and depressed. Hope enables people to find the will and the way to unleash greatness.

And yet, hope is not all. There's still one more final leadership lesson that we have learned. It's the secret to success in life.

When we began our study of leadership bests we were fortunate to cross paths with U.S. Army Major General John H. Stanford. We knew that he had survived military tours in Vietnam and was highly decorated, and that the loyalty of his troops was extraordinary. He went on to head up the Military Traffic Management Command for the U.S. Army during the Persian Gulf War. When he retired from the Army he became manager of Fulton County when Atlanta was gearing up to host the 1996 Summer Olympics, and then he was recruited to become superintendent of the Seattle Public Schools, where he sparked a revolution in public education.

All of his service was impressive, but it was his answer to one of our interview questions that most influenced our own understanding of leadership. We asked John how he'd go about developing leaders, whether at Santa Clara University, in the military, in government, in the nonprofit sector, or in private business. He replied,

> When anyone asks me that question, I tell them I have the secret to success in life. The secret to success is to stay in love. Staying in love gives you the fire to ignite other people, to see inside other people, to have a greater desire to get things done than other people. A person who is not in love doesn't really feel the kind of excitement that helps them to get ahead and to lead others and to achieve. I don't know any other fire, any other thing in life that is more exhilarating and is more positive a feeling than love is.

"Staying in love" isn't the answer we expected to get—at least not when we *began* our study of leadership. But after numerous interviews and case analyses, it finally dawned on us how many leaders used the word *love* freely when talking about their own motivations to lead.

Of all the things that sustain a leader over time, love is the most lasting. It's hard to imagine leaders getting up day after day, putting in the long hours and hard work it takes to get extraordinary things done, without having their hearts in it. The best-kept secret of successful leaders is love: staying in love with leading, with the people who do the work, with what their organizations produce, and with those who honor the organization by using its work.

Leadership is *not* an affair of the head. Leadership is an affair of the heart.

APPENDIX

Guide to the Research

The stories that we tell in this book bring the principles and practices of leadership to life. What gives credibility to these stories is our two decades of extensive research—research that clearly indicates that if you do more of what we've described in this book you *will* get better results in your work, in your relationships, and in your life.

In the two previous editions of this book we described our research in an appendix to the text. In this edition we've migrated the appendix—and much more—to the Web. We invite and encourage you to explore the research by going to http://www.leadershipchallenge.com/research.

We're excited about being able to post our data on the Web because it offers us opportunities that simply didn't exist when the second edition was published. The *Guide to the Research* includes a description of how we conducted the research underlying the Five Practices of Exemplary Leadership, the data supporting the model, the reliability and validity of that data, and summaries of key findings on the effects of exemplary leadership.

But there's more to the *Guide* than simply a report on our data. The *Guide* section of our leadershipchallenge.com Web site includes executive summaries of over 150 doctoral dissertations and other research projects based on *The Leadership Challenge*. You'll also be able to link to other resources and product information on the Web site, including the *Leadership Practices Inventory (LPI)* and other assessment instruments, information for college and university instructors, tips, and answers to frequently asked questions. Most important, we'll be updating the *Guide* every few months, and from time to time we'll be asking you to participate in exploring leadership issues with us.

We invite you to join us on the Web and to continue your own adventure in leadership and learning.

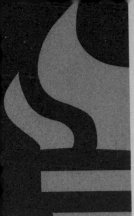

NOTES

PREFACE

1. The Five Practices of Exemplary Leadership® is a registered trademark of J. M. Kouzes and B. Z. Posner.

CHAPTER 1

1. Unless otherwise noted, all quotations are taken from personal interviews or from personal-best leadership case studies written by the respondent leaders. The titles and affiliations of the leaders may be different today from what they were at the time of their case study or publication of this volume. We expect many have moved on to other leadership adventures while we were writing, or will do so by the time you read this.
2. Additional information about Levin and the Whites Group can be found in a case study titled "Changing Gear," prepared by D. T. Jones (Lean Enterprise Research Centre, Cardiff Business School), October 1997, and in G. Golzen, "Driving Force," *HR* (March 1999): 28–31.
3. W. Bennis, *On Becoming a Leader* (Reading, Mass.: Addison-Wesley, 1988), 146.
4. Telephone interview with Jodi Taylor, Ph.D., Center for Creative Leadership, Colorado Springs, Colorado, April 1998.
5. "FC Roper Starch Survey: The Web," *Fast Company* (October 1999): 302.
6. Public Allies, *New Leadership for a New Century* (Washington, D.C.: Public Allies, 1998).

CHAPTER 2

1. For more information about the original studies, see B. Z. Posner and W. H. Schmidt, "Values and the American Manager: An Update," *California Management Review* 26, no. 3 (1984): 202–216; and B. Z. Posner and W. H. Schmidt, "Values and Expectations of Federal Service Executives," *Public Administration Review* 46, no. 5 (1986): 447–454.
2. We analyze these findings and discuss their implications in detail in J. M. Kouzes and B. Z. Posner, *Credibility: How Leaders Gain and Lose It, Why People Demand It* (San Francisco: Jossey-Bass, 1993).
3. Our own research is supported by a recent study by the Corporate Leadership Council, an organization that provides best practices to human resource executives in leading global corporations. They found exactly what we did—honesty is at the top of the list of what people look for in their leaders. Sixty-one

percent of their respondents said this was an important leadership attribute. See *Voice of the Leader* (Washington, D.C.: Corporate Leadership Council, 2001).

4. J. M. Kouzes, B. Z. Posner, and M. Krause, *Summary of the Executive Challenges Survey* (Executive Development Center, Leavey School of Business and Administration, Santa Clara University, 1986). Our own research is confirmed by a joint Korn/Ferry–Columbia University study. Seventy-five percent of respondents in that assessment ranked "conveys a strong vision of the future" as a very important quality for CEOs *today;* it was so ranked by an almost unanimous 98 percent for the year 2000. The desirability of this ability didn't vary by more than three percentage points across the regions studied (Japan, Western Europe, Latin America, and the United States). Korn/Ferry International and Columbia University Graduate School of Business, *Reinventing the CEO* (New York: Korn/Ferry International and Columbia University Graduate School of Business, 1989), 90.

5. For more on the role of positive emotions and leadership see D. Goleman, R. Boyatzis, and A. McKee, *Primal Leadership: Realizing the Power of Emotional Intelligence* (Boston: Harvard Business School Press, 2002); and B. L. Fredrickson, "The Role of Positive Emotions in Positive Psychology: The Broaden-and-Build Theory of Emotions," *American Psychologist* 56 (2001): 218–226.

6. F. F. Reichheld with T. Teal, *The Loyalty Effect: The Hidden Force Behind Growth, Profits, and Lasting Value* (Boston: Harvard Business School Press, 1996), 1.

7. F. F. Reichheld, *Loyalty Rules: How Today's Leaders Build Lasting Relationships* (Boston: Harvard Business School Press, 2001), 6.

8. F. F. Reichheld and P. Schefter, "E-Loyalty: Your Secret Weapon on the Web," *Harvard Business Review* (July-August 2000): 107. See also Bain & Company and Mainspring, "Bain/Mainspring Online Retailing Survey" (joint survey of 2,116 online shoppers in the categories of apparel, groceries, and consumer electronics) (Boston: Bain & Company, December 1999); and Reichheld, *Loyalty Rules*, 8. For additional information on Web credibility see B. J. Fogg and others, "What Makes Web Sites Credible? A Report on a Large Quantitative Study," Stanford University, 2001, available on-line at http://www.webcredibility.org.

9. For a study of the believability of politicians and journalists, and the difference in their roles, see Times Mirror Company, *The People and the Press* (Los Angeles: Times Mirror, 1986). For a more recent analysis of trust in major political institutions and prospective presidential candidates, see Times Mirror Center for the People and the Press, *The New Political Landscape* (Washington, D.C.: Times Mirror, 1994).

10. In a national study of the credibility of leaders and other public figures from a variety of settings, the Public Relations Society of America Foundation found that "the amount of credibility the public grants any particular information source . . . is an amalgam of specific issues, interwoven with demographics, attitudes, peer influence, experiences, ideology, and the level of the individual's participation in the working of society." See "National Credibility Index," Public Relations Society of America Foundation, 1999; available on-line at http://www.prsa.org/nci.

11. P. H. Mirvis, personal correspondence, January 1992. See D. L. Kanter and P. H. Mirvis, *The Cynical Americans: Living and Working in an Age of Discontent and Disillusion* (San Francisco: Jossey-Bass, 1989).

12. See F. Newport, "Military Retains Top Position in Americans' Confidence Ratings," Gallup Organization (June 25, 2001). Available on-line at http://www.gallup.com/poll/releases/pr010625.asp.

CHAPTER 3

1. M. De Pree, *Leadership Jazz* (New York: Currency Doubleday, 1992), 1–3.

2. De Pree, *Leadership Jazz*, 5.

3. D. S. Pottruck and T. Pearce, *Clicks and Mortar: Passion Driven Growth in an Internet Driven World* (San Francisco: Jossey-Bass, 2000), 97.

4. "Generation X Shuns Charismatic Leaders," *USA Today Magazine* (April 1999): 3; M. Dunne, "Policy Leadership, Gen X Style," *National Civic Review* (Fall 1997): 251–260.

5. M. Rokeach, *The Nature of Human Values* (New York: Free Press, 1973), 5.

6. For a discussion of the power of voice, especially in saying yes and saying no, see D. Whyte, *The Heart Aroused: Poetry and the Preservation of the Soul in Corporate America* (New York: Currency Doubleday, 1994), 117–144.

7. Rokeach, *The Nature of Human Values*, 14–15.

8. B. Z. Posner and W. H. Schmidt, "Values Congruence and Differences Between the Interplay of Personal and Organizational Value Systems," *Journal of Business Ethics* 12 (1993): 171–177.

9. For more on the importance of values, see C. A. O'Reilly and J. Pfeffer, *Hidden Value: How Great Companies Achieve Extraordinary Results with Ordinary People* (Boston: Harvard Business School Press, 2000). Also see J. C. Collins and J. I. Porras, *Built to Last: Successful Habits of Visionary Companies* (New York: HarperCollins, 1994).

10. Merriam-Webster's *Collegiate Dictionary, 10th ed.*, s.v. "care."

11. A. Lamott, *Bird by Bird: Some Instructions on Writing and Life* (New York: Pantheon, 1994), 199–200.

12. A. Roddick, *Body and Soul: Profits with Principles, the Amazing Success Story of Anita Roddick and the Body Shop* (New York: Crown Publishing, 1991), statements on pp. 17, 21, 25, and 117. You can also find her giving voice to these expressions in A. Roddick, *Business as Unusual: The Triumph of Anita Roddick* (London: Thorsons, 2001).

13. W. Zinsser, *On Writing Well: The Classic Guide to Writing Nonfiction* (New York: HarperCollins, 1998), 238.

14. For example, see his most recent book for an extensive research report on the qualities of successful firms. D. H. Maister, *Practice What You Preach: What Managers Must Do to Create a High Achievement Culture* (New York: Free Press, 2001).

15. D. H. Maister, *How's Your Asset?* (Boston: David Maister Associates, 1991), 1.

16. Maister, *How's Your Asset?* 3.

17. We were first introduced to a version of this exercise by C. A. O'Reilly (Stanford University).

18. The questions posed are based on the work of the original developers of the values clarification process; see S. B. Simon, L. W. Howe, and H. Kirschenbaum, *Values Clarification: The Classic Guide to Discovering Your Truest Feelings, Beliefs, and Goals* (New York: Warner Books, 1995).

19. J. M. McPherson, *Abraham Lincoln and the Second American Revolution* (New York: Oxford University Press, 1991), 95.

20. T. Branch, *Parting the Waters: America in the King Years 1954-1963* (New York: Simon & Schuster, 1988).

21. W. J. Bennett, *The Book of Virtues: A Treasury of Great Moral Stories* (New York: Simon & Schuster, 1993).

22. M. De Pree, *Leadership Is an Art* (New York: Doubleday, 1989), 107.

CHAPTER 4

1. See, for example, B. Z. Posner and W. H. Schmidt, "Values Congruence and Differences Between the Interplay of Personal and Organizational Value Systems," *Journal of Business Ethics* 12 (1993): 171–177; and B. Z. Posner, "Person-Organization Values Congruence: No Support for Individual Differences as a Moderating Influence," *Human Relations* 45, no. 2 (1992): 351–361.

2. B. Z. Posner and R. I. Westwood, "A Cross-Cultural Investigation of the Shared Values Relationship," *International Journal of Value-Based Management* 11, no. 4 (1995): 1-10; J. W. Haas, B. D. Sypher, and H. E. Sypher, "Do Shared Goals Really Make a Difference?" *Management Communication Quarterly* 6, no. 2 (1992): 166–179.

3. For example, R. I. Westwood and B. Z. Posner, "Managerial Values Across Cultures: Australia, Hong Kong and the U.S." *Asia Pacific Journal of Management* 14 (1997): 31-66; B. Z. Posner, J. M. Kouzes, and W. H. Schmidt, "Shared Values Make a Difference: An Empirical Test of Corporate Culture," *Human Resource*

Management 24, no. 3 (1985): 293-310; B. Z. Posner and W. H. Schmidt, "Demographic Characteristics and Shared Values," *International Journal of Value-Based Management* 5, no. 1 (1992): 77–87.

4. Posner and Westwood, "A Cross-Cultural Investigation of the Shared Values Relationship."

5. J. P. Kotter and J. L. Heskett, *Corporate Culture and Performance* (New York: Free Press, 1992).

6. Our colleague David Caldwell (Santa Clara University) originally shared this example with us.

7. J. C. Collins and J.I. Porras, *Built to Last: Successful Habits of Visionary Companies* (New York: Harper-Collins, 1994).

8. C. A. O'Reilly and J. Pfeffer, *Hidden Value: How Great Companies Achieve Extraordinary Results with Ordinary People* (Boston: Harvard Business School Press, 2000).

9. R. A. Stevenson, "Clarifying Behavioral Expectations Associated with Espoused Organizational Values," Ph.D. dissertation, Fielding Institute, 1995.

10. D. K. McNeese-Smith, "Increasing Employee Productivity, Job Satisfaction, and Organizational Commitment," *Hospital & Health Services Administration* 41, no. 2 (1996): 160–175.

11. "Continuous Journey," *Quality,* Association of Productivity and Quality Control (August/September 1993): 78–92.

12. This discussion draws upon T. J. Peters and N. Austin, *A Passion for Excellence* (New York: Random House, 1985); E. H. Schein, *Organizational Culture and Leadership,* 3rd ed. (San Francisco: Jossey-Bass, 1997); and E. H. Schein, *The Organizational Culture Survival Guide* (San Francisco: Jossey-Bass, 1999).

13. H. N. Schwarzkopf with P. Pietre, *It Doesn't Take a Hero* (New York: Bantam Books, 1992), 240–241.

14. J. A. Conger, "Inspiring Others: The Language of Leadership," *Academy of Management Executive* 5, no. 1 (1991): 31–45.

15. J. Conger, *Winning 'Em Over: A New Model for Management in the Age of Persuasion* (New York: Simon & Schuster, 1998).

16. M. M. Osborn and D. Ehninger, "The Metaphor in Public Address," *Speech Monograph* 29 (1962): 228.

17. See, for example, E. Borgida and R. E. Nisbett, "The Differential Impact of Abstract vs. Concrete Information on Decisions," *Journal of Applied Technology* 7, no. 3 (1977): 258–271; R. Zemke, "Storytelling: Back to Basic," *TRAINING* (March 1990): 44-50; T. Pearce, *Leading Out Loud: The Authentic Speaker, the Credible Leader* (San Francisco: Jossey-Bass, 1995); and S. Denning, *The Springboard: How Storytelling Ignites Action in Knowledge-Era Organizations* (Boston: Butterworth-Heinemann, 2001).

18. J. Martin and M. E. Power, "Organizational Stories: More Vivid and Persuasive Than Quantitative Data," in B. M. Staw (ed.), *Psychological Foundations of Organizational Behavior* (Glenview, Ill.: Scott, Foresman, 1982), 161–168.

19. S. Zuboff, *In the Age of the Smart Machine: The Future of Work and Power* (New York: Basic Books, 1988), 394.

20. "Brian Coleman, Manager, Tool and Dies, Ford Motor Co., Dagenham, England," *On Achieving Excellence* 8, no. 8 (1993): 3 (newsletter from TPG Communications, Palo Alto, Calif.).

21. R. P. Bagozzi and S. K. Kimmel, "A Comparison of Leading Theories for the Prediction of Goal-Directed Behaviors," *British Journal of Social Psychology* 34 (December 1995): 437–461.

22. C. A. O'Reilly and D. F. Caldwell, "The Power of Strong Corporate Cultures in Silicon Valley Firms," presentation to the Executive Seminar in Corporate Excellence, Santa Clara University, 13 February 1985; see also C. A. O'Reilly, "Corporations, Culture, and Commitment: Motivation and Social Control in Organizations," *California Management Review* 23 (1989): 9–17.

23. With one client we prepared an Aspirations Survey, which was distributed to over 2,500 managers throughout the company. The survey focused specifically on the company's aspirations (or values) and how well people understood them, supported and believed in them, and perceived that "living them" made a difference (that is, saw them as reflected in key actions and decisions). The results helped clarify which aspirations were clearly understood and where confusion existed, where there were discrepancies between personal alignment and work group congruencies with the aspirations, and to assess the inten-

sity to which aspirations were both held and being implemented. Analyses by function, as well as various demographic factors, helped pinpoint particular problems and opportunities. Subsequent administrations of the survey showed an ongoing commitment to aspirations and their continuing importance (not just a fad), and allowed people to see areas of consistency, change, and improvement.

24. A. Colby, L. Kohlberg, B. Speicher-Durbin, and M. Lieberman, "Secondary School Moral Discussion Programs Led by Social Studies Teachers," *Journal of Moral Education* 6, no. 2 (1977): 90–117.

25. F. A. Blanchard, T. Lilly, and L. A. Vaughn, "Reducing the Expression of Racial Prejudice," *Psychological Science* 2, no. 2 (1991): 101–105.

26. B. R. Schlenker, *Impression Management* (Monterey, Calif.: Brooks/Cole, 1980).

27. S. Benner, "Culture Shock," *Inc.* (Aug 1985): 73–82, quote on p. 80. Another example of this type of color-coding system is provided by S. Godin, "Is It Possible to Create a Maybe-Proof Company?" *Fast Company* (December 1999): 354–358.

28. Terry Pearce, e-mail correspondence with Jan Hunter, 12 July 2001. For more on using story, image, and ritual for common understanding, see D. S. Pottruck and T. Pearce, *Clicks and Mortar: Passion Driven Growth in an Internet Driven World* (San Francisco: Jossey-Bass, 2000).

29. S. Denning, *The Springboard*, 10.

30. Denning, *The Springboard*, 14, xiii.

31. D. M. Armstrong, *Managing by Storying Around: A New Method of Leadership* (New York: Doubleday, 1992).

32. Conger, *Winning 'Em Over*.

33. S. Taylor and L. Novelli Jr., "Some Basic Concepts of Innovation and Story Telling," *Issues & Observation* 11, no. 1 (1991): 6–9.

34. For more about being a storyteller, see J. Maguire, *The Power of Personal Storytelling: Spinning Tales to Connect with Others* (New York: Tarcher, 1998); and D. Lipman, *Improving Your Storytelling: Beyond the Basics for All Who Tell Stories in Work and Play* (Little Rock, Ark.: August House, 1999).

35. E. Aronson, *The Social Animal*, 8th ed. (New York: Freeman, 1999).

CHAPTER 5

1. In looking into the lives of ninety leaders, for example, professors Warren Bennis and Burt Nanus found that "attention through vision" was one of their key strategies. See W. B. Bennis and B. Nanus, *Leaders: The Strategies for Taking Charge* (New York: HarperCollins, 1985), 89. The personal behavior trait most frequently mentioned as desirable in a CEO by fifteen hundred senior leaders from twenty different countries (including Japan, the United States, Western Europe, and Latin America), was a "strong sense of vision of the future"; see Korn/Ferry International and Graduate School of Business, Columbia University, *Reinventing the CEO* (New York: Korn/Ferry International and Graduate School of Business, Columbia University, 1989), 90.

   In addition, management scholar and researcher Elliott Jaques has found in his extensive research that the only true differentiator between levels in an organization is what he calls the "time span of discretion." In lay terms, that's how many months or years ahead it takes for you to know how well those reporting to you are performing on tasks that are at their discretion. The longer your time span of discretion, the more money you make. See E. Jaques, *Measurement of Responsibility: A Study of Work, Payment, and Individual Capacity* (New York, Wiley: 1972); and Elliott Jaques, *Social Power and the CEO: Leadership and Trust in a Sustainable Free Enterprise System* (Westport, Conn.: Quorum Books, 2002). For a classic discussion of the role of vision and purpose in leadership, see J. M. Burns, *Leadership* (New York: HarperCollins, 1978).

2. E. L. Deci with R. Flaste, *Why We Do What We Do: Understanding Self-Motivation* (New York: Penguin Books, 1995).

3. Deci, *Why We Do What We Do*, 25.

4. For an excellent treatment of this subject, see K. W. Thomas, *Intrinsic Motivation at Work: Building Energy and Commitment* (San Francisco: Berrett-Koehler, 2000).

5. L. Ioannou, "Make Your Company an Idea Factory," *Fortune* (12 June 2000): F264N-F264R.

6. Envisioning and intuiting aren't logical activities, and they're extremely difficult to explain and quantify. Alden M. Hayashi, a senior editor of *Harvard Business Review* who has studied executive decision making, reports, "In my interviews with top executives known for their shrewd business instincts, none could articulate precisely how they routinely made important decisions that defied any logical analysis. To describe that vague feeling of knowing something without knowing exactly how or why, they used words like 'professional judgment,' 'intuition,' 'gut instinct,' 'inner voice,' and 'hunch,' but they couldn't describe the process much beyond that." Yet, as he points out, the leaders he studied agreed that these hard-to-describe abilities were crucial to effectiveness. They even went so far as to say that it was the "X-Factor" that separated the best from the mediocre. See A. M. Hayashi, "When to Trust Your Gut," *Harvard Business Review* 79, no. 2 (February 2001): 59-65. In fact, by definition, intuition and vision are directly connected. Intuition has as its root the Latin word meaning "to look at"—see E. Partridge, *A Short Etymological Dictionary of Modern English* (New York: Macmillan, 1977), 359, 742.

7. Tara Church shared this example with us, and she also wrote about it in T. Church, "Where the Leaders Are: The Promise of Youth Leadership," in W. Bennis, G. M. Spreitzer, and T. G. Cummings, eds., *The Future of Leadership: Today's Top Leadership Thinkers Speak to Tomorrow's Leaders* (San Francisco: Jossey-Bass, 2001).

8. O. A. El Sawy, "Temporal Perspective and Managerial Attention: A Study of Chief Executive Strategic Behavior," unpublished doctoral dissertation, Stanford University, 1983. Also see O. A. El Sawy, "Temporal Biases in Strategic Attention," research paper, November 1988, Marshall School of Business, University of Southern California.

9. El Sawy, "Temporal Perspective," VII-35.

10. J. James, *Thinking in the Future Tense: Leadership Skills for the New Age* (New York: Simon & Schuster, 1996), 28.

11. R. Chang, *The Passion Plan at Work: Building a Passion-Driven Organization* (San Francisco: Jossey-Bass, 2001), 4.

12. For extensive research on intuitive decision making under conditions of extreme uncertainty see G. Klein, *The Sources of Power: How People Make Decisions* (Cambridge, Mass.: MIT Press, 1998). Also see B. Breen, "What's Your Intuition?" *Fast Company* (September 2000): 290–300.

13. See G. Hamel, *Leading the Revolution* (Boston: Harvard Business School Press, 2000). Hamel observes, "One of the reasons many people fail to fully appreciate what's changing is because they're down at ground level, lost in the thicket of confusing, conflicting data. You have to make time to step back and ask yourself, 'What's the big story that cuts across all these little facts?'" (p. 128).

14. The Leadership Challenge Workshop™ is a trademark belonging to James M. Kouzes and Barry Z. Posner.

15. Market researcher and author Doug Hall has found that "dramatically different" levels in a new product or service increase the idea's probability of success in the marketplace from 15 percent to 53 percent. That's a 253 percent greater chance of success. The same is true for a vision; the more unique it is the higher the probability of success in getting people to buy in. See D. Hall, *Jump Start Your Business Brain: Win More, Lose Less, and Make More Money with Your New Products, Services, Sales and Advertising* (Cincinnati, Ohio: Brain Brew Books, 2001).

16. G. Hamel and C. K. Prahalad, *Competing for the Future: Breakthrough Strategies for Seizing Control of Your Industry and Creating the Markets of Tomorrow* (Boston: Harvard Business School Press, 1994).

17. H. Gardner, *Leading Minds: An Anatomy of Leadership* (New York: Basic Books, 1995), 9–10.

18. H. A. Shepard and J. A. Hawley, *Life Planning: Personal and Organizational* (Washington, D.C.: National Training and Development Service Press, 1974).

19. Hamel and Prahalad, *Competing for the Future*, 4.

CHAPTER 6

1. M. L. King Jr., "I Have a Dream," in C. S. King (ed.), *The Words of Martin Luther King, Jr.* (New York: Newmarket Press, 1983), 95–98. Reprinted by permission of Joan Daves, copyright © 1963 by Martin Luther King Jr.
2. D. A. Garvin, "How the Baldrige Award Really Works," *Harvard Business Review* (November-December 1991): 80–93.
3. A. Deering, R. Dilts, and J. Russell, *Alpha Leadership: Tools for Business Leaders Who Want More from Life* (London: Wiley, 2002).
4. B. L. Kaye and S. Jordon-Evans, *Love 'Em and Lose 'Em* (San Francisco: Berrett-Koehler, 1999).
5. Telephone interview with Dave Berlew, November 14, 1994. See D. E. Berlew, "Leadership and Organizational Excitement," *California Management Review* 17, No. 2 (1974): 21–30.
6. C. Caggiano, "What Do Workers Want?" *Inc.* (November 1992): 101–102; S. Caudron, "Motivation?" *Industry Week* (15 November 1993): 33; and E. Galinsky, J. T. Bond, and D. E. Friedman, *The National Study of the Changing Workforce* (New York: Families and Work Institute, 1993).
7. M. Novak, *Business as a Calling: Work and the Examined Life* (New York: Free Press, 1996); R. J. Leider and D. A. Shapiro, *Whistle While You Work: Heeding Your Life's Calling* (San Francisco: Berrett-Koehler, 2001); and P. J. Palmer, *Let Your Life Speak* (San Francisco: Jossey-Bass, 2000).
8. See, for example, H. Mintzberg and R. A. Norman, *Reframing Business: When the Map Changes the Landscape* (New York: Wiley, 2001); C. Handy, *The Hungry Spirit: Beyond Capitalism* (New York: Broadway Books, 1999); and G. Hamel, *Leading the Revolution* (Boston: Harvard Business School Press, 2000).
9. H. Mintzberg, "The Rise and Fall of Strategic Planning," *Harvard Business Review* (January-February 1994): 109.
10. J. M. Burns, *Leadership* (New York: HarperCollins, 1978), 20.
11. King, "I Have a Dream," 95–98.
12. B. M. Bass, *Leadership and Performance Beyond Expectations* (New York: Free Press, 1985), 35.
13. See, for example, H. S. Friedman, L. M. Prince, R. E. Riggio, and M. R. DiMatteo, "Understanding and Assessing Nonverbal Expressiveness: The Affective Communication Test," *Journal of Personality and Social Psychology* 39, no. 2 (1980): 333–351; D. Goleman, R. Boyatzis, and A. McKee, *Primal Leadership: Realizing the Power of Emotional Intelligence* (Boston: Harvard Business School Press, 2002); and J. Conger, *Winning 'Em Over: A New Model for Management in the Age of Persuasion* (New York: Simon & Schuster, 1998).
14. M. Pines, "Children's Winning Ways," *Psychology Today* 18, no. 12 (1984): 58–65.
15. C. Olofson, "The Ritz Puts on Stand-Up Meetings," *Fast Company* (September 1998): 62.
16. B. Decker, *You've Got to Be Believed to Be Heard* (New York: St. Martin's Press, 1993).
17. B. Hickson, E. W. Clayton, S. S. Entman, C. S. Miller, P. B. Githens, K. Whetten-Goldstein, and F. A. Sloan, "Obstetricians' Prior Malpractice Experience and Patients' Satisfaction With Care," *Journal of the American Medical Association* 272 (1994): 1583–1587.

CHAPTER 7

1. M. Korda, "The King of the Deal," *New Yorker* (29 March 1993): 43.
2. T. S. Bateman and J. M. Crant, "The Proactive Component of Organizational Behavior: Measures and Correlates," *Journal of Organizational Behavior* 14 (1993): 103–118.
3. J. M. Crant, "The Proactive Personality Scale and Objective Job Performance Among Real Estate Agents," *Journal of Applied Psychology* 80, no 4. (August 1995): 532–537.
4. Our sample involved managers from both the United States and Switzerland. See B. Z. Posner and J. W. Harder, "The Proactive Personality, Leadership, Gender and National Culture," paper presented to the Western Academy of Management Conference, Santa Fe, New Mexico, April 2002.

5. See A. Bandura, *Self-Efficacy: The Exercise of Self-Control* (New York: Freeman, 1997). Bandura offers a detailed discussion of ways to increase self-efficacy. He points out that there's a critical difference between self-efficacy and self-esteem. Self-efficacy is a belief in one's abilities, whereas self-esteem is a belief in one's worth. We prefer the concept of self-efficacy to self-esteem, because it's easier to offer suggestions on how to increase self-efficacy than to increase self-esteem. However, it is true that high self-esteem is positively correlated with speaking up. Also see J. A. LePine and L. V. Dyne, "Predicting Voice Behavior in Work Groups," *Journal of Applied Psychology* 83, no. 6 (1998): 853–868.

6. For detailed information on mental simulation, see G. Klein, *Sources of Power: How People Make Decisions* (Cambridge, Mass.: MIT Press, 1998), 45–77.

7. Blum's stirring account of this highly acclaimed adventure is chronicled in A. Blum, *Annapurna: A Woman's Place, Twentieth Anniversary Edition* (San Francisco: Sierra Club Books, 1998). Leadership lessons from Arlene Blum were also gathered from personal conversations and correspondence between Blum and the authors.

8. Blum, *Annapurna*, 3.

9. Blum, *Annapurna*, 6.

10. P. LaBarre, "How to Make It to the Top," *Fast Company* (September 1998): 72.

11. The finding that how we deal with challenge comes from the inside was dramatically reported by V. E. Frankl in *Man's Search for Meaning: An Introduction to Logotherapy* (New York: Touchstone, 1984) [first published in 1946].

12. See E. L. Deci with R. Flaste, *Why We Do What We Do: Understanding Self-Motivation* (New York: Penguin Books, 1995).

13. See A. Kohn, *Punished by Rewards* (New York: Houghton Mifflin, 1993).

14. M. Fox, *Reinvention of Work: A New Vision of Livelihood for Our Time* (San Francisco: Harper San Francisco, 1994), 49.

15. M. Wheatley, *Leadership and the New Science* (San Francisco: Berrett-Koehler, 1992).

16. R. M. Kanter, *The Change Masters: Innovation for Productivity in the American Corporation* (New York: Simon & Schuster, 1983), 125.

17. Economist Intelligence Unit, *Business, People, and Rewards: Surviving and Thriving in the New Economy* (New York: Economist Intelligence Unit, 2001), 6, 39, 23.

18. Warren Bennis, *Why Leaders Can't Lead: The Unconscious Conspiracy Continues* (San Francisco: Jossey-Bass, 1989), 15.

19. See R. Foster and S. Kaplan, *Creative Destruction: Why Companies That Are Built to Last Underperform the Market—and How to Successfully Transform Them* (New York: Currency Doubleday, 2001); and C. M. Christensen, *The Innovator's Dilemma: When New Technologies Cause Great Firms to Fail* (Boston: Harvard Business School Press, 1997).

20. R. Katz, "The Influence of Group Longevity: High Performance Research Teams," *Wharton Magazine* 6, no. 3 (1982): 28–34; and R. Katz and T. J. Allen, "Investigating the Not Invented Here (NIH) Syndrome: A Look at the Performance, Tenure, and Communication Patterns of 50 R&D Project Groups," in M. L. Tushman and W. L. Moore (eds.), *Readings in the Management of Innovation*, 2nd ed. (Cambridge, Mass.: Ballinger, 1988), 293–309.

21. Katz, "The Influence of Group Longevity," 31.

22. T. Kelley with J. Littman, *The Art of Innovation: Lessons in Creativity from IDEO, America's Leading Design Firm* (New York: Currency Doubleday, 2001), 28.

23. Kelley, *Art of Innovation*, 23–51.

24. P. F. Drucker, "Drucker on Management: The Five Deadly Business Sins," *Wall Street Journal* (21 October 1993): A25.

25. K. Brooker, "The Chairman of the Board Looks Back," *Fortune* 143, no. 11 (28 May 2001): 63–76. For a detailed, colorful look at Southwest Airlines see K. Freiberg and J. Freiberg, *Nuts: Southwest Airlines' Crazy Recipe for Business and Personal Success* (Austin, Tex.: Bard Press, 1996).

26. K. M. Hudson, "Transforming a Conservative Company—One Laugh at a Time," *Harvard Business Review* (July–August 2001): 48.

27. L. Yerkes, *Fun Works: Creating Places Where People Love to Work* (San Francisco: Berrett-Koehler, 2001). See also L. Yerkes and D. Hemsath, *301 Ways to Have Fun at Work* (San Francisco: Berrett-Koehler, 1997).

28. L. Downes, "What's the Big Idea?" *Industry Standard* (28 February 2000): 174. Also see L. Downes and C. Mui, *Unleashing the Killer App: Digital Strategies for Market Dominance* (Boston: Harvard Business School Press, 2000).

29. See W. Bennis and P. W. Biederman, *Organizing Genius: The Secrets of Creative Collaboration* (Reading, Mass: Addison-Wesley, 1997); and J. R. Katzenbach and D. K. Smith, *The Wisdom of Teams: Creating the High-Performance Organization* (New York: HarperBusiness, 1994).

30. S. Greco, "Letting Workers Play Customers," *Inc.* (October 1994): 119.

CHAPTER 8

1. H. Mintzberg, *The Rise and Fall of Strategic Planning* (New York: Free Press, 1994), 134.

2. K. M. Eisenstadt and B. N. Tabrizi, "Accelerating Adaptive Processes: Product Innovation in the Global Computer Industry," *Administrative Science Quarterly* 40 (1995): 84–110.

3. Kids F.A.C.E.® is a registered trademark.

4. "Melissa Poe," *Caring People* 6 (1993): 66, supplemented by an interview with Trish Poe on 3 November 1994.

5. S. Hollander, *The Success of Increased Efficiency: A Study of Du Pont Rayon Plants* (Cambridge, Mass.: MIT Press, 1965). Also see D. Ulrich, S. Kerr, and R. Ashkenas, *The GE Work-Out* (New York: McGraw-Hill, 2002).

6. D. Meyerson, *Tempered Radicals: How People Use Difference to Inspire Change at Work* (Boston: Harvard Business School Press, 2001).

7. *The Leading Edge,* video (Santa Cruz, Calif.: Langsford Communications, 1986).

8. A. Muoio, "Mint Condition," *Fast Company* (December 1999): 330–348.

9. Business volume per the U.S. Mint Web site; see http://www.usmint.gov/about_the_mint/.

10. M. Maidique, "Why Products Succeed and Why Products Fail," presentation to the Executive Seminar in Corporate Excellence, Santa Clara University, 29 May 1985; see also M. Maidique and B. J. Zinger, "The New Product Learning Cycle," *Research Policy* 14 (1985): 299–313; C. M. Christensen, *The Innovator's Dilemma: When New Technologies Cause Great Firms to Fail* (Boston: Harvard Business School Press, 1997); and Geoffrey A. Moore, *Crossing the Chasm: Marketing and Selling High-Tech Products to Mainstream Customers* (New York: HarperBusiness, 1999).

11. P. Carrick, *A Tribute to Fred Astaire* (Salem, N.H.: Salem House, 1984), 15.

12. L. M. Brown and B. Z. Posner, "Exploring the Relationship Between Learning and Leadership," *Leadership & Organization Development Journal* (May 2001): 274–280.

13. M. Dalton, S. Swigert, F. Van Velsor, K. Bunker, and J. Wachholz, *The Learning Tactics Inventory: Facilitator's Guide* (San Francisco: Jossey-Bass/Pfeiffer, 1999).

14. S. R. Maddi and S. C. Kobasa, *The Hardy Executive: Health Under Stress* (Chicago: Dorsey Press, 1984); and S. R. Maddi and D. M. Khoshaba, "Hardiness and Mental Health," *Journal of Personality Assessment* 67 (1994): 265–274.

15. S. R. Maddi, "Comments on Trends in Hardiness Research and Theorizing," *Consulting Psychology Journal* 51 (1999): 67–71.

16. In managers high in stressful events, the absence of all three of these buffers involves about a 93 percent likelihood of at least one serious illness. The presence of one, two, or all three of these buffers decreases illness likelihood to 72 percent, 58 percent, and 8 percent, respectively, suggesting a synergistic effect (and this pattern of illness likelihood holds up one year later). S. C. Kobasa, S. R. Maddi, M. C. Puccetti, and

M. A. Zola, "Effectiveness of Hardiness, Exercise, and Social Support as Resources Against Illness," *Journal of Psychosomatic Research* 29 (1985): 525–533.

17. L. A. Isabella and T. Forbes, "Managerial Mindsets Research Project: Executive Summary," Darden Graduate School of Business Administration, University of Virginia, Charlottesville, April 1994; and interview with the authors, 13 June 1994.

18. Isabella and Forbes, "Managerial Mindsets Research Project," 7.

19. It may be difficult to overcome a habitual pattern of avoidance, but it is possible to learn to cope assertively with stressful events through counseling and educational programs. See Maddi and Kobasa, *The Hardy Executive,* 59; D. M. Khoshaba and S. R. Maddi, "Early Experiences in Hardiness Development," *Consulting Psychology Journal* 51 (1999): 106-116; and S. R. Maddi, S. Kahn, and K. L. Maddi, "The Effectiveness of Hardiness Training," *Consulting Psychology Journal* 50 (1998): 78–86.

20. G. Calvert, *Highwire Management: Risk-Taking Tactics for Leaders, Innovators, and Trailblazers* (San Francisco: Jossey-Bass, 1993), 172.

21. K. D. Ryan and D. K. Oestreich, *Driving Fear Out of the Workplace: Creating the High-Trust, High-Performance Organization,* 2nd ed. (San Francisco: Jossey-Bass, 1998).

22. R. J. Kriegel and L. Patler, *If It Ain't Broke . . . Break It!* (New York: Warner Books, 1991).

23. E. J. Langer, *Mindfulness* (Reading, Mass.: Addison-Wesley, 1989); and E. J. Langer, *The Power of Mindful Learning* (Reading, Mass.: Addison-Wesley, 1997).

24. A. Taylor III, "Why Toyota Keeps Getting Better and Better," *Fortune* (19 November 1990): 66.

25. E. J. Langer and A. Piper, "The Prevention of Mindlessness," *Journal of Personality and Social Psychology* 53 (1987): 280-287; also see Langer, *Mindfulness,* 120.

26. J. Hyatt, "Ideas at Work," *INC.* (May 1991): 59–66.

27. C. Dahle, "Natural Leader," *Fast Company* (December 2000): 270–280.

28. W. Ury, *Getting to Yes: Negotiating Agreement Without Giving In* (New York: Penguin Books, 1991).

29. B. Breen, "What's Your Intuition?" *Fast Company* (September 2000): 290–300.

CHAPTER 9

1. For detailed analyses of alliances and partnerships in the competitive marketplace, see Y. L. Doz and G. Hamel, *Alliance Advantage: The Art of Creating Value Through Partnering* (Boston: Harvard Business School Press, 1998); and J. K. Conlon and M. Giovagnoli, *The Power of Two: How Companies of All Sizes Can Build Networks That Generate Business Opportunities* (San Francisco: Jossey-Bass, 1998).

2. Throughout this book we use *cooperate* and *collaborate* synonymously. Their dictionary definitions are very similar. In *Merriam-Webster's Collegiate Dictionary, Tenth Edition* (Springfield, Mass: 2001) the first definition of *cooperate* is "To act or work with another or others: act together" (p. 254). The first definition of *collaborate* is "To work jointly with others or together esp. in an intellectual endeavor" (p. 224).

3. For a history of the Internet see K. Hafner and M. Lyon, *Where Wizards Stay Up Late: The Origins of the Internet* (New York: Touchstone, 1996). For a history of the World Wide Web, see T. Berners-Lee with M. Fischetti, *Weaving the Web: The Original Design and Ultimate Destiny of the World Wide Web by Its Inventor* (San Francisco: Harper San Francisco, 1999). Berners-Lee, who is credited with inventing the World Wide Web, says, "The Web is more a social creation than a technical one. I designed it for social effect—to help people work together—and not as a technical toy. . . . The essence of working together in a weblike way is that we function in groups—groupings of two, twenty, and twenty million. We have to learn how to do this on the Web" (pp. 123, 125).

4. As author and university lecturer Alfie Kohn explains: "The simplest way to understand why competition generally does not promote excellence is to realize that *trying to do well and trying to beat others are two different things.*" One is about accomplishing the superior; the other, about making someone else

inferior. A. Kohn, *No Contest: The Case Against Competition* (Boston: Houghton Mifflin, 1992), 55. See also D. W. Johnson and R. T. Johnson, *Learning Together and Alone: Cooperative, Competitive, and Individualistic Learning* (Needham Heights, Mass.: Allyn & Bacon, 1999). For an extensive discussion of true collaboration and its role in the creative process and technology, see M. Schrage, *Shared Minds: The New Technologies of Collaboration* (New York: Random House, 1990).

5. See, for example, D. E. Zand, "Trust and Managerial Problem Solving," *Administrative Science Quarterly* 17, no. 2 (1972): 229–239; W. R. Boss, "Trust and Managerial Problem Solving Revisited," *Group & Organization Studies* 3, no. 3 (1978): 331–342; "Trust Traps," *Training & Development Journal* 48, no. 7 (1994); and V. Brunard and B. H. Kleiner, "Developing Trustful and Cooperative Relationships," *Leadership & Organizational Development Journal* 15, no. 2 (1994): 3–5.

6. *Innovation Survey* (London: PricewaterhouseCoopers, 1999), 3.

7. See M. B. Gurtman, "Trust, Distrust, and Interpersonal Problems: A Circumplex Analysis," *Journal of Personality and Social Psychology* 62 (1992): 989-1002. Also see G. D. Grace and T. Schill, "Social Support and Coping Style Differences in Subjects High and Low in Interpersonal Trust," *Psychological Reports* 59 (1986): 584–586.

8. Boss, "Trust and Managerial Problem Solving Revisited," 338.

9. Boss, "Trust and Managerial Problem Solving Revisited," 338.

10. Boss, "Trust and Managerial Problem Solving Revisited," 338.

11. J. W. Driscoll, "Trust and Participation in Organizational Decision Making as Predictors of Satisfaction," *Academy of Management Journal* 21, no. 1 (1978): 44–56.

12. C. A. O'Reilly and K. H. Roberts, "Information Filtration in Organizations: Three Experiments," *Organizational Behavior and Human Performance* 11 (1974): 253–265; and Boss, "Trust and Managerial Problem Solving Revisited."

13. M. Deutsch, "Cooperation and Trust: Some Theoretical Notes," in R. Jones (ed.), *Nebraska Symposium on Motivation* (Lincoln: University of Nebraska Press, 1962), 275–319; Zand, "Trust and Managerial Problem Solving."

14. Zand, "Trust and Managerial Problem Solving," and Driscoll, "Trust and Participation in Organizational Decision Making as Predictors of Satisfaction."

15. Sources include a personal conversation, Farmland Web site (http://www.farmland.com/), and A. Wolfe, "Can't Take the Farm Out of the Boy," *Ingram's* (August 1993): 31.

16. L. Tiger, "Real-Life Survivors Rely on Teamwork," *Wall Street Journal* (25 August 2000): B7.

17. S. Lumet, *Making Movies* (New York: Vintage Books, 1996), 17.

18. R. Axelrod, *The Evolution of Cooperation* (New York: Basic Books, 1984). Also see W. Poundstone, *Prisoner's Dilemma: John Von Neumann, Game Theory, and the Puzzle of the Bomb* (New York: Doubleday, 1992).

19. Axelrod, *The Evolution of Cooperation*, 20, 190.

20. R. B. Cialdini, "Harnessing the Science of Persuasion," *Harvard Business Review* (October 2001): 72–79. For a discussion of the principle of reciprocity, see R. B. Cialdini, *Influence: Science and Practice*, 4th ed. (Needham Heights, Mass.: Allyn & Bacon, 2001), 19–51.

21. R. Putnam, *Bowling Alone: The Collapse and Revival of American Community* (New York: Simon & Schuster, 2000), 134.

22. E. Zehnder, "A Simpler Way to Pay," *Harvard Business Review* (April 2001): 54.

23. D. W. Johnson and R. T. Johnson, *Cooperation and Competition: Theory and Research* (Edina, Minn.: Interaction, 1989), 63.

24. A. Van de Ven, A. L. Delbecq, and R. J. Koenig, "Determinants of Coordination Modes Within Organizations," *American Sociological Review* 41, no. 2 (1976): 322–338.

25. G. Homans, *The Human Group* (New York: Harcourt Brace Jovanovich, 1950).

26. The original research that led to "the six degrees of separation" concept was done by social psychologist Stanley Milgram in the 1960s. He wanted to explain the "small-world" problem, so he conducted an experiment to determine how long it would take a letter to get from a person in Omaha, Nebraska, to a

complete stranger, a stockbroker, in Sharon, Massachusetts. Most of the letters reached the stockbroker in five or six steps, hence "six degrees of separation." For a contemporary discussion of this phenomenon, see M. Gladwell, *The Tipping Point: How Little Things Can Make a Big Difference* (Boston: Little, Brown, 2002), 30–88.

27. For a detailed discussion of social capital, see Putnam, *Bowling Alone;* and Gladwell, *The Tipping Point.* For a practical application of social capital research to the world of business, see W. Baker, *Achieving Success Through Social Capital: Tapping the Hidden Resources in Your Personal and Business Networks* (San Francisco: Jossey-Bass, 2000). See also R. Levine, C. Locke, D. Searls, and D. Weinberger, *The Cluetrain Manifesto: The End of Business as Usual* (Cambridge, Mass.: Perseus Books, 2000).

28. See p. 48 of Gladwell, *The Tipping Point,* for one intriguing bit of evidence for this.

29. D. Cohen and L. Prusak, *In Good Company: How Social Capital Makes Organizations Work* (Boston: Harvard Business School Press, 2001), 20.

30. This exercise is drawn from "Broken Squares: Nonverbal Problem-Solving," in *A Handbook of Structured Experiences for Human Relations Training,* Vol. 1 (San Francisco: Jossey-Bass/Pfeiffer, 1970), 25–30.

31. D. Goleman, "Leadership That Gets Results," *Harvard Business Review* (March-April 2000): 80. Also see D. Goleman, *Working with Emotional Intelligence* (New York: Bantam Books, 1998); D. Goleman, *Emotional Intelligence: Why It Can Matter More Than IQ* (New York: Bantam Books, 1995); and D. Goleman, R. Boyatzis, and A. McKee, *Primal Leadership: Realizing the Power of Emotional Intelligence* (Boston: Harvard Business School Press, 2002).

32. Goleman, *Working with Emotional Intelligence,* 3, 32.

33. C. Fernández-Aráoz, "The Challenge of Hiring Senior Executives," in C. Cherniss and D. Goleman (eds.), *The Emotionally Intelligent Workplace: How to Select for, Measure, and Improve Emotional Intelligence in Individuals, Groups, and Organizations* (San Francisco: Jossey-Bass, 2001), 189. Portions of the information on EZI's approach and findings were also gathered from personal correspondence and conversations with Claudio Fernández-Aráoz.

34. See E. Aronson and S. Patnoe, *The Jigsaw Classroom: Building Cooperation in the Classroom* (New York: Longman, 1997).

35. To learn the details of how the jigsaw classroom works, go to http://www.jigsaw.org/. For a detailed description of hot groups, see T. Kelley with J. Littman, *The Art of Innovation: Lessons in Creativity from IDEO, America's Leading Design Firm* (New York: Currency Doubleday, 2001), 67–100.

36. See, for example, D. Kahneman and A. Tversky, "The Framing of Decisions and the Psychology of Choice," *Science* 211 (1981): 453–458; M. H. Bazerman and M. A. Neale, "Heuristics in Negotiation: Limitations to Dispute Resolution Effectiveness," in M. H. Bazerman and R. J. Lewicki (eds.), *Negotiating in Organizations* (Thousand Oaks, Calif.: Sage, 1983): 51–67; M. H. Bazerman and M. A. Neale, "Systematic Deviations from Rationality in Negotiator Behavior: The Framing of Conflict and Negotiator Overconfidence," *Academy of Management Journal* 28, no. 1 (1985): 34–49; and M. H. Bazerman, *Judgment in Managerial Decision Making,* 5th ed. (New York: Wiley, 2001).

37. M. H. Bazerman and M. A. Neale, *Negotiating Rationally* (New York: Free Press, 1993), 90-93.

38. This activity is found in *Positive Negotiation Skills Workshop* (Plymouth, Mass.: Situation Management Systems, 1980).

39. E. M. Hallowell, *Connect: Twelve Vital Ties that Open Your Heart, Lengthen Your Life, and Deepen Your Soul* (New York: Pocket Books, 1999), 125–140.

40. For more specific recommendations on how to build a network, see W. Baker, "How to Make the Right Friends Inside Your Company," which appeared originally in *Bottom Line Personal.*

41. R. Oldenburg, *The Great Good Place: Cafés, Coffee Shops, Bookstores, Bars, Hair Salons, and Other Hangouts at the Heart of a Community* (New York: Marlowe, 1999). This book is really a must-read for anyone interested in building community inside organizations. By the way, the first place is the home, and the second place is work.

42. "Alcoa: Form Follows Function," *Plants Sites & Parks,* February/March 1999.

CHAPTER 10

1. R. M. Kanter, *The Change Masters: Innovation for Productivity in the American Corporation* (New York: Simon & Schuster, 1983). For more recent studies by Kanter on power see R. M. Kanter, *When Giants Learn to Dance: Mastering the Challenges of Strategy, Management, and Careers in the 1990s* (New York: Simon & Schuster, 1989); and R. M. Kanter, *e-Volve!: Succeeding in the Digital Culture of Tomorrow* (Boston: Harvard Business School Press, 2001).

2. A. Bandura, *Self-Efficacy: The Exercise of Control* (New York: Freeman, 1997); K. A. Karl, A. M. Leary-Kelly, and J. J. Martocchio, "The Impact of Feedback and Self-Efficacy on Performance in Training," *Journal of Organizational Behavior* 14, no. 4 (1993): 379–394; C. M. Shea and J. M. Howell, "Charismatic Leadership and Task Feedback: A Laboratory Study of Their Effects on Self-Efficacy and Task Performance," *Leadership Quarterly* 10, no. 3 (1999): 375–396; and A. Bandura, "Social Cognitive Theory: An Agentic Perspective," *Annual Review of Psychology* 52 (2001): 1–26.

3. J. Thackray, "Feedback for Real," *Gallup Management Journal* 1, no. 1 (Spring 2001): 12-17. For a more detailed description, see M. Buckingham and C. Coffman, *First, Break All the Rules* (New York: Simon & Schuster, 1999).

4. The other six questions in this worker engagement scale: Do you have the materials and equipment you need to do your work right? In the last seven days, have you received recognition or praise for doing good work? Is there someone at work who encourages your development? Does the mission/purpose of your company make you feel your job is important? Are your associates (fellow employees) committed to doing quality work? Do you have a best friend at work?

5. "What Your Disaffected Workers Cost," *Gallup Management Journal* 1, no. 1 (Spring 2001): 32.

6. In fact, people with unpleasant bosses are four times as likely to leave than are people with nice bosses, according to a 1999 study conducted by Spherion, a staffing and consulting firm working with Lou Harris Associates. In the survey, only 11 percent of employees who rated their supervisor's performance as excellent said they were likely to look for a job in the next year, while 40 percent of those who rated their supervisors' performance as poor were likely to jump ship. As reported in A. Zipkin, "Management: The Wisdom of Thoughtfulness," *New York Times* (31 May 2000): C1.

7. S. Winston, "Being Effective with Today's Workforce," presentation at the Leavey School of Business, Santa Clara University, 3 April 2001.

8. See, for example, J. Borda, "Great Expectations," *Fast Company* (November 1999): 212–222; S. R. Williams and R. L. Wilson, "Group Support Systems, Power, and Influence in an Organization: A Field Study," *Decision Sciences* 28, no. 4 (1997): 911–937; and A. Tannenbaum and others, *Hierarchy in Organizations: An International Comparison* (San Francisco: Jossey-Bass, 1974).

9. D. A. Butterfield and B. Z. Posner, "Task-Relevant Control in Organizations," *Personnel Psychology* 32 (1979): 725–740.

10. See, for example, B. J. Avolio and B. M. Bass (eds.), *Developing Potential Across a Full Range of Leadership: Cases on Transactional and Transformational Leadership* (Mahwah, N.J.: Erlbaum, 2002); and C. C. Manz and H. P. Sims Jr., *The New Superleadership: Leading Others to Lead Themselves* (San Francisco: Berrett-Koehler, 2001).

11. L. A. Schlesinger and K. L. Heskett, "Enfranchisement of Service Workers," *California Management Review* (Summer 1991): 83–100; J. L. Heskett and others, "Putting the Service-Profit Chain to Work," *Harvard Business Review* (March-April 1994): 164–174; and J. L. Heskett, W. E. Sasser Jr., and L. A. Schlesinger, *The Service Profit Chain: How Leading Companies Link Profit and Growth to Loyalty, Satisfaction, and Value* (New York: Free Press, 1997).

12. As quoted in "Winners," *Sibson & Company* 1, no. 7 (October 1991): 2.

13. J. Sensenbrenner, "Quality Comes to City Hall," *Harvard Business Review* (March-April 1991): 4–10.

14. E. J. Langer and J. Rodin, "The Effects of Choice and Enhanced Personal Responsibility for the Aged: A Field Experiment in an Institutional Setting," *Journal of Personality and Social Psychology* 34, no. 2 (1976):

191–198; and J. Rodin and E. J. Langer, "Long-Term Efforts of a Control-Relevant Intervention with the Institutionalized Aged," *Journal of Personality and Social Psychology* 35, no. 12 (1977): 897–902. For more examples of how personal control influences personal well-being, see E. J. Langer and M. Moldoveanu, "The Construct of Mindfulness," *Journal of Social Issues* 56, no. 1 (2000): 1–9; and E. J. Langer and M. Moldoveanu, "Mindfulness Research and the Future," *Journal of Social Issues* 56, no. 1 (2000): 129–139.

15. See, for example, MICA Executive Survey, "Training Impact on Corporate Competitiveness," Toronto, Canada: MICA Management Resources, April 1991; *America and the New Economy* (Alexandria, Va.: American Society for Training and Development, 1990); and "The ASTD Training Data Book," a Web site that summarizes much of what is known about formal training provided by private sector organizations in the United States. See http://www.astd.org/members/data_book/data_toc.html.

16. CDR G. G. Gullickson and LCDR R. D. Chenette, "Excellence in the Surface Navy," Naval Postgraduate School thesis, Monterey, Calif., September 1984, 48–49.

17. D. Goleman, *Working with Emotional Intelligence* (New York: Bantam Books, 1998).

18. L. M. Spencer Jr. and S. M. Spencer, *Competence at Work: Models for Superior Performance* (New York: Wiley, 1993).

19. J. Stack, "The Great Game of Business," presentation for the Consortium on Executive Education, Santa Clara University, 11 November 1994; also see J. Stack with B. Burlingham, *A Stake in the Outcome: Building a Culture of Ownership for the Long-Term Success of Your Business* (New York: Currency Doubleday, 2002).

20. J. Stack with B. Burlingham, *The Great Game of Business* (New York: Currency Doubleday, 1994), 3.

21. Psychologists often refer to this as *self-efficacy.* See, for example, Bandura, *Self-Efficacy;* and R. M. Steers, L. W. Porter, and G. A. Bigley, *Motivation and Leadership at Work,* 6th ed. (New York: McGraw-Hill, 1996).

22. R. E. Wood and A. Bandura, "Impact of Conceptions of Ability on Self-Regulatory Mechanisms and Complex Decision Making," *Journal of Personality and Social Psychology* 56 (1989): 407–415. Managers in this study who lost confidence in their own judgments tended to find fault with their people. Indeed, they were quite uncharitable about their employees, regarding them as unmotivatable and unworthy of supervisory effort; given the option, they would have fired many of them.

23. A. Bandura and R. E. Wood, "Effects of Perceived Controllability and Performance Standards on Self-Regulation of Complex Decision Making," *Journal of Personality and Social Psychology* 56 (1989): 805–814.

24. A. M. Saks, "Longitudinal Field Investigation of the Moderating and Mediating Effects of Self-Efficacy on the Relationship Between Training and Newcomer Adjustment," *Journal of Applied Psychology* 80 (1995): 211–225.

25. For more on how coaches coach, see M. Goldsmith, L. Lyons, and A. Freas (eds.), *Coaching for Leadership: How the World's Greatest Coaches Help Leaders Learn* (San Francisco: Jossey-Bass, 2000).

26. C. Fishman, "Engines of Democracy," *Fast Company* (October 1999): 174–202.

27. J. A. Conger, "Leadership: The Art of Empowering Others," *Academy of Management Executive* 3, no. 1 (1989): 17–24.

28. Bandura, *Self-Efficacy.* See pp. 439–449.

29. C. Dahle, "Natural Leader," *Fast Company* (December 2000): 270–280.

30. P. F. Drucker, "The New Productivity Challenge," *Harvard Business Review* 69 (November-December 1991): 69–79.

31. T. A. Stewart, "Brainpower," *Fortune* (3 June 1991): 50.

32. J. M. Kouzes and B. Z. Posner, "Readiness Assessment Questionnaire," (Santa Clara, Calif.: Kouzes Posner International, 1992).

CHAPTER 11

1. D. Dorsey, "Andy Pearson Finds Love," *Fast Company* (August 2001): 78 ff.

2. A. Zipkin, "Management: The Wisdom of Thoughtfulness," *New York Times* (31 May 2000): C1.

3. For a discussion of "flow," see M. Csikszentmihalyi, *Finding Flow: The Psychology of Engagement with Everyday Life* (New York: Basic Books, 1997).

4. "Workers Drowning in Messages," *San Jose Mercury News* (20 May 1998): 7C.

5. Csikszentmihalyi, *Finding Flow*, 23.

6. See, for example, J. E. Sawyer, W. R. Latham, R. D. Pritchard, and W. R. Bennett Jr., "Analysis of Work Group Productivity in an Applied Setting: Application of a Time Series Panel Design," *Personnel Psychology* 52 (1999): 927-967; and A. Gostick and C. Elton, *Managing with Carrots: Using Recognition to Attract and Retain the Best People* (Layton, Utah: Gibbs Smith, 2001).

7. Blood tests taken during the march and again twenty-four hours later showed similar patterns. Blood levels of cortisol and prolactin (chemicals whose levels rise as stress increases) were, as expected, highest for the group that knew the least about the march and lowest for those soldiers who knew exactly where they were and how much farther they were expected to go. D. Eden and G. Ravid, "Pygmalion vs. Self-Expectancy: Effects of Instructor and Self-Expectancy on Trainee Performance," *Organizational Behavior and Human Performance* 30 (1982): 351-364; and D. Eden and A. B. Shani, "Pygmalion Goes to Boot Camp: Expectancy, Leadership and Trainee Performance," *Journal of Applied Psychology* 67 (1982): 194–199.

8. See, for example, R. M. Ryan and E. L. Deci, "Self-Determination Theory and the Facilitation of Intrinsic Motivation, Social Development, and Well-Being," *American Psychologist* 55, no. 1 (2000): 68–78.

9. P. A. McCarty, "Effects of Feedback on the Self-Confidence of Men and Women," *Academy of Management Journal* 20 (1986): 840–847.

10. Hundreds of research studies have since been conducted to test this notion, and they all clearly demonstrate that people tend to act in ways that are consistent with the expectations they perceive. See, for example, D. Eden, *Pygmalion in Management: Productivity as a Self-Fulfilling Prophecy* (Lexington, Mass.: Lexington Books, 1990); D. Eden, "Leadership and Expectations: Pygmalion Effects and Other Self-Fulfilling Prophecies in Organizations," *Leadership Quarterly* 3, no. 4 (1992): 271–305; and A. Smith, L. Jussim, J. Eccles, M. Van Noy, S. Madon, and P. Palumbo, "Self-Fulfilling Prophecies, Perceptual Biases, and Accuracy at the Individual and Group Levels," *Journal of Experimental Social Psychology* 34, no. 6 (1998): 530–561.

11. R. J. Blitzer, C. Petersen, and L. Rogers, "How to Build Self-Esteem," *Training and Development Journal* (February 1993): 59.

12. J-F. Manzoni and J-L. Barsoux, "The Set-Up-to-Fail Syndrome," *Harvard Business Review* 76, no. 2 (March-April 1998): 101-113, quote on p. 102.

13. CRM Learning (Producer), *Encouraging the Heart* (videotape featuring James M. Kouzes and Barry Z. Posner) (Carlsbad, Calif.: CRM Learning, 2000). Available from CRM Learning at http://www.crmlearning.com/ or call 1-800-421-0833.

14. D. L. Cooperrider, "Positive Image, Positive Action: The Affirmative Basis of Organizing," in S. Srivastva, D. L. Cooperrider, and Associates, *Appreciative Management and Leadership: The Power of Positive Thought and Action in Organizations* (San Francisco: Jossey-Bass, 1990), 103.

15. For a discussion of group effectiveness and positive images, see Srivastva, Cooperrider, and Associates, *Appreciative Management and Leadership*, 108, 115. Also see O. R. Lightsey, "Positive Thoughts Versus States of Mind Ratio as a Stress Moderator: Findings Across Four Studies," *Cognitive Therapy and Research* 23, no. 5 (1999): 469-482. For the original study on group images, see R. Schwartz, "The Internal Dialogue: On the Asymmetry Between Positive and Negative Coping Thoughts," *Cognitive Therapy and Research* 10 (1986): 591–605.

16. Cooperrider, "Positive Image, Positive Action," 114.

17. For a more in-depth discussion of personal credibility, see J. M. Kouzes and B. Z. Posner, *Credibility: How Leaders Gain and Lose It, Why People Demand It* (San Francisco: Jossey-Bass, 1993).

18. R. Fisher and S. Brown, *Getting Together* (Boston: Houghton Mifflin, 1988); and M. W. McCall, M. Lomdardo, and A. Morrison, *The Lessons of Experience* (Lexington, Mass.: Lexington Books, 1988).

19. R. Rosen and P. Dign, *Global Literacies: Lessons on Business Leadership and National Cultures* (New York: Simon & Schuster, 2000).

20. As quoted in F. Rice, "Champions of Communications," *Fortune* (3 June 1991): 111 ff.

21. J. A. Ross, "Does Friendship Improve Job Performance?" *Harvard Business Review* (March-April 1977): 8–9. See also K. A. Jehn and P. P. Shah, "Interpersonal Relationships and Task Performance: An Examination of Mediating Processes in Friendship and Acquaintance Groups," *Journal of Personality and Social Psychology* 72, no. 4 (1997): 775–790.

22. D. Jamieson and J. O'Mara, *Managing Workforce 2000: Gaining the Diversity Advantage* (San Francisco: Jossey-Bass, 1991).

23. J. L. Hall, B. Z. Posner, and J. W. Harder, "Performance Appraisal Systems: Matching Theory with Practice," *Group and Management Studies* 14, no. 1 (1989): 51–69.

24. J. T. Bond, E. Galinsky, and J. E. Swanberg, *The 1997 National Study of the Changing Workforce* (New York: Families and Work Institute, 1998).

25. B. Nelson, "The Power of Rewards and Recognition," presentation to the Consortium on Executive Education, Leavey School of Business, Santa Clara University, 20 September 1996.

26. R. M. Kanter, "The Change Masters," presentation to the Executive Seminar in Corporate Excellence, Leavey School of Business, Santa Clara University, 13 March 1984.

27. See, for example, E. L. Deci and R. Flaste, *Why We Do What We Do: Understanding Self-Motivation* (New York: Putnam, 1995); and E. L. Deci, R. Koestner, and R. M. Ryan, "A Meta-Analytic Review of Experiments Examining the Effects of Extrinsic Rewards on Intrinsic Motivation," *Psychological Bulletin* 125 (1999): 627–668. For an intelligent critique of incentive systems and the potentially detrimental effects of reliance on rewards on long-term performance, see A. Kohn, *Punished by Rewards* (Boston: Houghton Mifflin, 1993).

28. D. C. McClelland, *The Achieving Society* (New York: Van Nostrand Reinhold, 1961).

29. Eric Harvey suggests lots and lots of creative ways to recognize people in his handbook *180 Ways to Walk the Recognition Talk* (Dallas: Walk the Talk Company, 2000). Also see B. Nelson, *1,001 Ways to Reward Employees* (New York: Workman, 1994); and B. Nelson, *1,001 Ways to Energize Employees* (New York: Workman, 1997).

30. Nelson, *1,001 Ways to Reward Employees;* Nelson, *1,001 Ways to Energize Employees.*

31. A. E. Schnur and C. Butz, "The Best Finish First: Top Coaches Talk About Winning," Towers Perrin, San Francisco, 1994.

32. R.H.G. Field and D. A. Van Seters, "Management by Expectations (MBE): The Power of Positive Prophecy," *Journal of General Management* 14, no. 2 (1988): 1–33.

33. C. M. Steele, "A Threat in the Air: How Stereotypes Shape Intellectual Identity and Performance," *American Psychologist* 52, no. 6 (1997): 613–629.

34. Among the benefits that leaders see in leveraging diversity are greater profitability, enhanced organizational learning, flexibility, and rapid adaptation to shifting markets. See, for example, D. A. Thomas and R. J. Ely, "Making Differences Matter: A New Paradigm for Managing Diversity," *Harvard Business Review* 74, no. 5 (September-October 1996): 79–90.

35. As quoted in Gostick and Elton, *Managing with Carrots,* 37–38.

36. B. Greene, "Why Working for Some Bosses Is a Thankless Job," *San Jose Mercury News* (January 27, 1986): 14B.

37. Harvard researchers Robert Kegan and Lisa Laskow suggest a number of practical steps for giving praise that matters. See R. Kegan and L. Laskow, *How the Way We Talk Can Change the Way We Work: Seven Languages for Transformation* (San Francisco: Jossey-Bass, 2000).

CHAPTER 12

1. D. Campbell, *If I'm in Charge Here, Why Is Everybody Laughing?* (Greensboro, N.C.: Center for Creative Leadership, 1984), 64.

2. T. Deal and M. K. Key, *Corporate Celebration: Play, Purpose, and Profit at Work* (San Francisco: Berrett-Koehler, 1998), 5.

3. T. F. Deal and A. A. Kennedy, *Corporate Cultures: The Rites and Rituals of Corporate Life* (Reading, Mass.: Addison-Wesley, 1982), 63. Deal and Kennedy have updated their original work in *The New Corporate Cultures: Revitalizing the Workplace After Downsizing, Mergers, and Reengineering* (Cambridge, Mass.: Perseus Books, 2000).

4. See, for example, K. J. Fenlason and T. A. Beehr, "Social Support and Occupational Stress: Effects of Talking to Others," *Journal of Organizational Behavior* 15, no. 2 (1994): 157-175; and J. S. Mulbert, "Social Networks, Social Circles, and Job Satisfaction," *Work & Occupations* 18, no. 4 (1991): 415–430.

5. L. L. Berry, A. Parasuraman, and V. A. Zeithaml, "Improving Service Quality in America: Lessons Learned," *Academy of Management Executive* 8, no. 2 (1994): 32–45, quote on p. 41.

6. Hanker separated these celebrations from everyday work roles and work relationships. People across departments had the opportunity to interact with one another outside of the more formal and structured work context. Peter Tommerup, an ethnographer studying these events at UCLA, analyzed how they gave people permission to interact with one another in a friendly and intimate manner, increasing their feelings of camaraderie, cooperation, and appreciation of the reasons behind the hectic summer season. This social support network enhanced collaborative efforts and facilitated amiable interpersonal relationships throughout a stressful and highly productive period. P. Tommerup, "Inspiring Self-Management: On Symbols, Synergism, and Excellence," paper presented at the Western Academy of Management conference, Hollywood, Calif., 10 April 1987.

7. California Department of Mental Health, *Friends Can Be Good Medicine* (San Francisco: Pacificon Productions, 1981); and E. M. Hallowell, *Connect: Twelve Vital Ties That Open Your Heart, Lengthen Your Life, and Deepen Your Soul* (New York: Pocket Books, 2001).

8. L. F. Berkman and S. L. Syme, "Social Networks, Host Resistance, and Mortality: A Nine-Year Follow-Up Study of Alameda County Residents," *American Journal of Epidemiology* 109, no. 2 (1979): 186–204. See also S. Cohen, "Psychosocial Models of the Role of Social Support in the Etiology of Physical Disease, *Health Psychology* 7 (1988): 269–297.

9. The Beatles sang the same idea: "I get by with a little help from my friends." (J. Lennon and P. McCartney, "A Little Help from My Friends," On *Sgt. Pepper's Lonely Hearts Club Band* (Hollywood: Capitol Records/EMI, 1967).

10. R. F. Baumeister and M. R. Leary, "The Need to Belong: Desire for Interpersonal Attachment as a Fundamental Human Motivation," *Psychological Bulletin* 117 (1995): 497-529; H. W. Perkins, "Religious Commitment, Yuppie Values, and Well-Being in a Post-Collegiate Life," *Review of Religious Research* 32 (1991): 244-251; and D. G. Myers, "The Funds, Friends, and Faith of Happy People," *American Psychologist* 55, no. 1 (2000): 56–67.

11. See, for example, S. K. Kirmeyer and T. R. Lin, "Social Support: Its Relationship to Observed Communication with Peers and Supporters," *Academy of Management Journal* 30 (1987): 138–151; Fenlason and Beehr, "Social Support and Occupational Stress"; S. Cohen and T. A. Wills, "Stress, Social Support, and the Buffering Hypothesis," *Psychological Bulletin* 98 (1985): 310–357; and I. P. Erera, "Social Support Under Conditions of Organizational Ambiguity," *Human Relations* 45, no. 3 (1992): 247–264.

12. P. Gill, "Once Upon an Enterprise," *Knowledge Management* (May 2001), available online: http://www.destinationcrm.com/km/dcrm_km_article.asp?id=823.

13. D. Armstrong, *Managing by Storying Around: A New Method of Leadership* (New York: Currency Doubleday, 1992), 5. See also D. Armstrong, *Once Told, They're Gold: Stories to Enliven and Enrich the Workplace* (Stuart, Fla.: Armstrong International, 1998).

14. Armstrong, *Managing by Storying Around*, 6.
15. A. L. Wilkens, "Organizational Stories as Symbols Which Control the Organization," in L. R. Pondy and others (eds.), *Organizational Symbolism* (Greenwich, Conn.: JAI Press, 1983), 81–92.
16. Gill, "Once Upon an Enterprise."
17. For more information on this study and other story research, see G. Shaw, R. Brown, and P. Bromiley, "Strategic Stories: How 3M Is Rewriting Business Planning," *Harvard Business Review* (May-June 1998): 41–50.
18. G. Klein, *The Sources of Power: How People Make Decisions* (Cambridge, Mass.: MIT Press, 1998).
19. E. Ransdell, "The Nike Story? Just Tell It! *Fast Company* (January-February 2000): 44–46.
20. D. Hemsath and L. Yerkes, *301 Ways to Have Fun at Work* (San Francisco: Berrett-Koehler, 1997).
21. Deal and Key, *Corporate Celebration*, 28.
22. D. Goleman, "Happy, or Sad, a Mood Can Prove Contagious," *New York Times* (15 October 1991): B5. See also D. Goleman, R. Boyatzis, and A. McKee, *Primal Leadership: Realizing the Power of Emotional Intelligence* (Boston: Harvard Business School Press, 2002); and E. Hatfield, J. T. Cacioppo, and R. L. Rapson, *Emotional Contagion* (Cambridge, England: Cambridge University Press, 1994).
23. See, for example, Myers, "The Funds, Friends, and Faith of Happy People"; M. Csikszentmihalyi, "If We Are So Rich, Why Aren't We Happy?" *American Psychologist* 54 (1999): 821–827; and D. G. Myers and E. Diener, "The Pursuit of Happiness," *Scientific American* 274 (1996): 54–56.

CHAPTER 13

1. M. B. Cahill-Phillips, "The Demeter Effect: Trauma and Reparation in Mothers of Victimized Children," Ph.D. dissertation, California School of Professional Psychology, 1992.
2. A. M. Schlesinger Jr. *The Cycles of American History* (Boston: Houghton Mifflin, 1986), 419–420.
3. See, for example, D. C. Hambrick and S. Finkelstein, "Managerial Discretion: A Bridge Between Polar Views of Organizational Outcomes," *Research in Organizational Behavior* 9 (1987): 369–406; and R. G. Lord and K. J. Maher, *Leadership and Information Processing: Linking Perceptions and Performance* (Boston: Unwin-Hyman, 1991).
4. See, for example, J. R. Meindl, S. B. Ehrlich, and J. M. Dukerich, "The Romance of Leadership," *Administrative Science Quarterly* 30 (1985): 78–102; and J. Pfeffer, "The Ambiguity of Leadership," *Academy of Management Review* 2 (1977): 104–112.
5. See our Web site, http://www.leadershipchallenge.com/, for more information about these and other studies.
6. For example, see B. J. Avolio and B. M. Bass (eds.), *Developing Potential Across a Full Range of Leadership: Cases on Transactional and Transformational Leadership* (Mahwah, N.J.: Erlbaum, 2002); C. C. Manz and H. P. Sims Jr., *The New Superleadership* (San Francisco: Berrett-Koehler, 2001); D. H. Maister, *Practice What You Preach: What Managers Must Do to Create a High Achievement Culture* (New York: Free Press, 2001); B. P. Niehoff, C. A. Enz, and R. A. Grover, "The Impact of Top Management Actions on Employee Attitudes and Perceptions," *Group and Organization Studies* 15, no. 3 (1990): 337–352; A. B. Thomas, "Does Leadership Make a Difference to Organizational Performance?" *Administrative Science Quarterly* 33 (1988): 388–400; M. R. Barrick, D. V. Day, R. G. Lord, and R. A. Alexander, "Assessing the Utility of Executive Leadership," *Leadership Quarterly* 2 (1991): 9–22; and J. C. Sarros, *Leadership Report 1993: Australian Trends in Corporate Leadership* (Victoria, Australia: Leadership Research Unit, Monash University, 1993).
7. J. Kahn, "The World's Most Admired Companies," *Fortune* (11 October 1999): 267–275 ff.
8. This scene is from the film version of *The Prime of Miss Jean Brodie*, produced by Robert Fryer and directed by Robert Neame. Screenplay by Jay Presson Allen. Twentieth Century Fox Productions, 1969. Adapted from Muriel Spark's novel, *The Prime of Miss Jean Brodie* (London: Macmillan, 1961).

9. J. W. Gardner, "The Moral Dimension," in *On Leadership* (New York: Free Press, 1990), 67–80.

10. S. B. Oates, *Let the Trumpet Sound: The Life of Martin Luther King, Jr.* (New York: Mentor/New American Library, 1985).

11. S. Lumet, *Making Movies* (New York: Vintage Books, 1996), 17.

12. For more on the importance of humility in organizational success, see J. Collins, *Good to Great: Why Some Companies Make the Leap . . . and Others Don't* (New York: HarperCollins, 2002).

13. Collins, *Good to Great,* 27.

14. For a discussion of the role of hope in goal attainment, see C. S. Snyder and others, "The Will and the Ways: Development and Validation of an Individual Differences Measure of Hope," *Journal of Personality and Social Psychology* 60, no. 4 (1991): 570–585.

ACKNOWLEDGMENTS

We're both film buffs, and when we sit through the credits at the end of a movie we're always in awe of how many people contribute to the final product. In that respect, the making of a book is much like the making of a film. It's a highly collaborative effort, especially for the two of us, who've been a research, writing, and teaching team for twenty years.

We and this book have been the beneficiaries of the loving, caring, and generous assistance, advice, support, and encouragement of others. And since this is the third edition of *The Leadership Challenge,* we estimate there've been well over three hundred people who've contributed to these pages in one way or another. If it weren't for *all* of them, there'd be no book at all, let alone one that has stood the test of time.

It's hard to pinpoint the moment at which the idea for this book presented itself. We recall a parking-lot conversation with Donna Kouzes about the characteristics of individuals who perform at high levels. We thought it would be interesting to apply this idea to leaders. Another early memory is of a workshop we conducted at Santa Clara University with Tom Peters shortly after the publication of *In Search of Excellence.* Tom led the first day of the seminar, and we led the second day. In an effort to help participants apply the excellence lessons to their own organizations, we utilized a technique we called the "personal-best leadership case." That was the genesis of the research methodology we've subsequently used to study and understand leadership.

No book emerges whole from the minds of its authors. Throughout the years many scholars and students of leadership have strongly influenced our thinking. Their ideas have found their way onto the pages you read. We owe an immense intellectual debt of gratitude to these very special colleagues and friends: Wayne Baker, Warren Bennis, Dave Berlew, Ken Blanchard, Lillas Brown, David Caldwell, Mihalyi Csikszentmihalyi, André Delbecq, Claudio Fernández-Aráoz, Jerry Fletcher, John Gardner, Daniel Goleman, Marshall Goldsmith, Joe Harder, Roger Harrison, Frances Hesselbein, Rosabeth Moss Kanter, David Maister, André Morkel, Charles O'Reilly, Terry Pearce, Jeff Pfeffer, Warren Schmidt, Bob Tannenbaum, Noel Tichy, and Meg Wheatley.

From our social, educational, and business networks have come an incredible flow of cases, examples, and stories. We consider ourselves blessed to have such generous and inspiring colleagues. Unfortunately only a small portion of the anecdotes we received can actually fit in this book, so we hope to continue to highlight an ever-changing collection of new cases on our Web site.

Over the years, we continue to be moved to laughter and tears, awe and inspiration, as we listen in on the uplifting experiences of hundreds of men and women who accepted the leadership challenge. They're the ones who taught us what it really means to get extraordinary things done in organizations; they're the true heroes and heroines of this book, and of organizations. You meet lots of these courageous folks as you read *The Leadership Challenge.* We're forever grateful to them for sharing their lives with us, and we hope that we've represented them well.

One of the ways we've tested our ideas about leadership is through workshops and seminars. Our colleagues at the Tom Peters Company continuously uplift our spirits with their faith in and commitment to *The Leadership Challenge™ Workshop.* They provide us with that enriching opportunity to test our work with practicing leaders. We deeply appreciate their years of stimulation, support, and encouragement. Many people graciously agreed to be part of our early and our ongoing experiments in learning how to lead. Some of the many dedicated professionals who've added great value to our educational designs are Jo Bell, Ann Bowers, Boyd Clarke, Steve Coats, Sue Cook, Ron Crossland, Michael Doyle, Randi DuBois, Homeyra Eshaghi, Steve Farber, Dick Heller, Steve Houchin, Peter Jordan, Dianne Kenny, Marion Krause, Tom Melohn, Henry Miller, Linda Mantel, Joan McIntosh, Lynne Parode, Ranny Riley, Heather Shea, David Sibbet, John

Stanford, Reno Taini, Ricky Tam, Robert Thompson, Christy Tonge, and Cathy Weselby.

Moving from the realm of testing ideas to committing them to paper is always a test of teamwork. The first edition made it from ideas to print with the assistance of Liz Caravelli, Joy Congdon, Liz Currie, Judy Kasper, and Michael Malone. For the second edition, we relied heavily on Joan Carter for research assistance and case writing and Kathy Dalle-Molle for fact checking, permissions work, and attention to detail. For this third edition, we were challenged to address technological, cultural, and political changes in the new millennium—all in a finite space. We couldn't have written this third edition without the research and dedicated assistance of Leigh Gillen, Donna Perry, and Ellen Peterson, and of Elisabeth Pope, who provided some especially insightful suggestions on new leaders to study, and who collaborated on some of the most significant interviews. A great big thanks to Sheri Gilbert who covered all the permissions work, to JoAnn Johnson who so precisely and rapidly transcribed scores of hours of interviews, to Leslie Tilley for her expert fact checking, and to Hilary Powers for her thoughtful copyediting. Jan Hunter worked with us as developmental editor for both the second and third editions, pushing us for new material and then weaving it into the original, improving the readability of the book, and enabling us to come to consensus on the final text.

The community of professionals at Jossey-Bass masterfully practices the true art of editing and publishing. Their confidence in us and patience with us have been overwhelming. Without their support, there would be no book, only loosely connected ideas. Over the years and now through three editions we acknowledge the nudging, imagination, and encouragement of Josh Blatter, Cedric Crocker, Kathleen Davies, Mary Garrett, Bill Hicks, Rachel Livsey, Lynn Lukow, Trish O'Hare, Lisa Shannon, Laura Simonds, Bernadette Walter, Terri Armstrong Welch, and Susan Williams.

Our families are constant sources of love and warmth, inspiration and insight. We had to literally close the door on them on countless evenings and weekends. If there is one aspect of writing that we hate, this is it. Our parents, Tom and Thelma Kouzes and Delores Posner and Henry Posner, were early role models of leadership and their examples forever encourage our hearts. Donna Kouzes was an initial collaborator and, right up to her untimely death, an enthusiastic contributor of compelling cases and sparkling suggestions. Jackie Schmidt-Posner continues to provide perspective and balance as well as imaginative advice and a sense of humor. Amanda Posner has grown into a talented and wonderful person and continues to be a delightful and stimulating distraction. We can't express enough our appreciation for their sacrifices, their steadfastness, and their support. They embody what it means to love and to care about others.

As Don Bennett, the first amputee to climb Mount Rainier, told us, "You can't do it alone." We couldn't have done it without all of these folks, and the many others along the way. *You* made this book possible.

We love you all.

ABOUT THE AUTHORS

Jim Kouzes is chairman emeritus of the Tom Peters Company, a professional services firm that inspires organizations to invent the new world of work using leadership training and consulting solutions. He is also an Executive Fellow at the Center for Innovation and Entrepreneurship at the Leavey School of Business, Santa Clara University. **Barry Posner** is dean of the Leavey School of Business and professor of leadership at Santa Clara University (Silicon Valley, California), where he has received numerous teaching and innovation awards, including his school's and his university's highest faculty awards. Jim and Barry were named by the International Management Council as the 2001 recipients of the prestigious Wilbur M. McFeely Award. This honor puts them in the company of Ken Blanchard, Stephen Covey, Peter Drucker, Edward Deming, Frances Hesselbein, Lee Iacocca, Rosabeth Moss Kanter, Norman Vincent Peale, and Tom Peters, earlier recipients of the award.

In addition to their award-winning and best-selling book, *The Leadership Challenge,* Jim and Barry have coauthored *Credibility: How Leaders Gain It and Lose It, Why People Demand It* (1993)—which was chosen by *Industry Week* as one of that year's five best management books—as well as *Encouraging the Heart* (1999) and *The Leadership Challenge Planner* (1999). Jim and Barry also developed the highly acclaimed *Leadership Practices Inventory (LPI),* a 360-degree questionnaire assessing leadership behavior; the *LPI* is one of the most widely used leadership assessment instruments in the world. More than 150 doctoral dissertations and academic research projects have been based on the *Five Practices of Exemplary Leadership* model. CRM Learning has produced a number of leadership and management development videos based on their publications.

Jim and Barry are frequent conference speakers and each has conducted leadership development programs for scores of organizations including Alcoa, Applied Materials, ARCO, AT&T, Australia Post, Bank of America, Bose, Charles Schwab, Cisco Systems, Conference Board of Canada, Consumers Energy, Dell Computer, Deloitte Touche, Egon Zehnder International, Federal Express, Gymboree, Hewlett-Packard, IBM, Johnson & Johnson, Kaiser Foundation Health Plans and Hospitals, Lawrence Livermore National Laboratories, Levi Strauss & Co., L. L. Bean, 3M, Merck, Mervyn's, Motorola, Network Appliance, Pacific Telesis, Roche Bioscience, Siemens, Sun Microsystems, TRW, Toyota, the U.S. Postal Service, United Way, and VISA.

Jim Kouzes is featured as one of the workplace experts in George Dixon's book, *What Works at Work: Lessons from the Masters* (1988) and in *Learning Journeys: Top Management Experts Share Hard-Earned Lessons on Becoming Great Mentors and Leaders,* edited by Marshall Goldsmith, Beverly Kaye, and Ken Shelton (2000). Not only is he a highly regarded leadership scholar and an experienced executive, he's been cited by the *Wall Street Journal* as one of the twelve most requested non-university executive education providers to U.S. companies. A popular seminar and conference speaker, Jim shares his insights about the leadership practices that contribute to high performance in individuals and organizations, and he leaves his audiences inspired with practical leadership tools and tips that they can apply at work, at home, and in their communities.

Jim directed the Executive Development Center (EDC) at Santa Clara University from 1981 through 1987. Under his leadership the EDC was awarded two gold medals from the Council for the Advancement and Support of Education. He also founded the Joint Center for Human Services Development at San Jose State University, which he managed from 1972 until 1980, and prior to that was on the staff of the University of Texas School of Social Work. His career in training and development began in 1969 when, as part of the Southwest urban team, he conducted seminars for Community Action Agency staff and volunteers in the "war on poverty" effort. Jim received his B.A. degree (1967) with honors from Michigan State University in political science and a certificate (1974) from San Jose State

University's School of Business for completion of the internship in organization development.

Jim's interest in leadership began while he was growing up in Washington, D.C. In 1961 he was one of a dozen Eagle Scouts selected to serve in John F. Kennedy's Honor Guard at the presidential inauguration. Inspired by Kennedy, he served as a Peace Corps volunteer from 1967 through 1969. Jim can be reached at (877) 866-9691, extension 239, or via e-mail at jim@kouzesposner.com.

Barry Posner, an internationally renowned scholar and educator, is the author or coauthor of more than a hundred research and practitioner-focused articles in such publications as *Academy of Management Journal, Journal of Applied Psychology, Human Relations, Personnel Psychology, IEEE Transaction on Engineering Management, Journal of Business Ethics, California Management Review, Business Horizons,* and *Management Review.* In addition to his books with Jim Kouzes, he has coauthored several books on project management, most recently *Checkered Flag Projects: Ten Rules for Creating and Managing Projects That Win!* Barry is on the editorial review boards for the *Journal of Management Inquiry* and *Journal of Business Ethics.*

Barry received his B.A. degree (1970) with honors from the University of California, Santa Barbara, in political science. He received his M.A. degree (1972) from The Ohio State University in public administration and his Ph.D. degree (1976) from the University of Massachusetts, Amherst, in organizational behavior and administrative theory. He's a highly regarded seminar leader and conference speaker with a warm and engaging style, full of inspiring examples and practical applications. Having consulted with a wide variety of public and private sector organizations around the globe, Barry currently sits on the Board of Directors for the American Institute of Architects (AIA). He served previously on the boards of Public Allies, Big Brothers/Big Sisters of Santa Clara County, the Center for Excellence in Non-Profits, Sigma Phi Epsilon Fraternity, and several start-up companies. At Santa Clara University he has previously served as associate dean for graduate programs and managing partner for the Executive Development Center.

Barry's interest in leadership began as a student during the turbulent unrest on college campuses in the late 1960s, when he was participating and reflecting on the balance between energetic collective action and chaotic and frustrated anarchy. At one time, he aspired to be a Supreme Court justice, but realizing he would have to study law, he redirected his energies into understanding people, organizational systems, and the liberation of the human spirit. Barry can be reached at (408) 554-4523, or via e-mail at bposner@scu.edu.

More information about Jim and Barry, and their work, can be found at their Web site: www.leadershipchallenge.com.

INDEX

ALZA Pharma, 125–126
Ambiguity, tension and, 227
Ambition, 25
Amdahl, 150, 241–242
American Broadcasting Company (ABC), 89–90
American Demographics, 137
AT&T, 154–155
AmeriCorps, 21
Amputee Soccer League, 123, 138
Analogies: decision making and, 363; inspiring vision with, 155–156; teaching values with, 88–90, 104
Anderson, W., 292–293
Anderson Soft-Teach, 292–293
Animation studio case study, 8–12
Annapurna I, 183–184
Anthony, S. B., 45
Anxiety: challenge and, 178; high expectations and, 324; about public speaking, 164
Apache HTTP server, 201
Apology, 233–234
Apple Computer, 376
Applied Biosystems, 19, 279
Aráoz, C. F., 241, 264–265
Armstrong, D., 99, 360–361
Armstrong International, 99, 360–361
Aronson, E., 270
Arrogance, 396–397
Art, leadership as, 56–57, 84, 115, 390–391
Art of the Long View, The (Schwartz), 136
Article-writing exercise, 134
Artifacts, conveying shared values through, 97–98
Aspirations, time to fulfill, 119
Assessment centers, 64
Assignments, leader: as adventures, 195–196; seeking, with meaningful challenge, 197; seeking opportunities in, 181–182; using new, to question status quo, 200. *See also* Task assignments
Assumptions: defined, 137; testing, in regard to vision, 137–138
Astaire, F., 214
Attention: human moments and, 273; passion and, 121–122; paying, to constituents, 120–122, 327–331, 332; positive *versus* negative, 327–328, 343; recognition and, 327–331

Attitudes. *See* Employee attitudes; Mindsets; Positive attitude
Audits: collaboration, 266–267; I/We language, 270; internal, 60–61, 71–72; personal, about example setting, 103–104
Aural images, 155
Australia, admired leader characteristics in, 26
Authenticity. *See* Consistency; Example setting; Model the Way; Self-expression; Voice
Automotive metal stamping company, 253–254
Avery, T., 364
Awards, 333; commemorative, 372–374; presentation of, 338–339, 344–345; presenter of, 345. *See also* Celebrations; Recognition; Rewards
Axelrod, R., 254–255
Axpo, 359

B

Babb, A., 362–363
Babe Ruth, 214
Bach, J. S., 59
Backing off, 293–294
Bain & Company, 34
Baker, B., 297–298
Bali, S., 279–281, 292, 309
Bank of America, 173, 174–176, 259–260
Bar, raising the, 180–181, 207
Baskin-Robbins, 52–53
Bass, B., 158
Baxter Healthcare, 202
Behavior-change programs, 210. *See also* Change, individual
Behavioral evidence: of credibility, 33–34, 37–39; of honesty, 28; of leading by example, 77, 84–93, 103–104
Beliefs. *See* Values headings
Believability, 32–33. *See also* Credibility
Bell System breakup, 219
Belonging, sense of, 153–154
Ben and Jerry's, 109–110
Bennett, D., 123, 124, 138
Bennett, H. Z., 372
Bennett, W., 336–337
Bennett, W. J., 71
Bennis, W., 17, 189

for social support, 356–359, 370; story-telling in, 359–364; types of, 371
Center for Creative Leadership, 21, 352
Centers for Disease Control, 98
Centrigram Communications Corporation, 347
Ceremonies and rituals: for comfort and letting go, 371; conveying shared values through, 98, 354–355; rationale for, 351–352; types of, 371. *See also* Celebrations
Cessaris, A., 332–333
Cézanne, P., 215
Challenge, 171–237; action steps for, 194–204; adventure and, 173–174, 184, 194–196; in assigned work, 181–182; attitudes toward, 219–223, 224; creating, for others, 197–198; destructive extremes of, 396; example setting with, 86–88, 96–97; exemplary leadership practice of, 16–17, 171–237; experimentation and, 205–237; incremental steps and, 208–213; initiative and, 177–182; innovation and, 173–191; major change and, 174–177; meaningful, 182–186, 196–198; performance and, 176–177; psychological hardiness and, 218–223; risk taking and, 205–237; searching for opportunities and, 173–204; self-confidence and, 295–296; small wins and, 208–213; varieties of, 16–17. *See also* Innovation; Opportunities
Challenge the Process, 16–17, 22, 171–237; action steps for, 194–204, 223–237; Commitment Five of, 22, 173–204; Commitment Six of, 22, 205–237; credibility and, 38–39; destructive extremes of, 396; essentials of, 177, 207. *See also* Challenge; Experimentation; Innovation; Opportunities; Risk taking
Chan, L., 332
Chang, R., 121–122
Change, and changing times: action steps for, 194–204; being forward-looking in, 113–130; challenge and, 173–177; creativity and, 186–191; discipline and, 190–191; experimentation in, 205–237; fun and humor during, 198–199;

incremental steps in, 208–213; innovation and, 186–191; looking outward in, 191–194, 201–203; need for common purpose in, 153–154, 182–184; psychological hardiness and, 218–223; risk taking in, 205–237; routines and, 189–191, 199–200; small wins in, 208–213; stress and, 218–223; vision statement updates and, 136. *See also* Challenge
Change, individual: balancing forces in, 223; breaking mindsets for, 228–229; incremental steps and small wins for, 208–213; psychological hardiness and, 218–223
Character, 27–28; values and, 45–46
Characteristics, of admired leaders, 24–32; credibility and, 32–39; cross-cultural comparisons of, 26; enduring relevance of, 32; Five Practices and, 27, 38–39; learned *versus* innate, 385–387; listed, 25; top four, 24, 27–32
Charisma and charismatic leadership, 20; meaning of, 158; nonverbal expressiveness and, 158–159, 165; vision communication and, 144, 158–159
Charles Schwab & Co., Inc., 45, 97–98, 163–164, 332, 351, 354–355, 370
Chat rooms, 203
Chávez, C., 45
Checking up, 327–328
Cheer-manager, 347–348
Cheerleader, 347–348, 364, 376–377
Chef Allen's, 202, 203
Chen, W., 308
Chicago Tribune, 347
Chief executive officers (CEOs): competence of, 30; time orientations of, 118–119, 129–130
Children's Hospital Head Trauma Clinic, San Diego, 385
Choice, employee: for customer service, 289, 290, 306–307; designing in alternatives for, 291–292; for empowerment, 288–292; providing, 231–232, 288–292, 306–307; results of, 289–291. *See also* Empowerment
"Chow Now" program, 202
Church, T., 116–118, 119, 124
Churchill, W., 45

of, 317; focus on clear standards in, 318–321; high expectations in, 321–327; paying attention and, 327–331; personalized recognition in, 331–337; practice associated with, 22. *See also* Recognition

Commitment Ten: Celebrate the Values and Victories, 351–380; action steps for, 369–380; community of spirit and, 353–359; destructive extremes of, 396; essentials of, 353; example setting with, 364–369; practice associated with, 22; storytelling and, 359–364. *See also* Celebration

Commitments, Ten: Five Practices associated with, 22; overview of, 21–22

Committing style, 153

Common Cause, 393

Common purpose/common ground: discovering, 151–155, 161–162. *See also* Vision headings

Common vision. See Vision headings

Communication: in car dealership case study, 5–6; for collaboration, 258–265; defensive, 268–269; external and internal, 191–193, 195, 201–203; information sharing and, 262–264; for new ideas, 191–194, 201–203; nonverbal, 158–159, 165, 227; positive, 157–158. *See also* Employees, getting to know; Face-to-face interaction; Listening; Self-expression; Speaking; Storytelling; Values shared; Vision sharing

Communication skills: for vision sharing, 164–165. *See also* Listening; Speaking; Storytelling

Community, sense of, 95–96; celebration for creating spirit and, 352, 353–359, 370; common purpose and, 153–154. *See also* Values, shared

Compassion, expression of, 375–376

Compensation systems: to reward collaborative effort, 256–257; reward variety and, 333–336. *See also* Rewards

Competence, employee, developing, 292–298, 302–205, 308–309

Competence, leadership, 29–31; admitting mistakes and, 233; authentic voice and, 62–63, 71–72; credibility and, 32, 62–63; cross-cultural comparisons of,

as admired leader trait, 26; percentage of constituents who value, 24, 25, 26; self-audit of, 71–72; social and emotional, 264–265; technical competence and, 30

Competition: destructive, 243, 250–251; information sharing and, 263; rewards and, 257; success and, 242, 254–255

Competitive advantage, impact of shared values on, 81

Compliance, 112

Computing Resources, Inc., 315–316

Confidence, 398; employee, importance of, 295–296; speaking with, 96; trust building with, 268–269

Confidence building: coaching for, 298; encouragement for, 321; expectations and, 322, 325; feedback for, 321; modeling for, 305; power sharing for, 282–283, 284–288, 295–296; small wins for, 210–211. *See also* Enabling

Confusion, change and, 190

Connections: leadership and, 390; personal, 260–262, 358, 388

Connetics, 341

Consensus: on values, 81–83; on vision statement, 162–164

Consistency, between actions and words, 14, 22; as evidence of credibility, 37–38, 93–94; example setting and, 77–78, 83–94; finding one's voice and, 43–44, 45–46. *See also* Alignment; Example setting

Constituents: alternative rewards for, 272–273, 332–336; finding common ground with, 151–155, 161–162; getting to know, 148–151, 159–161; identification of, 148, 159–160; listening to, 148–151, 167–168, 329–330; seeking new ideas from, 202–203. *See also* Customer headings; Employee headings

Constitution, personal, 220

Consumer product companies, 224

Contemplation, 65–66

Continuous improvement, employee choice and, 289

Control, sense of: feeling powerful and, 282–283, 290–291; fostering, 221–223; psychological hardiness and, 219, 221–223; self-confidence and, 295–296

Controlling behaviors, 327–331
Cooperation. *See* Collaboration
Cooperative goals and roles, 252–253. *See also* Collaboration
Cooperative learning exercise, 270–272
Cooperativeness, leader, 25
Corporate Celebration (Deal and Key), 371
Correcting, 327–328
Costello, J., 361–362
Costumes, 378
Coughlin, B., 247, 248
Counseling, 64
Courage, 25, 398
Courage of convictions, 182
"Covering yourself," 281
Craft-making, 355
Crant, J. M., 178–179
Creativity: challenge and, 186–191; in rewards and recognition, 337–338; routine and, 189–190; transformation for, in animation studio case study, 8–12. *See also* Innovation
Credibility, 23–39, 398; admitting mistakes and, 233–234; behavioral evidence and practices for, 33–34, 37–39; in celebrations, 356, 367–368; characteristics of admired leaders and, 24–39; controlling behavior and, 328; dilemma of being forward-looking and, 34–37; example setting and, 93–94; expectations and, 322; feedback and, 102; Five Practices and, 38–39; as foundation, 32–39; impact of, on employee attitudes, 33–34; importance of, 32–34, 187; maintaining, 35–37; Model the Way practice and, 38, 62–63, 93–94; questioning of, by opponents, 35; source, 32
Credibility: How Leaders Gain and Lose It, Why People Demand It (Kouzes and Posner), 120–121
Credo Memo, 56, 68–70, 72; dialogue and assessment of, 69–70; writing, 68–69
Creed, personal, 394
Critical events, celebrations for, 371
Critical incidents, example setting with, 86–88, 104
Critical tasks, assigning, 302–304
Cross-cultural comparisons, of admired leader characteristics, 26

Cross-training, 280–281
Crozer Seminary, 393–394
Cultural differences: listening and, 329–330; personalized recognition and, 332–333; studying, 167–168. *See also* Diversity
Cultural Imprint, 152
Culture, celebration and, 356, 364, 377. *See also* Values, shared
Curtin University, 102
Customer focus groups, 4
Customer loyalty, leader credibility and, 34
Customer service: employee discretion and, 289, 290, 306–307; transformation for, in car dealership case study, 3–8; as value, 85
Customers: getting to know, 161–162; providing employees with, 304–305
Cyclical celebrations, 371
Cynicism: inconsistency and, 46; recognition and, 331; trend toward, 36

D

Daddow, A., 288
Daily Lineup, 160–161
Dalai Lama, H. H., 45
Dalin International Trading Corporation, 288–289
Damon, M., 202
D'Arcangelo, M., 109
Dayton, S., 121–122
De Pree, M., 43–44, 72
Deal, T., 354, 371
Dean, D., 156
Deci, E., 112
Decision making: under emergency conditions, 363; self-confidence and, 295–296
Deep listening. *See* Listening
Defensive climate, 268–269, 309, 310; moderating, 269
Defiance, 112
Delaney, M., 212
DeMartini, K., 284–285, 338
Demonstration projects, 211
Denning, S., 98–99
Department of Health, Education, and Welfare, 393

tional receptivity to innovation and, 187; power and, 283–284, 286–287; rewards and recognition and, 334, 340; small wins for, 209–210

Employee performance. *See* Performance, employee

Employees, getting to know: in animation studio case study, 10–11; caring by walking around (CBWA) and, 374–375; creating places and opportunities for, 275–277; data collection for, 161–162; face-to-face interaction and, 258–265, 273–277; focus groups and forums for, 160–161; leadership as relationship and, 20–21, 149; listening for, 148–151, 167–168, 249–250, 329–330; for recognition and praise, 327–331, 332; trust building and, 249–250, 329–331; unstructured time for, 150–151, 168–169, 274–275; vision sharing and, 148–151, 159–162; working side by side for, 14–15, 169. *See also* Communication; Face-to-face interaction; Listening

Empowerment: accountability and, 299–301; in animation studio case study, 10; benefits of, 281–284, 286–290; "can-do" attitude and, 287–288; choice and, 289–291, 306–307; through employee development, 292–298, 302–305; enabling others and, 18–19, 279–311; information and resource sharing for, 292–293; providing opportunities for problem solving and, 293–295; self-confidence and, 292–298, 302–205, 308–309; values as source of, 49. *See also* Power sharing

Enable Others to Act, 18–20, 239–311; action steps for, 265–277, 301–311; Commitment Seven of, 241–277; Commitment Eight of, 279–311; commitments associated with, 22; destructive extremes of, 396; essentials of, 243, 284. *See also* Collaboration; Empowerment; Enabling; Power sharing

Enabling, 239–311; exemplary leadership practice of, 18–20, 239–311; through fostering collaboration, 241–277; as a leadership competence, 30–31; through strengthening others, 279–311. *See also* Collaboration; Empowerment; Power sharing

Encourage the Heart, 19–20, 313–380; action steps for, 337–349, 369–380; Commitment Nine of, 315–349; Commitment Ten of, 351–380; commitments associated with, 22; credibility and, 39, 356, 367–368; destructive extremes of, 396; essentials of, 317, 353. *See also* Celebration; Recognition; Rewards

Encouragement, 313–380; celebration for, 351–380; exemplary leadership practice of, 19–20, 313–380; as feedback, 321; individual recognition for, 19–20, 22, 315–349; questions about, 339. *See also* Celebration; Feedback; Praise; Recognition; Rewards

Ends values, 48. *See also* Vision

Enlist Others in a Common Vision. *See* Commitment Four; Vision sharing

Enron, 36

Enterprise resource planning (ERP) system, 141–142

Enthusiasm: as admired leader characteristic, 31–32; for challenge, 177–178; for common vision, 16, 157–158, 164–165, 166–167; for shared values, 95–97

Entrepreneurs, 181

Entrepreneurship, 122

Environmentalist case studies, 51–54, 116–118, 209–210

Envision the Future. *See* Commitment Three; Envisioning; Vision

Envisioning the future, 109–139; action steps for, 130–139; essentials of, 114–115; imagining possibilities for, 114–115, 124–130; theme discovery for, 114–124, 131–134; time frames for, 129–130. *See also* Possibilities; Theme; *Vision headings*

Escalation, reciprocity and, 255

Essence, reducing items to, 212

Ethics of leadership, 28, 393–394

Eureka!Ranch, 378

Evans, J., 152–153

Events: celebration of, 371; for vision development and commitment, 163–164

Evert, D., 214
Evil leaders, 396–397
Example setting, 14–15, 75–107; action steps for, 93–105; and alignment of actions with values, 77–78, 83–105; behavioral indicators of, 84–93; in case study, 75–77; with celebrations, 364–369, 379; commitment and, 76–78; credibility and, 38, 93–94; with critical incidents, 86–88, 104; destructive extremes of, 395; essentials of, 77–78; shared values and, 77–83; storytelling and, 88–90, 98–101; time allocation and, 85–86, 103; words and, 90–92. *See also* Alignment, of actions with values; Model the Way; Values, shared
Excellence, feelings associated with, 222
Executive development programs, outdoor challenge, 205–207
Exemplary leadership. *See* Leadership, exemplary
Exercise, physical, 220
Exercises. *See* Action steps
Expectations: high, for constituents/employees, 321–327, 341–342; for leaders, 23–32; peer, 299; performance and, 323–325, 341–342; positive, fostering, 342–344; positive images and, 325–327; power of, 321–325, 326–327, 341–342; self-fulfilling prophecy and, 321–323
Experience: being the author of one's, 61–62; intuition and, 122–124; paying attention to, 120–122; relevant, as admired leader characteristic, 30
Experiment and Take Risks. *See* Commitment Six; Experimentation; Risk taking
Experimentation, 17, 22, 205–237; action steps for, 223–237; essentials of, 207; incremental steps in, 208–213, 229–231; learning from mistakes and, 213–218; psychological hardiness and, 218–223; safety for, 226–228; small wins in, 208–213; to test vision, 138
Experiments, setting up little, 224–226
Exploitation, 186
External communication, 191–194, 195, 201–203
Extra Mile Heroes, 377

Extrinsic motivation, 112, 183, 185–186. *See also* Motivation; Rewards
Extrinsic rewards, 335–336, 344–345. *See also* Rewards

F

Face-to-face interaction: caring and, 374–375; for collaboration, 258–265, 273–277; for communication, 161–162; creating places and opportunities for, 275–277; for durable relationships, 258–259; emotional intelligence and, 264–265; human moments and, 273–275; informal, 274–277; information sharing and, 262–264; networks and, 259–260; physical space for, 150, 161–162, 275–277; for power sharing, 310–311; social capital and, 260–262; for trust, 261–262, 329–331. *See also* Employees, getting to know
Failure: expectations and, 322–323; learning from, 17, 213–218; reframing, as learning experience, 157. *See also* Mistakes
Fair-mindedness, 25
Faith, 398
Family: admired leaders in, 388–389; connection and, 260; trust in, 249–250
Family history, psychological hardiness and, 221
Farmland Industries, 250
Farris, N., 364
Fast Company, 137
Fear: risk taking and, 207; trust and, 268–269. *See also* Anxiety
Federman, I., 149
Feedback: credibility and, 102; on Credo Memo, 69–70; for employee development, 305, 342; employee motivation and, 319–321; for employee performance improvement, 92–93, 319–321; encouragement as, 321; as gift, 64–65; for leader improvement, 102–103; real-time, 341; for self-awareness, 64–65; for self-confidence, 321. *See also* Recognition; 360-degree feedback
Feeling-oriented learners, 217
Fennell, L., 187–189

Honesty, 27–28; admitting mistakes and, 233–234; credibility and, 32; cross-cultural comparisons of, as admired leader trait, 26; evidence of, 28; percentage of constituents who value, 24, 25, 26

Honeywell-Measurex, 168–169

Hope, 20, 398

Hot groups or hot teams, 271–272

Hotel company case study, 160–161

Houghton Winery, 364

Hubris, 396–397

Hudson, K., 199

Human moments, 273–275. *See also* Face-to-face interaction

Humility, 216, 397–398

Humor, 198–199

Hyatt Hotels Corporation, 85

I

I-centric style of leadership, 397

"I Have a Dream" speech (King), 135, 144–148, 155, 166; imagery in, 155; techniques in, 146–147; text of, 145–146

I/We language audit, 270

Idea hot lines, 202

Ideal: finding meaning in, 125–126; focusing on, 125–126; values and, 126

Ideal self-image, 66–67

Ideas: positive *versus* negative attitudes toward, 227–229; sources of, 191–194, 201–203; as sources of little experiments, 224–225

IDEO, 193–194, 271–272

Illinois Bell Telephone, 219

Illness, stress and, 218–219, 220, 358

Imagery, for vision realization, 138, 155–156

Images: of the future, 128–129; positive, 325–327

Imagination, 25. *See also* Possibilities

Immersion: envisioning and, 122–124; inspiration and, 123; intuition and, 122–123

Improvisation, during critical incidents, 87–88

In-basket, personal audit of, 104

Incremental steps, 17, 207, 208–213; action steps for, 229–231; for agreements, 232–233; fast action and, 211–213; rationale for, 208–211. *See also* Wins, small

Independence, leader, 25

Indian Navy, 279–281, 292, 309

Individual recognition. *See* Recognition

Individualism, 258

Industrial Revolution, 18

Influence: enlarging people's sphere of, 306–307; openness to, 247–248

Informal interaction, 274–277. *See also* Face-to-face interaction

Information age. *See* Internet Age

Information Management Group, 241

Information overload: uniqueness and, 128; vision clarity and, 114

Information retention, stories for, 362–364

Information sharing: barriers to, 262–263; for collaboration, 262–264; for empowerment, 292–293, 307, 308; social networks and, 358–359. *See also* Self-disclosure

Information sources: for new ideas, 191–194, 201–203; trustworthy, 249–250

Information withholding and distorting, 248

Inghilleri, L., 160–161

Initiative, 177–182; encouraging, in others, 180–181, 301; positive expectations and, 343; seizing the, 178–179. *See also* Empowerment; Enabling; Opportunities; Power sharing

Innate characteristics, learned leadership *versus*, 385–387

Inner development, 43–73. *See also* Self-expression; *Values headings*

Innovation, 17, 22, 173–204; action steps for, 194–204; in assigned work, 181–182; challenge and, 173–204; change and, 174–177; destructive, 191; discipline and, 190–191; essentials for, 177; importance of, 186–189; incremental/small wins approach to, 208–213, 229–231; initiative and, 177–182; leadership and, 187–189, 195; looking outward for, 191–194, 201–203; meaningful challenge and, 182–186, 196–198; for mergers, 175–176; in New Economy,

187; praise and, 334; routines and, 189–191, 199–200; in secondary education, 187–189; sources of, 191–194; vision and, 113. *See also* Experimentation; Risk taking

Insight, 193

Insight-resolution, 88

Inspecting, 327–328

Inspiration, 107–170; common vision and, 141–170; exemplary leadership practice of, 15–16, 107–170; immersion and, 123. *See also* Envisioning; Vision; Vision sharing

Inspirational attribute, 31–32; credibility and, 32; cross-cultural comparisons of, as admired leader trait, 26; percentage of constituents who value, 24, 25, 26; vision communication and, 143–148

Inspire, defined, 155

Inspire a Shared Vision, 15–16, 107–170; Commitment Three of, 22, 109–139; Commitment Four of, 22, 141–70; commitments associated with, 22; credibility and, 38, 93; destructive extremes of, 396. *See also* Envisioning; Vision; Vision sharing

Institute for the Future, 362

Institute for Womens' Leadership, 308–309

Institutions, decline of trust in, 36

Integrity, 27–28, 81, 393–394

Intellectual capital, 260

Intelligence, 25

Interdependence, 250–257; accountability and, 299–301; developing cooperative goals and roles for, 252–253; importance of, 251–252; norms of reciprocity and, 253–256; rewards and, 256–257, 272–273

Internal audits, 60–61, 71–72

Internal communication. *See* Communication

Internal exploration: action steps for, 63–73; for leadership development, 390–394; listening to the masters and, 54–56, 59–60; for self-expression, 60–61; for values clarification, 51–56; for vision theme discovery, 115–120, 131–134

IBM Business Recovery Services, 179

IBM Institute for Knowledge Management, 359

International Committee of the Red Cross, Kenya, 383

International Women's Professional Softball League, 230

Internet: change and, 114; difficulties of differentiation due to, 127–128; publishing on, 119–120

Internet Age: collaboration in, 242–243, 260; social capital and, 260–262

Internet businesses: decline of, 36, 156–157, 184–185; paying attention in, 120–122. *See also* High-tech companies; New Economy

Internet skills, relative importance of social skills to, 21

Interpersonal interaction. *See* Face-to-face interaction

Interpreter, 168

Intrapreneurs, 181

Intraproject communication, 192

Intrinsic motivation, 112; celebration and, 372; common purpose and, 151–152; importance of, 185–186; meaningful challenge and, 182–186, 196–198; open-source movement and, 201; recognition and, 317

Intrinsic rewards, 334; extrinsic rewards combined with, 335–336, 344–345

Intuition: decision making and, 363; experience and, 122–124; learning climate and, 228; performance and, 222; vision and, 115, 122–124

Intuitive Surgical, 315

Inventors, 208

Investor loyalty, leader credibility and, 34

Involvement, power and, 282–284. *See also* Empowerment; Power sharing

Isolation: from external communication, 191–192; from social connection, 358, 370

Isomura, I., 228

J

James, J., 121, 137

Janus Effect, 118–120

Japan, admired leader characteristics in, 26
Jargon, organizational, 90–91
Jenkins, J., 224–225
Jenkins Diesel Power Company, 224–225
Jetsons, The, 8
Jigsaw Classroom, 270–272
Jigsaw groups, creating, 270–272
Job classification, 291
Job design, 304–305, 334. *See also* Task assignments
Job satisfaction: as common motivator, 151–152; as internal motivation, 185–186; managers and, 283–284, 288–289; power and, 283–284; rewards and, 334
Jobs: enriching, 304–305; projects *versus*, 186; work *versus*, 186
John Paul II, Pope, 45
Johnson, C., 216
Joint Commission for the Accreditation of Hospital Organizations, 297
Journal of the American Medical Association, 167
Journey metaphor, 156

K

Kaffer, G., 168–169
Kahl, J., 96–97
Kaiser Foundation Health Plans and Hospitals, 365–366, 377
Kanter, R. M., 187
Katz, R., 192
Keith, A., 3, 8–12, 13, 14, 18
Kelleher, H., 198–199, 378
Kelley, T., 193–194
Kermit, 120
Key, M. K., 354, 371
Key Communication, 332–333
Kido, K., 114
Kids for a Clean Environment (Kids F.A.C.E.), 209–210
King, M. L., Jr., 45, 53, 70–71, 135, 144–148, 155, 166, 393–394
King James Bible, 70
Klein, G., 235–236, 363
Klein Associates, 235–236
Knight, P., 363–364
Korea, admired leader characteristics in, 26

Kouses, J., 120–121, 242–243
Kouzes-Posner First Law of Leadership, 33, 46

L

Lam Research Corporation, 262–263
Lamott, A., 56
Landscape painting, 58, 59, 62
Language: collaborative, 270; of either/or mentality, 232, 272; learning others', 329–330; organizational, 90–92; power of, 57–58, 96, 155–156; for values sharing, 96; for vision sharing, 155–157. *See also* Communication; Speaking; Words
LaSandra, J., 58
Latitude, employee, 288–292. *See also* Choice; Empowerment
Lazar, I. "S.", 178
Leaders: biographies of, 131–132; characteristics of admired, 23–39; as coaches, 296–298; effectiveness of exemplary, 389–390; evil, 396–397; great, as role models, 45, 54–56, 59–60, 67–68, 388; impact of, 388–390; as learners, 215–217, 392–393; literary influences on, 70–71; mistakes of, admission of, 233–234; mobility of, 327; "ordinary" people as, 20, 383–399; outside pursuits of, 397; as possibility *versus* probability thinkers, 124; psychological hardiness and, 222–223; questions for, 392–393; role of, in celebrations, 364–369; trust and, 244, 268. *See also* Example setting; Historical leaders
Leadership, exemplary: as art, 56–57, 84, 115, 390–391; circle of, 368–369; credibility and, 23–39; as everyone's business, 383–399; Five Practices of, contrasts and contradictions in, 394–398; Five Practices of, overview, 13–20; innovation and, 187–189, 195; journey metaphor for, 156; as learned behaviors *versus* innate traits, 385–387; learning and, 215–218; moral leadership and, 393–394; myths about, 20, 385–387; questions for, 392–393; as relationship, 20–21, 23, 78, 110,

Motivation: celebrations for, 361–362, 363–364, 372; common vision and, 142; feedback and, 319–321; intrinsic *versus* extrinsic, 112, 151–152, 182–186, 335–336, 372; meaningful challenge and, 182–186, 196–198; peer expectations and, 299; recognition and, 317, 319–321, 335–336; stories for, 361–362, 363–364; values as source of, 49. *See also* Intrinsic motivation
Moumdjian, H., 229
Mount Everest, 387
Mount Rainier, 123, 124
Mountain climbing, 183–184, 387
Mueller, T., 374
Mutual dependence. *See* Interdependence
Myths about leadership, 20, 385–387

N

National Football League, 94
National Institutes of Health (NIH), 244–245
NationsBank–Bank of America merger, 174–176, 259–260
Navratilova, M., 214
Negative stereotypes, 343
Negativism, 227–228, 300
Negotiation exercise, with alternative currencies, 273, 274
Nelson, B., 340–341
Nettell, N., 173, 174–176, 259–260, 344–345
Network, 251
Networks and networking, human, 259–260; informal, 274–277; providing employees with opportunities for, 304; social capital and, 260–262; social support and, 356–359, 370
New Economy: collaboration and, 243, 258, 261–262; face-to-face interaction and, 258–259, 261–262; innovation and, 187; mercenaries *versus* missionaries in, 156–157, 185–186, 258–259; vision and, 113. *See also* High-tech companies; Internet Age; Internet businesses
New Focus, 173, 184–185
New Perspectives Quarterly, 137

New Zealand, admired leader characteristics in, 26
Newscasters, 34–35
Newsletter, company, 362
Newsweek, 362
Nichols, C., 344–345
Nicolo, J., 315–316, 339
Nietzsche, 394
Nike, 363–364
1970s, declining trust since, 36
Nissan, 304–305
Nonverbal communication: of "boss" behavior, 227; of charismatic vision, 158–159, 165
Nonviolence, 393–394
Norms, of reciprocity, 253–256, 262
North American Tool and Die (NATD), 162, 374
Nursing home case study, 290–291

O

O.C. Tanner, 344
O'Connell, C., 229
Oknaian, P., 332
Oldenburg, R., 275
ONE IN A MILLION, 117–118
One-on-one meetings, 310–311; human moments in, 273–274
1001 Ways to Reward Employees (Nelson), 340–341
One-way-mirror hypothesis, 119
O'Neill, P., 275–276
Open plan offices, 275–276
Open-source approach, 201–202
Open-source code, 201
Openness: to influence, 247–248; to outside information, 193–194; for trust building, 330–331
Operation Raleigh USA, 173–174
Oppenheimer, J. R., 45
Opportunities: action steps for, 194–204; in assigned work, 181–182; critical incidents as, 86–88; essentials of searching for, 177; fun, 198–199; initiative and, 177–182; looking outward for, 191–194, 201–203; meaningful challenge and, 182–186, 196–198; open-source approach to, 201–202;

problem solving and, 197–198; search-ing for, 173–204; seizing, 13, 177–182

Organizational change efforts, learning climate for, 309–310

Organizational communication, 192. *See also* Communication

Organizational practices and policies, questioning, 199–200

Organizational vocabulary, 90–91

Organizations: impact of shared values on, 78–80; impact of values clarity on, 49–51

Outdoor challenge programs, 157, 205–207, 213, 226

Outsight, 192–194, 195, 201–202

Outward, looking, 191–194, 201–203

Overwhelm, incremental approach and, 213

Ownership: in animation studio case study, 10; choice and, 231–232, 288–289; power sharing and, 287; of values, 81–83

P

Pacific Gas & Electric Company, 14

Palo Alto Research Center, 309

Paradigms, questioning, 10

Paraphrasing, 269

Passing the buck, 281

Passion: attention and, 121–122; celebra-tion and, 354, 375–376; expressing, 115–118, 375–376; meaningful chal-lenge and, 184, 196–197; vision and, 110, 112, 115–118, 121–122, 124, 165. *See also Vision headings*

Passion-Compassion game, 375–376

Past: future horizons and, 118–120, 132–133; reflection on, 115–120, 132–133

Paying attention, 120–122; listening and, 149, 329–330; recognition and, 327–331, 332. *See also* Attention

PCnet, 166–167

Pearson, A., 316–317

Peer instruction, 280–281, 309

PepsiCo, 316

Percy Priest School, 209

Perfectionism, 398

Performance, employee: climate and, 222; collaboration and, 242–243; expecta-tions and, 323–325, 341–342; fun and, 377–378; impact of exemplary leader-ship practices on, 389–390; impact of managers on, 283–284, 288–289; impact of measurement and feedback on, 92–93, 319–321; impact of model-ing on, 84; poor, 340–341; positive *ver-sus* negative attention and, 327–328, 343; power and, 283–284, 286–288; rewards linked with, 19–20, 315–349; shared values and, 79–80; trust and, 245–247, 330

Performance, organizational: collabora-tion and, 242–243; impact of exem-plary leadership practices on, 390; impact of shared values on, 80–81; power and, 283–284, 286–288; trust and, 245–247

Performance, team, communication and, 192

Performance appraisal, alignment of, with values, 92–93

Performance improvement, challenge and, 176–177

Permission, acting without, 212

Persistence, proactivity and, 179

Personal agenda, 112. *See also* Vision

Personal-best leadership experiences, 8; admired leader characteristics and, 27; challenge and, 176, 177; collaboration in, 241–242; Five Practices derived from, 13–20; impact of, on leaders, 122–123; possibilities and, 126; power sharing and, 284–285; vision buy-in and, 143

Personal creed, 394

Personal power, 18

Personal transitions, ceremonies for, 371

Personalized recognition, 331–337. *See also* Recognition

Pettingill, D., 365–366, 377

Philbin, K., 141–142, 143

Phillips, B., 234, 359–360

Physical capital, 260

Physical contact, 158–159

Physical presence, 273. *See also* Face-to-face interaction

Physical space: for interaction, 150, 161–162, 275–277; transformation of, in animation studio case study, 11

Picasso, P., 59

Pier 1 Imports' Stores, 19

Pigs, 110

Pilgrim's Progress, 70

Pilot tests, 211, 213, 224

Pioneers, leaders as, 17, 173–174, 184, 196

Planning, vision *versus,* 153

Play, celebrations for, 371. *See also* Fun

Podesta Baldocchi, 127

Podzilni, D., 150–151, 378

Poe, M., 209–210

Polaroid, 199

Political behavior, 46, 281

Position, leadership based on, 383, 386

Positional power, 286

Positive attitude, 31–32; of "can-do," 287–288; fostering hardiness and, 221–223, 224; safety and, 227–228; toward employees as winners, 327–331; toward ideas, 227–229; toward stress, 219–223; vision sharing and, 157–158

Positive communication, 157–158, 164–165

Positive expectations, fostering, 342–344

Positive images, 325–327

Positive self-talk, 138–139

Posner, B., 120–121, 161

Possibilities: either-or mentality *versus,* 272; envisioning with, 114–115, 124–130; focusing on the ideal and, 125–126; images and, 128–129; imagining, 114–115, 124–130; pride in uniqueness and, 127–128; probabilities *versus,* 124

Posters and pictures, 97

Postmortems, 234–236

Pottruck, D., 45–46, 97–98, 354–355

Power, temptations of, 396–398

Power paradox, 284–287

Power sharing, 18–19, 22, 279–311; accountability and, 299–301; action steps for, 301–311; benefits of, 281–284, 286–290; destructive extremes of, 396; through employee development, 292–298, 302–305; through ensuring self-leadership, 284–288; essentials for, 284; through providing choice, 288–292; resistance to, 285–286. *See also* Empowerment

Power sources, connecting others to, 260–262

Powerful, feeling, 282–283

Powerlessness, 281–282, 295

Practices, Five: admired leader characteristics and, 27; contrasts and contradictions of, 394–398; credibility and, 38–39; destructive extremes of, 395–396; effectiveness of, 389–390, 395; enduring relevance of, 13–14; learning tactics associated with, 217–218; listed, 13; overview of, 13–20. *See also* Challenge the Process; Enable Others to Act; Encourage the Heart; Inspire a Shared Vision; Model the Way

Praise: celebrations for, 370; importance of, 315–317, 334; reluctance to give, 315–316, 333, 347; ways to give, 347–349. *See also* Celebrations; Recognition; Rewards

Praklet, D., 16

Prefontaine, S., 363–364

Premortems, 234–236

Preparation, for speechmaking, 96

Presentation of recognition and awards, 338–339, 344–345. *See also* Celebration; Recognition

Presentation skills, 164

President's Summit for America's Future, 117

PricewaterhouseCoopers, 245

Pride: hubris and, 396–397; in uniqueness, 127–128

Primacy effect, 103

Prime of Miss Jean Brodie, The (Spark), 391

Prisoner's Dilemma, 254–255

Pritchard, M., 329

Pro-Action Associates, 157, 205–207, 226

Proactivity: conditions conducive for, 180–181; forward-looking thinking and, 129–130, 136–137; in search for opportunities and challenge, 178–180, 195

Probabilities, 124

Problem framing, 272

Problem solving: focus on gains *versus* losses in, 272; opportunities and, 197–198; providing employees with opportunities for, 293–295, 302–304, 343; stereotype threat and, 343

Problems, looking for, 327–328

Process, challenge the. *See* Challenge; Challenge the Process

Process innovation evaluation, 224

Professional communication, 192

Professionalism, 190–191

Profit sharing, 257–258

Project review, 234–235

Projects: breaking down new, 230; jobs *versus,* 291; pre- and postmortems of, 234–236

PSS/World Medical, 91

Psychological hardiness, 207, 218–223; factors in, 219–220; family background and, 221; fostering, 221–223; learning and challenge mindset in, 220–221; positive attitude and, 219–221, 224; stress of challenge and, 218–219; synergistic effect of, with other anti-stress factors, 220

Psychological health: social support and, 358, 370; trust and, 244

Psychological safety, 226–228, 268–269, 309–310

Public Allies, 21

Public celebrations. *See* Celebration

Public recognition, 339–341, 345–347, 348–349, 369, 371. *See also* Celebration; Recognition

Public speaking training, 164

Purpose, 112; common, 151–155, 161–162; meaningful challenge and, 182–186, 196–198. *See also* Vision

Purser, R. E., 136

Pursuit of Loneliness (Slater), 55

Putnam, R., 255

Puzzle-assembly exercise, 262

Puzzlement-recoil, 88

Pygmalion effect, 322–323, 328, 341–342

Q

Quad/Graphics, 378

Quadracci, H., 378

Qualifiers, 164

Quality programs, training for, 307–308

Question asking: to build trust, 269; to challenge the status quo, 199–200; to

convey values, 91–92, 101–102, 103–104; in learning mindset, 221

Questions, auditing, 103–104

Quests, 91–92, 101–102

R

Radius, 75–77

Ramans, A., 315

Rapid change. *See* Change and changing times

Rapid prototyping, 208

Rasmussen, H., 287

Raychem Corporation, 200

Raymond Bliss Army Community Hospital, 297–298

Razouk, L., 166–167

Reagan, R., 117

Real estate agents, proactive, 178–179

Reality-TV, 250–251

Recency effect, 103

Reciprocity, 253–256, 262

Recognition, individual, 315–349; action steps for, 337–349; in animation studio case study, 12; in car dealership case study, 6–7; clear standards for, 318–321, 342; creative, 337–339; destructive extremes of, 396; employees who don't deserve, 340–341; as encouragement, 19–20, 22, 315–349; essentials for, 317; expectations and, 321–327, 341–342; importance of, 315–317; one-size-fits-all approach to, 331; paying attention and, 327–331, 332; performance-linked, 19–20, 315–349; personalizing, 331–337; presentation of, 338–339, 344–345; public, 339–341, 345–347, 348–349, 369, 371; rewards combined with, 335–336; spontaneous and timely, 333–336, 337–338, 341; storytelling about, 100–101; thoughtful, 336–337, 345; values-based, 104. *See also* Celebrations; Praise; Rewards

Recognize Contributions. *See* Commitment Nine

Redundancy reduction, 175–176

Reflection: on past, 118–120, 132–133; spirituality and, 65–66

Rehearsal, mental, 138

REI, 387

Reichheld, F., 34

Relationship(s): celebrations and, 356–359, 368; durable, 258–259; leadership as, 20–21, 23, 78, 110, 296–297, 368; reciprocity in, 254, 255, 262; trust and, 244

Religion, 65–66

Research evaluation, 224

Resistance: to information sharing, 263; to power sharing, 285–286; small wins and, 211

Resource sharing: for collaboration, 262–264; for empowerment, 292–293, 307

Responsibility, 265, 298, 299–301. *See also* Accountability; Empowerment

Restructuring: challenge of, 174–176; cynicism and, 36

Retention, 151; impact of managers on, 283–284; rewards and, 334

Rewards: action steps for, 337–349; alternative, for diverse constituents, 272–273, 332–336; for cheerleading, 376; clear standards for, 318–321, 342; for collaborative effort, 256–257, 272–273; creative, 337–339; essentials for, 317; expectations and, 321–327, 341–342; extrinsic motivation and, 112, 183, 185–186, 344–345; feedback-linked, for leaders, 103; intrinsic and built-in, 334, 335–336; long-term, 257; paying attention and, 327–331, 332; performance-linked, 19–20, 93, 315–349; personalized, 331–337; presentation of, 338–339, 344–345; recognition combined with, 335–336; spontaneous and timely, 333–336, 337–338, 341; thoughtful, 336–337, 345; value-based, 93, 104. *See also* Recognition

Ricci, M., 252

Risk assessment, 218

Risk taking, 17, 205–237; action steps for, 223–237; essentials of, 207; incremental steps and, 208–213, 229–231; learning from mistakes and, 213–218; providing safety for, 226–228; psychological hardiness and, 218–223; small wins and, 208–213; trust and, 269; vision and, 113–114

Rituals. *See* Celebration; Ceremonies

Ritz-Carlton Hotels, 160–161, 306

Robbins, J., 52–54, 65–66

Roche Bioscience, 351, 352–353, 370

Roddick, A., 57–58, 61–62, 156

Rokeach, M., 48

Role models: obsession with being, 395; for personal values clarification and expression, 54–56, 59–60, 67–68; of proactivity, 181; recognized employees as, 339, 346, 374–375; stories about, 361–362

Role-play studies, of trust, 245–247

Roles, cooperative, 252–253

Roll-out, vision, 163–164

Roosevelt, E., 45

Roosevelt, F. D., 45

Root Learning, Inc., 163

Ropes course, 206, 213, 226

Rotating leadership, 277, 306

Routines: destructive, 189–190; innovation balanced with, 189–191; paradox of, 189–190; questioning, 199–200; useful, 190–191; values-linked, 190

Russo, V. J., 372–373

S

Safety: for climate of learning, 309–310; for climate of trust, 268–269; providing, for others to experiment, 226–228; specific actions for, 226–227

San Jose Sharks, 252

San Jose Water Company, 299–301

Sandvig, V., 163–164, 351

Santa Clara University, 97, 157–158, 161, 325, 348–349, 399

Sarhatt, T., 19

Scandals, 36

Scandinavia, admired leader characteristics in, 26

Scenario practice, for developing proactivity, 180

Schaer, H.-U., 241

Schallau, J., 347

Schiefer, J., 154–155

Schlesinger, A. M., Jr., 389

Schmidt, W., 49

Schwab. *See* Charles Schwab & Co., Inc.

Schwartz, P., 136

Schwarzkopf, H. N., 86–87, 88

Schweizer, C., 324

Scientific American, 137
Scientific experiments, 208
Scooby Doo, 8
Score-keeping: about one's leadership behaviors, 102–103; systems of, 92–93
Search Conference, The (Emery and Purser), 136
Search for Opportunities. See Commitment Five
Seattle Public Schools, 399
Seddeek, A., 43
Self-awareness, 64–65, 71–72; emotional intelligence and, 264–265; leadership development and, 390–394. See also Internal exploration; Values headings; Voice
Self-confidence. See Confidence
Self-control, 25
Self-determination, 295
Self-development, leadership development as, 390–392
Self-disclosure, leader, 248–249, 268, 330–331, 374
Self-discovery: action steps for, 63–73; leadership development and, 390–392; moral leadership and, 393–394; for self-expression, 60–61; for values clarification, 51–54; for vision theme discovery, 115–120, 131–134
Self-efficacy, 180; power sharing and, 282, 284–288
Self-esteem, employee: asking questions and, 100–101; pride in uniqueness and, 127; public recognition and, 339, 348–349
Self-expression, 44, 45, 56–62; action steps for, 63–73; art of, 56–57; authenticity in, 56–58, 60–61; competence and, 62–63, 71–72; importance of words in, 57–58; looking-in stage of, 60–61; looking-out stage of, 59–60; moving-on stage of, 61–62; stages of, 58–62. See also Communication; Speaking; Storytelling
Self-fulfilling prophecy, 321–323
Self-leadership, 284–288
Self-serving behavior, 250–251, 258–259
Selznick, D. O., 214
Senior executives: average time allocation of, for long-term envisioning, 136;

percentage of, who value forward-looking attribute, 29. See also Chief executive officers
Sense-making, retroactive, 119. See also Meaning
Sense of urgency, 212
Sensenbrenner, J., 289–290
Sensitivity to others, 149–151, 249–250
Sensitivity training groups, 64
Service quality, social support networks and, 357
Set the Example. See Commitment Two; Example setting
Set-up-to-fail syndrome, 322–323
Shakespeare, 70
Shannon, T., 69
Shared values. See Values, shared
Shared vision. See Vision sharing
Sharpnack, R., 230–231, 308–309
Shepard, H., 132
Signature authority, 306–307
Silicon Valley Bank, 156
Singapore, admired leader characteristics in, 26
"Six degrees of separation," 260, 261
Ski instruction, 215
Skill development, employee, 305
Slackers, 299
Slater, P., 55
Sloan School of Management, 192
Slogans, 135, 165
Small wins. See Wins, small
Smokenders, 210
Snowden, D., 359
Soccer team case study, 16
Social activist case study, 51–54
Social awareness and skills, 264–265
Social capital, 260–262
Social loafers, 299
Social psychology, 88–90, 322
Social skills, importance of, 21
Social support, celebrations as, 356–359, 370
Socratic dialogue, 343
Softball team coach, 230–231
Soldiers, importance of feedback to, 319–322
Solectron, 141–142, 308
Sonberg, K., 351, 352–353
Soul-wrestling, 393–394

Source credibility, 32

South Africa, reconciliation process of, 229

Southwest Airlines, 198–199, 378

Spark, M., 391

Speak Your Values. *See* Commitment One; Self-expression

Speaking: anxiety about, 164; developing skills in, 164–165; from the heart, 166–167; powerful, 96, 155–156, 164, 166; powerless, 96; about shared values, 95–97; about vision, 143–148, 164–167. *See also* Communication; Self-expression; Storytelling; Words

Speech communications research, 88

Speed: face-to-face interaction and, 258; incremental approach and, 211–213, 229

Spencer Stuart, 62

Spending authority, 289, 306–307

Sphere of influence, employee, 306–307

Spiritual practice, 65–66

Sports: learning, 215; mental imagery in, 325

Square D Company, Vision College, 375

SRC Holdings Corporation, 293, 304

Stack, J., 293

Staff meetings, listening in, 203, 305–306

Stafford, M., 102

Standards, high-performance: to encourage initiative, 180–181; expectations and, 321–327, 342; feedback and, 319–321; individual recognition and, 318–327, 342; as a shared value, 94; stories of role models and, 361

Stanford, J. H., 284, 302, 399

Stanford University, 210, 343, 393

Stark, M., 390

Start-over, 195

Start-ups, 195, 258–259

Status quo, questioning, 199–200. *See also* Challenge; Challenge the Process

Steele, C., 343

Stereotype threat, 343

Store, company, 12

Stories: celebrations and, 359–364; collecting, that teach values, 70–71; impact of, on rational discourse, 88–89, 99; memorable, 362–364; about others, 100; personal, 99–100, 359–360;

reading, about admired leaders and vision, 131–132; teaching excellence with, 362; teaching values with, 88–90, 98–101, 361–364; teaching vision with, 155–157

Storytelling: in celebrations, 359–364; examples of, 89–90, 98–99; to inspire vision, 155–157; on meeting agendas, 100–101; for motivation, 361–362, 363–364; for recognition, 337, 345–347; to teach values, 88–90, 98–101; tips for, 99–101. *See also* Speaking

Straightforwardness, 25

Strategic planning: incremental/small wins approach *versus*, 208–209; visions *versus*, 153

Strategic thinking, 153

Strengthen Others. *See* Commitment Eight; Empowerment; Power sharing

Stress: challenge and, 178; discipline and, 190–191; illness and, 218–219, 220, 358; positive attitude toward, 219–221, 224; psychological hardiness and, 218–223; social support and, 358

Strong, M., 137

Subjective well-being, 377–378

Subskills, 305

Success: celebrating, 376–377; collaboration and, 241–242, 251, 254–255; early, 230; expectations and, 321–327, 341–342; failure and, 214–215; feedback and, 319–321; interdependence and, 251; positive attention and, 327–331; positive images for, 325–327; secret to, 398–399; small wins for, 208–213; stories about, 361–362

Suffering, 51–52

Suggestion systems, 202–203. *See also* Ideas

Sullivan, L., 212

Summer Olympics, 399

Summit, 319

Sunnyvale Community Services, 323–324, 378

Sunset statute, for values statement, 95

Super Person of the Month award, 339, 374

Supportive relationships, celebrations and, 356–359

Supportiveness, 25, 302

Survey research, 13; on admired leader attributes, 24–32
Surveys, employee, to create values alignment, 94
Survivor, 250–251
Susser, A., 202
Swisher, D., 125–126
Swissair, 205
Switzerland Department of Economics and Labor, 330
Symbols: examples of, 165–166; teaching shared values through, 88, 97–98; teaching vision through, 165–166; words as, 88
Synergistic Systems, Inc. (SSI), 179

T

T-shirts, 12, 376
Taini, R., 205–207
Tanner, O. C., 344
Task assignments: for cooperative interactions, 253; critical, 302–304; incremental, 230–231; involving customers, 304–305; job design and, 304–305; for power sharing, 203–204, 280, 291–292; providing choice in, 291–292. See also Assignments, leader
Task force, celebration, 372
Taylor, C., 216
Taylor, J., 20–21, 136
Team building: in animation studio case study, 11; common purpose and, 154–155
Team life cycles, 201
Team meetings: informal interaction in, 276–277; listening in, 269; rotating leadership of, 277, 306; storytelling in, 100–101
Team recognition. See Celebration
Teams: in car dealership case study, 4–5; rotating new members in, 193, 201; shared vision in, 141–142
Teamwork: collaboration and, 241–277; destructive extremes of, 396; enabling others and, 18–19. See also Collaboration; Enabling
Technical competence, 30
Technological innovation, small-wins approach to, 210

Technovation room, 202
Telecommunications industry, in 1990s, 153–155
Tempered radicals, 210
Ten Commitments. See Commitments, Ten
Tentativeness, 164
Teresa, Mother, 45
Tests, 211, 224–226
Thank-yous, 334, 339, 345, 347–349. See also Praise; Recognition
Thatcher, M., 45
Theme: discovering, 114–124; immersion and, 122–124; passion and, 115–118, 121–122, 124; paying attention and, 120–122; reflection on the past for, 118–120, 132–133
Thinking in the Future Tense (James), 137
Thinking-oriented learners, 217
Thinking outside the box, 280
"Third places," 275
Thompson, R., 125–126
Thoughtfulness, 336–337, 345
301 Ways to Have Fun at Work (Lopes), 367–368
360-degree feedback: in animation studio case study, 11; credibility and, 102; for developing self-awareness, 64–65
Tiger, L., 251
Time, 362
Time allocation: as indicator of values, 85–86, 103; for listening, 150–151, 250; for long-term envisioning, 136
Time orientation: future horizons and, 118–120, 129–130; of strategic versus tactical leaders, 118–119, 129–130
Tithing, 66
Tivol, N., 323–324, 378
Tolerance for error, 216
Tom Peters Company, 120
Total process reengineering, 197
Total quality management, 197
Towers Perrin, 187
Town hall meeting, 269
Toyota, 228
Track record, 234
Training: in animation studio case study, 11; in business skills, 293; commitment to, in car dealership case study,

U.S. Forest Service, 133–134
Utne Reader, 137

V

Values: cultural, 333; ends, 48; goals and, 318; as guides, 47–49; ideals and, 126; importance of, 45–51; means, 48; moral leadership and, 393–394; routines based on, 190

Values, organizational, relationship between personal values and, 49–51, 78–80

Values, shared, 51, 77–83; action steps for, 93–105; celebration for reinforcing, 354–356, 370; common purpose and, 151; dialogue for, 80, 81–83, 94–95; diversity and, 78; example setting and, 77–93; examples of, 151; importance and power of, 78–83; providing rationales for, 95; speaking about, 95–97; stories and, 361–364

Values clarification, 44–56; impact of, on organizational commitment, 49–51; importance of, 45–51; internal exploration for, 51–54; role models and mentors for, 54–56, 59–60, 67–68

Values commitment, 14; character and, 45–46; example setting and, 75–78; honesty and, 28; shared, 78–83

Values expression. *See* Example setting; Self-expression

Values statements: dialogue and consensus on, 81–83, 94–95; sunset statute for, 95

Vanished Children's Alliance, 385

VEEM Engineering Group, 306

Vendor payment reviews, 175–176

Venture capitalist, 113

Vian, K., 362

Video, company, 362

Vincent J. Russo Leadership Award, 372–373

Virtual connections, 261, 273

Virtual organization, cooperation in, 18

Virtual trust, 261

Visa International, 334–335

Visibility, 302, 329–331

Vision: action steps for developing, 130–139; assumptions and, 137–138; being forward-looking and, 28–29, 111, 113–130; breathing life into, 165–166; cooperation and, 257; credibility and, 34–37; destructive extremes of, 396; ends values and, 48; essentials of, 114–115; of exemplary leaders, 15; giving life to, 155–159; imagining possibilities for, 114–115, 124–130; importance of, 111–112, 130–131; missionary *versus* mercenary, 156–157; questions for clarifying, 133; of smaller units, 127; strategic plans *versus*, 153; tangible expression of, 155–159, 160–161; teaching, 143–155; terms for, 112; theme discovery for, 114–124; uniqueness of, 127–128. *See also* Envisioning; Forward-looking; Inspiration; Inspire a Shared Vision; Possibilities; Theme

Vision sharing and enlisting, 141–170; action steps for, 159–170; celebrations for, 354–356; common purpose/common ground and, 151–155, 161–162; destructive extremes of, 396; essentials for, 148–159; exemplary leadership practice of, 15–16, 141–170; giving life to, 155–159; impact of, on constituents, 143; importance of, 112, 141–142, 143; inspirational attribute and, 31–32, 143–148; language and speaking for, 155–157, 164–167; listening to constituents for, 148–151, 159–161, 167–168; nonverbal, 158–159, 165; positive communication for, 157–158, 164–165; symbols, stories, and other aids for, 165–166. *See also* Inspiration; Inspire a Shared Vision

Vision statement: preparation for writing, 131–134; updating, 136; writing, 135–136; writing a collective, 162–164

VisionQuest, 163–164

Vista Test, 118–119

Visual imagery, 138, 155–156; symbols and, 165–166

Visualization, 128–129, 138–139

Voice, finding one's, 14; action steps for, 63–73; destructive extremes of, 395; elements of, 44–45; importance of, 43–44; internal exploration for, 51–54; role models and mentors for, 54–56,

67–68; values clarification for, 44–56. *See also* Self-expression; Speaking
Volunteer motivation, 319, 323–324
Volunteerism, 183, 197
Von Raesfeld, K., 325–326
Vulnerability, trust and, 248–249, 331

W

Wacker, W., 136
Waffle shoe, 364
Wal-Mart, 199
Walking around, caring by, 374–375. *See also* Employees, getting to know
Walt Disney Company, 89–90
Walt Disney World, 91
Walton, S., 378
Washington Mutual, 114
We, using, 270
Web shoppers, 34
Web site, The Leadership Challenge, 137, 401–402
Weight Watchers, 210
WellConnected, 89, 90
Wells Fargo Bank, 165–166, 212
Western Australia's Total Nissan, 304–305
Westpac Bank, 102, 152
"What would you do?" scenarios, 94–95
Where on Earth Are We Going? (Strong), 137
White water. *See* Change
Whites Group, 3–8, 225, 236
Whittaker, J., 387
Wilcox, K., 156
Wilderness School, 206
Williams, D., 301
Willingness, leader, 24
Wilson, G., 375–376
Winners: failures of, 214–215; treating employees/constituents as, 327–330, 334
Wins, small, 17, 208–213; commitment and, 209–210; fast action and, 211–213; importance of, 207; rationale for, 208–211
Winston, S., 283–284
Women's Health Initiative (WHI), 244–245
Words: collaborative, 270; for conveying values, 90–92, 104; either-or, 232, 272;

importance of, 57–58, 88–90; for inspiring vision, 155–157, 164–165; for self-expression, 56–62; that describe personal-best leadership experience, 177. *See also* Alignment; Consistency; Language; Self-expression; Speaking; Storytelling; Voice
Words and deeds consistency. *See* Alignment; Consistency
Work *versus* job, 186
World Bank, 98–99
World Trade Center tragedy, 19
World Wide Web: leader biographies on, 131; *The Leadership Challenge Guide to the Research* on, 137, 401–402; searching for new ideas on, 203
"Worst case scenario" technique, 236
"Worst Nightmare" exercise, 200
Wright-Patterson Air Force Base, 373
"Write Your Credo" exercise, 56, 68–70, 72
Writing, 55, 56
www.biography.com, 131
www.leadershipchallenge.com, 137, 401–402

X

Xerox, 90; Palo Alto Research Center, 309
Xilinx, 92, 216, 235

Y

Yang, G., 113
Yerkes, L., 199
Yes, saying, 232–233, 287
Yhtyneet Kuvalehdet Oy (United Magazines Ltd.), 276
Youth for Environmental Sanity (YES!), 52

Z

Zambia story, 98–99
Zapping, 7
Zárate, A., 253–254, 342
Zeder, M., 359
Zehnder, E., 62, 256–257, 397
Zhang, J., 288–289
Zinsser, W., 59
Zuboff, S., 90

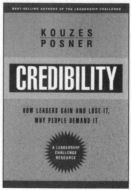

STUDENT LEADERSHIP PRACTICES INVENTORY

Designed to help develop the leaders of tomorrow, it includes a self-evaluation tool and an instrument for the gathering of feedback from peers, teachers, mentors, or other individuals.

Learn Anytime, Anywhere

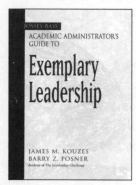

THE JOSSEY-BASS ACADEMIC ADMINISTRATOR'S GUIDE TO EXEMPLARY LEADERSHIP

This important resource clearly shows how anyone can develop the key leadership skills needed "to get extraordinary things done" on their campuses.

THE LEADERSHIP CHALLENGE WORKBOOK

Mixing up three of today's hottest business topics—leadership development, project management, and execution—Kouzes and Posner have created the ultimate change leader's workbook.

To learn more about these training tools or to place an order, visit us at **www.leadershipchallenge.com** or call **800-956-7739**.

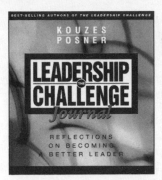

THE LEADERSHIP CHALLENGE JOURNAL

This personal reflection piece is perfect for readers (and writers) looking to start or continue their leadership journey.

WHAT FOLLOWERS EXPECT FROM LEADERS
How to Meet People's Expectations and Build Credibility

Make better use of your commute time. These two one-hour audio cassettes provide concrete examples and specific guidance on how to become a more effective leader.

THE FIVE PRACTICES OF EXEMPLARY LEADERSHIP
Article, Revised Edition

This 16-page article is perfect for leaders with limited time and budget. It provides a concise overview of Kouzes and Posner's model and overall thoughts on leadership.

THE LEADERSHIP CHALLENGE CARD

This handy pocket-sized card for desks, organizers, and wallets offers quick reference to the model used in *The Leadership Challenge* and the *LPI*.

THE LEADERSHIP CHALLENGE POSTER

A visible reminder of the Five Practices and Ten Commitments of Exemplary Leadership.

Plan a Leadership Workshop

The Leadership Challenge™ Workshop
This intensive two- or three-day program is based on the best-selling book and designed by its authors.

- Offered by the Tom Peters Company in onsite, public, and custom formats with pre- and post-consulting available for ongoing needs.
- Implemented by some of the world's most recognized companies, including Brooks Brothers, Cisco, Clorox, Rolls-Royce, Seagate Technology, Sun Microsystems, Unilever, and Wells Fargo Bank.

Leadership Is Everyone's Business™
A one-day workshop that develops the leadership practices of individual contributors at all levels of the organization.

To learn more about these learning opportunities, contact the Tom Peters Company in the U.S. and abroad at 888-221-8685, e-mail info@tompeters.com, or visit their website at www.tompeters.com/ implementation/solutions/challenge.

Get Connected With the Convenience of Online Learning

Instigo
Working with Instigo, Jim Kouzes produced several highly interactive online seminars. They are now available to you and your organization for your next learning activity.

To learn more, visit www.instigo.com.

Create Excitement With
The Leadership Challenge Video Collection

Video programs offer a compelling format for leadership training in both small groups and large gatherings. These *Leadership Challenge* videos are designed to educate, inspire, and liberate the leader in everyone.

Leadership Challenge: This compelling video shows that leadership is attainable; it is not the private preserve of a few charismatic people but a learnable set of practices.

Leadership in Action: Based on the best-selling book *The Leadership Challenge,* this must-have video describes the five practices common to all successful leaders through a single case study.

Closing the Leadership Gap: This exceptional video reveals how to cultivate and maintain credibility and fill the leadership gap—when leaders say one thing and do another.

Encouraging the Heart: This video illustrates the importance of employee recognition and presents examples of the types of rewards leaders can give to truly motivate top performance.

Credibility: This two-part video series explores the difference between a person in a leadership position, and a person whose direction you are willing to follow.

To learn more, visit www.crmlearning.com or call 800-421-0833.